Praise for

PETER MATTHIESSEN'S

The Birds of Heaven

"The poet laureate of nature writers applies his Zen-like intelligence to the world's fifteen surviving species of crane . . . Along with taxonomy, ethology, and field observation (including what must be the classiest description of crane sex ever written), we see natural history through the lenses of culture, economics, and religion." —*The New Yorker*

"Anyone whose heart has ever been suddenly pierced by an unexpected moment of wild beauty will be seduced by this book's accumulation of many such transcendent moments, simply and precisely rendered. In the end, Matthiessen's skill makes it impossible not to love the beautiful-but-doomed earth he portrays."
—Heather Dewar, *The Baltimore Sun*

"The story moves us—even uplifts us—because of the almost Quixotic persistence of craniacs such as George Archibald (and indeed Matthiessen himself) who ignore the odds in their efforts to change the world for the betterment of cranes."
—Tim Flannery, *The New York Review of Books*

"*The Birds of Heaven* inspires hope, despair, curiosity and, above all, awe . . . Matthiessen takes us on a journey of the mind, rich in detail on the ecosystems and people he encounters. But his real gift is the ability to engage our hearts . . . His greatest triumph is the extraordinary ability to convey spiritual moments in a book that reads as much like poetry as natural history." —Christine Shenot, *Orlando Sentinel*

"Perhaps no one is more qualified to examine these creatures, both as symbols and as a living ecological presence, than Peter Matthiessen . . . His nonfiction is consistently driven by a sense that personal truths emerge from the wilderness or at least from the imperfect quest to engage the wilderness on its own terms."

—Jason Roberts, *San Francisco Chronicle*

"Compelling . . . on the order of such classic Matthiessen works as *At Play in the Fields of the Lord*."   —Craig Nova, *Washington Post*

"Bard of the world's rarest creatures, from the snow leopard to the Siberian tiger, Matthiessen . . . is our finest chronicler of 'the lengths to which man is driven to salvage the last wild survivors of his own heedless course on earth.' "   —Caroline Fraser, *Outside*

The Birds of Heaven

PAINTINGS AND DRAWINGS

BY ROBERT BATEMAN

North Point Press

A division of Farrar, Straus and Giroux

New York

The Birds of Heaven

Travels with Cranes

PETER

MATTHIESSEN

North Point Press
A division of Farrar, Straus and Giroux
19 Union Square West, New York 10003

Copyright © 2001 by Peter Matthiessen
Paintings and drawings copyright © 2001 by Boshkung, Inc.
Foreword copyright © 2001 by George Archibald and James Harris
All rights reserved
Published in Canada by Greystone Books, a
division of Douglas & McIntyre Ltd.
Printed in the United States of America
Published in 2001 by North Point Press
First paperback edition, 2003

The Library of Congress has cataloged the hardcover edition as follows:
Matthiessen, Peter.
    The birds of heaven : travels with cranes/Peter Matthiessen ; paintings and drawings
by Robert Bateman.— 1st ed.
    p.   cm.
ISBN 0-374-19944-2 (hc. : alk. paper)
    1. Cranes.   2. Endangered species.   I. Bateman, Robert, 1930–   II. Title.

QL696.G84 M372 2001
598.3'2—dc21

                                                                            2001032986

Paperback ISBN: 0-86547-657-8

Designed by Jonathan D. Lippincott
Maps designed by Jeffrey L. Ward

1   3   5   7   9   10   8   6   4   2

For all those working to defend
the sanctity of Earth's precious land and life

The world?
Moonlit water drops
from the crane's bill.
— Zen Master Dogen, thirteenth century Japan

Our appreciation of the crane grows with the slow unraveling of earthly history. His tribe, we now know, stems out of the remote Eocene. The other members of the fauna in which he originated are long since entombed within the hills . . . And so they live and have their being—these cranes—not in the constricted present but in the wider reaches of evolutionary time. Their annual return is the clicking of the geologic clock. The sadness discernible in some crane marshes arises, perhaps, from their once having harbored cranes. Now they stand humbled, adrift in history.

— Aldo Leopold, "Marshland Elegy," 1937

Contents

Foreword

When we hear his call we hear no mere bird. We hear the trumpet in the orchestra of evolution. He is the symbol of our untamable past, of that incredible sweep of millennia which underlies and conditions the daily affairs of birds and men.
—Aldo Leopold, "Marshland Elegy," 1937

These eloquent words were penned in central Wisconsin in 1937, at a time when perhaps no more than twenty-five pairs of sandhill cranes remained in the state. Dr. Leopold feared they might soon follow the whooping crane, which disappeared from the midwestern United States after Europeans settled the land in the nineteenth century. But the sandhill's tenacity for life and a shift in the attitudes of the people of Wisconsin, who came to love and protect the crane, resulted in a remarkable recovery: an estimated twelve thousand sandhill cranes exist in Wisconsin today.

It is therefore appropriate that in 1973, central Wisconsin became the home of the International Crane Foundation (ICF), an organization dedicated to the study and preservation of the world's cranes. Once the dream of two graduate students in ornithology at Cornell University, the ICF has grown to a present staff of forty and holds a captive collection that includes all fifteen species of cranes, and additionally supports a network of kindred spirits around the world who work on behalf of cranes and the wetland and grassland ecosystems on which these birds depend. Through the ICF, cranes have inspired an extraordinary number of people to join efforts in a common cause.

Today eleven of the fifteen species may fairly be considered threatened or endangered. If we act quickly and concertedly, there is still a chance to save the rare cranes and a wide array of their beautiful wetland territories, but the opportunity may close in this decade or the next. Nevertheless, recent years have brought much good news for cranes. The whooping crane is making a slow but steady recovery in North America. In Europe, the Eurasian crane is increasingly adapting to wetlands close to human habitation and activity, and has begun to return to countries from which it had disappeared in centuries past. On the island of Hokkaido in northern Japan, the red-crowned crane has recovered from just thirty-three birds in 1952 to more than seven hundred, all because of the love the Japanese feel for their magnificent *tancho*.

Cranes are fortunate to have Peter Matthiessen and Robert Bateman, two eminent naturalist-artists who have observed these birds with great patience and care. Indeed, Peter has accompanied us into the field in Siberia, Mongolia, South Korea, and Australia, as well as in North America, while Bob has photographed and sketched all fifteen species of cranes at the ICF. During extensive travels, both men have encountered cranes in the wild landscapes of five continents and have come to know them extremely well. We believe that publication of this book is a wonderful event that will bring many more friends to the cause of cranes.

Through a remarkable combination of prose and art, this book explores the uncertain origin and natural history of these venerable birds. Peter Matthiessen's account has scientific as well as aesthetic significance in its contribution to the study and appreciation of this magnificent avian family of ancient and modern worlds.

George Archibald   James Harris
Chairman of the Board   President
International Crane Foundation   International Crane Foundation

Introduction

In a hard November in 1997, a young sandhill crane turned up at a salt pond on the coast near my house at Sagaponack and passed the winter in the company of a great black-backed gull.[1] Since this was only the third crane ever reported on Long Island, and since it arrived just as I commenced the writing of this book, I interpreted its appearance a half mile from my house as an auspicious sign—even more so when, departing in early spring, it passed right over the small shack where I was working. Hearing that wild summons, I ran outside in time to watch it cross the sky on a northeasterly bearing, bound for points unknown.

Seeing that lost crane—for it had wandered far off course—I recalled an evening in August 1992 when, on my return home to Long Island from crane travels in Asia, I was confronted by a woman at dinner who demanded to know where the hell I'd been all summer. Eastern Siberia and Outer Mongolia, I said. But why? she cried. Why?!—as if anyone who would forsake the summer Hamptons for such destinations must be mad. And when I offered my excuse of field research on endangered cranes and tigers, she drew back, aghast.

"Cranes?!" she squawked. "Who cares about cranes?"

I've remembered that exasperated outburst ever since. Whatever its provenance, that question echoes: Who cares about cranes?—and tigers and songbirds and sparkling streams and hoary ancient forests and traditional earth peoples clinging to old quiet ways of their language and culture—or cares enough to defend and protect what remains of the old world of unbroken and unpolluted nature on our ever more disrupted mother earth.

Like many people on many continents, I care profoundly about cranes and tigers, not only as magnificent and stirring creatures but as heralds and symbols of all that is being lost.[2] Working with dedicated conservation biologists and ornithologists in many countries, I set out to observe them in the wild and learn their evolutionary stories, as a means of persuading our consumer society to take responsibility for our fellow creatures while there is still time.

The crane family (Gruidae) occurs on every continent except South America, but the genus *Grus* (to which taxonomists presently assign all but five of the fifteen extant species) attained its greatest expansion in eastern Asia. Of those fifteen, eleven are threatened or endangered by *Homo sapiens*, either directly through hunting, poisoning, or trapping, or indirectly through despoliation of the earth's resources, most dangerously its dwindling fount of good freshwater.

These elegant birds, in their stature, grace, and beauty, their wild fierce temperament, are striking metaphors for the vanishing wilderness of our once bountiful earth; in addition, they function as "umbrella species" whose protection in the wild also protects a broad range of fauna and flora as well as the clean water, earth, and air of their extensive territories—in short, sustains the astonishing variety of forms in nature (with their habitats and ecosystems) known as biodiversity. Since most crane species are cosmopolitan in range, they offer an opportunity to protest the stunted industrial (hence political) vision behind the broad range of unrestrained, often senseless activities, from war to the ill-advised building of great dams, that degrade or destroy what is left of precious habitats around the world—precious not only to cranes and other wildlife but to our inheritors and to their children.

Surely a lingering sadness is unavoidable for those who revere the natural world and must bear witness to the ongoing degradation of our human habitat, tragically sacrificed to such narrow ideals as "gross national product" and diminishing hour by hour, day by day. "Of course I felt a special sympathy with your thoughts on 'the secret tension between love [of the earth] and despair' so that 'no carefree love of the planet is now possible,' " Rachel Carson wrote in a late letter to a friend. "Each day those words become more true!"[3]

And yet, to my astonishment, in the second summer of the new millennium, after four decades of lingering sadness and pessimism about the future and vain angry protest, a curious optimism has opened in my heart like a strange blossom. Paradoxically, in this scary period when out-of-date Western governments seem oblivious to any need except those of "big business"—and in particular "big oil" and the extractive industries—and just when the caravan of United States politics labors so heavily in its attempt at a U-turn back toward the past, signs of environmental heresy are appearing in the business world, a few thin cracks in the hard skull of the corporate mentality. For whatever reason, industry after industry and business after business are making a quiet shift toward environmental awareness.

In the end, it does not much matter whether this change of direction is mere "greenwashing" for public consumption; or a long-overdue realization that being socially irresponsible in this critical new century will be bad for business; or a growing awareness that, as resources decline and populations increase, taking care of land and life has become the world's highest priority, even for free-market capitalism. The corporate world that dictates policies to the Western governments appears to be coming to its senses.

Whether this enlightenment will evolve fast enough to spare endangered forests and rivers and unique and precious ecosystems (the Arctic National Wildlife Refuge, for example) and imperiled creatures such as cranes and tigers remains to be seen. It depends on all of us who would be world citizens, not mere consumers, and act accordingly.

One way to grasp the main perspectives of environment and biodiversity is to understand the origins and precious nature of a single living form, a single manifestation of the miracle of existence; if one has truly understood a crane—or a leaf or a cloud or a frog—one has understood everything. In the growing scarcity of good water and the impending competition for this resource—which may well become the greatest crisis for all life on earth in the new millennium—the plight of *Homo* may not differ very much from that of *Grus*.

Peter Matthiessen
Sagaponack, New York

The Birds of Heaven

ONE

Black Dragon River

> The immortal cranes call, their cries sound from afar, their
> thoughts circle upward into distant skies. Below, on the autumn
> rivers, stands a man, above him the bright moon. The man wan-
> ders aimless, trailing after the endless Milky Way. The wind
> blows past him. I, too, thinks the man, would like to be utterly
> free.
>
> —Jiang Yi Ning

On a rare clear morning—the first day of summer 1992—flying
across the Bering Strait from the Yukon delta toward the
Diomede Islands and the Chukotskiy Peninsula of Siberia, I
imagine the gray sun-silvered strait as seen from on high by a migrating
crane, more particularly, by the golden eye of the Crane from the East,
as the lesser sandhill crane of North America is known to traditional
peoples on its westernmost breeding territory in Siberia. The sandhill
commonly travels a mile above the earth and can soar higher, to at least
twenty thousand feet—not astonishing when one considers that the
Eurasian and demoiselle cranes ascend to three miles above sea level
traversing the Himalaya in their north and south migrations between
Siberia and the Indian subcontinent.[1]

That cranes may journey at such altitudes, disappearing from the
sight of earthbound mortals, may account for their near-sacred place in
the earliest legends of the world as messengers and harbingers of high-

est heaven. In Cree Indian legend, Crane carries Rabbit to the moon. Aesop extols the crane's singular ability "to rise above the clouds into endless space, and survey the wonders of the heavens, as well as of the earth beneath, with its seas, lakes, and rivers, as far as the eye can reach," and Homer and Aristotle comment on great crane migrations.[2] Every land where they appear has tales and myths about the cranes, which since ancient times have represented longevity and good fortune, harmony and fidelity.[3] Heaven-bound ancients are commonly depicted riding on a crane, or assuming the crane's majestic form for their arrival in the clouds of immortality.[4]

The larger cranes, over five feet tall, with broad strong wings eight feet in span, appear well capable of bearing aloft a wispy old-time sage. The cranes are the greatest of the flying birds and, to my mind, the most stirring, not less so because the horn notes of their voices, like clarion calls out of the farthest skies, summon our attention to our own swift passage on this precious earth. Perhaps more than any other living creatures, they evoke the retreating wilderness, the vanishing horizons of clean water, earth, and air upon which their species—and ours, too, though we learn it very late—must ultimately depend for survival.

In the large taxonomic order known as Gruiformes, the odd and elastic suborder Grues includes cranes and their closest relatives, the New World limpkins and trumpeters, and also the cosmopolitan jacanas, rails, gallinules, and coots; it does not include the smaller storks and herons with which they were traditionally grouped on the basis of common wading habits and similarities of rostra, bills, and feet. In 1735 Carl von Linné, or Linnaeus, in his *Systema Naturae* named the Eurasian or common crane *Ardea grus* or "crane heron," and in the nineteenth century Audubon would portray a heron as the "little blue crane." Herons were commonly called cranes in Ireland, Scotland, and South America, where no cranes occur,[5] and also in Australia (where the true crane was known, oddly, as "the native companion" because of its close association with the Aborigines). Even in flight and at a distance, cranes look nothing like herons, since cranes fly with neck outstretched rather than curved back onto the shoulders, while storks in flight display broad tails, which all cranes lack. (Crane tails are small and very short, a deficiency obscured by long loose feathers of the inner wing—the tertials, highly modified to form erect, handsome "bustles" or long trailing plumes when the bird folds its wings upon alighting. Otherwise this bird's extremities—bill, neck, legs, and toes—are unusually long.) Furthermore, crane voices with their wild, rolling *r* are far more musical than the strangled squawks of storks and herons.[6]

Cranes stand straight and erect with bodies parallel to the ground in the manner of ostriches. The hind toe or hallux, elevated like a cockspur, is vestigial in all but the two crowned cranes of the genus *Balearica*, whose longer hind toe may serve for balance in the perching habit, one of several that distinguish the "primitive" *Balearica* from modern or "typical" cranes of the genus *Grus*—primitive in the sense that in its anatomy and behavior, *Balearica* is closer to the ancestral form. Another is the fully feathered head, which crowned cranes share with the demoiselle and blue cranes of the genus *Anthropoides*. In all other cranes, the head is ornamented with a bare area of rough red comb or skin—bright crimson when the blood is up during the breeding season—located somewhere on the crown in most of the migratory northern cranes and in varying areas of the face and upper neck in the mostly nonmigratory southern species. (Among the latter, the sarus, brolga, and wattled cranes are additionally adorned with bald greenish brows.) Though the female tends to be smaller, the sexes of all cranes are otherwise indistinguishable when not interacting in pair bonding, courtship, and mating.

The brown coast of Alaska, falling away in the bright mists, gives way to rotted pack ice and the rough gray shallow seas of the vanished land bridge between continents, fifty miles across. Cold sea air over the North Pacific numbs the bright red skin on the sandhill's crown; the long stiff wings creak on the wind. "The flight of cranes, the way they form letters" was noted by the Roman poet Hyginus, among other early observers. Like wild geese, cranes often travel in V formation, presumably having learned—after millions of miles and long millenniums of buffeting by the great winds—the aerodynamic limits of formations in the shape of B or H.[7]

The Arctic distances flown at high altitudes by these dauntless creatures humble the seat-bound traveler on Air Alaska. Peering outward from my plastic aerie over the firmament of wind and light, mightily stirred by the unmarred emptiness of land and sea beneath, I could know with Goethe's Faust how "it is inborn in every man that his feeling should press upward and forward" when "over precipitous fir-clad heights the eagle floats with wings outspread, or over flatlands, over seas, the crane sweeps onward toward its home"—in German, *Heimgang* or "home going," the return to the lost paradise at the source of all man's yearnings.

Off the aircraft wing rises Nunivak Island, where thirty years ago I was a member of an expedition that captured ten burly musk-ox calves, the nucleus of a domestic herd to be raised in Fairbanks and turned over to the Inupiaq people in an effort to stabilize their economy.[8] On Nunivak, according to my notes from that expedition, "cranes on long black-fingered wings bugled sadly across the wind"—among the many far-flung sandhills which have brightened fine days in the field across all of North America, from Alaska to the northern Everglades.

Soon the islands known as the Diomedes—one in the New World, one in the Old—loom in northern mists, then Cape Dezhnev and the barrens of Chukotskiy, home of the Chukot or Chukchi aborigines, kinsmen of the Inupiaq and the Aleuts. Even in late June, the mountain tundra far below looks wintry, with hard, wind-worn snow in the ravines. Following old migration instincts, the Crane from the East will descend each spring to the great eastern peninsulas of Siberia, and some will wander west along the Arctic coast approximately fifteen hundred miles to the Yana River, where their breeding range meets that of the Siberian crane.

Off Asia's north Pacific coast, the airplane turns southward. In this clear weather, one can see most of Kamchatka, that vast and all but un-inhabited land of volcanoes and great bears, blue lakes, mountain meadows, swift cold streams, and hard bright coast. Extending a thou-sand miles north and south, with scarcely a scar or a raw scrape or glint of man, it fairly resounds with emptiness and silence, like the pristine New World continent of great mountains and rivers that astounded the early voyagers along its north Pacific coast.

Off Kamchatka's tip, the Kurile Islands march south through the Pacific haze toward the Japanese archipelago, which continues in a southwest arc approximately as long as the Atlantic coast from Maine to Florida. Eventually the plane descends to refuel at Magadan on the Siberian mainland, where even in late June, the barren Dzhugdzhur Mountains to the west are patched with snow. Beyond, the spruce tun-dra and boreal taiga, immense beyond reckoning, extend three thou-sand miles to the Ural Mountains and European Russia, in an all but unbroken forest composed of half the conifers and one third of the hardwoods left on earth.[9]

From Magadan the plane heads out across the Sea of Okhotsk. The Siberian coastline reappears in the sprawling delta of the Amur River, shining in braids and floodplains that stretch away under the western sun to far smudges of upland and small mountains. The Amur drainage is the great river system of eastern Siberia and northern China, draining a watershed of 716,200 square miles on its 2,700-mile journey from eastern Mongolia to the sea. With the Ussuri (in Chinese, Wusuli), which joins it from the south, the Amur serves as the north-eastern frontier between Russia and China, all the way from Inner Mongolia to great Lake Khanka—or Xingkai Hu—on China's border with Primorski Krai, Russia's maritime province on the Sea of Japan.

The Amur basin, where boreal forest or taiga meets the spruce muskeg tundra of the sub-Arctic, is a region of astonishing biodiversity. Here northern forms such as the Amur or "Siberian" tiger, wolf, lynx, brown bear, elk, and moose share an overlapping range with creatures of the broad-leaved forests, such as roe deer, Asian leopard, black bear, mandarin duck, and paradise flycatcher. A heartland of the Asian cranes, it is the only region in the world where six different crane species appear in each year (and where a seventh, the far-flung sandhill crane of North America, occurs regularly). Arguably the most beautiful of these seven are two species—the red-crowned and white-naped cranes—found in breeding season in the Amur drainage. Though this was not the only reason for my journey (the great Amur itself was an exciting destination), I longed to see such heraldic cranes in their Asian marshes.

The endless delta spreads away beneath the wings as the aircraft heads inland and upriver, descending eventually to the great bend at Khabarovsk. The Amur is the largest free, wild, unbridged, un-dammed river left on earth, as wondrous in the immensity of its basin as mile-deep Lake Baikal, off to the west. But in recent years, this last wilderness of the Russian Far East has been assaulted by international oil and mining development and timber exploitation, led by multina-tional corporations of South Korea, Japan, and the United States, and in its throes of economic stress, Russia may not act in time to save it.

From Khabarovsk I travel southeast to the coast range of Ussuria to join an expedition doing research on the endangered Amur tiger. From there I proceed to the Bolshe-Khekhstir Wildlife Reserve south-west of Khabarovsk, near the Ussuri-Amur confluence, where I join an international crane conference organized by Russia's Socio-Ecological Union (SEU), representing sixty environmental groups, and the Inter-national Crane Foundation (ICF), based in Baraboo, Wisconsin, with the support of American environmental organizations.[10] The two Mon-golian ornithologists fail to appear due to travel complications in their country, but China, Japan, and South Korea have all sent delegates, en-suring a chilly atmosphere. The future of east Asian wildlife, in partic-ular the migrant cranes, must depend at present on the cooperation of five nations more accustomed to addressing their disputes with xeno-phobia and war.

Among those attending the conference are the directors of the Amur basin's hard-pressed wildlife reserves, or *zapovedniki*, who are anxious to discuss ways to reconcile wildlife protection with lumbering and other compromises that have become necessary for the *zapovedniki* to survive.[11] In this dark time of myriad uncertainties, economic anarchy, and rapacious entrepreneurs, the regional governments have been leasing rights to mining and timber extraction, oil and gas exploration and development, hunting, fishing, and a tentative ecotourism, with little or no regard for sustainable development, wildlife management, or wilderness preservation. (There is even a rumor of negotiations with the Japanese for concession rights to the crystal water of Lake Baikal, which contains one fifth of all the earth's freshwater that is not locked in snow and ice.)

The Amur basin forests are accessible by navigable waterways to vast markets in South Korea and Japan (which have already destroyed most of their own forests); the timber, like every public asset, is being sold off at bargain rates by local officials and the military, with little or no accountability. The director of Bolshe-Khekhstir describes how its forest has been isolated from regional ecosystems by intensive clearing for agriculture and polluted by the runoff from stone mining. Mikhail Dykhan, who manages the Kurile Islands reserve on the island of Kunashir, deplores its shriveling support from the Russian government—a condition shared by all of the reserves, which are "demoralized and broke"—as well as the impact of military bases and petroleum dumping on his island's brown bears and its lone pair of red-crowned cranes, which return across the Nemuro Strait to Hokkaido every winter. Yet these dedicated people seem determined to find ways to keep their refuges alive, and they welcome suggestions and help from other countries. "We would like to work *with* you Americans on scientific projects," one Russian tells us proudly. "We are not here simply to beg."

The coordinator of the conference is Dr. Sergei Smirenski of the SEU, a tall, gaunt Russian always in a hurry and chronically exhausted, like the last man standing in a hopeless cause; he is an eloquent defender of the Amur region, generous with his energies, fiercely committed. "Sergei Smirenski might seem crazy to organize an international conference at such a chaotic time in Russia, when even simple things are hard to do," observes James T. Harris, then deputy director of the ICF, an indefatigably cheerful man with lank brown hair and a kind grin. "But he fears that freedom and free enterprise will unleash a wave of irresponsible development and destruction, and that we conservationists must use any opportunity to protect the Amur. In Sergei's mind, we cannot wait for better days in which to hold this conference—we must start right now forging international cooperation, however tenuous these first efforts may be."

In a few days, the conference will continue aboard ship on a voyage up the Amur, north and west from Khabarovsk to the floodplains of the middle Amur, where the red-crowned crane, *Grus japonensis*, shares its breeding range with the white-naped crane, *Grus vipio*. The co-director of the conference is Dr. George W. Archibald, head of the ICF, who is widely recognized as the world's leading authority on cranes. A native of Nova Scotia, Archibald is a round-faced man of forty-five with a puckish good humor that belies a firm sense of purpose and direction. Though he has explored most of the crane habitats on earth, this is his first visit to Siberia, which has been closed to foreigners for many years; he has never seen the mainland population of *Grus japonensis*. Dr. Archibald reminds the delegates that the red-crowned crane is revered as a symbol of long life, good fortune, harmony, and peace throughout the east Asian lands represented at the conference, where it has appeared in every form of art, design, and decorative motif, from screens and painted scrolls to royal robes and wedding cakes. "Just as cranes ignore international boundaries, real crane supporters pay scant heed to ideology and politics," he says, beaming straight into the dour faces of delegates whose countries have abundant cause for mutual suspicion and dislike. Archibald knows all about the obstacles to harmony, of course, but as I will learn, he is indomitable, a self-described "craniac" in love with life as gloriously manifested by the cranes. "Everything they do seems deliberate and graceful," he says. "There are birds and there are cranes, like there are apes and men."[12]

The Amur has always been a meeting place of many peoples, he continues, not only the Russians out of Europe but traditional Asian peoples such as the Udege and Buryat, the Mongols from the great steppes, the Manchurians from across the Ussuri—he points across the river—and the Han Chinese who have displaced them, spreading north into the region known as San Jiang, or Three Rivers, where the great wetlands—the heart of the Chinese breeding range of the red-crowned crane—are being drained to create what Chinese technocrats refer to as "the Great Northern Breadbasket." While much progress has been made, with new nature reserves recently established in every country represented at this conference—here Dr. Archibald smiles warmly in encouragement—human pressures are threatening irreparable harm to the rivers and forests and their wildlife. In short, he assures us, a more auspicious place for an international conference could scarcely be imagined.[13]

Increasingly, geopolitics must be perceived as a critical factor in crane survival. But observing the delegates' facial expressions as they hear out Dr. Archibald, one can only anticipate all sorts of trouble. A profound mistrust between Russia and China began with czarist expansion into Asia in the nineteenth century and was made permanent when the Trans-Siberian Railroad was forged across the central Asian states and along the borders of Mongolia and Manchuria. Hard feeling culminated in the Boxer Rebellion of 1900 against the "foreign devils" who were seizing the main Asian ports, commandeering commerce, and causing fires, flood, and drought by upsetting the natural harmonies of life.

The Russians, in the Chinese view, have no more business in the Amur basin than the Japanese, who made a puppet kingdom of Manchuria in the 1930s. In those days, Korea was also under Japanese control (it was colonized from 1910 to 1945), and South Korea remains fiercely resentful of Japan for failing to acknowledge its forcible abduction of Korean girls as "comfort women" for the Japanese troops. Japan, for its part, can never forget the obliteration of Hiroshima and Nagasaki by the Americans. Russia has chronic trouble with Japan over the Kurile Islands,[14] China has disagreeable memories of its war with South Korea and the United States, and the U.S. has not forgotten the

Japanese "day of infamy" at Pearl Harbor, China's role in the Korean and Vietnam wars as an ally of America's enemies, nor Soviet hostilities in the long Cold War. Under the circumstances, the delegations make little attempt to communicate with one another even when translators are at hand.

However, our Chinese colleagues, almost twenty strong, have come to Russia in a constructive spirit, to judge from the red banners raised on the first day, with gold letters proclaiming, "Just as these two rivers come together [the Ussuri and the Amur], so our two countries must inevitably come together." These worthy sentiments only inflamed the paranoia of their Russian hosts—that banner could be read to mean "come together under the flag of China," could it not? Through the translators, both delegations are talking volubly to George Archibald and also to Jim Harris, who has made numerous field trips to China, likes the Chinese, and has their trust.

If only because Manchuria has been eliminated from official mention, the Chinese agree to agree that "red-crowned" is preferable to "Manchurian" or "Japanese" as a common name for *Grus japonensis*, which breeds in three of the countries represented and winters in two others; they proudly inform us that the red-crowned crane has been decreed a Grade One Protected Species in their country, along with the giant panda and the yellow-haired monkey.

Despite ancient cultural traditions of invoking wild creatures in poetry and art, a genuine interest in protecting wildlife is very recent in the Asian nations. How the cranes' best interests can be reconciled with the national and cultural prejudices of their well-wishers remains the unspoken question that will underlie our urgent discussions in the coming days.

K habarovsk, a large industrial city of the Soviet era, sits at the confluence of the Ussuri and the Amur. Its summer atmosphere is white and hot and humid, dirtied with smog from the coal stacks and factories upriver. The town's huge and empty central square with its sterile Party headquarters and Lenin statue appears more stale and lonely than oppressive, but the well-kept elm-lined streets, waterfront park, and crowded public beach help the city appear less discouraged and decrepit than Siberian cities to the west, such as Irkutsk at Lake Baikal. On the broad river, large oceangoing ships moored in the current seem to await the brave new era of free-market commerce. Already Chinese peddlers are crossing the river from Heilongjiang to sell cheap clones of Western sneakers, jeans, and T-shirts, soft drinks, and CDs—the American monoculture that spreads like a plastic sheet across the world, stifling the last indigenous whiffs and quirks and colors. Among the few ethnic tatters to be found are shawls and scarves spun from the wool of the chiru or Tibetan antelope—fine things so light and wispy that the test of quality is to slip one through a wedding ring. (In recent years, international demand for this wool, known as *shahtoosh*, has grown so avid that the Tibetan antelope, like the Siberian tiger, has been hunted rapidly toward extinction.)

From Khabarovsk, the chartered steamer *V. Poyarkov* will forge upriver for seven hundred miles to the Amur's confluence with the Zeya River. Like its home port, the ship is named for one of the nineteenth-century Cossack explorers who helped to extend the Russian Empire from the Urals to the Pacific, extinguishing old central Asian kingdoms on the way. She is 250 feet long, with a draft of 5.7 feet—a bit deep, mutters the captain, for the upper river in this year of tardy rains. She belongs to an outfit called the Sputnik Youth Organization, and to judge from appearances, the Sputnik Youths are on the ball, for their ship is a rare emblem of what the new Russia must become in order to command a fair share of world tourism. White, with clean and spacious decks, she has air-conditioning and plentiful hot water, fresh food and fresh flowers on the salon tables, and a pleasant, sun-filled auditorium on the upper deck for meetings; almost all passengers have cabins with a river view.

Under the new Russian flag (a simpler version of the czarist tricolor, white, blue, and red), the ship churns west-northwest. Like the Mississippi, the Amur is almost a mile across, flanked on both banks by low wetlands and long reaches of broad flat savanna set about with wooded islands of pale willow and black oak. One cannot see far because the banks are high and the river already so low that sandbars have emerged on every side. To the Russians it is known as Amur Dear Father (the Lena is Mother), but to the Chinese it is Heilongjiang, Black Dragon River, which is also the modern name of the great northeastern province—formerly Manchuria—off our port bow.[15]

When the Amur became the border between countries in the middle of the nineteenth century, it was considered a Russian river to which the Chinese had free access. This state of affairs persisted until the end of the 1960s, when the U.S.S.R. responded to Chinese aggression by claiming control of the Amur to both banks. ("They were acting as if Russia were some small place between China and Finland," one Russian told me.) But after a series of bloody skirmishes, the Soviet Union withdrew its claim, yielding jurisdiction over the north bank in certain stretches and fencing it off in others, thereby preventing its own settlers from using boats or even from fishing or swimming. (Asked how the government could have let itself be bullied in that way, Dr. Smirenski sighs, "Russia," shaking his head in wry bewilderment.) With the easing of tensions in the past five years, the north bank, sparsely settled because of the disputed boundary, has been returned to the Siberians, but the settlers have left the fences and alarm systems intact—"to protect their gardens from our hungry city people," says Smirenski.

Russian and Chinese gunboats crisscross the river at the mouth of the Ussuri, where the border turns toward the west. Beyond the confluence, Russian guard towers rise every little way from the low willow banks, and soon these bony structures are the only sign of man for mile after mile of silent river. Beyond the limited agricultural strip behind the bank lie swamps, great grassland plains, and the vast taiga, all but uninhabited; to the south lies the great Three Rivers plain, where the triangle between the Amur and the Ussuri is divided by a third large river, the Songhua, which descends through Heilongjiang over a thousand miles from the North Korean mountains and Jilin Province, joining the Amur a hundred miles upriver. Until recent years, there were no towns in this region, only a few Manchurian villages; now the last of the Man people are losing their language, having been displaced by the Han Chinese, who are bringing this same fate to the Tibetans.[16] The Great Northern Breadbasket will require immense electric power, and the source of this power, if China has its way, will be a series of twenty-seven hydroelectric dams on the Amur River. We may be the first foreigners in many decades to voyage for hundreds of miles on the unspoiled Amur, but as someone observes, we may also be the last.

The Russians, too, have ambitious plans for timbering and clearing in the basin, where they have much more virgin forest and many fewer people than the Chinese; the old log-cabin settlements of the Cossack pioneers on the north bank are miles apart. In the Baikal region farther west, the logging is domestic, being largely devoted to supplying fuel for the local pulp and paper mills, but even so, vast areas of taiga are being destroyed, with accompanying pollution of earth, air, and water; this brutal development will mutilate the Amur, too, the more so because it is navigable far inland.

Most rivers and cities of Siberia have been horribly poisoned in the Soviet rush to industrialization. According to former president Yeltsin's ecological adviser, Alexei Yablokov, "About 75 percent of all the lakes and rivers in the ex-U.S.S.R. are so contaminated that the water is undrinkable." The situation in the Far North is worse, much worse, says Ivan Dyachovsky, a small bent man of the traditional people of Yakutia (now the Sakha Republic), a vast sub-Arctic wilderness that is the home of Russia's largest ethnic minority. Dyachovsky is attending the conference as a champion of the *sterkh*—the Siberian crane, *Grus leucogeranus*, whose eastern population in Yakutia crosses this river in its migrations north and south.

With the distinguished Russian wildlife artist Viktor Bakhtin serving as translator, I ask Dyachovsky why he is so passionate about this bird. He answers simply and directly, relating the story of his early childhood in the boreal taiga on Siberia's northeast coast, and how, as a boy of eight climbing a glacier, he broke his back in a bad fall and could no longer walk. One day, he explained, his father took him to a place in southern Yakutia where Siberian cranes stopped in their spring migration so that Ivan could see the beautiful white birds in their courtship dances. "Who sees this crane is happy, and who sees it dance is doubly happy, so my people say." The *sterkh* healed Ivan, he believes, by inspiring him to learn to walk again; later he would devote his summers to searching for their nesting territory in the Far North, which at that time was very little known. Eventually he took a job teaching physics at a village school in the sub-Arctic delta of the Indigirka River, spending the long days of the summer months walking the tundra marshes, studying cranes.

"I walked great distances, and usually I walked alone, the better to observe them. I carried a pack of fifty to sixty kilograms with cheese and dried fish and meat and vegetables, enough for forty-five days, but I wouldn't touch that food until I'd located the cranes and was obliged to remain quiet in one place. Before that, I'd live off the land, mostly on fish, though occasionally I was able to snare a duck."

Finding a nesting pair of cranes was often difficult, since the nests may be forty kilometers apart. "Yakutia is huge, three million square kilometers, and I have traveled most of it on foot. In the sixteen years that I have searched for cranes, I have found thirty-seven nests. Since childhood, my life has been dedicated to the *sterkh*."

Eventually, Ivan gave up teaching to devote himself entirely to the cranes. These days he spends much of his time fighting mining pollution in Yakutia's rivers in order to protect the main staging areas on the crane migration routes. On the Khroma River, he says, mercury pollution has already ruined at least one third of the nesting areas. "That river once had seventeen species of fish; now there is just one, and even that one is suffering mutations," he tells me. "The Siberian, Eurasian, and sandhill cranes living in Yakutia are threatened by pollution from the massive seepage from the oil fields. And of course the shorebirds, ducks, and geese are also greatly harmed." With its failed economy, Russia is feverishly mining gold to obtain hard currency, and extensive drilling for oil and gas is also planned. "Yakutia is the hard currency of

Russia," Ivan says. "We Yakuts are rich in resources and we live in poverty. The few thousand left in this whole enormous region subsist on fishing and hunting and reindeer herding. Most of the people in my village today are Ukrainians and Russians—the Yakuts people are what's left over."

In the present climate of national disintegration, Ivan wants independence for the Sakha Republic, with the white crane as the new national emblem. "Some of those who seek independence for Yakutia would like our emblem to be an eagle with three heads. This eagle faction is very concerned with power"—and here he glares fiercely, flexing his small biceps before adding wryly, "The Russian imperial eagle had only two heads, so perhaps that third head is the result of nuclear pollution."

His people have a long tradition of respect for wildlife. "Yakuts people treat life very carefully. We don't even break branches off the trees to defend ourselves against mosquitoes. All living things are sacred to the Yakuts, but the crane especially. Before we moved north from the Lake Baikal region in the eleventh century, there were old tribes in Yakutia, and each clan had a bird name—Eagle Clan, Gull Clan, Raven Clan, and so forth—but there was no Crane Clan because the cranes were the symbol of all clans, uniting them into one people."[17] The most popular of Yakuts dances, says Dyachovsky, is the dance of the white crane known to the Yakuts as *kitalik*, which nests in the northern taiga as well as on the tundra.[18] "That is our Yakuts name for the Siberian crane, and that is the name that our people have given to me— Kitalik Ivan!" Though he smiles, his olive eyes look worried. "It is difficult to carry such a name, a very great responsibility," Kitalik Ivan murmurs.

"It's a hard life here on this earth, but if you meet a crane, your difficulties and misfortune will be eased. Therefore every Yakuts child dreams of seeing a crane. Almost all of our songs have to do with cranes, and our artists use precious mammoth ivory to sculpt them.

"Our shamans say that this world is actually three worlds. We live in the middle one. The world below belongs to the dark spirits, and to fly down there to obtain power in order to predict the future and deal with someone's fears, the shaman must become a hooded crane [*Grus monachus*]. The hooded crane is black, so people fear it, because seeing one may bring about a death. To fly to the upper world, the shaman must become the white crane, *kitalik*. Only the shaman can travel to the upper and lower worlds and describe what he learns from cranes and eagles on these journeys."

In a misty sunrise, a bargeload of logs descends the river—bound for export, say the Russians. Their winces suggest that the very soul of great Sibir, the Silent Land, is up for sale to the multinational corporations—"the vultures," as Sergei Smirenski calls them bitterly, "who gobble up all they can get."

The river swarms with Chinese fishermen in high-prowed open skiffs propelled by archaic outboards. Some Chinese setting gill nets along the north bank swing alongside a Russian patrol boat to cadge cigarettes from her crew, with great banter and smiling on both sides. It seems a pity that our delegations aboard ship cannot meet in the free way of common men, who do not formulate grand schemes and ill-conceived development, merely suffer because of them.

Some barriers among the conferees are beginning to break down in response to a genuine interest—excitement, even—in the concept of international reserves; since all eight of Asia's crane species cross borders in their travels, their survival depends on such cooperation. Besides the proposed Russo-Chinese reserve north of Lake Khanka in Ussuria, there is fervent discussion of a much larger one in the Amur headwaters. Yet despite gallant efforts by the conference organizers and our tireless translators, Elena Smirenski and Simba Chan, the national delegations keep mostly to themselves; even the lone South Korean keeps his own counsel. A few English-speaking Japanese and Russians and the fifteen-odd Americans mingle a bit more, but in the end the language barriers and effortful civilities prove too wearisome, and each man returns to the companionable chatter of his countrymen.

Before any species can be systematically protected, its breeding grounds and migration routes must be discovered. The routes, territories, and wintering grounds of the red-crowned crane, *Grus japonensis*, have been so well mapped that in Japan, if not in mainland Asia, most pairs of this species can be tracked and accounted for. On the mainland, *japonensis* breeds almost entirely in the Amur drainage, often in sparsely populated border regions. It is essentially a bird of northern China, from Lake Dalainor in Inner Mongolia and Xianghai Nature Reserve on Inner Mongolia's border with Jilin Province east across Heilongjiang to Lake Khanka and the Ussuri; the heart of its territory is Heilongjiang, especially the environs of the Songhua River and the immense Zhalong marshes near the town of Qiqihar, some twenty-three hours by train northeast of Beijing.[19]

The main breeding grounds of *Grus vipio*, the white-naped crane, are still unknown; they may be in remote eastern Mongolia, where Jim Harris and I will explore later this summer. Both species represent what ornithologists know as the Oriental avifauna; the wetlands of the middle Amur lie at the north end of their range. According to Smirenski, the white-naped crane was once widespread throughout much of the Amur watershed, but with agricultural settlement and development encouraged by construction of the Baikal-Amur Railroad, and the Han settlement of the former Manchuria which increased rapidly after the Korean War, much of its habitat has been degraded or destroyed.

Neither crane flies much during the nesting season, and none have yet been seen on our upriver voyage. But toward dusk on the second day, an Oriental white stork (another rare species, already extinct in Japan and Korea, with less than three thousand left on the Asian mainland) is spotted from the conference room windows. The lone stork crossing our bow is traveling freely from China into Russia—a harbin-

Red-crowned crane (*Grus japonensis*)

ger of international unity which is not lost upon the delegates. Whether it encourages these men to set aside nationalist antagonisms on behalf of our common earth is quite another matter.

That afternoon, the *V. Poyarkov* arrives at Amurzet—the Jewish Autonomous Republic, as some maps call it, for that is its official name, bestowed in unholy apparatchik cynicism.[20] According to local memory, thousands of Jews from Ukraine and elsewhere were transported here during the vast purges and organized famines of the mid-1930s. For want of food and shelter, even firewood—most of the displaced were city dwellers, with no idea how to manage in the terrible Siberian winter—and because the few pioneers already on the land were desperate, too, and could not or would not help them, a large number of Jews died autonomously, without interference from the state. Others have since moved away or emigrated to Israel, and today the permanent Jewish families in this village of small cottages and log houses constitute less than 5 percent of the local population.

From Amurzet, a dirt road leads through broad communal fields of potatoes, soybeans, and wheat to a river floodplain and wet prairie of abounding wildflowers—meadows of daisies and the gold-and-purple Siberian iris, yellow daylilies, a red campion and a lavender geranium, blue cranesbill, purple vetch, a white bog orchid, and here and there a brilliant yellow flower called the Beautiful Lily. Known as Zhuravalini, this region is the largest undisturbed grassland in the Russian Far East, with tens of thousands of acres of good nesting habitat for cranes and storks. A gigantic stork nest fills the wide fork of an oak, and more nests hunker against the wind on some old survey towers; five white storks walk over a wet swale in single file. Birds are numerous—reed warblers and chestnut-eared buntings, garganey teal, a pair of pearl-gray Eurasian cuckoos, a black Amur or red-footed falcon darting away over the marsh between oak and willow. And finally, across the wind, comes that strong rolling cry of cranes that can sometimes be heard two miles away. A fine pair of *Grus vipio*, the white-naped crane—the first crane sighting of the voyage—cross the distant woods with heavy upward flicks of their great wings.

During the morning of July 7, as the ship moves north and west, the Amur lowlands of prairie and wet meadow give way to taiga and evergreen forest and low-rising foothills of the Dahinggan or Great Khingan Mountains. The region looks stunted and irregularly charred by the Great Khingan fire, known in the West as the Black Dragon fire, which broke out in Heilongjiang in May 1987 after a dry winter and burned for twenty days, consuming whole villages and crossing the Amur into Siberia, where it closed the Chita airport for two weeks with its shroud of smoke. Most of the burn was in Siberia, yet the Russians made no attempt to stop it, first because, with the high winds and drought, a great fire in a roadless land could never be brought under control, and second, because in the vast taiga of Siberia, the burn would grow back long before those trees were needed. But for China, with its diminished forests, the Black Dragon fire was a long-term ecological catastrophe; the world's worst forest fire in three centuries destroyed a third of its last great reserve of timber.[21]

In the hundred-mile gorge through the Great Khingan Mountains, the ship traverses a narrows that cannot be more than three hundred yards across; the captain tells me he has seen bears swim this channel. In July airlessness, the heat thickens, and the mist. Sun and shadow, whisperings of rain, a silver shimmering like uncoiling eels in the brown water. Facing upriver, the cormorants, terns, and tall grey herons have taken up stations on the banks as down the canyon between bluffs the wind comes in sudden puffs and buffets, raising white ridges on the current and leaving a strong scent of lime from flowering linden trees in the higher forests upriver. The squall passes and the air clears, turning cool.

Sergei Smirenski, at the ship's rail, reflects on his experiences in these forests, where he lived for months at a time while doing his doctoral dissertation on the birds of the Amur basin in the early seventies; he was astonished by the range of flora and fauna. He also discovered that its *G. japonensis* and *G. vipio* had never been studied systematically nor received protection. With Sergei Vinter, another crane man he had met out in the marshes, he fought successfully to have fifty thousand acres of these wetlands added to the Khingan Nature Reserve, which was expanded to its present size in 1977.

Smirenski knows the Amur basin as well as any man alive, and he is agitated and distressed by the proposed dams as well as by the free-for-all timbering in the region, which in addition to its endangered birds and mammals has sable, ermine, the Amur cat, and the yellow-throated marten, a big arboreal weasel. His days in the field as a young naturalist included skirmishes with aggressive brown bears, one of which drove him backward over a small cliff as he fired his gun into the air in an effort to hold it at bay.

The Amur, he says, has been logged since the late nineteenth century, but most of the clearing has occurred in recent decades. There are only a few settlements along the river, but more will come in consequence of logging and also the new Baikal-Amur Railroad, a northern spur of the Trans-Siberian which in just five years has opened up the taiga between Irkutsk and Khabarovsk. The accompanying disruption and the raw new towns, which are already polluting the north end of Baikal, have drawn hordes of the crows and magpies that prosper with human settlement, with great harm to local birdlife, cranes included. On the Chinese side, where timber clearing and development will be even more intensive, dreadful damage has already been done.

Next morning, Smirenski is on deck before seven, along with the hardcore bird-watchers who are prowling the ship's rails. "See that?" he cries, pointing a furious finger at the Chinese fishermen who stand up in their boats to watch us pass. "Fishing out of season! According to their own agreement with my country, they are not to fish during the spawning season! And I have spoken to the Chinese about it, and they pay no attention!" Smirenski deplores the fine-mesh nets used by the Chinese to drag even the smallest salmon from the river. He has counted a thousand nets, he says, between Khabarovsk and Amurzet; in consequence, the employees of two Russian hatcheries near Amurzet are out of work because spawning fish no longer come that far upriver. Such practices are responsible, he says, not only for the ruin of the salmon runs but also for the decline of the *kaluga* or Amur sturgeon, the largest of its family in the world.

What Sergei hates most passionately is the mid-Amur or Khingan dam proposed for the Khingan narrows, which threatens to flood the beautiful reserve he helped establish. " 'We have to do *something* with our great river!' That's the dam's main inspiration and excuse," he declares bitterly at a late-morning meeting in the upper-deck salon, where the sun pours through the windows on both sides. Sergei directs an impassioned talk against the dam at the few Chinese delegates who have bothered to turn up. Having consulted all concerned authorities, icthyologists as well as engineers, the SEU has serious doubts about the project, he reports.[22]

Because of monsoon rains, the Amur is high in the late summer when other rivers are low. Therefore the dam would inevitably raise the water level at the wrong season for the many species of flora and fauna adapted to Amur conditions; for example, masses of river ice blocked by the dam in early spring might later flood out river plains where the cranes breed. And despite the claims of the engineers, the reservoir could not help but raise the groundwater level and alter the plant community, with unknown effects upon the fauna. "Whether we shoot them, flood their nests, or destroy their habitat, we shall destroy the cranes!" he cries, with real emotion. Indeed, the proposed dam threatens critical habitat for many endemic and endangered species, not only the cranes but the white stork, Blakiston's fish owl, and the Chinese merganser. For many such species, the Khingan region lies at the north edge of a scattered and diminished range where their survival is already tenuous. "To this, the engineers say, 'So what?' " he exclaims despairingly. " 'Let those things go somewhere else if they don't like it.' But of course there is nowhere else for them to go.

"The Khingan dam will have no positive benefits in the long term. In 'conquering' the Amur, the engineers will not tame this wild river, they will kill it. We have the choice of being the biologists who let the Amur be destroyed for future generations, or the ones who saved it."

Sergei's passion is infectious, and the Americans and Japanese applaud him, but the Chinese harbor some grave doubts about his speech if relentless inscrutability is any clue. One by one, they turn toward the only member of their delegation who had been involved in the original dam proposals.

Dr. Ma Yiqing, director of the zoology department at the Institute of Natural Resources at Harbin, in Heilongjiang, has worked for many years in the region and is a leading authority on the Amur tiger as well as the cranes of China.[23] He advises the conference that although his country withdrew from the dam project in 1957, it continued to study land surveys, geology, economics, flora and fauna, even scenery and the cultural heritage of the local people. Therefore China was well prepared when in the early 1980s the two countries organized a "Committee on Joint Economic Betterment of the Amur Basin," which proposed two hydroelectric stations on Black Dragon River. Dr. Ma agrees with Dr. Smirenski that both salmon and sturgeon have been drastically reduced by man's activities.[24] However—do we see a glance over his shoulder at his dour colleagues?—his government has established two nature reserves where both species might spawn. Here Ma smiles enigmatically, confounding his audience.

The mid-Amur dam (known in China as Taipingtau, or "Peaceful Groove Channel") will have little impact on the Khingan Nature Reserve—that is official Chinese policy. However, Dr. Ma confesses, he has conferred with a Chinese engineer who agrees entirely with the data presented by his Russian colleague; he himself can only shrug in the face of such a paradox. On the other hand, he adds at once, the Chinese engineer arrived at a different resolution: "No matter," said the engineer, "we'll build it anyway, because only with electricity can we bring light to the People with minimum impact on the environment. It would be a waste of the Black Dragon River not to use this energy."

"Isn't it time we started thinking of other sources of power, other bases for the economy?" Smirenski demands; he dismisses the engineers, Chinese and Russian, as "the hydro-Mafia." Here Mr. Piao Xi Wang, the youthful director of nature reserves for the Environmental Protection Bureau in Heilongjiang (and apparently the Party man appointed by the authorities to monitor his colleagues' statements), stands up to respond stiffly, "There is no 'hydro-Mafia' in China. Our engineers work for the benefit of the People. Our studies prove that the Peaceful Groove Channel will have virtually no impact on the nature reserve. Anyway, only through dams can the People attain a decent life." He sits down.

"But even if you are right, the Khingan dam is only one of many problems we must face in regard to the Amur River!" Here Sergei stops short, knowing the uselessness of his emotions in the face of bureaucratic caution and inertia. He hurries to smooth things over, concluding the meeting by remarking how constructive these discussions have been, despite occasional small disagreements. But nobody imagines that our Chinese colleagues will change their minds, or dare to say so even if they do.

The Chinese are tough pragmatists who put great stock in statistics and are not much impressed by such fuzzy alternatives to massive dams as "ecotourism." They state that precisely 542 red-crowned cranes with 110 nests inhabit their great land. In private, the Russians complain that the Chinese are blindly addicted to official figures in the absence of meaningful ecological data from the field. They even claim to perceive in the Chinese a hostility toward the untamed forest and its wildlife that Russian people love, maintaining that the Chinese, having de-stroyed most of the wild land and life in their own country, have lost touch with nature.

Aware that Russia is suffering severe shortages, the Chinese have brought ample foodstuffs to be eaten in the privacy of their cabins; they plainly resent what they perceive as chronic Russian discourtesy and in-efficiency, not to speak of deficient hospitality toward themselves. The Chinese have not had their fair share of the limited places in the vehi-cles during shore excursions; while that is true, it is also true that more than once, they have chosen to shop at the local market rather than go bumping off on rough dirt roads. As the Russians are too quick to point out, the Chinese delegates' clothes are quite unsuitable for fieldwork—most wear street shoes and white shirts at all times—and only three have binoculars (which are scarce in China and not easy to borrow, Jim Harris explains).

In the Chinese view, as patiently translated by the indefatigable Simba Chan, the Japanese receive favored treatment because they are mainly scientists and naturalists, whereas the Chinese, through no fault of their own, are mostly bureaucrats. No place was made for naturalists during the rigors of the Cultural Revolution and the Great Leap For-ward, in which millions of people died; in consequence, trained field bi-ologists such as Dr. Ma Yiqing are elderly and few.

Dr. Ma, to be sure, has come equipped with binoculars and field clothes and even a pair of brownish shorts for this warm weather. He is also more fraternal than his compatriots—in fact, boisterous and amus-ing—not only because he speaks some English but because he has worked with George Archibald for the past twelve years and understands the critical significance of crane reserves. Dr. Ma is working hard to persuade his delegation to arrive at some sort of agreement with the Russians, but perhaps he is mildly resented by his compatriots, who feel less free to wear brown shorts and voice opinions. Each man is polite and friendly when encountered on deck by himself, his face opening with shy pleasure upon being greeted, but as a group our Chinese associates relax only in the security of their own quarters, where to judge from the bursts of toasts and merriment—*Gan bei!*—from behind closed cabin doors, they are very relaxed indeed.

Considering their nation's population pressures and industrial priorities, Dr. Archibald points out, the Chinese deserve credit for recent efforts to spare what little wildlife they have left. Therefore he warns his grumbling colleagues that the good faith of their delegation in regard to international cooperation on behalf of wildlife and the environment must be taken seriously.

The Japanese, who have brought their own television crew, are English-speaking ornithological associates and friends of Dr. Archibald.[25] They avoid the Russo-Chinese skirmishing, taking no sides and moving unobtrusively, all the more so because their government is withholding aid to the new Russia until the Russians agree to relinquish the southern Kurile Islands. On this ship, to be sure, we are bird men first and nationalists second. (Says Mikhail Dykhan, the young director of the Kurile reserve, "We don't really care who owns the place. We care about the cranes.") For their part, the Japanese suspect that the few Kurile cranes might be better off if Russia kept the islands, since the Russians are probably less inclined to drain crane breeding areas and "develop" them as golf courses.

Days and evenings aboard ship are largely taken up with research meetings on endangered species and discussion groups on such corollary threats to wildlife as surging human populations, watershed destruction, unsustainable forestry, industrial pollution, and other problems that do not seem to concern the corporations and their minions in public office. At meals, Archibald and Harris do their best to nurse rapport between the delegations, promoting future communication between countries and coordinated protection of known flyways. As one delegate observes, it's time the red-crowned crane was perceived as a single biological unit, not as five endangered populations in five different lands.

And so, with increasing difficulty due to the low water level and emerging sandbars, our ship proceeds on this symbolic voyage up the great watercourse parting two nations. Even on the Chinese shore, the red-bricked settlements are becoming small and few, though one sees an occasional factory stack off in the distance. Along a dike on the south bank, a mare draws two men on a farm cart with big wooden wheels, trailed at a little distance by her foal.

Toward noon on July 9, the ship arrives at Innokentievka, a nineteenth-century Cossack settlement that has been farmed communally since the 1930s, when the grain harvest was confiscated and a hard famine induced to improve the local attitude toward collective farming. Like most of the river settlements at this time of year, it has a broad brown beach where a few robust Siberians take the sun. In Stalin's day, these folks relate, local people lived on grass and whatever they could gather from the taiga; occasionally a villager would wander here with hook and line in quest of fish only to die of starvation at the river's edge, too weak to return home.

In early afternoon, a brown-and-orange Aeroflot helicopter lands on the beach. Groups of delegates are flown in relays to survey the Khingan Nature Reserve, and once again the Chinese are missing from the party. Weren't they invited? Are they not interested? No one seems to know.

The Arkhara plain lies inland from the village, a huge savanna of bog and wet meadow wandered by creeks and scattered with islands of willow, birch, and poplar. A roe deer, then another, flushed from the swale, streak away through the birch islands like shoots of fire in the white trees. Waterbirds flee in all directions as the chattering helicopter slides out sideways to investigate four or five treetop nests of the white storks, coming so close that the black-and-white young crouch hard on the bare sticks in the battering roar and wind.

At this time of year, still tending unfledged young, the cranes are rarely seen aloft, but two white-napeds, long necks outstretched, traverse the distance, and farther on, the helicopter startles a molting pair that goes flapping wildly through the reeds, unable to fly. Of the red-crowned crane, alas, there is no sign.

According to its young director, Dr. Vladimir Andronov, the Khingan Nature Reserve comprises 130,000 acres of swampy plain in the Arkhara lowlands and 50,000 acres of oak foothills with Korean pine and linden in addition to the spruce and fir of the northern taiga—a mixed deciduous and coniferous woodland where the fauna and flora of Siberia, Manchuria, and Ussuri Land all come together.

On a lake on the Arkhara plain, the reserve maintains a crane breeding station that obtains its eggs and chicks from nests threatened by the fires that sweep over the reserve almost every spring. Rampant burning of the marshes, illegal hunting, and insufficient territory and protection are its main problems. Reserve staff includes nineteen scientists and researchers who are studying birds of prey as well as cranes, also ecological effects of fires and other factors which might diminish the dwindling crane numbers in the Amur basin.[26] Since the station was founded a few years ago, one male *vipio* has raised three chicks all by himself, a pair of orphaned *vipio* have joined the wild flock in migration, and a female *japonensis*, though too young to breed, has been borne away by a migrating male, which if all goes well will become her mate for life.

At present, three red-crowneds are resident at the station— one chick, one yearling, and one adult male—together with a solitary white-naped chick. In their confiding curiosity and sweet peeping, the big-footed young, warm golden brown, resemble immense long-legged baby chickens. The red-crowned chick has been reared mostly by the yearling in the absence of any parental impulse in the male, a cranky bird that hisses like a snake as it stalks the nervous visitors, bringing a Japanese TV crewman to a rigid halt with a smart peck between the shoulder blades. "I am *attack*," the poor man cries, scarcely daring a look behind him. Captive cranes can be feisty indeed, requiring safety precautions, and the feistiest of all, Archibald says, is the Siberian crane—though the red-crowned, largest of the cranes and fast and smart, may be more formidable.

I have hardly begun to scan the marsh from a point of wooded shore along the lake when a vivid red-black-white head rises from tall reeds two hundred yards away, withdraws, rises again, joined this time by another. In a moment, two brilliant white cranes stalk warily into the open, the shining black tertial feathers of the folded wings draped elegantly on the hidden tail. Standing side by side, they stretch white necks and long black bills to the sun, bugling a duet response to a cry from the captive male at the research station, whom perhaps they perceive as an intruder on their territory. Generally the duet is initiated by the male with one strident syllable, which the female answers with a rapid two or three; then the male gives a long series of low calls counterpointed by the high-pitched yelping of the female. The duet will be echoed in synchronous chorus by any other pairs in the vicinity.

All cranes are exceptionally sharp-eyed and wary, and almost at once, the twin heads turn toward me, the crimson afire in the green of marsh and woods for just that instant before the birds withdraw into the wind-waved reeds. Not until the first exultation passes does it occur to me that the pair is too close to the research station to be truly wild. As it turns out, these two have been raised by man from wild eggs removed from the path of a spring fire. Having grown accustomed to the research station, they have not responded to the calls of the wild cranes that might have led them southward in migration, although their chicks have flown away each autumn. And yet how beautiful they were in those instants when I first saw them—bugling tricolor cranes in a shining marsh surrounded by dark forest, unaware that their wild nature had been lost.

Most crane species establish breeding territories in open wetlands or the environs of water, as far as defended territories permit from the closest pair of their own species. The mated pairs nest annually, and they are long-lived; those young which survive the dangerous first year may breed in their fourth year and annually thereafter for at least fifteen years in the wild and a good half century in captivity.

Among cranes, the first nesting attempt and quite often the second are apt to fail. Despite tradition to the contrary, cranes do not pair for life unless reproduction is relatively successful soon, since the precious nesting season cannot be wasted every year trying to hatch infertile eggs. However, the mate is loyal, even in time of danger, and this loyalty may persist after its mate's death. (There is a record of a starving *japonensis* in Korea's demilitarized zone guarding the frozen corpse of its companion.) Attentive mates contribute more genes to the population than flighty ones, and biologically, the advantage of strong and continuous breeding outweighs the risk. The pair bond is strengthened by the elaborate dancing and displays that characterize this family and by the strong "unison call" made by all *Grus* species. An elongated trachea coiled like a French horn in the sternum permits those wild horn notes on the wind, which may resound from the gray skies before the dark skeins of their companies come through the clouds.

In the spring, the red-crowned crane, *G. japonensis*, arrives first in the Amur basin, staking out its breeding territories as far as possible from any sign of man; it rarely leaves the sanctuary of its wetlands. The white-naped crane, *G. vipio*, generally selects the outer areas of the same nesting habitat in reed beds and wet meadow, although usually closer to the agricultural lands where it does much of its feeding. Because *vipio* mostly probes for tubers in a limited patch of boggy ground while *japo-*

nensis wanders the water's edge, hunting small creatures and picking at the vegetation, there is little competition and small conflict.

As Archibald admiringly points out, the eggs of the red-crowned crane are elegantly smooth, as befits such a grand bird, not "pitted and pimpled" like those of other species. Oddly and inconsistently, however, *japonensis* lays dimorphic eggs, which are sometimes clear white, as in the subtropical species (the crowned cranes, sarus, and brolga), and sometimes bluish or of a mottled pattern, as in most northern cranes. The occurrence of an occasional white egg among *japonensis* suggests that its ancestors nested in a more southerly region of east Asia, where the white shell would reflect the sun's heat. (Cold-climate species such as the Siberian and the black-necked crane of the Tibetan plateau lay the darkest and most heat-absorbent eggs.)

Because red-crowned cranes will not nest except in high dead reeds, fire is a great risk to nests and may prevent nesting from taking place at all. One year when no red-crowned nests survived due to drought and fire, Sergei Smirenski observed a *japonensis* destroy a nest of *vipio* and usurp the nest site. Even when the nest is successful, only three out of five chicks live long enough to fly. In all crane species, both parents incubate and tend the eggs and young, which leave the nest soon after hatching. Ordinarily, one chick dominates in the competition for food and the other, stressed and starved, perishes quickly.[27] However, wild red-crowned chicks are fairly tolerant of each other, Sergei observes. For that reason and perhaps others, *japonensis* pairs often raise two chicks.

I row on the lake and swim and explore the oak woods, enjoying the great crested grebe and eastern curlew and pied harrier, the nuthatches, rose finches, and tricolored flycatchers. At night, with Archibald, Harris, and a few others, I sleep in a research station tent in order to join a helicopter expedition to capture and fit radio harnesses to those molting *vipio* early next morning.

With the free-spirited hospitality one meets everywhere in Russia, our kind hosts prepare a delicious supper of fresh vegetables and spicy sausage, with the usual fulsome toasts of beer and vodka. We are joined by an archeologist who has a small dig in the oak woods on a knoll overlooking the lake—a site, he says, of early man (probably *Sinanthropus*) and also of later Paleolithic nomads perhaps related to the Jomon of Japan, who were replaced in their turn by the small Mongol tribe known as the Dauri who gave their name to the Daurian steppe off to the west and to the Daurian crane, as *G. vipio* is known here in Siberia. Apparently the Dauri were obliterated one way or another at the time of Chinghis Khan and his successors. Among the artifacts the archeologist displays are bone harpoons and walrus-tusk choppers, apparently acquired by the Dauri in trade from a northern tribe such as the Chukchi, also agate scrapers, an iron mirror with carved figures, and a bronze bell with a tiger-head motif that he thinks might be about fifteen centuries old. Ancient as these objects are, they only remind me that cranes were flying in their modern form more than sixty million years before man fashioned them.

Next morning, we set off in the helicopter after a sunny breakfast of thin blinis with fresh blueberries and a light white honey from the linden tree. Soon that pair of molting *vipio* is sighted, flapping and running at astonishing speed over wet prairie. The copter pilot, skidding his big machine around, manages to turn them; when they finally tire, Smirenski and Vladimir Andronov are dropped off to run them down. Even with more helicopter herding, their run turns out to be long and exhausting, and eventually the larger male escapes entirely. Smirenski tackles the female, who cuts him badly across the arms with her razor toenails.

An adult of a large crane species is a very strong animal indeed, and its long, hard, pointed bill and claws are fearsome weapons; its flapping attack is generally claws first, but if this fails to bowl over or drive off its opponent, it may use its bill, aimed at the head or face. Several pairs of hands are needed to subdue and band the bird without doing it harm; one man holds and tapes the legs and another grasps it by the neck as a Japanese ornithologist, Dr. Kiyoaki Ozaki, slips a bag over its head (the darkness calms it) and wraps a cloth straitjacket around the body to pin

its wings close to its sides and control its thrashing. Next, it is banded—
a numbered red band on the right leg and a green on the left. Once it is
sexed and weighed and measured, Ozaki fits it with a small radio in a
back harness, to permit satellite tracking during its migrations. When
the bag is removed, the enormous bird, its fierce flame-colored eye
blinking at electronic speed in the carmine skin, hisses in distress like its
reptile ancestors; in this frayed, molting condition, it can neither fly nor
properly defend itself, as it might do in full plumage.

In the summer silence, in this sunlit wet savanna of iris and lilies, I
am struck abruptly by the spectacle of so much manpower and machin-
ery, noise, time, and cost devoted to the capture and banding of one
ragged bird—the lengths to which man is driven to salvage the last
wild survivors of his own heedless rampage on this precious earth. After all this trouble and expense, in the shock of this scarifying and dis-
orienting episode, and the peril of the obstacles it may meet in the
thousands of miles of a migration encumbered by its backpack and
transmitter, this bird may never be heard about again.

Jim Harris acknowledges that the radio-transmitter pack may increase
the bird's risk during migration. However, he thinks the crucial information to be gained justifies that risk for the benefit of the species as a whole.
Satellite tracking cannot solve the mystery of unknown migration routes
and destinations unless many transmitters are attached to many cranes,
but knowing where this middle Amur population goes when the birds
cross the frontiers provides a better understanding of which staging areas
along its route should be monitored, the better to protect it.[28]

A t dawn next day at the village of Poyarkovo, I awake at six to find
the ship docking at a coal depot, with long-necked cranes (the machines took their name from *Grus*) elevated all about us in the morning
mist. Delicate Amur falcons course the river like huge swallows in pursuit of insects, but the falcons are small consolation for the news that the
river is too low for the ship to proceed farther. The captain has counted
on monsoon rains that are already weeks late; she will never reach her

destination at the old frontier town of Blagoveschensk, at the confluence of the Amur and Zeya rivers.

A car for hire is located, and a small party of Russians and Japanese journeys fifty miles upriver to the village of Muraviovka, where the local people vote to lease to Sergei's SEU an eleven-thousand-acre "nature park" protected within an existing game refuge which surrounds *Grus* breeding territory.[29] The historic signing of July 10 takes place in a town-hall ceremony attended by a throng of seventy, marking the first time since the 1917 revolution that a private organization has acquired Russian land for a reserve. Meanwhile, we indulged ourselves in excited talk of a three-nation crane reserve in the central Asian steppes. With the encouragement of the ICF, Inner Mongolia's Dalainor Nature Reserve, with its huge lake and surrounding steppe—nearly two and a half million acres—was established in 1986 and Russia's Daurski Nature Reserve, another half-million acres, including the broad Tari lakes on the Mongolian border, in 1989. This year Outer Mongolia has established its own Daguurin, or Daurian, reserve of a quarter-million acres, most of it adjoining the Russian tract at the Tari lakes. In the next fortnight, Harris and I would travel to eastern Mongolia to verify reports of breeding white-naped cranes in the remote Kerulen River.

On the way downriver, still muttering about discrimination, the Chinese delegates sign a nonbinding resolution to work for the preservation of the Amur. Their mood seems lighter, but only Dr. Ma and the smiling Mr. Piao are relaxed enough to participate in the singing at the evening parties in the dining salon. Translator Elena Smirenski and the Yakuts friend of the Siberian crane, Kitalik Ivan, lead the crowd with their fine voices, while South Korea's representative, Mr. Cho, contributes a few peculiar riffs on his guitar. The monsoon is on the way at last, for next day the Black Dragon skies are low, with a rumor of the sullen rain that will greet us at Khabarovsk.

From Khabarovsk, George Archibald, Jim Harris, and I, with Viktor Bahktin, Dr. Ma, and other Chinese delegates from Heilongjiang, take the night train south to Spassk, a town on the Ussuri plain east of Lake Khanka and west of the Amur tiger region in the coastal mountains.

Like all Siberian cities, Spassk is drab, in sad need of a patch and a lick of paint, but it is also clean and prosperous, thanks to its cement factory and the rich agriculture of the old lake floor. As in Khabarovsk, a statue of Lenin still stands in the town square, a monument not to ideology but to indifference—these towns are several thousand miles from Moscow and are slow to change. The streets are lined with dark and dull-leaved poplars, and the houses are mostly a dark leaden green or a soiled blue, with sprawling vegetable gardens out behind. In this hot midsummer weather, the citizens line up for bread and beer, dispensed from a large tank on a cart down at the market. The most picturesque spot I come across is an old cemetery, overgrown and dark under mourning trees and long sad grasses that stray and whisper. "Our friends are here, and our co-workers," one young woman says of the gaunt monuments and plastic flowers, "and our parents, too. So our cemetery is called the Second Town."

On the evening of July 15, a farewell party at the Hotel Lotos became an occasion of boisterous festivity. Thanks to the patient mediation of the ICF, the Chinese and Russians had survived one another's company for two weeks, and now they toasted and vowed to meet again to work together on crane problems—the main hope and purpose of the Amur conference. "The Chinese and Russians and Japanese *must* work together. If we give up on that, we give up on the Amur and much else besides," Jim Harris said. In an agreement signed at Spassk the following morning, the Russians undertook to provide a helicopter for a crane survey of Xingkai Hu the following year, with the Chinese providing logistical support and biologists from both countries participating.[30] Unlike the rhetorical Amur Declaration, this was a firm, practical agreement, recognized by everyone present as the critical first step in establishing an international reserve for endangered cranes. Fragile though it was, an armature of harmony had been created; already Noritaka Ichida of Japan's Wild Bird Society had flown off to the Kuriles with *zapovednik* director Dykhan to establish a cooperative program on behalf of the islands' small *japonensis* population.[31]*

On our last morning, with Harris and Yuri Shibaev, a crane biologist from Vladivostok, I accompany two Chinese officials on a helicopter survey of the border region where it is hoped that an international crane reserve might be established.[32] The Chinese led the way in 1986 with the establishment of what they called the Xingkai Hu Reserve, which they have since expanded; they claim that about 60 of the lake region's 130 red-crowned cranes live on Chinese territory. On the Russian side, the Lake Khanka Reserve, created four years later from five isolated sites surrounded by developed land, includes two million acres of wetlands and open lake, with a buffer zone of drier marsh and a prohibition against fishing or hunting within a mile of the shoreline. Where the two tracts abut in the northeast corner of the lake is a promising location for an international reserve.

For many years, this flat wetland east of Khanka, with a few farms of Korean immigrants in Kazakhstan, provided all the rice grown in the U.S.S.R. Since this is Siberia's richest agricultural land—grains, soybeans, tomatoes, rice, most of it in vast communal fields that stretch to the horizons—the proposal that the wetlands near the lake be made into a crane reserve has been fought hard. Similarly, on the Chinese side, the Xingkai Hu Reserve lies too near the valuable farmlands of the Three Rivers plain. In any event, according to Dr. Ma, no provincial government can authorize an international reserve, and Mr. Hu Zheng Wu—deputy director of the Heilongjiang Forest Bureau and the highest-ranking official in the delegation—must make a request of the minister of forestry in Beijing, who will have to approve any agreement and its proposed financing as well. "Sometime money not okay, sometime money yah okay," predicts Ma Yiqing.

The small aircraft crosses the grainfields west of Spassk, turning north over the rice paddies and marshes of the buffer zone between town and lake. Khanka, shining silver in the mist, is a shallow egg-shaped basin some fifty miles from north to south, and thirty-seven

---

*See the brief summaries of significant developments with respect to the cranes' situation in each region at the head of the notes for each chapter, pp. 303 ff.

miles across at the widest.[33] Not counting the Aral and Caspian seas and
Lake Baikal, it is the largest lake in Russia, but its average depth is only
about twelve feet.[34] Lake Khanka is severely polluted by heavy metals
from the coal mining industry as well as herbicides and pesticides from
the huge farms.

Spassk is still in sight when three immense white birds appear in
measured flight to the northeast, on a course that seems bound to inter-
sect our own. I lean forward and yell, *"Red-crowneds!"* at Jim Harris,
who nods and smiles and waves assent over his shoulder. The cranes
swing off toward the north, increasing speed with the short hard upward flick of wingtips that is characteristic of this family. Through
binoculars, I can see their elegant red-black-white heads.

The birds turn toward the sun and vanish as the helicopter clatters
on over the marshes. The wind of its rotors bends green reeds and riffles the sparkling black sloughs. The water is sprinkled with large
white birds—swans, storks, egrets—that cannot compare in size or
majesty with those great cranes.

Perhaps fifty miles north of Spassk, the aircraft approaches the frontier at the small river that divides the Khanka and Xingkai Hu reserves,
flowing eastward through wet meadows from the misty lake to the Ussuri, which channels Khanka's overflow north to the Amur. Here the
machine turns south again, following a wooded ridge that forms the
rim of this huge saucer. Just east of the ridge, stalking the open savanna
between ponds, is a family of four *japonensis*, the sedate adults striding
swiftly, without flutter or commotion, leading big brown chicks from
pale green meadow into the deep green reeds at water's edge.[35]

We turn back for a second look, swinging wide so as not to flare the
cranes. In the vast marsh, the giant birds with their huge chicks evoke
those ancestral crane-like birds that walked among the dinosaurs in the
morning sunlight of the Eocene, sixty million years ago.

TWO

On the Daurian Steppe

At Changanor the Khan has a great Palace surrounded by a fine
plain where are found cranes in great numbers. He causes millet
and other grains to be sown in order that the birds may not want.
—Marco Polo

The white-naped crane, *Grus vipio*, which has been described as
"very rare and possibly becoming extinct,"[1] was known to
breed in various locations in the Amur-Ussuri watershed of
southeastern Siberia and northern China. These small populations migrated south to wintering grounds in the Han River estuary and the demilitarized zone (DMZ) that crosses the Korean peninsula; others went
farther, crossing the Korea Strait to the village fields of Izumi and the
Araseki plain, in Kyushu, the great south island of Japan. Others still,
apparently from farther west, appeared in numbers in the Poyang and
Dongting lakes region of the Yangtze River basin of southeast China—
a great mystery, since the wintering population at the Poyang lakes,
undiscovered until 1981, was more than twice the number that could be
accounted for by the known breeding territories in the upper Amur
drainage. According to Dr. Ma Yiqing, the few breeding *vipio* in northern China were outnumbered everywhere by *G. japonensis*, and the
same was true north of the Amur in Siberia, where the species was in

serious decline. Conservationists were at a loss to help *G. vipio*, since the heart of its northern breeding grounds and its precise migration routes remained unknown.

During the Cold War decades, Siberia and central Asia had been closed to Western ornithologists, who had no opportunity for fieldwork or even good communications with isolated Asian colleagues. Not until 1991, with the implosion of the Soviet regime, did the ICF receive a report that the white-naped crane was breeding on the Daurian steppe in northeastern Mongolia; it had also been sighted farther south, in remote marshes where the wild Kerulen River crossed the border into Inner Mongolia, in the farthest western headwaters of the Amur watershed. (Excited by the report, the ICF had invited two Mongolian ornithologists to the crane conference on the Amur River, but they had not arrived, flights having been canceled in their country for want of fuel.) Jim Harris and I hoped to confirm the report of critical *vipio* breeding territories in that region.

B ound for Mongolia, Jim Harris and I joined some of the Chinese delegates on their return from the Amur conference to Heilongjiang. We would journey by train from the Russian Far East across the border to Harbin, and from there to Beijing, in order to catch the twice-weekly flight to Ulaan Baatar, where we would travel to eastern Mongolia in search of the main breeding territories of *G. vipio*.

From Spassk our group traveled by bus to catch the train that travels to Harbin from the small border town of Kamen-Rybotov. There a customs official—a Colonel Savin—decreed that the Amerikanski's passport and visa were not in order. To leave Russia, said the colonel, the Amerikanski must obtain some sort of certification from higher authorities that these papers were acceptable. In effect, this required a four-hour bus trip back to Spassk and a night train to Khabarovsk, six hundred miles in the wrong direction.

Nyet pro-blem, my Russian friends assured me. Waving their hands in fine Russian style, they remonstrated with Colonel Savin. Perhaps in this isolated place, word had not arrived about the end of the Cold War? But in the end, this obdurate official closed eyes, ears, and mouth, dead to all pleas. Stunned, I went out onto the platform and waved goodbye to Jim Harris and Dr. Ma as the whistle blew and the train jerked, then moved slowly away across the border into China.

Viktor Bakhtin, who had accompanied the party as translator, was profoundly distressed. "I am ashamed of my country," he kept saying, no matter how often I pointed out that mean-spirited bureaucrats in every land have ever made life miserable for the undefended. Nevertheless, this Savin had done me a very serious disservice, since I held a hard-won ticket on the biweekly flight from Beijing to Ulaan Baatar that was scheduled to leave in three days' time, and if I missed it, I would never overtake Jim Harris and the crane expedition to eastern Mongolia.

Much disheartened, we returned in the bus to Spassk. Awakened in the dead of night to lend me a few rubles, George Archibald gallantly pulled pants on over his pajamas and walked with us to the railroad station. Though none of us had serious hope that I would reach Beijing in time, I caught the train to Khabarovsk at 3:15 that morning.

At the Khabarovsk station, I was met by Sergei Ivanov, a young ornithologist who had been with us on the Amur. He conducted me straight to the visa office, which said my papers were in order, *Nyet pro-blem*. Sergei Smirenski also said *Nyet pro-blem* and rushed me to the airport, where we learned that there were no flights to Beijing and that both of the biweekly flights to Harbin, where I might hope to catch a train, were overbooked. *Nyet pro-blem*, Smirenski said, worried but gallant to the end. Since the first flight to Harbin left that same evening, he returned me to the airport at 8:30 P.M. to wait about in case of a cancellation. Sergei thought a bribe might help conjure up an empty seat, and of course it did; he waved goodbye and hastened off into the night. He had hardly left when the customs official at the final barrier slapped my passport down and picked up a red phone in order to confer with some unknown authority—Colonel Savin? Hard minutes passed as those behind me fretted, openly suspicious of the innocent expression—*Nyet pro-blem!*—that I maintained on my face while I screeched inside. Then, abruptly, the official waved me through, perhaps because it was simply too much bother to detain this pesky Amerikanski whose duffel was already on the plane.

I arrived at Harbin's Swan Hotel at two next morning. At daybreak, with the spirited assistance of my corridor attendant, a delightful young person named Miss Chen Shih—the only soul at the Swan Hotel who had some English—I ascertained that the daily Beijing train was departing even as we inquired about it, and that the first space on the daily flight would not become available until four days hence. Undaunted, Miss Chen Shih tracked down my Amur shipmate Dr. Ma, who was scarcely off the train from Kamen-Rybotov. Dr. Ma turned up promptly on his bicycle, instructed me to wait, then pedaled off to the chaotic airline office. I passed a long day of suspense in the hotel lobby before he came back beaming, having worked more wonders with the lowly bribe.

Ignoring my gratitude, refusing to be my guest in his own city, Ma bundled me off to his small apartment, stopping to buy white peaches, tomatoes, and cucumbers along the way. After steamy hot towels and tea, peaches, and beer, then a delicious supper in which we were joined by his son and a few friends, we celebrated something or other with a series of straight shots of *bai jiu*, a perfumed and highly lethal Chinese vodka. "*Gan bei!* Three times *Gan bei!* Three is Chinese *prin*-ciple!" cried my jolly savior. Ma insisted that I address him in the future as "Lo Ma," or "Old Dog."

The worse for wear, I bid adieu to the Swan Hotel at four next morning. Because of China's policy of maintaining the same time zone throughout a country approximately two thousand miles from east to west, it was already broad daylight. Despite the frantic crowding in China, there is a sense of cleanliness and order in marked contrast with the decrepitude of Russia, and street sweepers in white masks with long straw brooms scoured the boulevards, dodging the swarms of tiny tractors hauling old farm carts to street markets. Vegetable gardens sprout and flourish in every odd-sized corner of the city and all along the highway to the airport, where an immense sign reads HAPPY ON THE WAY.

Flying south over Heilongjiang and the vast collective farms of Jilin Province, I was awed by the regimented landscapes. The neat red villages and towns are well contained and do not straggle out into the farmland as they do elsewhere. This is refreshing to the eye until one realizes the extent and multitude of these brick outcrops, like spreading molds in the green seas of machine agriculture. With China's population at well over a billion—about one out of five of all human mouths on the planet—one perceives in an instant why there are no trees, why the meanest city lot must be induced to produce food, and why the future of the cranes—and the tiger and the panda—is shrouded by the dark shadow of mankind.

I astonished Jim Harris at his morning coffee in the lobby of Beijing's Beautiful West Park Hotel. Since he had appointments at the zoo, I collected myself in a long walk around Tiananmen Square and the Forbidden City. Somewhere above, the day was sunny—that is to say, the sun glinted dimly through the smog and grainy mists that shroud Chinese cities even in fair weather, due to the pervasive burning of low-grade coal. The pollution is compounded by the hordes of honking vehicles that stink and fume in the choked traffic girding this sanctuary of space and silence, and yet the vast square and monumental palace remain serene.

Outside the Hall of Supreme Harmony, two noble bronze cranes awaited me on the high terrace; the most famous crane statues in the world, they originally stood guard on either side of the emperor's throne in the imperial palace as symbols of long life and good fortune, and like most creatures depicted in Chinese art, they are beautiful. By now, however, I had encountered what seemed to be an aversion to wild things in Chinese life. Entering a taxi at the Beijing airport, I was met by a loud cry of dismay emitted by the driver upon discovering a small

pinkish gecko on his windshield. Before I could protest—for having pioneered who knows how many miles of airport concrete, this brave
lizard surely deserved a better fate—the man mashed it to death with
repeated blows of his windshield wipers, then turned to me with a great
smile of triumph and relief, as if he had slain a dragon. And now in the
Forbidden City, a youth walking ahead of me past a stone wall attempted to obliterate a harmless wall lizard with a rolled-up magazine,
dancing in and out in high excitement, as if the tiny desperate thing was
on the point of a savage attack. Fortunately, the young man was too
frightened to be effective, and indeed seemed grateful to escape with his
life when the three-inch lizard whisked into a cranny, leaving behind a
small, sad, twitching tail.

Especially since 1949, China has been afflicted with appalling abuse
and mismanagement of its land and life, with consequent public alien-
ation from its wild creatures. A great man-made famine in a three-year
period in the early 1960s was followed by the so-called Cultural Revolution, beginning in 1966, which through famine and violence destroyed
more than thirty million people, with widespread cannibalism reported
in the barren south. On its western plains, whole herds of antelope and
kiang, or wild asses, were slung onto trains for shipment to the starving
millions in the eastern cities. The last Chinese tigers, leopards, wolves,
and dholes were hunted down and killed as "vermin"; street sparrows,
rats, and locusts were condemned to death as "class enemies" and
"pests" for eating up too much of the People's grain. (The sparrows
were purged in a three-day country-wide campaign that deployed every weapon from poisoned grain to firecrackers, and millions of other
small vertebrates perished with them; more recently, it has been
decreed that sparrows compensate for their counterrevolutionary activities by their consumption of insects, and the common bedbug has replaced them on the death list.)

Jim Harris says, "The Chinese like the idea of nature as an abstrac-
tion, as a metaphor, which is why it is prominent in their art, but the re-
ality makes them uneasy. The new generations have no experience of
wilderness, far less wild creatures." The campaigns against wild ani-

mals coincided with official disregard for wildlife science education in the universities. Although the government has changed its conservation policies, there is still a dearth of field biologists—hence the bureaucratic makeup of the Chinese delegation to the Amur.

I bought a watermelon slice to quench my thirst on a walk across the park. Next morning, "happy on the way," we departed on the bi-weekly flight to the People's Republic of Mongolia, accompanied by young Tsuyoshi "Go" Fujita of Japan's Wild Bird Society.

Northwest of Beijing, the teeming plain is left behind, the soft farm greens cut off abruptly by dark forest jades on the evergreen slopes of sudden mountains. Here the Great Wall—begun in the third century B.C., and the one evidence of man said to be visible from the moon—winds like a stone serpent along wooded ridges. Soon the mountains descend to the drier, less fertile landscapes of Inner Mongolia, which subside in turn into the harsh grays and yellows of the Gobi Desert.

By air, the Gobi is scarcely an hour from Beijing. The proximity of this wild and remote land of Chinghis Khan (whose cavalry, sweeping Eurasia, caused tremors in the imperial courts of Jin) led to the construction of a barrier all the way from the Yellow Sea to the western borders of Nei Mongol Zizhiqu (the Inner Mongolia Autonomous Republic), and also to the farther region that became Outer Mongolia, with its ancient capital at Karakorum. The Great Khan's grandson Kublai Khan would have his throne in the Chinese capital called Dadu, which became Peking under the emperors and is now Beijing. All that is left of Karakorum is a great stone turtle, solitary on the plain, that has weathered the fierce winds of central Asia since the thirteenth century.

The border between Mongolias is lost in the dry wastes of the Gobi. Gradually, the sands give way to arid plains, then grassy steppe, which in the summer monsoon season, when the land receives most of its meager precipitation, is a rain-rich green that deepens where small river valleys wander the high plateaus. Stretching away to the horizons is an endless rolling grassland without roads or fences. Infrequent small clusters of round nomad tents crop up from the steppe as white as mushrooms, and here and there, herds and lone riders flow across the landscape—horses, cattle, sheep and goats, a camel. All seem to tend toward the edges of a glinting city to the north, more than four thousand feet above sea level. Beyond, low foothills crested by dark manes of conifers climb toward the Hentei Mountains, which march northward across uninhabited frontiers into Siberia.

Mongolia's nomadic, shamanistic culture, in the thrall of local deities and the Sky God Tengri, has mostly died out since the late sixteenth century, when the Gelugpa sect of Tibetan Buddhism (the reform sect headed by the Dalai Lamas) became the state religion; Gandar Lamasery at Yihee Huree (known to the outside world as Urga) became the seat of a lama known as the Living Buddha of Mongolia, the most exalted holy man in all the Buddhist hierarchy after the Dalai and Panchen lamas. Though the society would remain nomadic, the tough warrior spirit of the Tatar horsemen was apparently softened by the peaceful Buddhist teachings, for the territory was eventually absorbed by the Chinese Empire that it had conquered formerly and ruled. Mongolia became a virtual colony of the Qing dynasty, and not until the last emperor was retired, in 1911, did Outer Mongolia—Mongolia—reclaim its independence, turning to Russia for protection.

In 1921, the newly formed Union of Soviet Socialist Republics used the founding of a "Mongolian People's Party" as a pretext to invade the country and set up the first satellite Communist government. Four years later, Yihee Huree, now the capital of the brave new People's Republic of Mongolia, was renamed Ulaan Baatar, or Ulan Bator, meaning "Red Warrior."

In 1928, when Stalin's puppet Horloyn Choybalsan rose to power, the national pride in Chinghis Khan was severely repressed, and in the 1930s—in part because Mongolia's Buddhism had degenerated and its priests showed no interest in reform—the national religion was condemned as an obstacle to progress. In a reverberation of the anticlerical purges already taking place in the Soviet Union, the three thousand Buddhist temples in the country were destroyed, their property seized, and their monks and lamas disrobed, executed, or driven into hiding. The one lamasery spared was Gandar, the "Big Monastery," which became a sort of ramshackle museum. Not until the 1970s were a few old monks permitted to creep out of hiding and practice their religion in a token manner, and a reformist monastery, Tashi-choeling, was reopened in the city. In 1979 the Dalai Lama visited Gandar, an occasion used by the Red Chinese to denounce his evil influence on Tibet.

In 1989, with the departure of the Red Army, Buddhism and Chinghis Khan were officially restored to the cultural heritage of the Mongolian people, and two years later, in September 1991, the Dalai Lama returned to Gandar on the wings of a religious yearning so pent up by decades of oppression that tens of thousands came to welcome him. The pilgrims traveled by bus and truck as well as on horseback, raising clouds of spiritual dust over all the land. (Like His Holiness's first visit, this second coming brought indignant protest from Beijing, which was anxious to return Outer Mongolia to its sphere of influence and denounced any upsurge of nationalism, any "lamaist" revival, that might give Inner Mongolia the wrong idea.)

We are met at the airport in Ulaan Baatar by the Mongolian mammalogist Sharaid Sugarragchaa Chuluunbaatar. Sharaid is a family name among the Buryat Mongols of this region, north into Siberia and Trans-Baikal, and Chuluunbaatar may be translated as "Stone Warrior." "Perhaps that name is too much of a responsibility," sighs this small man, whose sad demeanor and soft dejected voice hide a sudden delighted smile and sense of humor. Chuka, as he is called by friends, has been accompanied to the airport by Drs. Ayurzaryun Bold and Natsagdorjin Tseveenmyadag (hereinafter "Bold" and "Tseveen"), the two eminent Mongolian ornithologists who had notified the ICF about the crane nesting grounds in eastern Mongolia but had been unable to join us on the Amur. Bold and Tseveen are very happy, they declare, to be our guides on the journey east to the Kerulen, from where we shall travel north to the Daurian steppe and the remote river valleys near the Siberian border. As organizer of our expedition, Chuka has arranged quarters at the Balgal Hotel, where the towels are folded like lotus blossoms on the beds and food is prepared each little while by a large motherly Russian woman who is much amused by the unfathomable things that foreigners do and say.

After seven decades as the capital of a puppet state, Ulaan Baatar's barren boulevards and lifeless gray constructions are final monuments to Soviet domination and the swarming technocrats who imposed polluting industries on a pastoral society and all but eradicated religion and ancient culture. With the collapse of the U.S.S.R. after 1989, the rebuilding of the city was left half finished; for want of funds, for want of fuel, the silenced cranes hunch like huge mantises over the rusting armatures of concrete blocks—the ugly ruins of committee inspiration and makeshift construction, already decrepit while they were being built. As in the Siberian cities, the disorderly stacks of shoddy building materials, thrown down any old way as if discarded, bear witness to the apathy inspired by this soulless "progress." Everything is wasted, even space—the structures erupt randomly from vast dusty broken lots, crossed by hurrying lone figures like survivors.

One imagines these figures in the dead of winter, when the average temperature is −6 degrees Fahrenheit and an acrid air pollution from the primitive industries descends upon the city like a shroud. In 1991, these factories produced $85 million worth of goods that found no market because of the poor quality inherent in the system. Even worse, Russia announced that past aid grants to Mongolia would be regarded retroactively as debt. The removal of Russian aid and trade, together with new austerity measures to satisfy the punitive loan demands of the International Monetary Fund and the World Bank, ensured that an already tottering system would collapse entirely.

The Western nations and Japan have promised $200 million to help the country shift to a market economy, not nearly enough to make competitive an industrial base as rickety as this one. Last month (June 1992), a people in dread of chaos and a hungry winter rejected the new democratic candidates and returned to power the Mongolian People's Revolutionary Party—the old Communist Party (though not the old regime). This land of dire economic want has immense mineral resources, but until these can be developed, all agree, it must suffer instability and hardship.[2]

During our stay, electricity in the capital was intermittent, and meat, flour, sugar, matches, and vodka were strictly rationed. Yet as in Russia, the dark cold stairs within the rust-streaked walls of concrete buildings lead to warm private apartments, and in the street, where one still sees the traditional *deel*, or high-collared knee-length cloak—worn by the men with sash and boots, and by women cut full length in traditional style—the people appear cheerful and energetic, considering the chronic shortages they have suffered since Russia demanded hard currency for its oil.

Today the gold-green temples and halls of the walled cloisters of Gandar Lamasery are the one balm to the eye in all Red Warrior. While its pagoda-roofed six-story main temple is being restored—the only construction site in town where work appears to be under way—its hundred-odd monks worship and hold chanting service with conch horns and drums in a side chapel in a small pine court scented with incense. By the roofed gate, in hope of attracting tourists (at present fewer than three hundred a year in all Mongolia), local artists set out small paintings that mostly depict the white nomad dwellings called *gers* (in Russian, *yurtas*) and the horsemen and horses and the old ways of the steppe economy that must see these city people through the endless winter.

Most Mongolians remain nomadic, and even here in the small capital, almost half of the half-million people dwell behind wood palisades in *ger* encampments that can be disassembled and moved back out onto the steppe in about an hour. This half million represents nearly one fourth of the population of a country the size of Western Europe—at fifteen hundred miles from west to east, the largest landlocked country in the world. Most of Mongolia is uninhabited and unspoiled, not only the deserts to the south and west but the remote plateaus and marshes of the far northeast, where the endless horizons of the Daurian steppe, our destination, stretch away into Inner Mongolia.

I n the evening our hosts bring excellent *arak* (Mongolian vodka) and comprehensive maps of those eastern regions of the country, and the discussion is lively and exciting. After years of enforced sociability in Asian crane countries whose languages he does not speak, Jim Harris has perfected a missionary manner that counts on an unflagging smile and jolly laugh to convey bonhomie in the absence of substantive communication. Jim's good nature and enthusiasm are sincere, as his hearers recognize, and behind them lie sound ornithological knowledge and a quick humor that make him an excellent companion. Chuka speaks some English, and Go Fujita somewhat less, though he swaps scraps of Russian with Bold and Tseveen, who address us mostly in Russo-Mongol pidgin and taxonomic Latin. Otherwise we shall have to make do with international goodwill and an intense shared passion for the cranes.

Mongolia in summer is notorious for hard and sudden changes in the weather. In the late afternoon of the next day, we leave Ulaan Baatar in a storm of rain and hail that brings mud rivers in flash floods through the streets, stranding cars and stalling buses and causing the goats to press against the walls, yet in no way fazing the pedestrians, who scarcely quicken their pace in search of shelter from the deluge. This hardihood, this indifference to the elements, is very apparent in Mongolia, and helps explain the whirlwind that was Chinghis Khan, and the barrier of the Great Wall, and why the walls in the imperial palaces in old Peking are five feet thick in places, the better to keep barbarians at bay.

The expedition was scheduled to fly east to Choybalsan, then travel overland down the Kerulen, but because of fuel shortages, all domestic flights have been cancelled until further notice. Instead, we will make a four-day drive on the "east-west highway" in two four-wheel-drive vehicles, hauling a two-wheel trailer load of tools, tents, stove, and rubber boats. Our spirited and obliging drivers, Dorj and Dawa, will assist with the cooking and the camp.

A few miles east of Ulaan Baatar, the highway turns to either mud or rigid ruts, according to swift changes in the weather. "We hope you will be tough enough to make this journey," warns the taciturn Dr. Bold. His name means "rock," and at fifty-six, he is a rough old badger in dark glasses and a brown business suit that will answer his field needs throughout our safari. From a physiognomy as weathered as a stump, quick, humorous eyes peer out through elliptical leather holes, unsurprised by anything, good or bad, that humankind might have to offer. His associate, Tseveen, thirty-seven, is also competent and hardy, as he will demonstrate unobtrusively throughout the journey. (As befits a man so shy and quiet, Tseveen wears camouflage clothing of Mongolian manufacture, perhaps unaware that its peculiar tropical greens make him an exotic feature in every landscape.) Both are members of Mongolia's Academy of Sciences, which pays them a scant subsistence salary. In addition, Bold directs the Mongolian Ornithological Foundation, of which Tseveen is secretary. Together with their friend Stone Warrior, they represent one fourth of the national membership.

At the edge of town, the road crosses the Tuul River, which flows west and north to the Orhon, thence to the Selenga, which flows down out of Mongolia into great Baikal. An hour to the east, the east-west highway, now dirt track, climbs a high valley to the continental divide. West of this ridge, all streams flow to the Arctic or subside into the central Asian desert, whereas east of this point, all waters descend to the Pacific. The Kerulen, which we shall reach the day after tomorrow, flows into Lake Dalainor in China, which overflows into a tributary of the Amur.

At the pass, a large cairn, or *obo*, stands adorned with rags and liquor bottles, rusted cans, broken thermoses, and other offerings, including two pairs of old crutches and a few tattered Buddhist prayer flags. Though cairns set up by trepid wayfarers to placate wrathful regional deities are an ancient custom in mountain lands, this one is a debased form of the Buddhist stupas or chortens found on passes throughout the Himalaya and the mountains of central Asia. The Mongolians circumambulate the *obo* and deposit roadside rocks, but when asked if they are Buddhists, they look wary, shaking their heads. Not so long ago, to be a Buddhist might have cost one's life. "We are all a *little* bit Buddhist," Chuka murmurs.

Long after dark, we pitch our tents in a small grassy basin. Here on the steppe, the July night is very cold. Scorpius and Cygnus bristle with ancient light, and the Milky Way descends in swathes all the way to the horizon. In the morning, my first Mongolian lark jauntily awaits inspection on a grass tuft before the tent; not far away stands a pale isabelline wheatear, an old acquaintance from its winter range on East Africa's Serengeti Plain. Walking the grassland in the early sun, I find puffballs and other mushrooms that Dorj and Tseveen cook up for breakfast.

Eventually, we are en route again, descending the grassland plateaus toward the Kerulen. Steppe marmots stand upright at their burrows like huge prairie dogs, and a sick one lies beside the track, its fur—gold and ivory in the morning sun—rising and falling with each failing breath. The Mongolians wave me away from it, honking their horns and shouting in great agitation; they indicate that a sick marmot, broadcasting bacilli on its breath, can transmit a deadly pneumonic plague to human beings.[3]

A steppe fox whisks through the blowing grass, a steppe eagle stoops on a young marmot. The eagle glares at the oncoming vehicles as it tears away red shining shreds. Neatly, then, it eviscerates the rodent, leaving the heavy guts behind as it takes wing, dragging the rest away over the grass tips.

In high tablelands, a pair of elegant gray birds, hurrying a chick, traverse a barley field. At a signal from the parents, the chick presses itself flat in the thin barley. Affecting to feed, the adults move away, then take off with a ratcheting horn-note call reminiscent of the sandhill, though less musical. Almost at once the birds circle back, alighting at a

Demoiselle crane (*Anthropoides virgo*)

little distance, "craning" long necks in distress in our direction. By now we have found the flattened chick, like a gray pullet with long legs and huge feet. Handled quickly by Go Fujita, the first crane banded on the expedition runs off wearing a green leg band that reads "Y-01."

The demoiselle crane, *Anthropoides virgo*, is a small grassland species that has adapted to semidesert and wild pasture, provided that water may be found not far away.[4] Unlike most cranes, it prefers a dry climate, firm soil, and low grass cover near lakes and rivers, where it lays two greenish or yellowish-gray eggs without attempting to scratch out a depression among the stones and pebbles. Yet the bird is loath to leave its humble home, write Bold and Tseveen, and one may approach within fifty yards before "the disturbed bird leaves the nest without any sign of alarm, as if just standing up after [resting from feeding]. Calmly pecking the ground, it goes away towards its mate, which has already moved a considerable distance from the nest and is showing more signs of distress than the one which has just left." Many clutches are destroyed by the trampling of herd animals, which may explain why most broods in this species are limited to two chicks. A day after hatching, these nidifugous chicks have been seen to swim after their wading parents, making their escape across a shallow river. Both chicks usually survive to fledge (as they rarely do among *Grus* cranes), and at six weeks are ready for migration.[5]

The demoiselle is an upland feeder, as evidenced by its short seed-eating bill, but it may also forage in shallow marsh; on the steppe, we rarely saw it far from water. (Not surprisingly, this generalized feeding habit is shared by the two other cranes that remain relatively abundant, the widespread Eurasian or common crane *Grus grus* and the sandhill crane *G. canadensis* of North America and northeastern Siberia; by contrast, all three of the rare white cranes are largely restricted to the marshes.)

The very simplicity of its silvery blue-gray plumage, set off by a black bib of pointed plumes that lie pendant on the breast and long white head plumes that lead straight back from the red iris of the eye, makes the demoiselle one of the most beautiful of the crane family. Tradition has it that this species received its name from Queen Marie Antoinette, who admired the demure elegance of her new pet. Called by Mongolians "the lovely bird," the demoiselle is found everywhere throughout the country except the northern forests and high mountain plateaus, and is widely distributed all the way east to the Great Khingan Mountains of northern China and westward across central Asia to Ukraine and the Crimea. Formerly its range extended to the Iberian Peninsula and northwest Africa, and a small nonmigratory population may still persist on the Atlas plateau of central Morocco. From its western range, it migrates through Turkey and the Caucasus, Iraq, and Saudi Arabia to winter along the great rivers of northern Africa—in short, a far-flung bird. I first saw it many years ago in Equatoria, in the Sudan; I have seen its likeness in the old mosaic floor of the Church of the Holy Sepulchre, in Jerusalem.

Though not uncommon on the Mongolian steppe, the demoiselle has been much diminished by the spread of land cultivation and development that has already reduced its populations farther west and across the northern border in the Trans-Baikal regions of Buryatia and Tuva. In Buddhist Mongolia, killing wild creatures is a sin, made worse when orphaned chicks are left behind, but like all cranes that resort to croplands, the demoiselle is vulnerable to power lines and pesticide. Bold and Tseveen blame the hasty economic development brought by the U.S.S.R., which was devoid of ecological understanding or concern; they fear for "the lovely bird" in their own country.

In wildflower prairie, in the strong scent of sage (*Artemisia*), the track follows a small stream that must be one of the farthest headwaters of the Amur; it arrives eventually at a lake and mineral spring where fifteen or twenty demoiselles stalk the surrounding grassland. Midday is hot, and in the spring, a large flock of ruddy shelduck, gold-cinnamon in the fresh light, has been joined by nomad human beings, who smear their pale bodies with medicinal mud under the patient gaze of their waiting horses.

Already the plateaus subside into the high rolling plain of the open steppe, islanded by white solitary *gers* with dark strings of horses. Over grassy seas pass the swift shadows of white clouds in the high blue sky—much as the Great Plains were first described in a North America we shall never see again. The steppes of eastern Mongolia, one hundred thousand square miles in extent, are the last great grassland ecosystem left on earth, comparable only to the Chang Tang plateau of north Tibet. The wild Przhevalsky's horse, extirpated in 1951, has been reintroduced in recent years, and the steppe still supports vast companies of Mongolian gazelle, up to fifty thousand in one herd, and perhaps as many as two million altogether—"one of the great wildlife spectacles left in Asia," as field biologist George Schaller has remarked, "and one of the greatest wildlife populations in the world, and nobody has ever heard of it."

Toward noon, the stream crosses broad wet floodland meadows to

join the upper Kerulen, a swift torrent fresh and cold out of the Hentei
Mountains where it widens in a great bend toward the east. In the afternoon, the demoiselles increase in number, and in one flock of sixty or
more, we capture and band a pair of chicks as six Tatar boys, three of
them riding bareback, come galloping up to inspect the vehicles and
gawk at the operation. In their soiled cloaks and dusty boots, their skin
sun-blackened and hair uncropped (save the two youngest, whose heads
are shaved to deter lice), they look wild and proud and shy. Backing the
horses when we draw too near, fighting to conceal their wonder, to appear aloof, the six boys stare as Go Fujita opens his shamanic kit of glittering equipment—he is training the Mongolian bird men, who assist
him—and with great care draws a white muslin bag over the bird's
head; he tapes its legs and binds it in a jacket to restrain it while he fits
and glues green plastic rings to the upper leg, then measures and
weighs the bird while the glue dries. Unrelenting in his precision—he
even attempts to measure the grass height at each chick location until
asked to desist in the interests of reaching the lower Kerulen before
winter—Go inscribes the last detail of data in his book before cutting
the tape, removing the bag and jacket, and releasing the chick to run
away over the plain.

Asked by Chuka if they ever catch young cranes, and if they eat
them, the nomad boys say proudly, Yes, we do! Perhaps this is bravado.
The chicks would be easily caught by boys on horseback, yet the adult
demoiselles here are not wary, drawing near man's herds and habitations with a confidence suggesting that they pass undisturbed. The only
dead crane we will come across on this expedition lies beneath the
power lines of one of the administrative centers (school, meeting house,
mechanic shop, hospital, and veterinary clinic) set up for wintering nomads in each steppe district and mostly deserted at this time of year.

We camp that night on the riverbank, to the calls of cranes and
cuckoos, redshanks and an owl. The night cries give way at
dawn to the alarmed bark of marmots and the skylark's daybreak song.

The day begins with fitful rain and cold. Since this is the season of monsoon—Mongolia gets almost all of its precipitation in midsummer—we anticipate more rain and rather dread it. Already the red ruts are so rough that earlier travelers—mostly truckers, to judge from the few vehicles we have seen—have carved their own tracks across the grasses to avoid deep potholes. In places, as many as ten or a dozen tracks fan out and wander, mile after mile, before braiding again where the original track forded a stream or traversed a hillside.

The myriad tracks erode and blight the grassland, and a day of reckoning must arrive. Those who come from lands already worn out by human beings know how fragile such vast emptiness can be, even on a steppe inhabited outside the small settlements by only one human being per square mile. But for now the steppe seems endless, like a long-haired green hide tight fitted to this earth of rolling steppe and ancient hills. Though most of the plateau is undulating, there are glimmering flat regions where the horizon seems so near that giant horsemen rise between the grass and sky. In their traditional hats and *deels*, the booted figures appear mythic, and their "Mongol ponies" seem more ancient still, with their chunky bodies and thin legs and lumpy heads reminiscent of *Equus caballus przhevalsky*. Like the American mustang—the "Indian pony"—Mongol ponies come in many colors, but most are chestnuts, blacks, and grays, with heavy black manes and wary stares. The nomads' goats, too, seem archaic, with crazy yellow eyes and outsized horns. Only the sheep and cattle look domestic—that is, dull and sluggish in gaze and comportment, content to be shunted hither and yon in bawling herds.

This is a landscape of great saker falcons—two adults flying, then two juveniles perched on marmot mounds, then a single bird, another, and another, all within the space of a few miles. In taking off, the saker's sharp wings slice the air like two knives sharpened one against the other. This huge sand-colored raptor has the heavy flight of a gyrfalcon—the peregrine would appear "light" by comparison.

The Holy Roman Emperor Frederick II hunted cranes with gyrfalcons, it was said; cranes were also hunted by the hawks of Kublai Khan. "He derives the highest amusement from sporting with gyrfalcons and hawks," wrote Marco Polo. One may suppose that these "gyrfalcons" were sakers, which, unlike gyrfalcons, could be captured on the steppes.

Camels roam untethered in aloof and stately parties, awaiting their next call to duty, which may occur in a month or four, depending on the condition of the wild pastures. These are the two-humped Bactrian camels, whose wild forebears still persist—a few—in the Gobi and other desert regions. They are used almost entirely as draft animals, dragging the two-wheeled covered carts piled with household gear. Once a new camp is made, these carts, parked in a line and tilted forward on their shafts, are used for storage; they serve also as hitching posts for horses, which are kept saddled near the door from daybreak until nightfall. The poorest *gers*—those with the most disreputable adults and dirtiest children—tend to be located on overgrazed ground scattered with human litter.

Having heard about the savagery of nomad dogs, I anticipated a thickset brute similar to the mastiffs met with on the Tibetan plateau. Instead, these creatures have more kinship with the Russian wolfhound, and perhaps were bred originally for the same purpose, being mostly lean and rangy, on long bounding legs, the better to run down the gray wolves still common in this country. Some bark absently as strangers pass, even when so far away that often the dog itself is not in sight; others lope out in deadly silence and pursue vehicles a mile or more, so close alongside that one must keep one's hand inside the window. At a strange *ger*, one never dismounts to approach on foot until a face peers from the low doorway and the disposition of the dog is ascertained.

West of the town of Ondor Chaan (Great King), a small lake marsh is an oasis for migrating shorebirds, many still in breeding plumage: black-tailed godwits, Eurasian curlew, common and spotted redshanks, lesser golden plover, and sharp-tailed sandpipers consort on the margins with white-winged black terns, shelduck, gadwall, and green-winged teal. Six ornithologists must make do with two spotting scopes, one of them a gift from the ICF to the Mongolian Ornithological Foundation in appreciation of its practical participation in this journey. Even

Dorj and Dawa love the telescopes and are learning quickly to identify the larger birds; they ignore the citrine wagtails and gray starlings at the swamp edge.

O ndor Chaan, with an economy based in wheat flour, is the main settlement between Ulaan Baatar and Choybalsan. Since but 1 percent of Mongolia is arable (90 percent is grassy steppe or desert and the rest is forest, mostly in the northern mountains; more than half the country is locked all year in permafrost) and since both rainfall and the date of the last frost of spring are as capricious as this monsoon weather, field agriculture is necessarily of small importance. Where soil permits, as in this region, a few communal farms grow grain, but in these hard years when no fuel is available, the red combines and harvesters of Soviet aid, penned up in barbed-wire enclosures high with weeds, seem as archaic as the dinosaurs whose mighty bones protrude from the Gobi Desert.

Ulaan Baatar is linked to China by both rail and air, with additional air service to Irkutsk, near Lake Baikal, while Choybalsan can claim rail connections to Moscow and Vladivostok by way of a trunk line north to the Trans-Siberian at Chita; Ondor Chaan's only connection to the outside world is this rough track, which skirts *ger* clusters and wood shacks, sullen industrial detritus, half-built, burned, or decrepit public buildings, hard windy lots. Only briefly does it become a dusty stretch of pavement between rows of poplars; at the eastern outskirts, it subsides into the earth of the great steppe.

Within the hour, the axle shears and one wheel spins off the two-wheel wagon; it leaps and bounces behind Dorj's car, bringing the expedition to a sudden halt. *Kaput*, Dorj explains. That useful term is pervasive in Mongolia, much like *nyet pro-blem* in Siberia. With Dorj and Tseveen, Chuka sets out for a mining settlement some fifteen miles off to the north. While Bold guards the dumped cargo, the rest of us take advantage of the delay to run down, catch, and band demoiselle chicks.

From a *ger* with a large corral on a nearby hilltop, a big Mongol mounts his horse and, trailed by his boy, rides down to the road with his ancient hammer rifle. Hitching his horse to our kaput cart, this man in night-blue *deel* with orange sash relates that in this drought year even wildflowers are few—he looks astonished—obliging him to move his *ger* to fresh pasturage in the next fortnight instead of in early August, as he had planned. He wants his son to learn some English, but since neither Bold nor Dawa can comprehend far less translate a single word we say—even Go Fujita, organizing his stiff phrases, speaks English a great deal better than he understands it—the shy and silent boy in purple *deel* and crimson sash is none the wiser when they spring onto their bony wooden saddles and ride away. They cross the hard plain at the stiff-legged run, not quite a gallop, which tough Mongol horses can maintain for hours—the dogged pace that made possible the lightning campaigns of Chinghis Khan. Even today one never sees a Mongol walk his horse, and only rarely does he trot or canter, preferring to stand up in the stirrups and whip the animal into a run from the first step.

Toward twilight the nomads, called *arats*, return with a fresh-killed marmot, which they fling to the ground before our camp in gracious token of steppe hospitality. As delicacies of the local diet, these heavy rodents are often extirpated over broad areas, and this one had been taken out of season, warns the *arat*. He crouches behind a tussock to skin and clean it, lest he be spotted from the road, although not one vehicle has passed in the several hours since our calamity.

As nomads of high windy plains, contemptuous of any work not done from horseback, the *arats* place more emphasis on traveling light than on property and extended clans; they consort in loose bands of related families that manage common herds. After so many centuries of independence, they fought hard to evade the compulsory collectives, and sometimes slaughtered their animals rather than see them appropriated by the state farms. As in most pastoral societies, not only their wealth but their sense of their own existence is manifested by their herds, especially the sheep, which are the mainstay of their diet—mutton served with noodles in a soup, together with *ayrag,* or fermented mare's milk, pressed sour-milk curd, cheese, and yogurt, accompanied by sweet biscuits or bread. In spring and summer, milk products replace the dried and frozen meat consumed once all but the strongest animals are slaughtered in the fall. (Though fish are plentiful in Mongolian rivers, they are scarcely bothered with, and the hunting of wildfowl and game is limited by Buddhist tradition; as for fruit and vegetables, none are available excepting a few apples and potatoes—not that we see any, but at least they are referred to.) Today the self-sufficient *arats* are far better off than those countrymen who were drawn into the mines, mismanaged industries, and despondent cities. With twenty million herd animals, or about ten for every human being, the *arats* must sustain their city relatives. Animal husbandry is the main support of the domestic economy, just as it was in the days of Chinghis Khan. It is also the foundation of an export trade (to Russia, mainly) of wool and hides as well as meat.

No matter how remote our camp nor how foul the weather, there is always an *arat* on the horizon who will ride over to investigate intruders. The nomads are astonished by our strange doings with the cranes but not unfriendly, seeming to welcome the experience of new faces and behavior in a silent land where any change except the weather comes so slowly. Often, when we pass *gers* at a distance, the young people ride or even run from afar simply to stand beside the track and watch us pass. They smile when the young cranes are set free after capture, not so much because they love the cranes but because cranes manifest powerful spirits, and harming these creatures might bring evil luck.

Not until long after dark do our friends return with a tough old cart bought at the mining village, by which time we have made camp beside the track, confident that on the east-west highway there will be no vehicle to disturb our rest.

Because six ornithologists tend to halt the cars for bird study too frequently, the expedition is already two days behind schedule. To make up time, we rise next morning before six and dispense with cooking breakfast, feeding instead on the cold and fatty marmot, which is not improved by tepid coffee and cold rice. No doubt the marmot would have been delicious when fresh-fried in its own fat, but over the cold night it had turned rank and greasy.

Already two hours have passed on a cool morning that promises to grow long and hot, and still we have not finished loading the new cart and heaving the old one upside down on top. Breaking camp seems to require nearly three hours each day, no matter how hard the Americans try to hasten it. Dawa and Dorj, tired from long days of hard driving that sometimes continue past ten o'clock at night, help pitch the tents and cook, wash, and fetch water; they are therefore excused from preparing breakfast or even rising from the back of the car until their preferred hour, which in Dawa's case is precisely one hour after everybody else. Mongolians rarely rush, far less hurry others, and this morning, due to the great amount of gear, the artful loading of the busted cart requires an extra hour before the last man has satisfied himself that we are roadworthy. We break camp finally at about 8:30, just as a trucker comes along who agrees to haul the broken cart back to Ulaan Baatar, and so another hour passes in negotiation and off-loading. By this time the day is warm and, needing water, we delay our journey with a visit to a solitary *ger* where the side panels have been hoisted to permit the passage of the hot dry summer wind. The two dogs look old and leery, but Dawa will not set foot out of the car until they are safely penned inside.

The track tends east along the river. Though the steppe is treeless, lacking even a poor shrub, the grass is becoming taller and less sparse. Cranes are fewer in this long-grass country, and the falcons, unable to see prey, have vanished, but wheatears and larks seem undiminished in species and numbers, and hoopoes flourish in a variety of habitats, from marsh to dry hillside to the empty winter stock sheds in an old corral. There are more wandering camels, too, and great running herds of feral horses.

As the day wears on, the grass becomes longer, thicker, until even the larks are few. The cranes disappear entirely, and man, too, all but a lone horseman in the distance. Earth and sky are an unbroken green and blue. On a plateau that overlooks distant Choybalsan are the ruins of huge pyramidal bunkers of a missile site, abandoned two years earlier; under the blind eye of its sagging sentry hut, infiltrated by coarse weeds, it will not rise out of the grassy wastes many seasons longer.

In the distance rises what looked at first like the broken stack of another Soviet ruin, left behind by history. It turns out to be a strange octagonal brick tower—"an ancient military tower," ventures Chuka, who has seen one like it near the old Mongol capital at Karakorum. Asked how old it is, he shrugs and says, "Nobody knows." Fork-tailed swifts chitter in and out of the ancient structure, which shelters two pairs of hill pigeons—the first wild pigeons observed on the steppe. Perhaps at some time centuries ago, wandering pigeons sighted the lone tower on the empty plain and made it an outpost of their habitat. Unlike the Soviet constructions, this old edifice of small archaic bricks has weathered the centuries, perhaps because such pains were taken with the work. The beauty of the simple tower is set off by the jagged window on the sky left by the fallen turret, the sun shards, dust, the soft croonings of the winged inhabitants on nesting ledges sheltered from the wind.

O utside Choybalsan, the only settlement of any size in eastern Mongolia, stand more broken-windowed military barracks. "Russki," growls Bold, with a dismissive wave at the whole stultified town, which was named for the late dictator, a Stalin puppet. Here we welcome two Chinese colleagues from Inner Mongolia who will join our search for white-naped cranes and participate in preliminary discussions of the proposed international wildlife reserve here in the border regions. Since the frontier between Mongolias is not a friendly one, the newcomers had to travel into Siberia from Lake Dalainor and make their way northwestward to Chita, where they returned south by train into Outer Mongolia.

Our road next day leads north and east across plateaus above the river plain and over long hills of empty grassland. Birds seem scarce, but we record a gruid relative, the great bustard, which carries itself like a short-necked, short-bodied, short-legged crane—much less graceful than the cranes, but just as dignified. Wings flaring white, the bustard propels itself heavily from the thick grass and pounds away over the steppe as we all cheer, for this mighty species, much diminished, is one of the rare birds we had hoped to find.

Not far away, the sharp-eyed Dawa spots a Siberian polecat (*Mustela sibirica*), a large, black-masked ferret related closely to the almost extinct black-footed ferret (*M. nigripes*) of the North American Great Plains. Chased on foot over the prairie as we try to corral it for a better look, the big quick fire-colored weasel castigates its pursuers with hard chitterings before whisking down a burrow at my feet.

Farther east, where the thick grass gives way to short, sparse growth, stands a flock of more than sixty demoiselles. At this season, such flocks are composed of immature birds as well as those that failed to pair or nested without success, losing eggs or chicks to predators; already these birds are gathering in the first stirrings of the migratory instinct that will lift them one September day and bear them south on their long journey across the Gobi and the great Takla Makan Desert, the arid Kunlun Mountains and Tibet, and on across the Himalaya to the Thar Desert and the flat plains of western India.

The track works eastward, crossing the plateau, and below, broad curves of the Kerulen appear. This river plain—the primary destination of our journey—looks wild and uninhabited, but also too brown and dry in this dry year to attract the white-naped crane. As the track descends the plateau toward the river, however, we see that the reedy margins swarm with waterbirds and our hopes rise.

On open ground overlooking a broad shallow lagoon known as Tsagaan Sum (White Church Lake) stands a mound of earth and rubble—all that remains of a Buddhist temple torn down during the anticlerical purges in the 1930s. The faded track and this mute heap are the only evidence of man in the silent landscape.

On a high bank on a deep bend, Tseveen and Bold locate the stretch of river where they first sighted white-naped cranes along the Kerulen a few years earlier. The campsite lies across the river from Wolf Island, and beyond Wolf Island lies an expanse of marsh and hidden lake—a haunt, says Bold, of the aggressive wolves that, with the mosquitoes, deter herdsmen from this region. Bold produces his set of small red cups and his bottle of *arak*, relating wolf tales as his friends absorb the warming spirits and the murmur of the river, the wail of lapwings and the cry of crakes and the primordial woodblock rattle of the demoiselles. Lacking the extensively coiled trachea found in the *Grus* species, *Anthropoides virgo* has little of the bugled resonance of its larger relatives, including the white-naped crane, which we listen for that night but fail to hear.

A dawn rain ends and the sky clears early. Not having to break camp, we depart quickly on a downriver hunt that will take us all the way east to the border, and the morning begins auspiciously with the discovery of two great bustards close to camp. Like yesterday's bustard, they seem to be consorting with demoiselle cranes, as if in some dim recognition of their ancient kinship. A few miles south, a pair of wolves lopes away over a ridge. Beyond, the track slowly descends toward a pale expanse called Khoyor Melkhit (Two Frog Lake), and as we draw near, I see an immense bird in the southwest corner of the lake, beyond a convocation of grey herons. "See that bird?" I point, and Jim Harris hollers, "*Stop!*"

A superb adult *vipio*, still at a distance, stands transfixed by the sound and dust of vehicles; then it rises from the shore with hard upward flicks of its great wings. Its wariness and its hard-flicking flight (a trait shared with the bustards) suggest the agitation of a breeding bird, and we hope that somewhere in this river system, a mate and chicks await the majestic creature that crosses the silver lake, long neck and legs in silhouette against the sun now rising from the blue mountains of China.

To the south, the river turns and turns in its broad green meadows, and all around this valley rise dry, windy plateaus, with scarcely a white tent or horseman, scarcely a horse. According to Bold and Tseveen, the river meadows do not flood until after May's ice melt in the northern mountains—a little late to attract the white-naped cranes, which arrive on their known breeding territories in the Amur basin in late March or early April and lay their eggs within the month.[6] This year, the monsoon rains are late, but even so, these meadows look too dry.[7] In good *vipio* habitat of the kind seen a few weeks earlier in the Amur, the marshes and swamps have no distinct channel, since the river flood spreads wide over the meadows. Here a shallow marsh perhaps a mile across looks promising, but we search in vain for a bright red-faced head and serpentine white neck, rising and coiling down again into the reeds.

At the border post, a company of demoiselles moves about among perhaps two hundred horses, blowing and stamping, heads together, in a large consortium of black-tailed rumps of every shade. The soldiers welcome their infrequent visitors with dried curd (*aruul*) and weak milky tea served with sweet biscuits, after which a young officer escorts us past a barrier into the no-man's-land, where a promontory overlooks a vast sedge meadow a mile or more across and several miles in length. From riverine woods, the valley rises to a grassy rim—the China border, to judge from the formidable high fencing; beyond, the great steppe continues eastward along the river flowing onward in its long descent to the great Dalai Nuur or Dalainor, the "World Ocean," fifty miles around. Much of the lake and its surrounding grasslands have been set aside as the Dalainor Nature Reserve, nearly a million acres in extent, with a sparse human population—very different from China's reserves farther east, Jim Harris says, where many human beings must make a living among what is left of the wildlife.

Connected by a man-made canal to the Amur River, Dalainor is the westernmost breeding territory of the red-crowned crane, a fact noted early by Przhevalsky: "About Dalainor we met with few of these cranes and consequently think they do not go far into the interior of Asia."[8] From the lake eastward, throughout the Amur basin, *japonensis* shares its general habitat with the rare *vipio*, which it outnumbers in most of their shared range. This may be because the high reed beds and deeper marshes frequented by the more aquatic *japonensis* dominate the Chinese lakes, while in Mongolia, the sedge meadows and shallow swamp preferred by *vipio* are more common. (Apart from a single nesting record in the 1920s, sightings of *japonensis* in Mongolia have been rare, but the lower Kerulen, which has both types of wetland, is where one seems most likely to occur.)

The Inner Mongolians, Wul Ji and Li Ming, come from Dalainor, where Li Ming's father is the director of the nature reserve and Wul Ji is attached to the Environmental Protection Bureau. The two could scarcely be less alike. The chubby, ebullient Ji has turned up with his shirttail out, wearing loose-laced white sneakers, while the handsome, lean, enigmatic Li wears a crisp, well-fitted camouflage outfit, with matching cap and footgear. Nonetheless the two are friends, and relatives, too, since both are named Borjin—they say this proudly because Borjin is the family name of Temujin, or Chinghis Khan, who they say is buried in their province.

Outer Mongolians are often scorned as bumpkins and hustlers by the Inners and Chinese, while Inners are disdained by Outers as tame Mongols exploited as ethnic curiosities by their Chinese masters. (Another million Mongols live across the Russian border in the Buryat and Tuva regions of Trans-Baikal.) With 3.5 million indigenous people, the Autonomous Republic of Inner Mongolia—approximately as "autonomous" as Tibet—is far more populous, but already its natives are outnumbered five to one by the Han immigrants sent there by Beijing. China has invested heavily in this province to keep it from emulating its neighbor to the west in notions of democracy, a resurgence of lamaism, and other counterrevolutionary evils; even so, its Mongol people resent the imposition of a Han culture and bureaucracy with Chinese as the official language, which confers an inferior status in their own land. (During China's Cultural Revolution, some forty thousand Mongolians lost their lives, although Mongols constituted less than half of 1 percent of the national population.)

Outer Mongolia, too, was China's colony until the fall of the Qing dynasty in 1911, when it fled straight into the bearish embrace of the Soviet Union; having escaped—and knowing what took place when the Han took over in Manchuria, Tibet, and Inner Mongolia—it is all the more anxious to retain its independence. As good bird men, however, these Inners and Outers clearly wish to set aside political antagonisms and make friends as fellow Mongols of the steppe.

Fortified at the border post with hot mutton soup containing gobbets of hard fat from the sheep's tail, we proceed north to some small lakes where Dr. Bold thinks our lone *vipio* might have headed. In this dry summer, the lakes are little more than shadows in the grass haunted by nondescript, shy birds—young Oriental plovers. But nearing camp, the vehicles flush three cranes out of the marsh, which Harris, snatching up binoculars, identifies as the first Eurasian or "common" cranes, *Grus grus*, recorded on this journey.

Carefully we walk to where the cranes have glided in under the bluffs; they are not far from a pair of demoiselles, which provide a good comparison in size and voice. In fact, their calls are somewhat similar, though the black-and-white-faced *grus*—the red is restricted to a modest crown patch—is distinctly larger than the demoiselle (and distinctly smaller than the white-naped) and its voice is stronger, with a lower pitch.

Grus grus is notably shy and wary, even among cranes—one reason for its persistent success. Once the nest site is chosen near a remote lake or in forest swamp or floodlands, it becomes secretive and silent, to safeguard the whereabouts of eggs and chicks. Before we can draw near, the three *grus* take flight and cross into the marsh north of our camp on the Kerulen River.

Exhilarated by the sight of three species of wild crane in a single day, I set off by myself on a long walk upriver. Near Tsagaan Sum and the temple ruin, two more *grus* rise—perhaps two of our three birds—and fly back toward the plain, crossing a rainbow far off to the east, arching all the way down to its pot of gold in the blue hills of China.

A northern harrier is harried hard by a young saker as it crosses over the camp early next morning. The huge falcon is so much faster and more agile that it chivies its quarry from below, but it is playing and makes no attempt to kill the other raptor.

On the camp table sits a jade-green tin with gold Chinese characters inscrutably transcribed into French and English: CHINA GREEN TEA. TEMPLE OF HEAVEN. SPECIAL GUNPOWDER. Over the night, a truck bound for the border post has broken down along the track, and the man who walks into our camp is glad to get gunpowder tea; along with *deel*, sash, and boots, he wears a tractor cap marked "U.S. 101."

Chuka looks after the camp while Go Fujita goes crane-hunting with Wul Ji and Li Ming; he is teaching them techniques of banding. Jim Harris, Bold, Tseveen, and I take two rubber boats a few miles upriver, where Dawa drops us off. Bold carries his old twin-hammer fowling piece, intent on provisioning the meager larder. In the hope of glimpsing a white-naped head erupt out of the reeds, we will drift and row down the Kerulen where it winds through the backwaters of the marsh until the swift current brings us out again at camp.

Through high swale and tortuous side channels, we haul the boats a mile or more across the marsh to the main channel. At one point our route follows an oxbow, all but dry in this parched year, and here Bold points out some fine big wolf tracks, then a wolf scat. "*Canis lupus!*" Accompanying these prints is some fresh sign of a gazelle, which he thinks the wolf might have been tracking. Another pile of scat, too small for wolf, too large for fox, he identifies as the raccoon dog (*Nyctereutes procyonoides*), a squat, black-masked canid that preys heavily on cranes and other ground-nesters. This execrable creature, Bold avers, is no native of Mongolia, but has sneaked in recently from Russia and China. "*Nyet Mongolica fauna—immigrantski!*" The raccoon dog reminds him unpleasantly of the New World muskrat we saw last night, swimming across the river by our camp. "*Nyet Mongolica! Amerikanski immigrantski!*" Bold had cried.

In this time of low water, we cannot see over the high willow banks and reeds, yet our drift is pleasant and productive, as Bold and Tseveen collect molting mallards to leaven our daily fare of goat and hard-boiled mutton. Alas, our quest for breeding *vipio* has so far come to naught. Since the white-naped crane has adapted its feeding habits to human agricultural activity, with almost all of its recorded nests within easy flying distance of croplands, this dry steppe country begins to seem unlikely habitat.

When finally we emerge from the reeds, weary from our four-hour expedition, we are astonished by Dawa's report that on his return along the marsh, he has observed a white-naped crane with chick less than a mile from camp; we search his face in mixed joy and disbelief, appraising his ornithological credentials. As we grill him, eight cranes fly over from the marsh, four together, then four more, and Jim, still flustered by Dawa's news, yells, "*Grus monachus!*" He is convinced that the first four birds were hooded cranes, an uncommon migrant in this region. "*Nyet! Anthropoides!*" snaps Dr. Bold.

Despite their comparative differences in size, species identification of cranes in flight is rarely as simple as one might imagine, and even less so in a land where six different species have been recorded. Most of the time, the wary birds are far away, and angles of light distort the coloration in strange ways, turning the soft grays to black and the silvers to white, changing the entire aspect of the bird. The smoky-gray Eurasians often look white; even the dark gray neck can be bleached out by intense sunlight, especially when reflected skyward from snow mountains; this may account for occasional reports of "Siberian cranes" crossing the Himalayas.

Leaving the identification dispute unsettled, we pile into the cars and take off upriver, in the small hope that Dawa's *vipio* sighting can be confirmed. But no white-napeds are present between track and reeds where Dawa thinks he spotted them, nor is there any sign of Jim's hooded cranes, which were seen to have alighted near that place. He stares balefully at a pair of demoiselles, blithe and beautiful and utterly unsatisfactory in this moment.

In silence, we wander west along the marsh, doing our best to admire the fresh beds of bright yellow water lilies and the migrant shorebirds, including several sandpiper species I have not seen previously on this journey nor, for that matter, in all my life—Temminck's stint and the rufous-collared stint, its whole head a red-gold-copper in the morning sun, and the broad-billed sandpiper, consorting with some sharptails, and large groups of black-tailed godwit and spotted redshank. The shorebirds—the "wind birds"—and their globe-spanning migrations have been a lifelong passion:[9] I am delighted.

Perhaps a quarter mile away across a shallow slough, against a wall of tall, sun-bathed phragmites, four demoiselles stalk a bright green sward that is like close-cropped lawn, and fifty yards west of the demoiselles, in full sunlight, a pair of white-naped cranes move in long strides, trailed by a big golden chick, still in its down. Overjoyed, we crouch low and in rapt silence study the *vipio* family until the birds vanish into the green reeds. These cranes with young have called not once during the past three days at White Church Lake.

Dawa's fine grin mocks us. While the learned researchers were ransacking the swamp, the humble driver, unaided by binoculars, found their bird for them—the first breeding record of the white-naped crane, *Grus vipio*, in the Kerulen River valley of eastern Mongolia.

Today we row across the river and forge our way on foot into the marsh, bound for two hidden lakes where Tseveen collected some birds for specimens two years ago. For a hard half mile, we push and slog and wade through thick willow scrub and inner swamps of sloughs and coarse phragmites up to nine feet high, emerging at last at the edge of a large lily lake crowded with waterfowl, including gold-necked whooper swans with two big cygnets. The swans take heavy flight and climb and circle against soft white clouds in the blue sky, round and round a round horizon of wind-tossed lavender tassels of tall sedges; the wind brings back their musical soft plaints of distress about the cygnets, which press themselves against the reeds on the far side. The phragmites walls are shelter against buffets of strong wind which back at camp will overturn the boats and blow and tumble them a good two miles downriver with Dorj and Dawa in pursuit.

At dusk, as the wind diminishes, bank swallows course the river, up and down and up and down. Then, in an instant, they funnel together like a cloud of giant midges, swirl upward, and are gone. Where hundreds flickered a moment before, not one is left, only the twilight reflections of the willows in the silent river.

When dawn comes, the wind is still, and from a distance, at the lily lakes, a swan is calling, solitary, mournful. We are breaking camp when two *vipio* fly in from the east, low against the valley rim, and setting their wings, descend toward the lagoon edge beyond the ruined temple, not far from where the pair with chick was seen the day before. Was this the same pair? If so, why had they left their chick? I walk west to the ruin and on past the north end of the lake, circling the bed of yellow blossoms at the marsh edge.

The two cranes rise from a low slough, but instead of fleeing, they alight a little farther on. Ignoring me, they stalk restlessly around the flats, crisscrossing each other's paths, entering the reeds from separate directions, coming out again, in what appears to be a systematic search. All the while they utter an odd call, a simple *ka-kuk—ka* is the high note—and sometimes simply *ka*.

Surely the two are calling to that golden chick, as if to coax it out of hiding. In a few minutes, they rise and cross a stand of reeds and alight on that greensward where they had posed yesterday. There they resume the intent search, the calling. Not once do they seem alarmed by my presence, nor pick and feed in the "displacement behavior" with which birds ease stress. Still calling, they hunt in and out until finally they disappear among the reeds, fall still, and do not emerge again.

Surprised that a downy chick would be left untended by both adults (though often chicks may be left for several hours by this species when the feeding grounds are distant), I wonder whether this pair could be different from the birds seen yesterday, but in that case, why is their chick so close to where the other pair had been? This makes no sense, or at least less than the unwelcome explanation that is already thrusting itself forward—that the golden chick was taken by the wolf or raccoon dog whose tracks were so close to it yesterday morning. That explanation might account for why the pair wandered away over the plain, and why they returned to hunt the chick, perhaps in a last spasm of parental instinct.

I have scarcely imagined this sad ending to the first recorded nesting of *Grus vipio* in the Kerulen when a young crane appears out of the farther reeds and crosses quickly to the break in the reed wall into which the adult birds, still calling now and then, have disappeared. I am so excited that I almost yell, because this is not yesterday's chick but a much larger one—larger, even, than the two adult grey herons which it runs past on its way into the reeds. Yesterday's small chick was downy, uniform gold-brown excepting the rich gold on the nape; this one is scruffy and already graying where pin quills have replaced the natal down. Suddenly the tragedy has been reversed. If this is indeed a second chick, what is the explanation? Could there be two breeding pairs so close together? I do not believe I confused a small gold chick with a large gray one.

The cranes remain silent and do not emerge, presumably because they are reunited with their chick. Yet the proximity of two pairs is most unlikely. In the days that follow, we decide to be conservative and assume that the second chick must have been the larger of two siblings, in which case the younger bird seen the day before might have been lost.

I am happy and grateful for my great good luck in the chance to observe *Grus vipio* at close range and in good light against the fresh morning reeds. With its brilliant mask of carmine skin and fire-colored eye, and the alabaster column of its nape extending down to the warm silver of the mantle, and the throat and belly of slate gray that in certain lights may turn a lustrous black, it is surely the most "oriental" of the cranes, an effect enhanced by the red legs that it shares with the Siberian; to my mind, this bird rivals the red-crowned in its pristine elegance.

Though the expedition has confirmed that *vipio* breeds in the Kerulen, the few birds here cannot account for the large flocks wintering in southeast China. Still in search of the heart of the bird's range, we set out on an old track toward the northeastern border.

The track winds over high hard plains wandered by steppe eagles and Mongolian gazelles—husky, long-faced animals, creamy-rumped but otherwise tawny in pelage—which move off in the pronking gait of gazelles everywhere. To the west is the embankment of the lone railroad track north from Choybalsan to the Russian border, and on the horizon rise the immense red shapes of the harvesters and combines of a communal wheat- and barley-growing enterprise, stilled by neglect and drought and want of fuel. Swift pigeonlike sand grouse in small flocks crisscross a dim track which arrives eventually at an abandoned depot with weed-split concrete and dusty windows, broken out by stones. "Another Soviet ruin," Chuka mutters. "This one hasn't even got a name."

Farther north, the grassland thickens once again, with lavender aster, night-blue spiky thistle, and yellow lilies, and the track turns eastward for some miles to Khukh Nuur, or Blue Lake, six miles across, a mirror of sky in the dry straw-colored land. On its lee shore, at the foot of a grass slope brightened by iris, gabble thousands of assorted waterfowl, and across the south bend of the lake strays a herd of perhaps eighty gazelles. Dr. Bold, who holds a permit to kill two gazelles to victual our expedition, has passed up a number of easy shots to avoid carrying a dead animal in midday heat. Now that he is ready, the herd is too far distant; we do not see another that day.

Blue Lake lies at the heart of the Daurian steppe (from the Mongolian *Daguurin*, after the Daguur nomads, who were the Old People in this region even in the days of Chinghis Khan, and who still inhabit remote corners of the steppe—Li's wife is a Daguur, he tells us). Little frequented by man, Dauria extends into Siberia as well as China, and retains a large variety of wildlife. We discuss the prospects for the proposed Daurian wildlife reserve in the corners of all three countries; the possibility excites all of us, even the guarded Li Ming. As an international reserve, the whole could never be contiguous—both the Russian and the Mongolian reserves include separated tracts, and Dalainor in Inner Mongolia is a hundred miles from either—but all of it lies on the Daurian steppe and contains good habitat for *Grus vipio* (known in Siberia as the Daurian crane).

The vague track crosses the rail line once again, wandering northwest over a plain where multitudes of new-fledged larks and pipits swarm low along the grassy path ahead, trying weak wings, perhaps for the first time, and too inexperienced to rise a little and plane away over the steppe. We make camp on a high bluff at Duroo Nuur, a round and rather lifeless lake at the headwaters of the Uldz River. With Jim, I walk along the lake, but we see no cranes and record few birds of any kind. A young *arat* from the *ger* on the far shore rides down to the water, lugging a black inner tube. Dismounting, he strips down to his shorts and paddles across to inquire about our business. Since we have no answers, only smiles, he trails us in suspicious silence as far as the place where the Uldz River, low and slow, departs the lake on its journey north to the Tari lakes on the Russian border.

This is an empty country of horse nomads, with few cattle; one herd seen next morning has at least three hundred head. The horses separate themselves into groups of a half hundred and form companionable circles around some point of interest, turning their tail-swishing rumps to the world as they contemplate a resting foal.

Vainly scouring a series of small lakes for a rare bird called the relict gull, we travel far into the northeast corner of the country without encountering a single *vipio*, perhaps because these lakes are brackish and the meadows salty. Finally we turn back north and west to the border town of Ereentsav ("Striped Riverbed"), across from the Russian village of Salavioski, a local name for the thrush nightingale. Here we learn from Bold's old friend Mr. Choijilsuren, director of the District Council, that the suspicious young *arat* in the inner tube had ridden all the way north to Striped Riverbed to report that two spies armed with binoculars were encamped with their confederates at Duroo Nuur. A ruddy Buryat with an erect shock of silver hair and a surprised smile, Mr. Choijilsuren, who had been expecting us, assured the young man that we were crane fanatics but otherwise quite harmless. The director also instructed a Buryat friend who was returning into Russia to notify the bored soldiery over there not to shoot at peculiar figures prowling the border with binoculars.

A latecomer to conservation, Choijilsuren destroyed ninety-seven wolves before "I lost my taste for killing them." He also killed numerous cranes, hanging them from poles around the fields in warning to their kind to leave the crops alone. The *tsen toguru* ("crane of metallic color": the white-naped crane) being larger, he told us, "did more damage than the others, not only in the amount it ate but in all its damned stalking about, trampling crops. However, the local people came to me and begged me to stop shooting it, saying that killing *tsen toguru* would surely bring calamity upon them." Today he leads the local support for international wildlife.

After a pause for cakes and yogurt, we head off on crane explorations along the largest of the Tari lakes. A first sighting is made several miles west of Ereentsav, and although our quarry is far away and nearly hidden in great reed beds between track and lake, the shifting white patch is too prominent in the tall reeds to be any bird except a crane. Excited, we set off on foot through the sedge meadows. The only two white cranes in Asia are the red-crowned and the Siberian, both of them rare or accidental in Mongolia—indeed, there are only three records for *Grus japonensis*, although it breeds not far away at Dalainor. Tseveen and Bold, who have traveled all over the country for decades, have never recorded it, whereas they have seen the Siberian three times between them. Since a Siberian turned up across this lake only two years ago, that species seems far more likely than the red-crowned to occur here.

Four of us hike a mile or more into the marsh, stopping every few hundred yards and using the spotting scope to fix the location of our quarry in the blowing reeds; we do our best to spot the head, which would tell us the species. In the tall reeds swaying back and forth, there sometimes seem to be two fragments of white, making us wonder if we might not have a pair. Perhaps a quarter of a mile away, the failure to spot a head has begun to trouble us, but finally the head emerges while Jim Harris has it in the scope. He straightens abruptly. "White horse," he mutters. So it is—a white horse deep in tall green reeds, the sole white horse as far as the eye can see in all directions. Our party of crane experts wheels without a word and begins the long trudge back to the road.

From a high bluff a hundred feet above the lake, one can scan long prospects of the marsh and shore. Almost at once cranes are located, *G. vipio* and *G. grus*, both with chicks. Earlier we had passed a demoiselle family, and perhaps to console us for *G. equus*, Jim remarks how uncommon it is to see three species of wild cranes with chicks in a single day. We count ten more Eurasian cranes, some standing on a grassy point, some flying over the grass islets that extend far out into the lake.

G. grus is an ash-gray bird tinged with brown above; its throat and foreneck as well as its primary and secondary flight feathers are sooty black, and the curved secondaries form the most elevated bustle of all cranes when folded upon its modest tail after alighting. Head, nape, chin, and throat are blackish, while the sides of the head from the eye back through the ear coverts and down the sides and back of the neck are white. Like the bare black skin of the lores and forehead, the modest patch of red skin at the back of the crown is haired sparsely with small black bristles. Its red-black-white head is less striking than those of *japonensis* and *americana* (though it is close to the whooping crane in its general head pattern and DNA).

The Eurasian crane was formerly an uncommon nester on Mongolia's northern borders, but in recent decades it has moved south, no doubt because of the intense cultivation of the borderlands by Russian

agriculture, and today it breeds widely in river floodlands of this country. Adapting its diet to man's seeds and sprouts—in Mongolia, wheat,
oats, and barley—it is often seen gliding in wide circles on the sky as if
scouting the terrain before making a slow descent into the fields. Unlike
the demoiselle, which uses the deep valleys, it habitually crosses the
peaks of the Himalaya.

> In Kansu . . . our tent was pitched at an absolute height of 10,600
> feet, but these birds [*G. grus*] were flying at such an enormous
> altitude that they could hardly be seen. During the whole day
> one flock seemed to follow another. At Koko-nor they arrived on
> the 17th of March. We did not find *G. communis* in the Ussuri
> country.
>
> —Nikolai Przhevalsky, *The Birds of Mongolia, the*
> *Tangut Country, and Northern Tibet,* 1875

The track follows the frontier west until the lake has been left behind. To the north, on a low hill of Siberia, is a mixed stand of
conifers and poplar—a last patch of relict forest, the Mongolians say,
where the Daurian steppe meets the Palearctic taiga. Farther on, the
track follows the border fencing; here huge red machines of the Siberian collectives stand idle at the ends of grain fields sown between long
poplar windbreaks, and here a pair of white-naped cranes, rising from a
reed pond in Mongolia, flies low over the track and the barbed wire and
glides down into the Russian grain to join eleven more of their species,
together with seventeen demoiselles and two Eurasian cranes, all in one
flock. I jump from the car and run along the fence as a new flock of
mixed *grus* and *vipio* cross into Russia. The *vipio* alight among the rest,
but the *grus* sail over the poplar break to the next field, where they join
two more groups of demoiselles.

Some of the cranes in the second field look small and dark, with a
heavy-set appearance, and when they raise white heads and necks, I yell

Red-crowned crane (*Grus japonensis*)

White-naped crane (*Grus vipio*)

Eurasian crane (*Grus grus*)

Hooded crane (*Grus monachus*)

Siberian crane (*Grus leucogeranus*)

Sarus crane (*Grus antigone*)

Demoiselle crane (*Anthropoides virgo*)

Black-necked crane (*Grus nigricollis*)

out, "Hoodeds!" Harris, coming up the road, thinks this unlikely, but a moment later, he cries out, "You're right! *Monachus!*" From where we stand, we count forty demoiselles, sixteen Eurasians, thirteen white-napeds, and thirteen hoodeds—four crane species in one place, including the first *G. monachus* I have ever seen.* I am elated, and Jim is, too. For all his experience with wild cranes in many countries, he has never before seen four species in a single sighting. "I know how lucky I am," I assure him, grinning. "You needn't tell me."

The hooded crane, scarcely three feet tall, is the smallest of all cranes except the demoiselle. It has a dark gray body with a cloudy-white neck and head, yellow eyes, and greenish bill, and like its close kin among the northern *Grus*, it has the roosterish arrangement of elongated tertials adorning its tail and the obligatory bare red skin on the head—in this species, on the forehead, separating the white of the crown and nape from the patch of bare black skin between eye and bill, and somewhat obscured beneath fine black feathers resembling down or hair. Like *G. vipio*, this species can contract its bare skin under its head feathers.

The name *monachus* comes from "monk crane," as it is known in Germany, due to its white cowl or hood. Little is known of the natural history of this wary and elusive bird except that it nests in forest swamps or larch peat-moss bogs with small and scattered trees; perhaps its short-limbed, heavy-looking shape, which gives it an inelegant appearance, at least by comparison to other cranes, is an adaptation to the more constricted flight demanded by its wooded habitat, as is its relative modesty in wing display. The first *monachus* nest was not discovered until 1974, in the Bikin River of Primorski Krai in the Russian Far East, which is the last stronghold of the Amur tiger.[10] This is partly because its breeding range was closed to foreign researchers until recent years and partly because its nests are hard to find. While the gray cryptic cranes of modest size require smaller wetlands than the white cranes, the blackish *monachus* has pursued obscurity into the very shad-

---

*The Latin names for three of the *Grus* species—the hooded, brolga, and whooping cranes—are spelled variously in the scientific literature as *monachus/a*, *rubicundus/a*, and *americanus/a*. Throughout this book, I have used *monachus*, *rubicundus*, and *americana*.

ows. As recently as the late nineteenth century, the hooded crane was widespread in eastern Siberia west to Lake Baikal, wintering in southeastern China and on Kyushu, the south island of Japan. Hybrids are uncommon among cranes, but *grus* and *monachus*—both exceptionally wary of human beings—regularly interbreed, with young in the second generation showing up in the winter in Kyushu.[11] (Though *monachus* tends to replace *G. grus* in northeast Asia, a few Eurasians turn up regularly in Japan.)

> [*G. monachus*] is very numerous during the spring migration *between* Lake Dali-nor and the town of Kalgan: further west it does not occur. It is very common about Lake Baikal, and must consequently migrate thither along the borders of the Gobi Desert ... A few of these cranes were seen about Lake [K]hanka in spring.
> —Nikolai Przhevalsky, *The Birds of Mongolia, the Tangut Country, and Northern Tibet,* 1875

We make camp after dark on a high plateau overlooking a tributary of the Imalkha River; a solitary light on the far side is revealed at dawn as a Russian border post that still bears the C.C.C.P. insignia of the Soviet Union. The border here is so uninhabited and uncontested that Russian Buryats come across to cut their neighbors' hay.

Still searching for breeding *vipio* in numbers, we return south, crossing the high country under Blue Mountain in light rain and descending again to the Uldz valley. In three hours of travel, the only cranes seen are a single pair of *vipio* which reveal by their reluctance to depart their reed marsh that they have a chick. We cannot find the chick, only the nest, a round platform of pressed vegetation built up above water level by the nesting bird, which plucks the vegetation all around, creating a moat. During the hunt, Tseveen shows me two gray raccoon-dog pups, which peer up beady-eyed and black-masked from their tunnel in the sedgy labyrinths.

At the Uldz River, cranes are plentiful—so plentiful, says Bold, that Uldz farmers complain about crop damage in the early autumn—and a cold rain is falling hard, as if the monsoon has arrived at last. This is the first real rain in a month, says Bold's friend Mr. Dorjpurev ("Bell Thursday"), a prosperous *arat* who welcomes us warmly to his house.

Mr. Dorjpurev is a jolly man with a jolly Buryat wife and a strong son named Khureltogoo ("Bronze Kettle") and also a winsome daughter-in-law in purple *deel* with a high collar and gold trim on her broad cuffs, neat slippers, and white stockings; she serves us milk tea gracefully before slipping away through the low wood door to help her mother-in-law prepare our meal. Everywhere in backcountry Mongolia, we receive a noble hospitality from the people of the steppe, who go about their age-old customs and economies quite unaffected by the chaos in the cities.

Retired now, Bell Thursday lives in a double *ger* and enters his horses in races held at Ereentsav. As one of the uncommon members of the Mongolian Ornithological Foundation, Bell Thursday keeps track of crane numbers in the Uldz valley. He once lassoed a hooded crane so strong, says he, that it lifted him right out of his saddle, but luckily the rope broke and he fell back to earth. Laughing, he cocks his head to see if these tall foreigners are enjoying his fine story.

Bell Thursday's *ger* is unusual in having a wooden vestibule at the entrance, as well as a generator and electricity. Otherwise it is much like all the rest, a compact round tent made from wool felt that is rolled, then compressed with water. Most *gers* are about twenty feet across, with walls held upright and reinforced by sections of wood lattice four to five feet high. From the lattice walls, the poles that support the sloping roof extend upward at a forty-five-degree angle toward the peak, where they are braced and held apart by a round light wood framework in the form of a spoked wheel. The wheel, which permits light to enter and the stovepipe to exit, may also be supported by a wooden upright, sometimes two. Ordinarily the stove is in the center of the *ger*, but this one has a gas stove that stands against the wall, as do the clothing chests, the several small beds that we are sitting on, and such items as a sewing machine and rolled winter rugs. The effect is that of a ship's cabin, neat and spare, with nothing extra, yet with small luxuries like a glass cabinet containing souvenirs and family photos, and ample space in the center of the room in which to stand up straight and move around. The circular space and agreeable proportions made me feel I could live permanently in such a dwelling, with no more possessions than such a space could comfortably contain. Almost everything the family uses is made by hand, and made to last. It occurs to me that the *arats* are the last true artisans in an unlucky country, driven from self-sufficiency into dependence on a technology that failed it.

Since Fujita and Harris and both of the Chinese are amateur photographers, the family dresses up in its best cloaks and comes outside in a rain lull to have its picture taken. Bell Thursday has replaced his leather *deel* with a rich red one, together with traditional Mongol hat and shining boots; for this occasion he hauls himself onto his horse, where all true Mongols know that they belong.

At a campsite that overlooks Goose Lake, not far away, we set up our tents quickly as the rain sweeps in. A strong wind brings a shift of air like the first turn of autumn, and in this storm light, a passing flock of white-naped cranes are silver-winged on the shining iron skies.

The small southerly part of the new Daguurin reserve is a stretch of valley where the river Uldz winds gracefully through wet meadows. Here we find a flock of forty-six Eurasians and band two more demoiselles. We cross the river at a ford and turn back westward. In last year's grainfields we meet a fox and three gazelles, a fair number of white-napeds, a few Eurasians, and seventy-five hooded cranes—an unusually large flock of *monachus* anywhere except on the crowded winter grounds in south Japan.

A huge black goat has been presented to us by kind Bell Thursday, and that evening we return to a goatly feast. With most of the meat removed for drying and curing in the smoke of a dung fire, the goatskin has been stuffed with its own meat and bones, together with heated rocks, then sewn up tight in its skin bag so it might cook itself. When it is ready, the guests are offered hot, greasy black rocks, to be pressed hard between fingers and palms to ensure good health, after which the rocks are assembled in a little cairn. Straightening, we make a slight bow to the cairn, palms together in gratitude to the goat for its sacrifice. The ceremony is Buddhist in its reverence for awareness of this moment, moment after moment, and also its gratitude for what is given to support our life; yet the Mongols seem shy about discussing this, after so many decades when Buddhism was outlawed.

Bronze Kettle has ridden across the marsh to serve up the goat meat and bones along with bowls of hot melted fat dipped up from the charred skin bag. He tells us that the crane is a fierce and angry bird according to Mongol tradition. He also says, "My grandfather was a lama, and so is my brother. We are a very religious family. We believe that Crane will bring bad luck to those who raise a hand against him, but if Crane is left alone, he is just a bird." As if to bear witness, a hundred hooded and Eurasian cranes appear, flapping and sailing across the lake and alighting in a sedge meadow down the shore.

Two youths on a motorcycle turn up; they squat by the feast until they are invited to take part, which they do gladly. Asked who they are, Chuka says calmly, "Nobody knows." Soon Bold's little red cups appear, and his good *arak*, and all sides offer toasts to our friends from Lake Dalainor, who will return that evening to the border at Striped Riverbed, cross to Thrush Nightingale, and make their way home to Inner Mongolia as best they can.

Rain comes and goes. Toward midnight, a strong wind jumps up, knocking down tents. It rains till morning.

August has come, and the *vipio* chicks, grown too big to crouch and hide, flee across the marsh or attempt to lose themselves in heavy cover. We hunt in vain through the bulrush and phragmites, then form a line and make a long sweep back, and still we lose them. A few days ago, two young demoiselles, fledged, flew off with their parents when we tried a capture, and this happens more often with each passing day. "The lovely bird" is the last crane to arrive in spring (late April to early May) and the first to depart, gathering in large flocks in the last fortnight of August; by the end of this month, it will be gone.

Our road returns west, up the long valley of the Uldz. On a gray day of impenetrable cloud and restless wind that give the steppe the strong monotone cast of Arctic tundra, two swans cross the rolling grasslands with sad callings, and Eurasian curlews, and a saker falcon. Where the nomad herds have been, the wild pasture is cropped short, and at one place I find a Daurian hedgehog that has rolled itself into a tight small ball in the thick grasses. Turning it gently and pulling apart the quills at the belly uncovers an alarmed black eye and a black shiny nose.

Many swans ride the dark chop at White Shears Lake, where in June 1981, Bold and Tseveen saw a Siberian crane. In the nineteenth century, they have learned, the white cranes passed through Dauria in spring migration, but unlike the other cranes, they were hunted, and now they have disappeared. From a river bluff, we count eight black storks, another rare species in this region; the black stork migrates to India and Africa, where I last saw them circling the Zimbabwe sky above the gardens of the Victoria Falls Hotel. Near the storks, a pair of demoiselles flutter and dance on the greensward of the riverbank—not in courtship but strengthening the pair bond. We run out into the marsh to capture and band the near-fledged chick of another pair, putting to flight a pair of white-napeds in a stubble field which seem to circle back a bit too soon. Sharp-eyed Chuka gets a glimpse of the chick's head, and eventually Dorj finds it—the tenth chick banded and the first *Grus vipio*, at last.

Alighting not far away, the searching adults crisscross the field in swift broad sweeps until the larger bird, probably the male, is only yards away from where I crouch in the field stubble, craning and peering, bill agape, gold eye flashing red reflections in the wild red face. A more formidable eye I have never beheld in all my life. *Vipio* has a harsh voice for a crane, low and loud at the same time, and like all cranes will "purr" or "growl," according to the listener; I expect a parental snarl at the very least. But no second chick reveals itself; the parents have been searching for the captured one. When it is released, they keep their distance, neither responding to its frantic peep nor moving toward it. Nor does the chick run after them, seeming to know it should move at once toward the cover of the river vegetation. Its parents follow, silent and aloof.

In Bayan Dun, we pay a call on Chuka's uncles, Lkhamjar and Bazarsad, two peaceful elders with Buryat faces carved like old mahogany who keep summer cabins by the river for the manufacture of yogurt, cheese, and curd. Next day, in the picket-fenced and rain-puddled village of Bayan Uul, we meet a handsome woman with a horse cart full of kids who turns out to be Chuka's cousin Dolgorkhand. She invites us to call upon her father.

With old bones carved around deep-set falcon eyes, Uncle Jamst at eighty is a warlike replica of his two brothers. At one time he was a champion archer, and in his modest way he is proud to show us his Buryat double bow of ibex horn strips glued to birch, and its eagle-feathered arrows. As a young man, Jamst was celibate, a lama, and he is still religious, but alas, he was forced to marry to escape the oppression of all Buddhists by the socialists. He does not appear unhappy about this, and neither does Aunt Regzedmaa, his serene wife. In purple *deel* and long white braids, Aunt Regzedmaa bears a startling resemblance to a friend, a Navajo elder from Big Mountain, Arizona. As children and grandchildren come and go, we are plied with fine milk tea and clotted sour cream (*zookhii*) and also good husky bread and sweetish biscuits.

A falcon morning—a kestrel, a red-footed falcon, many sakers. A white-naped crane at the Dalt River tributary, then five more, with dancing, leaping, bounding. Two more *vipio* near the track and then two more, then ten pairs in one small valley, with seven more *grus* and eight great bustards on the river plain—we are astonished. Those ten pairs of *vipio* with young in a single mile of river meadow are by far the greatest breeding concentration we have heard of anywhere, and the most exciting thing we have seen on our whole journey, confirming the theory of Tseveen and Bold that the heart of *tsen toguru*'s breeding range is the Daurian steppe, and more particularly these long valleys east of the Hentei Mountains.[12] With Russian Dauria so modified by agriculture, the last stronghold of the white-naped crane appears to be these river basins of Mongolia. Here the species has adapted to domestic cattle, walking around and through the herds, which do not barge far enough into the reed ponds and sedge floodlands to disturb its nests. (However, the fires set to renew wild pasture in late spring and swept by wind across these valleys may destroy a large number of the nests and young.) In this backcountry, G. *vipio* nests within sight and sound of human habitation, perhaps protected by the superstitions of the herders. We even find them in a place where ten *gers* have been raised on three sides of a large pond with minimal reed cover. Furthermore, they tolerate others of their species on breeding territories much smaller than considered necessary elsewhere—a thousand acres per pair in China's Zhalong reserve, for example.

With summer passing, more juveniles flee as the cars approach, but our capture system is efficient. Today a second *vipio* is caught after a prolonged chase, thanks to hand signals by spotters with binoculars, who keep the fleeing bird in sight and direct the banders to the place where it finally takes cover in deep reeds.

In late afternoon, the track descends to an open plain where twenty-four demoiselles, two white-napeds, four Eurasians, and a lone hooded crane stand within a hundred yards of one another—the second time in the past few days that these four species, getting ready for migration, have appeared together. These cranes are mainly diurnal in migration (although when at high altitude over the mountains, they may keep flying under the night stars). They take to the air in the mid-morning when the air warms and thermals develop, soaring and gliding north and south on ridges of high pressure at altitudes of 3,870 to 13,000 feet, at 25 to 37 miles per hour (and up to 50 miles an hour with a tailwind).

This day, four falcon species are observed—sakers, kestrels, red-footeds, and just at dusk, a hobby, stooping on a lark put up by Dorj's car. Missing it, the husky falcon—the size of a merlin—seems to somer-sault, so swiftly does it double back, the beak and head with its bold malar stripe twisting in the air to snatch the lark even as its sharp scis-sor wings bear it away.

All the way west, we census, band, check sightings, pausing only briefly to admire golden and white-tailed eagles. Gradually the valley narrows between grassy hills, rising to dark-maned ridges of larch and pine; the random bursts of white are wheeling flocks of wild hill pi-geons. Perhaps 120 miles upstream from the Tari lakes, the track enters the Hentei foothills, with mountains rising higher in the west. The strands of conifers on the highest ridges descend as the track gains alti-tude; in silhouette, a boy on horseback follows the horizon, trailed by a long unhurried line of camels.

The track descends. At the far end of a plain, under gray storm light and the shrouded western sun, clouds mill and drift chaotically on the dark peaks. The monsoon has overtaken us. After four days' rain, the plain is an interminable slough, and the vehicles lurch drunkenly and churn and skid. In the floodlands, the river is braided widely through the willows. A hare of narrow brain, dodging the headlights, bounds crazily ahead for minute after minute before jumping aside; later the beam picks up the eyes of Pallas's cat, small, silver-gray, and spotted. It crouches and withdraws into the road-edge tussocks.

The dim path traces a strange elevation in the plain, rounded and grassed over long ago like an old railroad bed. "Chinghis's Wall," say Bold and Chuka, claiming it wandered all over Mongolia. Whether Chinghis built it, whether it dates from the days of the Golden Horde, "nobody knows." I think of those Soviet missile sites, already over-grown, concerning which some Mongol of the future might well say, "Nobody knows."

It is past ten and still raining when camp is made on a grassy hill above a stretch of the old wall.

A cold wind from the western steppe is holding back the rains, which lie massed above the hills where we have come from. A bright sunrise warms the tents, and across the steaming grass comes the strange seesaw calling of the demoiselles. (These demoiselles of eastern Mongolia must cross the Himalaya to winter on the plains of western India.[13]) We drag on clothes still dank and cold from the crane hunts of the day before. The bread is gone, so Chuka makes chapatis. Everyone is in the best of spirits, and the most cheerful is Dorj, whose open, undefended face is a tonic every morning.

An early visitor is a boy of great beauty who rides up on an ugly measle-spotted horse attended by two dogs; a Buddhist design—the endless knot—is tooled into the leather of his saddle. Then another boy comes, this one not beautiful, evoking instead some squint-eyed violent warrior in the campaigns of the Great Khan. The two ride after us as I take the wheel in pursuit of two demoiselle chicks spotted from camp (Dawa has not completed his toilette or is otherwise indisposed). A short-eared owl flutters up before the car, only to dive straight down again into the grasses.

The track continues westward, still following Chinghis's Wall. A cinereous vulture crosses the sky, a red-footed falcon plucks a vole from its daily round not thirty yards from the front tires. Soon the track turns north, departing the Uldz valley and climbing to a ridge of dark pine and pale larch before descending to the Onon River, which flows north to an Amur tributary in Siberia. At the small town of Bayan Adraga (named for a holy mountain), it turns westward once again, up the Onon valley.

In early afternoon we pause to fish for supper. Chuka drags in a small taimen, a primitive salmonid that in larger Asian rivers such as the Lena may attain a weight of well over one hundred pounds (and can only be subdued, so it is said, if the nimrod has a confederate on hand to blaze away with a heavy-gauge shotgun when the monster breaks the surface). On an open river bar, I catch two small fish on my fly rod and miss a good strike in a strong riffle as a black storm rushes in between the peaks and thunder comes crashing all around. Chary of lightning, I flee the river, thrashing across two tributary streams, and am midway across the second stream when kind Dorj comes to find me. We race for cover, reaching the cars as an avalanche of rain and hail buries the river plain in ghostly slush.

This lowland may be hit by a flash flood, and the Mongolians are out packing up camp even before the storm relents; we reach the higher ground in time, but the main track west is already flooded out. Heading cross-country in four-wheel-drive, the cars climb the hills above the track, traversing an evergreen ridge and descending once more to a high bluff over the confluence of the Onon River with the Khurkh (pronounced backward—*Hkruhk!*).

Our camp on the bluff has a dramatic view of the Hentei Mountains. Up there, Bold tells me, pointing northwest, is the sacred mountain called Burkhan Kaldun, which gave shelter from his enemies to the young Temujin before he became known as Chinghis Khan. Despite the claims of those Inner Mongolians, the Great Khan lies buried near Burkhan Kaldun. Japanese archeologists are of the same opinion, he says, having come there this summer, searching for the tomb.

Bold is preparing to go night fishing for taimen, which he hopes to entice with a crude furry lure the size of a young muskrat; the lure is twitched slowly across the surface like a rodent struggling in a swift current. But the rain continues and the night is black and all we hook are heavy river weeds torn out by storms. We give it up until 3:15 A.M. when, awakened by Bold's ferocious old alarm, I slip and slide down the bluff in the pitch darkness to my preselected casting ledge only to find that it has disappeared beneath the rising river. The muddy flood is roiling, and there is no place under the steep bluff to strip out fly line, far less cast it. But miraculously, in the black daybreak, my emergency rig (a saltwater jig heavy enough, when snapped hard up and outward from the rod tip, to yank the fly line coiled up on my boot toes out over the river) hooks a taimen on a slow retrieve over the bottom. The big fish missed its rough swipe at the lure that passed it in the murky water and has foul-hooked itself behind the gills, making it difficult to turn with my light fly rod. Hearing its primordial thrashing, Chuka races upstream even as I shout at him to keep away. We are shoulder to shoulder in the shallows when at last I work the fish in close, and he stoops and heaves it with both hands onto the shore, then up the steep bank to safety on the bluff.

The dull metallic green-gray fish with its red tail and pelvic fins measures out at forty inches long—a pretty fair fish for the Khurkh, if not the Lena. The taimen provides a delicious respite from Bronze Kettle's black goat with its bared teeth, which is not less rank for its many days of unrefrigerated travel. Only Bold continues to chisel stray bits from the fire-blackened skull and eat them from the point of his old clasp knife.

Headed west again under gray skies and intermittent rain, we have to wonder just how far we are going to get. Apart from the dissolution of the track, the small settlements we pass have no fuel whatever, not even for the tractors that must cut the precious hay for the coming winter. But that evening, after two hours spent in Tseveen's brother's village of Omondelger, we manage to scrounge thirty liters of diesel fuel. However, each of our two cars needs at least forty liters to reach Ulaan Baatar, which is still more than two hundred miles away.

Next day toward noon, at a huge cairn topped by a Soviet soldier's helmet, we meet a procession of camel-drawn carts—each camel hitched to the back of the cart ahead—that is moving an *arat* family and its *ger* to a late-summer pasture. While the girls and women and young boys with long pole lassos herd the horses, sheep, and cattle, the *arat* himself, in purple hat, finds a saddled horse for Tseveen, then accompanies him in wild pursuit of two *vipio* chicks spotted at the far side of a reedy marsh.

From the higher elevation of the track, I use hand signals to guide riders and runners in pursuit of the swift half-flying chicks, which are often hidden. (Alas, I have become more useful as a spotter than a runner, but spotting, while critical, is not for a man who loves to run.) When the chicks finally tire, Tseveen overtakes one on his horse, and soon the runners have corralled the other. Beyond the knot of men and horses surrounding the two chicks, the parent cranes pretend to feed, straightening long white necks every few moments to peer over the reeds at the distressing scene, then lifting off the ground to flap and glide and alight and peer at it all again from another angle. Perhaps these white-napeds are the last ones we shall see, for we are close to the west end of their range in the Khurkh drainage.[14]

I climb to a rock outcrop on the ridge from where I can see up and down the lake-eyed valley. White *gers*, cattle herds, the black-maned horses reflected in still pools, the *arat* camel train and prayer-flagged cairn, the grass and grass and grass and grass, rolling away toward purple peaks of the storm-shrouded mountains—in the midst of this ancient landscape of central Asia, I feel wistful. Our expedition is coming to an end, and already I miss the Daurian steppe. Is it the knowing that in all likelihood I shall never see this land again, or is it something else?

Toward six that evening, in a broad valley of shallow lakes, twenty-six *tsen toguru* come in sight at once, the largest group observed on the whole journey. We can no longer doubt that this western region of the Daurian steppe, in the upper valleys of the Uldz and Khurkh, is the heartland of the Daurian crane and the probable source of the large winter flock at the Poyang lakes.[15]

Inspired, Tseveen goes to the nearest *ger*, and within a few minutes, he is galloping with a young *arat* across the two or three miles of steppe to where a fawn-colored chick, too big to hide, has set off on a wild flapping run across the marshes, through a reed bed, and out onto the plain. Jouncing and swerving to keep up, the car cuts off its escape and we jump out to surround it.

In the end it is Jim Harris who grasps it by the neck and struggles to subdue it without harming the young bird; he is nicked by the sharp toenails in the process. At this size, so nearly fledged, it is quite danger-

ous, for its dagger bill has hardened. When Go Fujita bands and releases it, the young crane makes no attempt to flee but turns to confront
him, crossly shuffling its new pin feathers, spreading its wings and
dancing upward, long claws spread to rake him.[16] Only when Go has
hastily retreated does it turn and stalk away across the plain in no great
hurry, shaking the bright green ring around its leg.

The *arats* of Targalant Lakes ("Lucky Guy Lakes," Chuka assures
me) set out a warm mutton-and-noodle soup before permitting us to
continue on our way. Very low on fuel, we camp that night on an open
plain and set out early next morning for the upper Kerulen. Marmots,
which have been scarce, are reappearing, and with them the small
golden ground squirrel of the plains. At midday, we visit a *ger* owned
by a bent widow in gold head scarf whose son labors in the mines but
whose grandchildren have come for the summer to help with the animals. She offers fermented mare's milk, cheese, pressed sour-milk curd,
and fresh yogurt, and the yogurt is sprinkled with a few small dark
wild berries, the only fruit we have tasted on the expedition.

The upper Kerulen, in flood after the rains, is a swift torrent between hills, but to the west, the old low mountains are marred by mine
scars, coal smog, and the industrial mine stacks at Baga Nuur. Here at
last we acquire diesel fuel from a passing truck. On a high hill flowered
by sky-blue scabia and night-blue delphiniums, we make a light meal of
the last taimen and chapatis, then continue south and west across the
continental divide into the valley of the Tuul.

One hundred demoiselles in the hills west of the Kerulen are the last
cranes recorded. In late August, they will dance up from the steppes
and rise in the blue skies, circling higher and higher on the thermals before heading south in flocks of thousands on the long journey across
central Asia and Tibet and the Himalaya, setting tired wings at last for
the long gliding descent into the Indian subcontinent. Many will trace
the silver thread of the deepest gorge on earth where the Kali Gandaki
River parts the snow peaks of Dhaulagiri and Annapurna before burst-
ing forth in the sun of the Ganges Plain.

THREE

Gujarat and Rajasthan

What is the color of snow like? It is like a white crane.
                                                    —Nirvana Sutra

Because of airline strikes in northern India, the plane southwest
from Delhi to Ahmedabad in Gujarat ("Land of Herders") on a
hot January day in 1993 was a TU-154, one of seven on lease
from Uzbekistan—soon to be six, since one would crash while landing
at Delhi the next morning. In Ahmedabad, there was violent strife
caused by Hindu destruction of the Muslim mosque at Ayodhya in the
hours before; at the bridge over the Sabarmati River, a crowd pointed
excitedly at a high plume of black smoke where rioting was taking
place. The official death toll at Ahmedabad that day would be seventeen, but other reports would claim a much higher count. With the old
town cordoned off by soldiery, the bus made a tortuous passage out of
the city, headed west.

Peering out the window in the seat behind me was my old friend
Victor Emanuel, with whom I had been observing cranes since 1976,
when I joined him as a field leader of his new wildlife safari company
that operates out of Austin, Texas. That year we took our pioneer
clients to observe wintering whooping cranes on the Texas coast and
sandhill cranes on the coastal prairies. Here in India, with our friend

Raj Singh, an expert ornithologist from Delhi, we were guiding a band of intrepid travelers to observe northwestern India's wildlife in Gujarat and Rajasthan, where the four species of cranes includes the dangerously diminished western Siberian crane. From India, we would travel on to Bhutan, China, and Japan, where with luck, perseverance, and good weather, we hoped to observe all eight species of Asian cranes.

From Ahmedabad, a narrow road leads west across flat delta country to Zainabad, one of eleven villages in the former principality of the same name. Zainabad's unofficial leader is a Muslim *nawab* (the Hindu equivalent would be *rajah*). "Here is not like Bombay or Ahmedabad, where the British separated Hindu and Muslim as they did in Pakistan," says the nawab, Dr. Shabeer Malek, shaking his head over the senseless rioting which was taking the lives of hundreds in Bombay. "Here in the villages we need one another, and so we live nicely together." His own wife is a Hindu, and his son-in-law, too, and all live together as nicely as you please.

Dr. Malek's big house in a walled grove of figs and neem mahogany overlooks the bare-dirt village and the thick brown pond to which animals and humans come for water. Women in bright saris pound their wash on rocks as water buffalo and bullocks, sheep and cattle muddy the shallows.[1] In an acacia grove on the west side of the pond, the nawab maintains a camp of tents and thatched rondavels. Protected from wandering livestock by a thornbush compound, the camp is a refuge in the midst of the abounding village life—almost too peaceful, one feels uneasily, in light of the human strife and suffering we have left behind us in the cities. At dusk on that first night at Zainabad come jackal yips and the heavy grunting of an eagle owl; toward dawn the night sounds are replaced by the water-bottle song of coucals.

Out of the sunrise comes the rolling cry of cranes. I emerge from my rondavel in time to see two immense pale gray-silver birds cross the acacia scrub right behind camp. When they flare off only yards away, the fresh red of the bare face and nape gleams in the new sun, which turns the soft pearl hues of the great birds to a rare blue. A broad white collar separates the red skin of the upper neck and face from the lower neck and body, which is a uniform pale gray except for the gray-white tertials of the wing.

The male of the Indian sarus (the name comes from its call) may be well over five feet tall, taller than the average male of *Homo sapiens*; *Grus antigone* is the tallest flying bird on earth. A common species of the northern subcontinent before its arable lowlands, from the floodplain of the Indus in Pakistan to the Brahmaputra floodplain in Bangladesh, produced one of the earth's greatest densities of human beings, the sarus is a holy messenger of Vishnu, the Hindu deity. In Gujarat, says Dr. Malek, its name is a synonym for goodness, since like most cranes, the species is popularly supposed to mate for life, even to remain celibate after its mate's death, and is therefore a symbol of virtue and fidelity. A sarus struck down in its courtship dance by a hunter's arrow—and the gallant fidelity of the female, trying to help it to its feet until she too was killed—inspired the great Indian epic called the *Ramayana*, which is beloved throughout southern Asia. If a crane is killed, country people say, its mate will shortly pine away, perhaps destroy itself (how its suicide is carried out is not related), and a person who kills one is fated to lose his own mate shortly thereafter. That it has been protected since the earliest days of the Hindu religion might perhaps be the source of the Buddhist love of cranes, for the reputation of cranes as sacred creatures appears to have spread with Buddhism from India to other Asian lands.

The clarion calls of the sarus crane herald the beginning of the village day here in backcountry India, where it requires little in the way of breeding territory. Adapting to small seasonal wetlands, it lives most of the year in scattered pairs near the farm villages, often nesting in a field, a rice paddy, or the tall reeds of the village pond and gleaning harvest grains in village croplands. Though ordinarily a monsoon nester (August to October), it may attempt a second nest in February or March in places where water seeping from irrigation canals creates a marshy

shallow-water habitat all year round. Like other *Grus*, the sarus produces two eggs, but unlike those species with long migrations, it often
raises both, since conserving the precious energy spent in arduous travel
permits more efficient breeding.

More than other cranes (with the possible exception of the Florida
sandhill, which may frequent airports or be laid low by golf balls), the
beloved sarus has lost its fear of man, and will stalk within yards of people in the fields. Even so, it has been driven ever farther into the hinter-
lands by increasing human densities, mechanized agriculture, wetlands
drainage and development, and fertilizer and pesticide pollution, and
has commenced an inevitable decline. Its very adaptability has worked
against it, since its pairs may become so widely scattered that protection
in reserves is of little use.

Not far from Muslim Zainabad—an hour's walk away across flat
fields—is the old whitewashed Hindu village of Mulala, where
black-faced white sheep consort with white-faced black goats, and wild
peafowl—also sacred birds—are fed by the reverent on special platforms erected for this purpose. The peacocks perch boldly on the thatch
of the village roofs and strut like glorious green turkeys through the
earthen streets. Cattle, too, are sacred, but not water buffalo, which are
perpetually yoked by a dull karma to ponderous wood-wheeled carts.
The camels, too, are mere draft animals, an insolent, flea-bitten lot
whose cold hauteur and contemptuous loose lip, curling back on their
big yellow teeth, give fair warning to the prudent traveler to keep his
distance.

Mulala's fields are planted in wheat and millet, and also an archaic
cotton with a small, tight boll. From a slough between fields, two sarus
rise trumpeting and sail away over yellow-blossomed cassia and acacia.
Though Mulala is Hindu, a young woman from another village who
has married here comes down the stone street with her face veiled by
her sari—a reflection, says Raj Singh, of the strong Muslim influence in

these desert regions. Scattered across the countryside are stone monuments to warriors from those ancient days of the twelfth century when the Muslims, in a series of invasions, sought control of all this western country.

A few miles west of Zainabad is a broad, shallow pan where the last of the monsoon waters has collected. Here hundreds of Eurasian cranes circle and call before drifting down on the far side of the pan, whereas a pair of sarus flies straight in, low and direct, alighting calmly on the bank within a stone's throw of passing villagers before setting off to forage in field margins. Graceful women in brilliant saris thread the slow old paths, copper water vessels shining on their heads, and lone herders rise out of the land, trailed by slow companies of livestock and slow camels, all along the flat horizon of the Rann of Kutch, in a scene unchanged since the time of the *Ramayana*.

In the past few decades, this western race of the sarus crane has vanished from Pakistan and Bangladesh and is now largely confined to northwest India—Gujarat, Rajasthan, Uttar Pradesh—with a small population just across the border in Nepal. There, in the Tarai lowlands of the upper Ganges, the cranes glean crops at certain times of year, but they also feed on harmful insects and field rodents and are generally considered beneficial by the Hindu Nepalese, who protect the pair in the belief that the mournful cry of a lone bird hunting its lost mate is an evil omen. Such beliefs mean little to the hungry hill peoples who have settled the Tarai since the 1960s (an estimated two hundred thousand in the single decade after 1971) in the wake of a malaria-eradication program that encouraged wetlands draining, new dams, reservoirs, and irrigation projects for ever-swelling human populations. Further deterioration of crane habitat was caused by sedimentation and the flooding of wetland ecosystems due to overcutting of the forests and consequent soil loss and erosion from the foothills. New roads provided access to armed hunters from the towns for whom the cranes were tame and easy targets, and children competed with the hogs in raiding nests for the few eggs that cattle and buffalo had not trampled.

Although new parks and reserves such as the famous Royal Chitwan were created in Nepal for the rare one-horned rhino and the tiger, most wetlands were left entirely unprotected. The last significant sarus habitat (which also serves endangered storks, ibises, and spoonbills) is a region around Lumbini, a village that has scarcely changed since the birth of Sakyamuni the Buddha in Lumbini's gardens more than twenty-five hundred years ago. Developed by Buddhist groups since the 1960s as an international shrine constructed around a simple pillar erected in 236 B.C. by the emperor Asoka, Lumbini is surrounded by a three-square-mile reserve that shelters a number of uncommon species—a suitable homage to the Buddha, who taught his followers to revere all forms of life. In 1988, a census estimated about one hundred sarus in the Lumbini district, the densest population in Nepal.

The so-called eastern sarus, or Sharpe's sarus, *Grus antigone sharpii*, of Southeast Asia[2] is smaller and darker than the huge *G. a. antigone* of the Indian subcontinent, and lacks the broad white neck band of the larger bird as well as the pale gray tertials on the wing. Since ancient times, the eastern sarus has been seen as a messenger from heaven sent to fetch departed souls destined for immortality. A sarus alighted on the broad back of a turtle symbolizes virtue and harmony in Buddhist temples throughout the region; in the huge black ruins at Angkor Wat, in Cambodia, are bas-reliefs of dancing cranes. But while the Indian sarus, more than other cranes, has adapted to life with *Homo sapiens* and even adjusted to his battered lands and muddied waters, the eastern sarus, which rarely enjoyed the religious protection afforded the Indian birds, was less confiding, and in recent times has disappeared almost everywhere throughout its range, from Burma[3] and southern China south to Southeast Asia, the Philippines, and New Guinea. With violence widespread in Indochina, it was commonly trapped or hunted down with dogs during the molting season, with many brought back alive for sale in the world wildlife trade.

The rich farmlands in the great delta of the Mekong River, which descends twenty-six hundred miles from the Tibetan plateau through Cambodia and Vietnam to the South China Sea, are restored annually with a rich silt that, when the floodwaters recede, grows three crops of rice each year, food for half of the Vietnamese people and for export as well. During the wars with the Japanese and French, then the "American War" (as it was known to the small countries that suffered its devastation), the delta was a stronghold of the Vietcong. The French and the Americans dug two huge canals to drain the Dong Thap Muoi lowlands in southwest Vietnam near the Cambodian border, a natural flood basin of the Mekong known to foreigners as the "Plain of Reeds"; subsequently the plain was napalmed, leaving the scorched earth poisoned by acid sulfates. In the lean aftermath of war, the last scattered cranes were trapped or killed with poisoned bait and eaten by hungry villagers whose farms and paddies had been mostly destroyed, or hunted by helicopter crews for sale and trade in Ho Chi Minh City (Saigon).

By now it was feared that *sharpii* was extirpated from Southeast Asia and endangered everywhere throughout its range. In Thailand no wild sarus had been reported since 1968. In China's southern Yunnan Province, evidence of sarus was confined to an alleged footprint and some village rumors; from across the border in Burma, where a military dictatorship had seized control, there were no reports whatever. In the Philippines, where *sharpii* had occurred on the main island of Luzon, it was beset by the same problems as in Southeast Asia—man's warfare and uncontrolled hunting for food, as well as crane habitat that could not be protected because the political situation was so dangerous.

In Vietnam, in the mid-1970s, certain wetland areas were set aside where the people were persuaded to stop trapping, in the hope that the cranes might return as the habitat recovered. However, no sarus reappeared. In the early 1980s, dikes were rebuilt to restore water levels in the Mekong basin, and in August 1984, twenty-odd cranes miraculously reappeared in the Dong Thap Muoi floodplains—the first authenticated sighting of *G. a. sharpii* in Southeast Asia since the Vietnam war. With the encouragement of the ICF, local officials set aside a part of Dong Thap Muoi as the Tram Chin ("Bird Swamp") Nature Reserve, fifty thousand acres in extent.[4]

In 1988, more than a thousand *sharpii* were counted at Tram Chin, restoring hope for the future of this race, though where these birds

might be breeding remained unknown. It was supposed that they were
nesting somewhere in Cambodia, which remained mostly undeveloped,
with vast areas of open forest and scattered wetlands. This low-lying
country includes Tonle Sap, the Great Lake, seventy-five miles long
and twenty miles wide, the largest body of permanent freshwater in Indochina; in the summer monsoon, Tonle Sap swells to fifteen times that
size, flooding forest and fields for hundreds of miles around. However,
it could not be searched, since it lies about ten miles south of Angkor
Wat, and the Angkor region—scene of much of the death and terror
between 1975 and 1979—was still the stronghold of the Khmer Rouge.

(In 1994, breeding grounds of the eastern sarus would finally be discovered, not at Tonle Sap but in small scattered wetlands in savanna
habitats of northeast Cambodia from where, at the onset of the dry season in December, the crane flocks travel to the Mekong Delta.[5] Although its Philippines population is presumed to be extinct, *G. a.
sharpii*, taking advantage of the lull between the chronic wars, has made
a tentative recovery in Southeast Asia.)

Not far from Zainabad is the border of the Little Rann of Kutch, a
vast pale desert and saline marsh that extends, when dry, eighty
miles from east to west and from ten to forty miles north to south. *Rann*
signifies a "desolate place," as in a wasteland in the wake of war, Raj
Singh informs us. Kutch, or "Marsh Land," the largest district in the
state of Gujarat (in all of India, for that matter), also includes the Great
Rann, which lies off to the north on the borders of Rajasthan and Pakistan. The Great Rann is watered by one seasonal river and is dry most
of the year, whereas the Little Rann, during the strong southwest winds
of the monsoon (when solar tides are forced onto the desert from the
Gulf of Kutch and the Arabian Sea), may be flooded by four rivers and
an ocean. In certain seasons of certain years, much of southern Gujarat
disappears beneath six inches to six feet of water. (Though one hundred
miles north of the coast, Zainabad lies only three feet above sea level,

and most of the roads are constructed on embankments to keep the villages from being isolated during the monsoon.)

The low-lying flats of the Little Rann connect the mainland to the broad peninsula of Saurashtra, most of which is low-lying and drained for agriculture. However, considerable thorn scrub lies inland and also a dry, deciduous forest—the Gir Forest, last stronghold of the lion, which was formerly widespread throughout northern India. From October to February, great companies of Eurasian cranes and demoiselles from central Asia and Mongolia descend on Saurashtra's peanut crops and grainfields, joining the resident sarus in one of the largest crane aggregations left on earth.

While the sarus may gather in large flocks in the dry season, awaiting their breeding season in the monsoons, and the Eurasians, picking here and there, tend to scatter in family groups, the demoiselles move through the crops in flocks, doing severe damage if nobody is there to scare them off. (Later in the season, the cranes have competition from the nomadic poor, who slip into the fields after the harvest to glean ungathered peanuts.) Roads and vehicles are increasing with the population, and although crane hunting is illegal, some are inevitably taken for food. The pressure of human numbers on land and life together with the prevailing drought and desertification has blighted these latitudes in Asia as in Africa, and in Gujarat (where promised water from the discredited Narmada River dam projects has never gone much farther than Ahmedabad) the companies of migrant cranes may gradually disappear.

Kind Dr. Malek, an ironical small man in foulard and a broad Aussie hat that does not quite suit him, escorts us in his lorry out onto the *rann* in search of the rare *ghor khar*, or Indian wild ass, *Equus hemionus khur* (from the Sanskrit *gaura khara*, or "white ass"), one of the last three species of wild horse left on earth. A half century ago, the wild ass had all but vanished from the Great Rann and from Pakistan;

it was dying out in its last redoubt in the Little Rann when India's
Board for Wildlife intervened. Despite unseemly partisan cries—
"There is no shortage of asses in this country!"—a sanctuary was finally
established. By 1976, its estimated population was 720 animals, together
with 96 large nilgai or "blue bull" antelope, 191 Indian gazelles, and
some 62 wolves, which prey on all the hoofed fraternity without dis-
tinction. Two other races of *E. hemionus* occurred sparsely in the Iran-
ian deserts and in central Asia, but none survive in Iran and only ten in
Pakistan. Some authorities believe that *E. h. khur* is the only true (non-
feral) wild ass in the world besides the little-known kiang of western
China and Tibet.

Our host soon locates a small herd of *E. hemionus*, which drifts away
across the cracked pale alkali of the dry *rann*. Wary of men as well as
wolves, the sharp-eyed animals feel more secure out on the open pan.
From a distance, the wild ass appears white, since its hindquarters and
hind legs are white and it is usually observed going away. Seen closer,
the animals have pale fawn saddle marks and rump, and the black dor-
sal line of the short stiff mane continues all the way to the base of the
tail.

Drifting across sere distances, the asses shimmer like mirages. Ten
stallions following the edge of the low bushy islands known as *bets*
pause to peer back at us over their shoulders. A lone stallion tends a
herd of mares, five trailed by foals. He leaves his harem to go sniffing
off into the scrub after a single mare with a yearling and foal, but the
mare pays his horsy itch no heed, and he, too, seems to tire of it, stopping short as if coming to his senses, then turning back, head hanging.
Five sarus come from the horizon to alight near the wild horses—"very
unusual," comments Dr. Malek, observing that two adults with chick
form the largest group of sarus usually seen here. (Large flocks may
gather near water in the dry season, before the monsoon, after which
they return to their breeding areas and split up again.) The immature
bird is smaller, with a shining white nape instead of a pearl-gray one.
At all ages, *Grus antigone* has pale pink legs, though the tibia or lower
leg is usually caked over with dried mud. The five sarus remain silent,
cocking their heads as if listening for something far away.

Long skeins of Eurasian cranes appear on the horizon, until at least a thousand gray-brown migrants from northern Asia are drifting in over the desert; it's fun to think I might have seen a few of these same birds last summer in Mongolia. The Asian *grus* will overwinter in Iran, India, Burma, and southern China, with a few in Southeast Asia. European *grus* migrate to the Iberian Peninsula and northwest Africa, where sixty thousand may overwinter; a like number from Scandinavia, gathering in Hungary in autumn, will migrate across southern Italy to Algeria; a third population comes south from Russia through Turkey and Israel to northeast Africa, then up the Nile to southwestern Ethiopia and the Sudan.

In this region of the *rann*, the groundwater beneath the pan is a brine several times more saline than the sea, and 40 percent of India's salt is mined here. Shining mounds of salt, as white as bone, are scattered across the brown horizons. Here and there rise lone thatched huts of the Koli people who tend the crude bore holes and ancient pumps that sluice the brine toward the center of the pan, where the salt is crystallized by evaporation and piled up to be trucked away. (The salt tenders work knee-deep in brine, and their leg bones become so impregnated with salt, says Malek, that they won't burn in the ritual cremation; those impervious tibiae must be buried intact, in contravention of Hindu precepts.) One family which keeps goats in a small fenced yard must take them indoors every night because of a wolf that comes boldly to the hovel door.

Though the Koli salt miners are very poor, they are not Dalits or "untouchables"—or "Sons of God," as Mohandas Gandhi called them. Gandhi himself was a Gujarati, born at Porbandar on the seacoast, and his first social action upon his return to India from South Africa was the famous Salt March from his ashram at Ahmedabad south to Dandi, in protest against the harsh British tax on an already exploitative enterprise that still pays human beings less than one dollar a day for toiling in the white-hot light of hell.

As the sun rises and the cool of the night desert disappears, strange liquid mirages manifest all along the merciless horizon that recedes for a hundred miles south to the sea. Flights of northern *grus* circle down to alight near the wild horses, just as the sarus did yesterday, as if here in this white place, living creatures instinctively draw near one another. A mile beyond, a solitary camel passes in the silver shimmer, then a lone human figure in wavering silhouette, fallen far behind; in the hallucinatory light, the dark vessel on her head is an outlandish crown. The two creatures in their vague relation have appeared from nowhere in the desert, rising minutely from the landscape and inching onward across the mirror of white sun and on down the line of the horizon. In the mirage, they walk on water, with only light beneath them.

From Gujarat, our road leads north to Rajasthan, then west to the Thar or Great Indian Desert, and on beyond the exotic desert town of Jaisalmer to India's Desert National Park on the Pakistan frontier, where we search for and find that rare crane relative called the Indian bustard. On the return eastward, we turn off on a lightly traveled road that leads from Jodhpur one hundred miles north-northwest to Phalodi, in the country of those Vishnoi Hindus who 250 years ago defied the maharajah of Jodhpur's order to cut down a grove of the "tree of life"—the *khejri* acacia whose taproot famously descended ninety feet in search of water, and whose beans and leaves were staple food and fodder for humans and livestock. Some sixty Vishnoi were destroyed in that early conservation battle, but they still protect all wildlife and have made sacred animals of the dwindling blackbuck antelopes, which may not be hunted anywhere in the region.

From Phalodi, a humble track arrives eventually at the village of Khichan, where fences are constructed of tall slabs of blood-red rock, like leaning gravestones. Here an association of Jain and Hindu merchants has undertaken the care and feeding of hundreds of wintering demoiselle cranes. More than 150 years ago, they say, a king of Jodhpur banned the hunting of these birds, and they have gathered in Khichan every fall and winter for no less than 115 years. Many Jain people lived at Khichan, and since the Jain philosophy is based on nonviolence and charity to all living things, the people took pity on the dainty cranes, which appeared to be pecking up the dust and eating pebbles. A custom of crane feeding was initiated that has grown each year as the number of cranes increased. *Anthropoides virgo*'s original benefactors have mostly gone away to live and work in Delhi, Madras, and Bombay, but the families maintain large shuttered dwellings in their dark red village.

The first demoiselles appear in December at the end of the monsoon rains; they remain until early March, when the last birds depart on their trans-Himalayan journeys. The cranes gather each day at two ponds at the village outskirts, where a waste of hard-packed yellowed desert stretches westward toward a few bent *khejri* in the distance. From the water edge and sand dunes all around, they honk, rattle, and creak in response to calls of inquiry from the legions which circle and descend the dusty skies, until the silver flocks cover several acres. Unlike the sarus, the demoiselles are wary, yet they are so acclimated to Khichan that camel and bullock carts and women in flame-red, orange, and saffron saris, passing them within stoning distance, cause only a light shifting in the ranks.

The demoiselle's voice, higher and thinner than that of larger cranes, is nonetheless audible from far away. *Kurr-kurrj*, it seems to say, and so it is called *koonj* or *kuraj* or *kurjan*. *Kurajo te mharo dekh chhillariyo tal* is a folk song about crane messengers from the days when many local men were absent, working as laborers for large landholders elsewhere: *Oh crane, arrange that I meet with my beloved.*

As a grain eater with a taste for young shoots, the demoiselle does serious damage, not only in agricultural Saurashtra but in arid regions like Khichan, where the critical concern is growing enough food in the monsoon to last the people through the chronic droughts. Yet the Khichan folk welcome *kurjan*, ignoring the harm done to meager local crops by these little cranes with fiery red eyes that are fed well twice a day.

The feeding is supervised by Mr. Prakash Jain, a devotee of the controversial guru Bhagwan Raj Neesh (lately of Oregon, where his vast fleet of Rolls-Royces awed the rural populace); the radiant visage of his guru illuminates Mr. Prakash's modest dwelling, where he serves us tea with a smile that rivals that of Raj Neesh for pure beneficence. Eight years ago, our kind host renounced the world to see to the protection of the cranes.

Like the peacocks and sacred cattle, the birds were fed irregularly in the early years, and their numbers rarely exceeded several hundred. It was only when the villagers started a cooperative and a grain offering was made twice daily at appointed hours that *A. virgo* started appearing in large numbers, with *H. sapiens* close behind. (The first few tourists turned up in 1990, and the first bird-watchers two years later.[6])

Today the Khichan flock, estimated at 5,500 birds, consumes 70 gunnysacks of grain at 220 pounds each, or more than 15,000 pounds every day throughout the season; with the help of local donations, this offering has been made for twenty years. The cranes fly over the village twice a day, alighting on bare dunes just beyond a 200-by-300-foot enclosure with a barbed-wire fence designed to exclude hogs, dogs, and children. In midafternoon, from the house of Jain, we hear the flocks rising from the pond edge to the west, and as the cranes pass noisily over the village, as if to bear it away with all their racket, we walk through dark red empty streets of hollow family houses. To the dunes outside the fence, to the large pen at the east edge of town on the side farthest from the houses, the cranes are already falling slowly, long legs dangling, long toes straining to touch the fine brown sand; none presume to enter the pen before Mr. Jain's assistants have scattered the fine white millet seed from large metal bowls. Even then, the courtly birds hold back a little and they do not crowd and jostle, for cranes are not like chickens, gulls, and ducks, which rush their food. But finally the hungriest or boldest dances up into the air and circles the pen about fifty feet above the ground before dropping into the corner farthest from the onlookers.

The bird ranks are restless, rising and settling in place, and soon they run a few light steps, rise into the wind, and circle unhurriedly over the low buildings and the oblivious children bicycling home from school. (One inspired small boy with a large school backpack operates a man's bike from below by hanging on with one thin arm around the bar and managing the handles with the other, while the rest of him, well below the seat, labors the pedals. I long to cheer as he arrives home, neatly dismounts, and lugs his pack inside, his nonchalance making quite clear that this hard-won feat is no less and no more than his daily practice.)

A single crane, then two and three, then squadrons of demoiselles drop in slow against the wind, line after line, as more long V's of calling birds cross the village from the ponds. On black-fingered wings, they join the spirals that drift slowly down the sky and disappear among the the feeding birds. Perhaps five hundred occupy the pen at the same time. I abandon my search for those green-ringed birds I had helped to band in Mongolia the previous summer, being unable to make out legs in the thronged pen.

Already the cranes are returning to the dunes to rest and preen before recrossing the village to the pond edge. Toward twilight, when most of them are gone, we leave Khichan. At the edge of the village stands a lone nilgai antelope. This beast, too, has been befriended by the people, for it does not run but merely climbs the dune a little way before turning its head to observe our departure for the Keoladeo Ghana National Park at Bharatpur in east Rajasthan, where we hope to see the last few Siberian cranes that still fly to India in winter.

"Just as in medieval Europe when the color white had important symbolic significance, white plumage in cranes has come to signify a special status—great rarity and an uncertain future," the ICF's Ronald Sauey wrote in his doctoral thesis on the Siberian crane. "Only three of the fifteen crane species are predominantly white and these three are by far the most endangered members of this small and declining family."[7]

Grus leucogeranus, slightly smaller than the other two white cranes, resembles the whooping crane of North America in its almost identical arrangement of white plumage and black primaries, or "flight feathers," but its vivid red face and long decurved bill give it an appearance very different from all other *Grus*. What *leucogeranus* brings to mind—to this mind, at least—is a very large American white ibis, even to the tropical pink legs. To German immigrants brought to Russia by Catherine the Great, it evoked the beloved white stork of home, which delivered babies and nested on chimney tops; they called it *Storch* (which became *sterkh* in Russian), or *Nonnenkranich*, the nun crane, due to the white cowl or coif of feathers surrounding the red facial disk.

The Siberian differs from other *Grus* in its almost complete dependence on wetlands—though when tundra bogs and marshes are still frozen upon its arrival on the sub-Arctic breeding grounds, even this most aquatic of the cranes stalks higher ground, hunting voles, lemmings, and old berries. Because it has never adapted to man's farmlands, it has suffered considerable harm from wetland pollution and destruction by ever-increasing human activity on its northern breeding grounds as well as in its winter sanctuary. The whooping crane has made a slow but steady gain in numbers, while the red-crowned crane appears more or less stable in its east Asian and Japanese populations. However, those species have been zealously protected for more than a half century, while the Siberian is hunted along all three of its arduous migration routes. Despite its higher numbers, it is presently regarded as the most endangered of the three.

"Cranes are relict birds and do not withstand anthropogenic pressure well, whether direct (hunting) or indirect (habitat alteration or destruction)," Dr. Sauey notes. They do not breed until their fourth or fifth year, and there is high mortality among young birds; even after receiving full protection, the wild whoopers took twenty years to raise their population from thirty-one to fifty-seven, averaging scarcely one per year. The last western Siberians, unprotected and separated from the much larger eastern population by a sub-Arctic wilderness of swamp and forest—more than a thousand miles—from the Ob delta to beyond the Lena, have an even more daunting task.

Siberian crane (*Grus leucogeranus*)

In late Pleistocene Asia, when receding glaciers left behind vast low-lands of shallow lakes and marshes, the great white crane of northern Siberia is thought to have been widespread, although not plentiful. The earliest known illustration of the bird was made by a court painter of the Moghul emperor Jahangir (1569–1627) named Ustad Mansur, whose likeness showed that the bare red of the face included the nares and the base of the long heavy beak—a detail which many modern bird artists (including the impeccable Roger Tory Peterson) were to miss.[8] Its first scientific description was recorded by the distinguished German naturalist and geographer Peter Pallas, who explored the Russian Empire between 1768 and 1774, collecting among other trophies the huge bones and hairy hides of mammoths and woolly rhinoceroses; Pallas made a crude but unmistakable drawing of a bird he named *Sarcogeranus leucogeranus*, which nested in "vast swamps, interspersed with large lakes and extensive waterways in the vicinity of the rivers Isim, Irtys, and Ob, and regions farther north."

By the nineteenth century, the Asiatic white crane's distribution on its northern breeding grounds was already discontinuous, to judge from its scattered winter range. In 1890, when nests were discovered in east-central Siberia, in the sub-Arctic tundra to the east and west of the Lena River delta, it was assumed that this "eastern flock" wintered in China; the breeding territories of the "central flock" that wintered in India and Pakistan, and the "western flock" that migrated south to lakes and marshes in Iran and Turkey, would remain unknown for almost another century.[9]

Allan Octavian Hume, the British dean of Indian ornithology who saw his first *leucogeranus* in Ladakh, near Leh, in 1854, was so taken with this striking creature that he called it "the snow wreath" and "the lily of birds"; he praised its "extreme elegance of form" which presented "a series of the most graceful and harmonious curves," and deemed it "the rarest and perhaps the finest" of the four crane species found on the subcontinent—though not, apparently, so rare that he refrained from shooting one, which he deemed "unfit to eat."

A decade later, the white crane was described as a "rare winter visitant to several parts of northwestern India" by the great biogeographer T. C. Jerdon, who in fact had never seen one when he wrote *The Birds of India* in 1864. The snow-white bird with glossy black primaries or "flight feathers" was a favored target for hunters and collectors; in India, the native *mirshikars*, or bird trappers, prized it for market sale.

At the turn of the century, *leucogeranus* still occurred in several localities in the Ganges basin, in the myriad small lakes and jheels, or monsoon ponds, which mostly vanished in the dry season. With human increase and agricultural development, its dwindling bands became confined to one of the last undeveloped wetlands in the region, a marsh area of some eleven square miles near Bharatpur, in Rajasthan, one hundred miles south of Delhi and thirty-six miles upriver from the Taj Mahal; originally the marsh had been maintained as a shooting preserve by the maharajah of Bharatpur and frequented by the viceroys of India and other sporting notables. Here the monsoon overflow from the Gambhira River, stored behind the Ajan dam from June through September, was channeled through gates and canals, creating an artificial ecosystem of shallow wetlands which supported a wild profusion of aquatic life.

The first reports of the Siberian crane at Bharatpur were made in 1937 by Dr. Salim Ali and Richard Meinertzhagen, who found eleven of them (like Hume, these excellent ornithologists felt obliged to shoot and eat one). Since then, *leucogeranus* has rarely been recorded elsewhere in India. When the first annual count began, in 1964, two hundred Siberians wintered at Bharatpur; there were seventy-six in 1975, a decline of two thirds in little more than a decade. Since few mortalities occurred in these winter marshes, it was assumed that the missing birds had perished on the breeding grounds or in migration, likely both. Unfortunately, there was no way of protecting them once they departed Bharatpur in early spring.

By 1973, the winter distribution of *leucogeranus* across southern Asia had been reduced to "the lower Yangtze, northern India, and northeastern and central Iran." "The lower Yangtze" denoted a few wetlands near the river settlement of Wu Cheng, which sheltered about one hundred birds. "Northeastern and central Iran" were represented by a few wetlands near the south shore of the Caspian Sea; "northern India" was, in effect, the Keoladeo marsh near Bharatpur.

Crane numbers at Keoladeo continued to diminish: by the winter of 1979–80, a year of savage drought, there were just thirty-three. Feeding had been difficult for the Siberians in the baked mud of the drying jheels,[10] it was reported, and some of the birds had gone elsewhere in the Ganges basin. Their destination was mysterious, since in over-populated northern India, Keoladeo is the one body of water that has survived man-made disturbance—roads, noise, pesticides, fertilizers, detergents, industrial pollution, and trampling herds. Somewhere during that parched winter, the white birds clung to their fragile existence, and twenty-nine of the thirty-three survived to return to Bharatpur in 1980–81. The number rose in the next year, to thirty-eight, and hopes rose with it.

Even before its drastic decline in India, the Siberian had disappeared from wintering areas farther westward, such as Pakistan and Turkey and the south-shore wetlands of the Caspian Sea, in Iran, where the last white crane was recorded in 1925. In 1977, Dr. Ronald Sauey of the ICF and his associates spotted fifty-six *leucogeranus* at saline, shallow Lake Ab-e-estada at six thousand feet in south Afghanistan—almost certainly the same flock, minus one, that they had seen four days earlier at Bharatpur; presumably these northbound birds had crossed the great Thar Desert, the Punjab, and Pakistan along the way. Another leg of the migration route had finally been established, though the location of the breeding grounds was still a mystery.

In Afghanistan in the late 1960s, a French visitor had found a Siberian for sale in the Kabul market, no great distance up the Kabul valley from Lake Ab-e-estada. The greatest threat to the species during migration was thought to be the uncontrolled hunting in this war-torn, hungry country. The recent emergence of well-armed militia of the Taliban, who doubtless destroy cranes as well as ancient stone Buddhas, has not improved things.

In the Punjab, all crane hunting, trapping, and trade had at last been banned, but in Pakistan, Pathan tribesmen of the Zhob District of

Baluchistan and the North-West Frontier Province near the Afghan border made their living hunting cranes, using captive birds which called out to the migrants passing overhead and hurling *soias*—long hemp cords with metal weights—into the decoyed groups in order to ensnare them. Crane migration is normally diurnal, to take advantage of the thermals; that the hunting was mostly done at night suggested that in hard-hunted regions, the birds may have adapted to nocturnal travel. Demoiselles and Eurasians are wary, hard to hunt, and almost never fooled except by live decoys; once caught, however, the demoiselle especially is easily tamed. Both species, kept in cages or walled yards or gardens, serve commonly as watchdogs.

Inevitably, the rare Siberians were taken, too. In 1983, only thirty-six white cranes were recorded in migration across Pakistan. The following year, attempting to control live capture, especially in spring, the government imposed new laws and fines and required licenses for the crane camps, and the country's few bird-watchers urged the public not to harm white cranes, especially in the Kurram River valley, where a refuge was established to help protect them.

In the summer of 1978, a very large, long-legged bird was spied on a sandbar by tourists floating down a tributary of the great Ob River, east of the Ural Mountains that separate European Russia from Siberia. Run down and captured, the unfledged chick was turned over to a local villager, who seems to have banished it beneath his hut to compete for fish scraps with his sled dogs. In the late fall, a rumor reached Russian crane authority Dr. Vladimir Flint in Moscow that a cranelike bird had been captured near the Ob. Taking no chances, he dispatched a young biologist named Alexander Sorokin to Siberia to pick it up. The villager came to the airstrip on his motorbike, the large bird bulging beneath his coat; when its red face and big-billed head popped out, "Sasha" Sorokin fairly whooped for joy. The home of those last *leucogeranus* that flew south to India (the so-called central Siberians, as opposed to the western group that migrated to the Caspian) had been found at last.

In 1981, Sorokin organized an aerial survey of the lower Ob, near the Arctic Ocean—"the Ob in its furthest northern reaches," just as Peter Pallas had described it two centuries before—about 125 miles southeast of the frontier settlement at Salekhard. Near the Kunevat River, just south of the Arctic Circle, seven nests with five eggs were located in open areas of marsh in the transition zone between riverine forest and open tundra. The Kunevat, an eastern tributary of the Ob not far upriver from its Arctic delta, drains a wilderness homeland of the tepee-dwelling Hunte, who say that a hunter who slays a bear must don a crane costume and dance in celebration, since it is the crane spirit that has protected him.

The longest migration of any crane—and one of the longest known migrations among nonpelagic birds—could now be roughly charted. The Kunevat is approximately twenty-four hundred miles due north of Bharatpur, but the route traveled in the two-month migration is considerably longer; the northbound birds follow a great arc of thirty-one hundred miles, crossing the Great Indian Desert to the Indus River in Pakistan, tending northwest to Lake Ab-e-estada in the Kabul valley of eastern Afghanistan, then north across the Hindu Kush before turning northeast across central Asia, risking assault from *Homo sapiens* all along the way. In this manner they avoid the high ranges of the Himalaya and the Karakoram, taking their time at the wetlands on their route, since the arid plateaus of central Asia are still hard frozen.

Following the same path south in autumn, spiraling on thermals, gliding and flapping as the earth turns and the continent unfolds beneath, they descend here and there to rest and feed and preen before flying onward; at the long-term resting places known as "staging areas," they may congregate for a month or even more, gathering strength for the last leg of their great passage.

In the mid-1970s, Iran was creating a number of large refuges in a program to restore all species of its indigenous birds and mammals, and it welcomed the ICF's offer to help in the possible restoration of the vanished *leucogeranus*. Before the plan could be initiated, however, this cranky species reappeared of its own accord. In 1978, during a water-fowl survey for Iran's Department of the Environment, a field natural-ist named Ali Astiani found a little flock of nine white cranes in flooded rice fields a half mile southeast of the village of Fereydunkenar, just south of the Caspian Sea—the first good record of wintering Siberians since 1925. Oddly, the cranes had selected a wetland within a system of circular ponds and channels in the heart of a large duck-trapping operation used since the nineteenth century; in an old Persian tradition of market hunting, vertical nets hung from the trees kill all species in-discriminately. George Archibald arrived in time to see the flock of nine, but shortly thereafter, as he put it, "the paths of Iran and the United States diverged" in the great hostage crisis. The new wildlife refuges no longer interested the government, and for three years, the ICF's letters to environmental contacts were returned. Once the hostages were released, however, communication was quickly reestab-lished, and Iran's Department of the Environment sent word that six-teen white cranes were now overwintering in Iran, and that even the duck trappers took great pride in their rare visitors and would not harm them.

A few Siberians were also reappearing at Astrakhan Nature Re-serve, at the mouth of the Volga on the west Caspian shore; there had also been sightings south of Baku at Lenkoran (where the last tigers of the Caspian race had been reported in 1964). The researchers concluded that this westernmost flock, arriving from some unknown northern re-gion near the Urals, stopped over at Astrakhan to feed and rest before proceeding down the west coast of the great inland sea to Fereydunke-nar.

In 1981, the Keoladeo Ghana Bird Reserve near Bharatpur was made a national park, thanks mainly to the dedicated efforts of India's great ornithologist Dr. Salim Ali, who enlisted the support of Prime Minister Indira Gandhi; it became a World Heritage site in 1985. Often referred to as Bharatpur, it is essentially a wetland 7,165 acres in extent, about one third of which is flooded in the time of the monsoon and through the winter; with its astonishing total of 364 bird species, including several that are uncommon and endangered, it is the foremost bird sanctuary on the subcontinent and perhaps on earth.

Unfortunately, the new park is so closely surrounded by humanity that hunting and poaching, firewood harvest, air and water pollution from local industries, and relentless overgrazing by the region's fifty-six hundred cattle and water buffalo threaten its future. In 1982, all grazing in its marshes was prohibited to minimize disturbance to endangered birds, in particular *leucogeranus*, which won't mix with buffalo, apparently because they muddy up the water. When an earthen wall constructed around the perimeter caused rioting, five protesters were shot dead at the main gate by the police, and in the end, the closure was of doubtful benefit, since a number of the ungrazed marshes became choked with a wetland grass which eventually closed over many areas of open water, permitting encroachment by terrestrial grasses and wild bush.

In 1986, thirty-eight white cranes appeared, but three years later, there were only seventeen, of which nine soon vanished and did not return. The situation of the Indian flock was desperate. Encouraged by ongoing experiments with sandhill and whooping cranes in North America, in which surplus whooper eggs from the nesting grounds in northern Canada were placed in sandhill nests in Idaho in efforts to establish a new migratory flock, and by the fact that these Idaho sandhills were successfully rearing whooper chicks and leading them on migration to New Mexico, Russian and American researchers had high hopes that Sibe productivity might be doubled (and a new winter range established) by placing the second eggs in the nests of the Eurasian cranes which bred in the same area.

Like all *Grus*, the Siberian lays two eggs, yet it rarely succeeds in raising two chicks;[11] thus, the surplus egg could be removed without harm to the species. Also, the blotched green-brown eggs of *leucogeranus* are very similar to those of *grus*, and the two species are compatible in other ways, to judge from the proximity of their nests in the Far North. Like the sandhill crane, its ecological counterpart in North America, *grus* smears its back feathers with mud or clay, apparently for camouflage; to a lesser degree, *leucogeranus* does the same, daubing a modest collar at the base of its snowy neck. The main problem was that while both birds build nests with the snow still on the ground, *leucogeranus* may refrain from laying eggs before late May or early June, when the chicks of *grus* have already quit the nest.

The solution was a complicated scheme to transfer wild Siberian eggs to the ICF in Wisconsin in late June, when the embryos would be sufficiently developed to withstand the stress, yet not so old that they would have to undergo the trauma of hatching before they'd had time to rest and recover from the trip. Once a small captive flock had been raised from the wild eggs, artificial illumination simulating the spring light in the Far North would induce this group to nest two months early, in late March, after which their eggs would be sent to Siberia to hatch under the bellies of wild *grus*, in the hope that as fledged juveniles, the young would follow their surrogate parents on migration.

Proposing this scheme to Vladimir Flint, who had done extensive fieldwork with *leucogeranus*, George Archibald requested surplus eggs from the Siberian's more numerous eastern population near the Lena, in order to establish a captive flock whose eggs might be used to restore the Kunevat population near the Ob. In 1978 (when the total population of the species, east and west, was estimated at a maximum of 250), four wild eggs were transferred to the ICF in the lap of Archibald's colleague, Dr. Sauey. (One hatched en route, thereby relinquishing its status as an egg and causing Sauey's detainment by U.S. Customs for the illegal importation of a live wild bird.) Though the eggs survived the ten-thousand-mile journey, two turned out to be infertile. The following year five fertile eggs arrived intact and were hatched by incubators. With the aid of four more Siberians on loan from zoos, a captive flock was established at the ICF and a second flock was started at the Oka State Nature Reserve, southeast of Moscow.

Breeding this species in captivity was a great challenge. Cranes reared in captivity are often extremely aggressive, and even within their own species may develop intense dislikes. The strong pair bonds necessary for successful reproduction need time to develop, especially among the fractious Siberians, which are second only to the red-crowneds in their hostility not only toward their keepers but toward prospective mates, which are often penned separately to prevent their deaths. (A pair penned next to each other for seven years at the ICF reserved the unison call that was supposed to bond them for threatening each other and railing at human observers.) Understandably, the abused females may become too wary and discouraged to mate or lay eggs under such conditions.

The first captive flock included Wolf, an old male that had survived two World Wars in European zoos and had fathered chicks when in his seventies (when he finally died, this bird was at least eighty years old). His mate was Hirakawa, so called because, having become lost in her 1969 autumn migration and making a lucky landfall on Okinawa, she was removed from a ditch in semistarved condition and taken to Japan's Hirakawa Zoo to recover. At the ICF, this energetic creature built nest after nest, producing an amazing total of thirty-eight eggs, every one of them infertile: despite his chronic willingness to mate, Wolf's ancient gonads had proved insufficient. Finally, in 1980, assisted by a second male from a breeding facility at Vogelpark Walsrode near Hanover, West Germany, Hirakawa produced three fertile eggs. Incubated by white-naped cranes and sandhills (cranes incubate eggs more efficiently than incubators), one hatched but quickly died, a second perished in the egg, and the third survived—the first Siberian crane ever born in captivity.[12]

Meanwhile, intensive efforts were devoted to "cross-fostering" as a means of strengthening the Ob River group. Finding *grus* nests was not easy, since Eurasian cranes are cryptic in coloration and secretive, shy, intelligent, and difficult to deceive, but in early June 1982, Dr. Sorokin successfully insinuated a *leucogeranus* egg from the ICF into a wild *grus* nest near the Kunevat. The Eurasians hatched it and raised a healthy chick that departed with them on migration to great rejoicing, never to be seen again.

Meanwhile, the search for the breeding grounds of the remnant Caspian Siberians was under way. Those grounds were finally discovered in 1986, when the last Siberians of the western flock radiotelemetered by Russian researchers at Fereydunkenar were tracked to a remote region not far east of the Urals and almost a thousand miles south of the central group along the Kunevat; ten nests were located the next year. In the next decade, this central flock remained at the dangerous level of nine to twelve birds.

In 1990, Sasha Sorokin, now the leading authority on the breeding biology of *leucogeranus*, made a desperate effort to reverse the fatal trend. Seven eggs from the ICF's Wisconsin flock were hatched and raised at the Oka Reserve in isolation from human contact. As fledged juveniles, they were introduced among the last cranes on the Kunevat, and to the great excitement of the researchers, they flew southward in the early fall with their wild kin. Like the Kunevat bird raised by surrogate *grus* parents in 1982, they were never seen again. Four others released subsequently at Tyumen, to the south, were destroyed by hunters.

(In Siberia in the summer of 2002, under Sorokin's supervision, a group of ten young Siberian cranes who had been imprinted on an ultralight airplane–surrogate parent at the Oka Reserve were transferred to Kushevat near the Ob River, from where the ultralight, piloted by an intrepid Italian, Angelo d'Arrigo, would lead them south on a 5,500-kilometer migration in an attempt to restore the imperiled flock that winters in Iran, near the south end of the Caspian Sea. Leaving the Arctic Circle on August 27, they flew over long stretches of western Siberia; at last report, September 16, 2002, they had reached the north border of Kazakhstan, where political complications may put an end to an exciting experiment that appeared to be theoretically successful.)

In 1992, only six birds turned up at Bharatpur. "This last small flock has knowledge that no other cranes have," George Archibald reflected. "Cranes learn from their parents, and no other bird can teach them their migratory pattern. If we lose these six, we have lost the knowledge of fifteen million years." In this winter of 1993, the same flock, reported from Pakistan, was down to five; according to Raj Singh's latest communication from the Indian ornithologist Mr. Bhoulu Khan at Keoladeo, no cranes had arrived at all. Siberians migrate mostly in small groups, three to ten together, and they usually turn up at Keoladeo between late October and the end of the year. Most appear by the end of November; it is now almost mid-January. In the half century or more since the first Bharatpur record in 1937, the tardiest birds had come on January 14, the day after our scheduled arrival. The marshes are readily surveyed from the dikes and roads, and the large white birds are impossible to overlook. We still hope they will appear in the next days, while we are visiting Jaipur and Ranthambore, but this seems most unlikely.

The Rajasthan desert gives way to neem and *khejri* savanna, and as this is a Vishnoi region where wild things pass undisturbed, small herds of nilgai, sometimes attended by demoiselle cranes, are now quite common. Though these big antelope look clumsy with their humps and their small heads, they can outrun the tiger and lion that used to abound in this region. Today the lion is entirely gone from Rajasthan, and the tiger is confined to scattered enclaves such as the maharajah of Jaipur's former hunting tract at Ranthambore, where we are headed.

Along the road goes a white-robed party of Jain monks and nuns, and a man riding an elephant, and young girls with gold rings in their left nostrils, and a bride-to-be escorted on foot under a canopy woven of every color of the sun, bound for a very different sort of wedding from the one we will witness this evening at the grand hotel in Jaipur—an immense ceremony on an artificial stage in the formal gardens, under the burning eye of a tiny spotted owlet that flies in out of the dark to perch on a lamppost and cock its head, glaring askance at this immense disruption of the night.

In three fine days at Ranthambore, the many beautiful creatures seen do not include a tiger.[13] Still awaiting word on the Siberian cranes, we travel on to Bharatpur on the *Frontier Mail,* the slow old train of colonial days that still journeys the long arc from Bombay to Delhi and on to the Punjab on India's northwest frontier—so slow that through its dusty windows I spot three pairs of sarus in three village fields.

In the railway station at Bharatpur, a sadly bent boy drags his body down the platform like a stepped-on insect, using felt pads to protect his hands. Despite the gray teeth and lifeless skin of bad diet and ill health, he brandishes an angelic smile that disarms the travelers entirely; indeed he is the prince of the young beggars, humping himself into the vestibule as the train departs, the better to hustle a fresh crop of new patrons at the next station. He is very good at what he does, and knows it, for when one nods in admiration of heroic con and an indomitable spirit, that seraphic smile of his turns saucy, gleeful, even a bit disdainful.

At Keoladeo we are delighted to learn from Mr. Bhoulu Khan that the five Siberians reported from Pakistan earlier this winter turned up yesterday (January 13). The sixth, according to Mr. Bhoulu, may have been the immature bird reported taken this past autumn in Afghanistan by a golden eagle.

By the time we arrive, it is too close to dusk to go out hunting for the cranes, which have been resting in the farthest part of the reserve since their arrival. Instead we walk one of the broad dikes that fan across this old wildfowling marsh. Bharatpur's great waterfowl assembly includes many species of ibises and herons, eight thousand pairs of painted storks, and fifteen species of ducks. From the flocks soon in view, one can readily believe that at the turn of the century the viceroy of India, Lord Curzon, with his friend Lord Kitchener and others, destroyed 540 ducks here in a single day. On November 11, 1938, a later viceroy, Lord Linlithgow, with a huge shooting party of 38 guns, slew 4,273 ducks, or over 100 birds per man; the viceroy alone fired 1,900 shells on that grand occasion.

With Mr. Bhoulu, Raj, and Victor, who have all seen these white cranes at Keoladeo, our group is in good hands, so I set out alone early next morning, anxious to locate the five Siberians before they take it into their heads to keep on going, like the nine that vanished from this place just four years ago. Motor travel on the dikes is wisely forbidden, and one travels the longer distances by bicycle-powered rickshaw. My guide, Mangal Singh, is well acquainted with most of the reserve's more exotic species, and as we creak along the dike path, his sharp eye picks out four young spotted owlets, bunched close as pinecones in a tree fork, and two collared scops owls in the cavities of old kadamba trees, and some white spoonbills and painted storks and the gaudy purple moorhen, and nilgai antelope and sambar deer and mongoose. At one point he leads me off into the scrub—dry deciduous forest dominated by *Acacia arabica*, known as babul—to view an Indian rock python of his acquaintance, a large quiescent animal wrapped around the base of a small bush. I entreat Mangal Singh to take me directly to the cranes lest they fly away into extinction while we dawdle on the path; we must not even pause for his "special birds" that frequent the temple grounds on a point of higher land. Fatalistic, he turns east on the embankment road and pedals into the fire of the sunrise.

The chilly morning on the marsh warms quickly, raising fine smells of thorn and mud and reeds and the heavy gobbling of thousands upon thousands of greylag geese and a single flock of the beautiful bar-headed goose (*Anser indicus*)—two striking black bars across the crown of its white head—which nests near high wetlands on the Tibetan plateau with *Grus nigricollis*, the black-necked crane, and migrates over the high Himalaya to the Ganges Plain at altitudes estimated at 29,500 feet.[14] With its powerful strokes, this huge-winged goose has been known to fly at fifty miles per hour with no tailwind; it is thought to travel the thousand miles of its migration from Tibet to the subcontinent in a single direct flight, conserving energy by heading straight over the massif instead of navigating the deep ravines between its peaks.[15]

Beyond the bright-headed Tibetan geese, not eighty yards away in the open marsh, stand two white cranes with startling red faces and red bills, fresh as roses in the light of the new sun. Like most cranes, *G. leucogeranus* prefers open areas with unobstructed views, and since it is wary, I am scared I might flare the first snow wreaths I have ever seen, or cause them to move farther from the bank. I sink to my knees behind a bush, watching in relief as they resume feeding: they probe wet gleaming bills through the bronze duckweed or immerse red faces to the eyes to grasp sedge tubers and tug them from the mud. Between probes, they glare with livid eyes—the iris is a strange pale yellow—yet they do not take alarm at my close presence but on the contrary seem curious and confiding.

Like whoopers, the Siberians defend feeding territories on winter grounds, but unlike whoopers, they give these up as winter passes and migration nears, when they begin to feed in groups. At Bharatpur, they feed more than half the day, digging and foraging for tubers, in particular *Cyperus rotundus*; though almost entirely vegetarian except in early spring, *leucogeranus* is a general feeder like all cranes, and occasionally will eat aquatic life, including young ducklings.

The second pair is feeding among the greylags in a grassy pool half-shaded by a large water-tolerant acacia (*A. nilotica*); they are far enough from the first pair to maintain their own loose territory without scattering the cohesion of the group. (The fifth Siberian, a mile away across the marsh, will remain apart throughout the day.) Nearby in this parliament of fowls stand other white birds ordinarily considered large— white spoonbills, open-billed and painted storks, and three species of white egrets of assorted sizes—but in the company of *G. leucogeranus*, they look like mere attendants.

The cranes call intermittently and are noisy all day long: this species possesses the longest unison call (up to three minutes' duration) of all its family. "Suddenly the male ducks his head comically," Ronald Sauey wrote in his doctoral thesis on this species, "as another crane swoops low over the family. With a stiff but splendid bow the male utters a nasal 'Yaaah!' Immediately he pulls up his great white wings tipped with black and forms a huge fan of feathers. 'Toodle-loo, toodle-loo, toodle-loo,' cry the male and female in duet. (The female's higher voice

forms the 'toodle' part of the three-part 'toodle-loo.') So perfectly synchronized are the calls of male and female that at a distance the call
sounds like the work of a single bird."[16]

The ringing three-part *toot-toot-toot* heard in time of migration
maintains contact within the flock; it may also be the origin of *karekhur*,
the three-part Hindi name for the species heard in Hume's day. Here at
Bharatpur, the Siberian's local names are *rai kunj* (presumably, "royal
crane") and *tunhi* (a local word for flute, in recognition of its melodious
clear call).[17] Like all cranes, it is easily heard a mile or more across the
marshes, yet unlike most other migratory species, it has a short and simple trachea that is only slightly convoluted, a character it shares with the
nonmigratory wattled crane of Africa.[18]

Bringing up tubers, the Siberians rinse the mud off quickly with a
sideways flourish of the bill, which because of its deeper-water feeding
trait is markedly longer and heavier than in most cranes, also slightly
curved and toothed at the tip for grasping. Feeding in water sometimes
two feet deep is a *leucogeranus* habit that demands great effort; pulling
at the sedge tubers, which may be six inches deep in mud, their bodies
shudder with exertion. As George Archibald says, "Primitive species
must suffer their handicaps."[19] (Besides this deep digging, "primitive"
denotes such nonadaptive characters as the simple trachea that limits
the Siberian's voice in variety as well as volume.)

In the day, the Siberians may skirmish with the sarus cranes over a
feeding pool. The sarus usually initiates the conflict by flying into the
pool with its loud rolling call, attempting to usurp the shallow water.
Though the larger bird usually dominates, the Siberian may protest and
drive it off with strutting, wing-shaking, and splashing, often accompanied by low "growling." In threat posture, Dr. Sauey noticed, it lifts its
wings to expose its puffed-out thigh feathers, pulling its bill down to
its expanded breast. In combination with the long, elaborate tertials
hoisted up over the back, these adjustments make the bird look bigger;
it stalks about in stiff slow gait, lifting its legs higher, wing-shaking and
splashing, tugging at weeds to ease its agitation.

Feeding, then preening, is the main activity, though *tunhi* may sleep and laze and gaze about; it seldom dances on the winter grounds. Unlike the sarus and Eurasian cranes in Keoladeo, the Siberian has not adapted to large local animals; it seems to be disturbed by peasants and tourists on the dike paths, by water buffalo and cattle, and even by large wild mammals such as nilgai antelope and sambar deer.

Exhilarated by the Siberians, I say goodbye to Mangal Singh, for I plan to spend the day here on the marsh; he seems astonished when I say I will walk home, peering about as if on the lookout for stray tigers.

Farther east down the dike road, a sarus family, two adults and two fledged juveniles, is probing soggy ground and shallow water twenty feet from the embankment; the heads and necks of the young birds are a rich golden brown. Unlike the "primitive" Siberian, the sarus rarely feeds in water deeper than twelve inches and can adapt somewhat to degradation of the habitat as well as livestock and human beings. The great calm birds permit me to come so close that I can study the black "down" on their long bare throats and the small gray auricular tuft that protects the ear in the otherwise naked red wattled caruncle behind the golden eye: the tuft is all that remains of the ancestral feathered head in this bald-faced bird (and also its close kin the white-naped and the brolga).

Moving off without haste, the family splits into two pairs, an immature bird trailing each adult. Although eighteen sarus were lost here between 1988 and 1990—apparently poisoned by the pesticide aldrin, used by the farmers in surrounding fields—there are presently ten pairs in Keoladeo.

Four boys on bikes come down the path from their village school on the far side of the sanctuary. Excited, they wish to show me three large pythons they have discovered sunning at their holes, off a side path. The pythons lie in a shining pile of bronze-and-golden coils, but at our approach, the pile comes to life, uncoiling and sliding and whispering into the ground in a seemingly unhurried yet accelerating process, so swift that it is difficult, in the golden blur, to keep track of which is which. Two of the animals are twelve foot or better, of a girth and strength much more impressive than my biceps.

On the far side of the main dike, another path leads to open scrub where a dusky horned owl has two big chicks rearing and straining in the nest. In the distance, like giant ancestors of cranes back in the Eocene, a pair of sarus stands isolated in the sunset. Nearby, on a high bush, is an imperial eagle, of the great *Aquila* genus that includes the golden eagle of North America and Eurasia. Soon, from the west, comes the loud two-note horn blast of flying sarus, in seeming counterpoint to a more distant rattle of Eurasian cranes. As the light fails, *G. grus* appears, crossing the sky in broken strings and ones and twos and threes. Soon two black-necked storks fly across the dike and out over the marsh—one of the several disappearing species of Asian wading birds that still occurs here.

Returning down the dike, I notice that the fifth Siberian has drawn closer to the others, to a distance of perhaps two hundred yards. Bhoulu tells me that before dark, the feeding territories are given up in the interest of cumulative wariness and protection. Next morning, the two pairs maintain a discreet distance in the same location, but the fifth bird is nowhere to be seen in the broad marsh. Though it arrived here with the others, it will not associate with them again until late March, when these last five Indian migrants of the Ob River population—should they make it through the winter—will reconvene, calling out to one another as they rise from the marsh, circling higher before embarking on the great drift north and west across the Thar Desert and the Indus River drainage to the dangerous lake called Ab-e-estada, in Afghanistan, and from there north through the Kabul valley and high over the Hindu Kush to the Amudarja and Syrdarja river systems. Like wisps of desert cloud, the white cranes will flap and glide and soar past Samarkand and over Kazakhstan to the river valleys which lead north to the spruce muskeg, then the tundra lowlands near the delta of the Ob at the Kara Sea.

FOUR

At the End of Tibet

> ... my hands ... reaching
> soundlessly,
> like the mountain ash climbing after a flight of cranes.
> To fly like the cranes and not look back!
> Haughtiness
> would be mine, and in death's country ...
> —Marina Tsvetaeva, "Separation," 1921

O f all the planet's far-flung cranes, the least-known and most difficult to see is *Grus nigricollis*, the black-necked or Tibetan crane; it was also the last to be discovered,[1] in 1876, in the region of Koko Nor (Qinghai Lake), by the same Lt. Col. Nikolai Przhevalsky who discovered lakes Dalainor and Khanka, and first described the wild horse of the steppes named in his honor.

A supernatural or "fairy" creature in Tibetan folklore, the black-necked crane inhabits remote regions of the Tibetan plateau as high as eighteen thousand feet, from the sources of the Indus River east along the upper Brahmaputra and northern Himalayan regions to southern Tibet. The *yan-e*, or "blackheads," also breed in small numbers in the Qinghai and Sichuan provinces of western China, and a few pairs nest in Indian Ladakh,[2] where a mummified bird collected about 1805 by an early explorer hangs to this day in front of a religious painting in Lhyang Monastery. Indian soldiers guarding Ladakh's tense border with Tibet shot the only pair near the village of Hanle, where the revered *trung trung* had lived as far back as Buddhist villagers could re-member; the soldiers were seized in a citizen's arrest and sent to prison. After Indian conservationists changed its name to "the Tibetan sarus," the black-necked crane became a sacred bird to the Hindu soldiery, and no further incidents occurred, but across the border in Tibet, Ladakhis say, cranes are still killed intermittently by soldiers and immigrant Chi-nese. (It has been remarked that the species would be extinct today were it not for the precepts against killing among Buddhists and Hindus; the suppression of Buddhism in the region will inevitably threaten *G. nigri-collis* and other creatures.)

The migrations of *G. nigricollis* are more altitudinal than geograph-ical: the freezing of the streams and marshes on the Tibetan plateau forces the birds to descend about five thousand feet into mountain val-leys farther south, where they can forage in unfrozen fields after the harvests. In China, in 1979, an important winter grounds for about four hundred *nigricollis* was discovered at eight thousand feet on the Guiyang plateau in Guizhou Province, among mountain peaks in an

Black-necked crane (*Grus nigricollis*)

ancient marshland known as Cao Hai ("Sea of Grass"). A few were reported from remote corners of India's northeastern state of Arunachal Pradesh before the species disappeared in the mid-1970s: the last known pair, alighting near Hang village in the Api Tani valley, was killed for the pot within an hour of its arrival.[3] (Before the advent of firearms in the valley, said the villagers, the bird they called *kengda* had been common and rather tame.) A number of cranes crossed the Himalaya to the remote kingdom of Bhutan, where fifteen to seventeen were found in 1978 by Indian ornithologists led by Dr. Salim Ali of the Bombay Natural History Society, the man chiefly responsible for the establishment of the Keoladeo bird sanctuary in Rajasthan.

Essentially, *nigricollis* was a breeding species of Tibet, surviving in a Buddhist land where wildlife had been generally spared. It was seriously threatened by the surge of human activity that followed China's seizure of Tibet in the 1950s and the inevitable environmental destruction in a land where water is a scarce and precious resource in many regions, a threat made ever worse by the wane of Buddhism on the Tibetan plateau and China's chilling indifference to the natural world.

In the 1980s, in the wake of the assault on wild creatures that accompanied the so-called Cultural Revolution, China reversed its policies in an effort to save what little wildlife it had left, including its last cranes, tigers, and giant pandas. Wildlife refuges were created throughout the country, including the "autonomous region" of Tibet, and among the first beneficiaries were the cranes: *nigricollis* alone had eight locations set aside for its protection on both wintering and breeding grounds in Tibet and China.

The Tibetan plateau has always been one of the least accessible regions in the world, and since most of the region, until recent years, has been closed to foreign travel, the breeding range and natural history of *nigricollis* remained little known; the Beijing and Shanghai zoos, with two and three birds respectively, had the only captives. In 1982, an Indian authority estimated that perhaps one hundred black-necked cranes survived on earth; barring immediate intervention, he predicted, *nigri-*

collis would be extinct in the wild within the year. As late as 1987, it was still assumed that the species was rapidly vanishing, and the following year, when the first *nigricollis* was hatched in captivity at the Xining Zoo in Qinghai, the news account called it "the second-most endangered and least known of all the cranes."

In the winter of 1991–92, new surveys made by an ICF associate, ornithologist Mary Anne Bishop, indicated that past reports had been fragmentary and unduly pessimistic. Exploring with Tibetan and Chinese researchers, she returned the species to good health with an astonishing count of 3,910 cranes found in Tibet. Today (A.D. 2000), *nigricollis*, inaccessible as ever, has an estimated population of 5,500 birds.

The royal government of Bhutan now protects the species in the three known places where wintering *nigricollis* have been reported, including the vicinity of a fifteenth-century monastery called Gantey, in the Black Mountains. It was this flock that, in late January 1993, Victor Emanuel and I took our clients to see.

B hutan remains a remote destination, cut off from the world by the high Himalayas of Assam, Sikkim, and Tibet. In a nation the size of Switzerland or Denmark, a population of just over one and a half million is scattered among a few small towns and the isolated mountain villages. Not until 1962 was a road constructed from Thimphu, the capital city (or small town, according to the eye of the beholder), to Phuntsholing on the Assam border—the only road connecting the mountain kingdom to the outside world. For another twelve years, the country remained closed to foreigners, and even in 1993, it limited tourist visas to three thousand per year and maintained sensible restrictions on journalists from abroad and other troublemakers.

On the flight from Delhi, on a clear winter day, the bright wall of the eastern Himalaya passes in formation, from Dhaulagiri and the Annapurna cirque to great Chomolungma (Mount Everest) and Chomo

Lhari, a conical peak twenty-four thousand feet high that separates Bhutan from the Chumbi valley of southeastern Tibet. The snow peaks press down upon the country from the north-northwest, while lesser peaks in the southwest and in the east cut it off from the Indian states of Sikkim and Arunachal Pradesh. Its south frontier with Assam and Bengal lies in the lowlands. Like the Terai in Nepal, this narrow strip, eight to ten miles wide, is only the threshold (the *duars* or "gates") to the steep mountains that encircle Bhutan and break it up into north-south ranges between thirteen and sixteen thousand feet high. The mountains are parted by tumultuous ravines and narrow valleys, and each valley is separated from the next by a high pass; all streams and rivers flow eventually to the great Brahmaputra, which descends from the Tibetan plateau to the Bay of Bengal.

With its small population and ample rainfall, Bhutan remains largely forested, and the country is dedicated to sustained reforestation, a wise precaution against erosion and ruined rivers that Himalayan lands such as Pakistan and Nepal have failed to take. In a world spinning out of ecological balance, this country is an oasis to environmentalists such as Victor and myself, who are here en route from India to China, the two most populous and battered landscapes in the world.

The Paro valley, forty miles southwest of Thimphu, is the only place in west Bhutan wide enough and long enough to accommodate an airstrip. Even here the strip appears too narrow and too short, and often it is closed down entirely by billows of thick cloud that pour out of the mountain passes into the small valley. Even in fair weather, the Druk (Dragon) Airways flight into Paro from Bangkok or Delhi is not one the visitor is likely to forget, since the descending aircraft must curve close around a mountain wall.

Paro lies at seven thousand feet, in what is known as the Lesser Himalaya. This foothill region where most of the population is located is well watered due to its proximity to the Bay of Bengal and a climate influenced by the monsoons. Paro has orchards of apples, plums, and peaches as well as fields of asparagus and rice, which can be grown up to elevations of eight thousand feet. Since the snowfall is greater in

Bhutan than in most lands of the Himalaya, the flat roofs used elsewhere for winter storage of fuel, fodder, and dried food are replaced
here by steep open-sided peaked roofs of slates, shingles, or corrugated
iron, held in place by heavy stones and unencumbered by TV antennae
(which would not reach Bhutan until six years later, in 1999). The
houses are comparatively large and separate, not bunched in clusters for
defense as they are elsewhere, and their clay walls are inset with bright-
painted wood windows. A hostel sign in the main street offers "Food-
ing and Lodge," and an archery tournament is under way in the small
park.

This one-street town with willow trees overlooks the gray torrent of
the Pachu River, where Victor's sharp eye spots the rare and beautiful
mountain sandpiper known as the ibisbill, pearl-gray with a black-
white breastband and a red curved bill; this doughty bird is breasting
the swift glacial riffles of a shallow channel between bars of rock and
gravel.

Bhutan, or Bhot Ant, is generally translated "Eastern Bhot" or "End
of Bhot"—that is, "End of Tibet," with which it shares much of its
history and religion. Western Bhutan is known as Ngalong, or "First to
Rise"—the first Bhutanese region to adopt Tibetan Buddhism. The
seventh- or eighth-century temple called Kyichu Lakhang is the nation's oldest, and a national museum in the round guard tower of Paro
Castle contains superb Buddha figures and *thankas* or religious paintings on silk. Since 1988, however, foreigners have been excluded from
most of Bhutan's holy sites, to protect ancient treasures from thieving
hands and prevent exploitation that might destroy the integrity of sacred ceremonies—all excellent precautions, to judge from the looted religious sites found throughout the Buddhist Himalaya.

A fine climb through mountain oak and rhododendron and an-
dromeda is enhanced by the rush of waterfalls and chime of bells, the
prayer wheels turning in the steep current, the squall of nutcrackers

and song of laughing thrushes (not at all like laughter), lavender primula in sheltered sun patches, and red cotoneaster berries higher on the path, and everywhere fine smells of smoke and cow dung mixed with spruce. Emerging at last on a ledge bedecked with prayer flags, I am set upon by three black mastiffs, which turn away when I stoop to pick up rocks; they soon permit me to put down my missiles and make friends.

The teahouse has a splendid view of the white monastery called Taktsang—"Tiger's Nest"—perched on a ledge high up on the sheer cliff face across the valley. This fabled *gompa* commemorates the place where in the eighth century (A.D. 747) the great Padma Sambhava, or Guru Rinpoche, arrived from Tibet and transformed himself into a tiger, the better to banish the old B'on religion and affirm the Buddhist faith. The Druk-pa or "Thunder Dragon" sect (thunder was thought to be the dragon's roar) of the Kagyu school of Tibetan Buddhism was founded in the thirteenth century as the official religion of Bhutan, which is known to its people as Druk Yul, "Land of the Thunder Dragon." Below Taktsang, a flight of snow pigeons circles the black cliff face and settles in a dead tree on a ledge like a sudden crop of strange white blossoms.

Our guide in Dragon Thunder Land will be Mr. Ugyen Dorjee, whose name (like most given names in Bhotian lands) has spiritual significance, "Ugyen" being a diminutive for Guru Rinpoche and "Dorjee," or "Dorje," the sacred thunderbolt or diamond (*vajra*) that symbolizes enlightenment. Similarly, Ugyen's assistant is named Karma. Like all Bhutanese men, they wear the traditional central Asian *kho* or long formal robe that can be hitched up with a belt when riding horses or walking about town, where hitched-up *khos* look much like kilts, worn with well-shined Western street shoes and knee stockings.

Traveling southeast to the Wang-Chu River, our bus arrives at the main east-west road across the country, turning north at a bridge where three large stupas or chortens (oddly square-topped in Bhutan) stand side by side at the river confluence. Simtokha Dzong, at the entrance to the Thimphu valley, is the oldest castle in the country; it now serves as a Buddhist school. These huge *dzongs*, or fortress-monasteries, at prominent points along the mountain rivers are one reason why, throughout the centuries, despite small wars with Tibet, India, and even Great Britain, Bhutan has been able to maintain its independence.

In 1907, when Britain meddled in the Tibetan Himalaya, it replaced Bhutan's traditional leader with a royal family of its own devising. Since then, a hereditary king of the Wangchuk family (the present incumbent is Jigme Singye Wangchuk) has been the nation's Druk Gyalpo, or "Precious Ruler of the Dragon People." Serfdom was legal until 1958, but today the kingdom is roughly democratic, with full women's rights and no caste system as in Tibet and India; on the other hand, the government exercises stiff control and keeps progress at bay to protect its people. (In 1999, in a referendum, the people voted not to try democracy.)[4]

From Simtokha Dzong, the road climbs a pretty valley of brown winter rice fields and pale green winter wheat, arriving at last in the colorful main street of the nation's capital at Thimphu, where the government buildings and the Druk Gyalpo's residence are located. Responding to our curiosity, the people are friendly, although somewhat restrained in the mountain way. Tonight it snows, and it is still snowing when we depart early next morning, passing a village of Tibetan refugees as the road climbs slowly through evergreen forest of hemlock, spruce, and fir to the Dochu Pass at 10,200 feet. On this cold, heavy winter day, the fine view of the northern peaks promised by Ugyen Dorjee is lost in the thick weather.

Crossing Dochu La, the road descends from the dark evergreens into an oak-rhododendron forest where birds are numerous—redstarts, finches, laughing thrushes of several species, the large whistling thrush (a fine dark blue), and the lovely gold-billed magpie. Along the way are some primitive huts that house the Bangladeshi laborers conscripted to maintain these narrow, winding mountain roads, which have a tendency to fall away into the gorges. Gradually, with the descent, the forest opens out in a walnut-tree plantation, in temperate woodland at about five thousand feet.

More than four fifths of Bhutan's people, engaged in subsistence agriculture, live in small medieval villages far up the mountains from the nearest road. In the Punakha valley, in the village of Mesina, communal house building and wheat threshing and garden maintenance are all in progress. No nails are used in house construction (which is why the roof slates are weighted down with heavy stones), and the walls are erected in wooden forms or molds into which clay is pounded from above by enthusiastic teams of singing, stamping girls wielding big pestles.

According to Karma, the girls are singing "The Flying of the Cranes," composed by the fifth Dalai Lama, who is said to have been a sometime poet. A prisoner sentenced to death is enclosed in a box and thrown into the river. Through the slats, he spies two flying cranes and implores them to lend him the help of their wings. Asked if they did so, Karma shakes his head. "That prisoner was probably a romantic sort," he says.

The road climbs the foothills and descends to the brilliant green-blue Mochu-Tangchu River, which it follows as far as Wangdi Phodrang, an immense *dzong* overlooking sand beaches at the confluence. As in other *dzongs*, the walls curve outward as they descend to the thick fortress base; a broad red band encircling the white walls signifies that this *dzong* belongs to the Kagyu sect. From Wangdi Phodrang, the main road leads south into Assam, but our route turns off to the northeast, climbing gradually along high cliffs above the Mochu-Tangchu tributary into the Black Mountains.

At about sixty-five hundred feet, after crossing a steep streambed in a narrow ravine, the bus stops on the next incline for the striking spotted forktail, working a rivulet that comes down through fern and moss off the steep mountain. Dense forest climbs steeply to lost canopies above and falls away just as steeply across the road, so that the crown of a large red-fruited tree is just at eye level. This tree and lesser trees and vines and tangles all around have attracted an array of brilliant birds—

barbets, bulbuls, yellow-naped woodpeckers, and laughing thrushes, sibias, yuhinas, sunbirds, fantail flycatchers, and a shy, covert forest bird called the long-tailed cuckoo dove. Hearing a harsh rush of air, I look up just in time to see the beak and folded wings and talons of a goshawk pass close overhead, aimed at the bright green of a Himalayan barbet in the treetop. At the last second, the raptor flares, put off by the spectacle of the big strange mammals milling on the road, and keeps on going down the mountainside; up the ravine, a second goshawk, possibly its mate, causes a red feather burst where a flushed tragopan pheasant hurtles noisily into the brush.

In the sun, the day is warm—though not warm enough, alas, to bring out such fabled butterflies as the golden bird wing, the Krishna peacock, the painted Jezebel, the Bhutan glory. Just down the road at a stream crossing, a startled cry comes from a bird-watcher who has retired behind a bush; a terrific fracas, filled with eerie squalling, has broken out in a tree over her head, where an otter-sized animal has been driven to the very tip of a bouncing branch by two snarling and spitting foes of its own kind. The tawny, white-chinned creature, yellowish across the throat with a long black bushy tail and bright beady eyes in a glossy black mask as triangular and fierce as an adder head, is the yellow-throated marten, a very large and not uncommon arboreal weasel whose scat I had met with frequently in mountain forests in Nepal, and again on the Taktsang path two days ago. Having never before seen the creator of that scat, I add my own shouts of excitement to the general din.

The attacking martens, distracted and displeased by the intruders on the road below, whisk up and down the tree trunk and back and forth among the hillside rocks as if seeking reinforcements, only to swiftly reappear and race to the attack again, lest the cornered one make its getaway. So intent are they on their savage business that we watch their agile acrobatics at close hand for minute after minute, so enthralled that we scarcely notice the arrival of a rough truck. Poking his head out, its driver offers to shoot those damned things for us. "Make a nice hat," he says. His kind proposal, translated, is spurned by outraged cries from the animals' well-wishers—the fatal distraction, for that instant the beleaguered one shoots past the rest and off the tree in a great leap toward the mountainside, up which his enemies pursue him with the harsh, hideous squalling for which the disputatious weasel tribe is known so well. The local vehicle, departing, leaves behind a miasma of black fumes in the ravine.

Just up the hill a rhesus monkey, then a small barking deer, peer out from the hillside leaves. This region, Ugyen says, is the royal hunting preserve, containing tiger and leopard and also the melanistic leopard called the black panther. At Pele Pass, at 11,000 feet, it is already snowing, and the clouds leave a beautiful frosted mist on the *Usnea* lichens in the trees. From somewhere in the snow comes the *chirr* of nutcrackers, then the clatter of stones falling, no doubt caused by one of the skittish yak-cattle crossbreeds known as *dzos* that wander everywhere in the steep forests.

At the forlorn road-fork hamlet of Dungdung Nesa, the main route continues eastward over the Black Mountains, which separate the watersheds of western and central Bhutan. Our own route—no more than a muddy track in this wet weather—must climb to Lawala Pass before descending into the Phobjika valley. Since the bus is useless in the snow, the resourceful Ugyen has arranged for a four-wheel-drive truck to haul us higher. From the pass we can trek down into the valley while the pickup returns to the stranded bus for the gear and sleeping bags.

From Lawala La, the crane valley looks empty and dead silent, its alpine pastures and dark evergreens shrouded by snow. The Phobjika is one of the few glacial valleys in Bhutan, too high and wet to grow much besides potatoes and barley and some winter wheat. At these altitudes, the main winter inhabitants are the seminomadic yak herders whose yak-hair tents are scattered like black glacial boulders on the hillside. Only gradually, as the road descends, do small farm dwellings appear in the mists below.

In winter, the black-necked crane seeks valleys wide enough to provide waste barley in the harvested, unplowed fields and a stream broad enough to ensure safe roosting. Since most of these high valleys lack wetlands for foraging, the winter cranes depend almost entirely on harvest gleanings, as they have for centuries. (One wonders how they managed before man.) Such dependence is dangerous, since agricultural practices may change; in their winter territories in southeast Tibet, a shift to planting winter wheat instead of the traditional spring wheat and barley has meant that the new shoots do not appear until late February, when the cranes are preparing to fly north.

In late afternoon, in a light snow mist, three pale forms take shape in the dark plowed corner of a field, down in the valley. When Victor comes, we stand quietly on the mountain road, content and happy, observing our first *Grus nigricollis* cranes together. When our clients catch up and everyone has seen the cranes, we walk on down the mountainside, locating a few more distant cranes along the way.

In the almost empty street of the fifteenth-century village of Gantey (*gang* is "mountain," *tey* is "summit") it is nearly dark; the ancient roofed chorten in the square seems full of mystery. Gantey Gompa, founded in 1613, is the only Nyingma-pa (the "Old Sect," founded by Padma Sambhava) monastery east of the Black Mountains—it shelters ten monks and 140 *gomchens*, or lay disciples, of the high lama, Gantey Tulku Rinpoche, who according to Ugyen has retired from this world on a spiritual retreat of three years, three months, and three days.

Gantey is located on a ridge that sticks out like a narrow butte into the valley. Using flashlights, we make our way down a rough and narrow footpath through the forest, rejoining the road near a bridge that crosses the small Phobjika River. Beyond the bridge, on a low rise, is the guesthouse where we spend the night. On the colorful walls of the main room is a collection of ancient weapons from seventeenth-century battles with Tibet.

The Dragon People know the crane as *cha thung thung* (in Ladakhi, *cho trung trung*), "bird with long legs." Local people say that just ten years ago, when perhaps twenty *cha thung thung* were first reported in this valley, the birds were still hunted, mostly by boys practicing archery, Bhutan's national sport. Far from revered, as they are in most countries, the cranes were discounted as "the thing with a bird's head and a sheep's body." Not until they were finally adopted by the Royal Society for the Protection of Nature did hunting cease, doubtless because the penalty for killing one is life imprisonment. (These days, the *cha thung thung* is threatened less by arrows than by barbed wire, which is replacing the old wood fences and is much more difficult for flying birds to see.) In recent years, the Phobjika valley's winter population has increased to about two hundred cranes—the actual count this year is 210—with another hundred birds or so in the Laool valley, across the main ridge to the east, and another hundred at Bongdeling, in eastern Bhutan. In addition, there are—or were—four birds that wintered near Bumthang. Thus this valley shelters about half of Bhutan's *nigricollis* population.[5]

The cranes roost each night at a location within sight of the farmhouse. Anxious to observe the flock before it scatters for the day, I rise at six and walk out on the road, where Victor soon joins me. The frozen dawn is clear and windless. The flock roosts on the north side of the wet meadows of the Chu Nap (Water Black) stream that winds down through the dwarf bamboo marsh at the center of the valley. Like many other northern cranes, *nigricollis* chooses gravel bars and shallow river channels for roosting, but in the absence of this habitat in the Phobjika, they are making do with stream bank and bamboo marsh.

Heads beneath their wings, the birds stand hunched against the cold at the foot of snow-misted pasture hills that rise to a forest of blue pine. The pale lumps of the cranes are as still as boulders. We try to move closer, but the marsh is not hard-frozen, and we break through the ice and soak our boots before clambering free of the black mud and retreating to the road, with mud, pants, and laces ice-locked into one hard bond.

A cold dawn light swells up from behind the hairline of black conifers on the ridge to eastward. Even as we stamp and watch, the first dark heads of the roosted birds rise one by one, and a crane trumpets loudly as if to awaken the unsociable few hunched here and there along the stream farther down the valley. In the mountain silence, an occasional distant dog or rooster can be heard, but no smoke rises from the scattered houses, since most of the inhabitants move away in winter to make a rice crop in a lower valley.

Soon the cranes are calling, though without much heart. We are too far away to hear them well, and after breakfast, we cross the small bridge over the Water Black and walk along under a pine wood to a place where the marsh can be crossed dry-shod with judicious leaps. The far bank rises to a grassy small plateau, at the end of which two cranes, heads raised, stand tail to tail against the valley mist, the early-morning light reflecting from their mantles. Three take wing, gliding across a meadow to alight by a grove of pines, but the rest remain roosted on flat pasture by the marsh edge, scarcely two hundred yards from where we crouch. Over the shining marshland hunts the silvery raptor known as the pallid harrier.

The cranes are restless. Though we mammals are careful to move slowly and sit quietly, Ugyen warns that the birds may be alarmed by our modern colors and take flight; those few already flying are performing the crane "threat flight" in which the stiff wing tips are flicked upward with each stroke. Like *A. virgo* and *G. vipio* in Mongolia, *G. nigricollis* will forage fearlessly among man's herds, and is not disturbed when two local men, much smaller than most Westerners, walk past them scarcely fifty yards away. The worn, earth-colored *khos* of the mountain peasants and the calm ease of their movements hold no threat, unlike the gait of strangers, whose movements appear intrusive and erratic.[6]

The black-necked crane is smoky-white except for the black head and neck (the darker juveniles are speckled on the back, with a brown bustle), and George Archibald speculates that this whitish species of open alpine country is slowly evolving into a white bird. Through binoculars, the *cha thung thung* are so close that one can study the golden eye with the white spot behind that gives this species a strange double-eyed appearance. The frontal red patch of bare skin, extending from the base of the bill back past the eye, seems smaller than in most *Grus*—perhaps a cold-climate adaptation, like its legs and neck, which are noticeably shorter than in other species. (As in many northern creatures, the larger body mass relative to its short extremities reduces heat loss and causes this medium-size crane to look stocky, even heavy.) The bustle on its rump is large, and perhaps a comfort to its small hind end in this frosty season.[7]

Nigricollis is thought to be an alpine race of *monachus*, the hooded crane, just as *monachus* may originally have been a population of *G. grus* that adapted to tamarack bogs and forest swamps. Another *Grus* offshoot, and probably the most recent, is the whooping crane, *Grus americana*, which developed farthest from the source, in North America.

Eventually, the cranes lose interest in the queer intruders and proceed with their preening and calling, mixed with brief flurries of February dancing—elevating bustles, leaping upward, posturing with wings, or moving stiffly in the threat displays that are often included in the dancing. The calls and two-note bugling grow more intense, as one family group after another runs a little toward the sun and dances aloft and moves out over the winter fields to glean and forage. Some defend a winter feeding territory in a harvested field, but the local men say that the cranes also feed on roots and tubers of the dwarf bamboo. (In Ladakh they feed mostly on the tuber of a marsh sedge with a name something like "George," availing themselves where practicable of lizards, fish, aquatic insect life, and freshwater shrimp.)

The last *cha thung thung* I observed would circle high up over the ridges to at least twelve thousand feet, calling and calling, as it will do again later in February, gathering its flocks on the warmed thermals that will lift them skyward for the two- or three-hour flight north across the mountains to the valleys near Shigatse in southern Tibet. There the cranes may spend most of March and April before flying onward to their breeding grounds on the high plateau. They will not lay eggs until late May or early June, depending on the coming of the spring.

According to tradition, the birds will return to the Phobjika valley in late December, arriving at midday when the sun is highest. Invariably, say the villagers, they circle three times over Gantey Gompa, crying out to the lama for his blessing before gliding slowly down into the dark-walled valley. Only a few arrive each day, so that their coming is spread across a period of weeks.

The departure a few weeks from now will be quite different. The northbound birds will take flight in groups of forty or fifty at a time, so that all vanish within several days. Despite the urgency of spring, however, not a single *cha thung thung* neglects its ceremony, circling three times over the monastery before heading north.

Already the conifers have lost their white frosting of snow, and the bright, clear mountain day is warming rapidly. At the Pele La, snow blown from branches is sparkling like diamond dust in the sun rays piercing the blue pines. On the road down to the Dong Chu valley, the body of an old woman, tiny on her bier, descends the mountain carried by two bearers, with others trailing. Ordinarily the deceased would be bound uphill, on her way to an air burial—chopped to pieces and set out on a crag to be consumed and scattered to the winds by the wild creatures—but sometimes, says Ugyen, corpses such as this one bound downhill may be chopped into small bits and fed to the fishes in the rivers. These rites return the deathless beings to the mountains and the rivers, the air, soil, and water of the earth, and to the endless life cycle from which they came.

Eventually, the long snow-peaked border with Tibet comes in full view, from Jejekangphu Kang in the northwest all the way east to Gangkar Punsum, known as "White Glacier of the Three Spiritual Brothers." At 24,784 feet, this is the highest mountain in Bhutan. Because it is a holy place, ascending to the glistening peak is not permitted.

FIVE

In the Nine Rivers

The crane cries in the Nine Marshes,
 its voice carrying to Heaven.
By the islet the fish lies, or plunges into the deep.
 —*The Book of Odes*, collected by Confucius, sixth century B.C.

At Poyang Hu, or Poyang Lakes, a vast labyrinth of lake and marsh in Jiang-xi Province, in the lower Yangtze River basin of southeastern China, vast assemblies of migratory cranes of four different species may be found in winter. *Jiang* is "river" and Jiang-xi means "West River," a contraction of an older name signifying "Western Part of the Province South of [Yang-tze] River." At least eight provinces border on the south bank of the Jiang-tze, or Yangtze, which means "long river" and is, after the Amazon and Nile, the third-longest river in the world, descending almost four thousand miles from its headwaters in the high glaciers of Qinghai and Tibet to the East China Sea—so long and so broad, it is said, that the Mongol legions, seeking to invade south China in the days of Chinghis Khan, took fourteen years to work their way around the headwaters. Where Poyang's shallow waters pour north into the mighty Yangtze is the city of Jiujiang, or Nine Rivers, and I like to think that this name echoes the Nine Marshes in the lines from *The Book of Odes* quoted above.

In recent years, it has been discovered that the Poyang lakes—not the main lake, which in summer flood absorbs the others to become the largest lake in China, but a cluster of smaller lakes among the river deltas on the northwest shore—were the long-sought destination of the last significant winter flock of the Siberian crane: in effect, 99 percent of all *G. leucogeranus* left on earth. For centuries, this eastern population was scarcely known, despite scattered sightings of white cranes, and the scattered and imprecise reports from nineteenth-century travelers and explorers in eastern Asia of white cranes with pink legs and red faces in Heilongjiang and in marshlands on the China coast only confused those ornithologists who sought to determine its range. An 1877 account called this species "very rare" in China, whereas an 1891 report called it "common" along the Yangtze in the winter. Then the species seemed to vanish. Not until 1961 was the first known nest of *leucogeranus*—"two goose-sized olive-green eggs"—located by Russian ornithologists east of the Lena River near the Arctic Circle, in one of the most remote regions of the planet. Subsequently, more nests were found on mudflat hummocks and grassy mounds in the moss-lichen tundra surrounding Chokurdakh village.

In other days the breeding territories of this species ranged at least as far west as the Ob River drainage and the Urals, where the relict flocks that winter in north India and on the south coast of the Caspian Sea are nearing extinction. In 1981, when the first nests of those western *leucogeranus* were discovered near the Ob, it was still assumed that the eastern population located two decades earlier was similarly precarious, since only a few nests had been found in that vast Yakutian wilderness between the Yana and Kolyma rivers; based on the distances between known nests, Russian ornithologists Vladimir Flint and Alexander Sorokin had concluded that the eastern *leucogeranus*, scattered across a breeding range 50,000 square miles in extent, might number no more than 300 birds with territories averaging 240 square miles.[1]

Subsequently, migrating Siberians were reported from mountainous valleys between the Argun and Onon rivers, not far from the Mongolian border country where Jim Harris and I had searched for the white-naped crane, and estimates of the Yakutian population grew; this intensified the mystery of the eastern birds' main destination after leaving the tundra in the autumn. It was now realized that the few birds reported from the lower Yangtze could not nearly account for the known breeding population in or near the Lena River delta, and that the main wintering grounds of the eastern *leucogeranus*, although presumed to be somewhere in south China, had yet to be discovered. Unable to pursue the migrants into China, and frustrated by the absence of information from that country, Dr. Flint was beginning to think that these eastern cranes might be traversing China on their way to unknown marshes in Southeast Asia. But because at least a few Siberians were known to fly south along the Yellow Sea and winter in marshes of the lower Yangtze, most authorities continued to assume that the main winter grounds must be somewhere in the Yangtze basin. Already George Archibald was speaking worriedly (and presciently) of China's plan to build a colossal dam at the Three Gorges of the middle Yangtze and to deepen and rechannel the lower river to improve transportation, agriculture, and industry; the inevitable disruption of the seasonal flow and change of water levels in the lowlands might obliterate the last sanctuary of *leucogeranus* before anyone could discover where it was. And in fact, the precious Poyang ecosystem may be destroyed by the construction of a gigantic hydropower dam fifteen hundred miles upriver on the Yangtze, whose flooded tributaries and river backflow replenish its immense wetlands in monsoon season. China's greatest building project since the Great Wall (an earlier grand folly of enormous cost which failed to bar the Mongols from the Celestial Kingdom), the Three Gorges dam will be sixty stories high and 1.3 miles across—the largest hydroelectric system facility on earth and the largest works project of the millennium, according to the boasts of the Chinese government. Approved in 1992, it will raise the river 560 feet and create a reservoir 360 miles long, engulfing more than a hundred towns and countless villages.[2] Its proponents claim that it will control the Yangtze floods that wash away the rich farmlands of the lower river and have taken perhaps a half-million lives in this century alone; by replacing coal-generated power, the hydroelectric dam will clean up air pollution in addition to propelling the economy.

The $20 billion dam, scheduled for completion in 2009, was endorsed by loans from the dam-besotted bureaucrats of the World Bank, whose well-intentioned policies and practices have done serious harm to the long-term world environment, not to speak of the hopes for a better life of defenseless millions; its grandiose and ill-considered "Big Dam" projects in the Amazon, Africa, India, and elsewhere are typified by the Sardar Sarovar dam across India's Narmada River, which will displace hundreds of thousands of people, drown precious forestlands, and ruin land and life in the name of very problematical power and irrigation schemes in Gujarat.[3] In 1991, the Bank's own internal report concluded that "involuntary settlement resulting from the Sardar Sarovar Projects offends recognized norms of human rights." Almost without exeption, the Big Dam projects have ignored the social and environmental ruin in their wake.[4]

International opposition by environmental groups had sparked a new concern in China for its battered environment and wildlife, and a systematic search for *leucogeranus* got under way. In 1981, an estimated one hundred "great white cranes"—the Chinese will not refer to their own cranes as "Siberians"—were discovered in the northwest Poyang lakes by Drs. Zhou Fu-chang and Ding Wen-ning of the Beijing Institute of Zoology. A winter air survey the following year confirmed the report, counting 230 *leucogeranus*, with 19 juveniles.[5] In 1985, a team of observers organized by the ICF located 1,350 Siberians at Poyang, a number that nearly doubled the following year.[6]

It has now been determined that in early spring, small groups of the last large flock of *leucogeranus* forsake Poyang's mighty silver disk and fly northeast across the Yangtze, continuing cross-country to the coastal wetlands near Pei-tai-ho beach on the Gulf of Chihli; from there, they

will head north over Heilongjiang to their staging area at the huge
Zhalong Nature Reserve near Qiqihar, west of Harbin.[7] There they
linger for some weeks while winter relents on their breeding grounds
in the sub-Arctic. Though their course from Zhalong onward is not yet
clear, it is widely supposed that they continue northwest across the
Amur to the upper Aldan River, then the lower Lena, which they follow downriver to the tundra. Where the white horizon of the Arctic
Ocean comes into view, the cranes tend northeast toward their breeding
grounds, which may still be frozen under snow.

A lighting at Hong Kong on our way from Bhutan to Japan, Victor
Emanuel and I fly north next day in high anticipation. A letter
from Jim Harris warned that good sighting conditions would depend
on seasonal water level in the lakes as well as the vagaries of a shifting
winter climate known for its copious mist and rain; in this drought
year, Jim recommended that we allow at least three days for locating
the four crane species at Poyang.

Po seems to be an ancient place-name, while *yang*, "south" or
"sunny" in this usage, is the opposite of *yin* ("north" or "dark"); Poyang
signifies "south side of the mountain." According to my map, the
mountains of Poyang Lake's watershed include Stone Bell Mountain
and the Immortal Water Crags and Mount Dragon-and-Tiger, all of
which sound most auspicious to an old Zen student. Another location is
"the Palace of the Taoist Founder," whom I took to be the immortal
Lao Tsu; Lu Shan, or "Hut Mountain," I imagined, commemorated the
simple hermitage of some ancient sage. It pleases me that this province
was the birthplace of Lin Chi (Rinzai in Japan), the great Zen patriarch
of the Tang dynasty, whose name is revered by his adherents in Japan
and America even today.

At Nanchang, the ancient capital city of Jiang-xi Province, our contact is Ms. Sheng Xao Lan, who prefers to be called Pauline. Pauline
says we can scarcely fail to enjoy a heavenly visit to Poyang, especially

the boat ride to the lake village that will complete our delightful three-hour journey through the Chinese countryside. Anxious to arrive at the reserve by nightfall, we decline a visit to Prince Teng's pavilion, which rises and vanishes in the smog and fumes and winter ground mist of the city. (I will regret this decision later when I learn that this huge pagoda was allegedly the site of the monastery of Ma Tsu—in Japanese, Baso— one of the greatest masters of Zen's golden age, famed for "the stride of an ox and the roar of a tiger.") We depart at once in the company of Song Xiang Jin, public relations officer of the Poyang Lake Migratory Bird Nature Reserve, a sad-faced, bespectacled young man in a leather jacket who had looked somewhat uneasy during Pauline's rapturous evocation of Poyang. But apparently Mr. Song's command of English did not permit him to demur, far less explain what lies in store for us. Claiming to suffer from carsickness, he sits up front with our chain-smoking driver, who presses his hand hard to the horn as we set off and keeps it there as we go honking through Nanchang's broken streets and swarming human beings.

What we behold through the car windows scarcely evokes Zen's golden age, far less the Immortal Water Crags and Mount Dragon-and-Tiger. In a gloomy winter mist, the dingy, depressed roadsides and deep potholes of Nanchang's outskirts seem to straggle forever into the battered countryside. Utilitarian brick structures are the rule, as if for long millenniums the entire landscape, with its cutbanks, gouges, and piles of raw red earth, had been dedicated to furious brick manufacture. Even the weeds which patch these wounds in most eroded landscapes are missing from this wasteland with its last trees bent like survivors of a cataclysm, made all the more desolate by doomed plantings of meager conifers, ghostly in cold shrouds of winter dust.

Cities such as Harbin and Beijing appear lively and clean by comparison to this provincial city. One would like to suppose that Nanchang and its environs are the exception, but to judge from scaring recent reports of environmental destruction in the Yellow River basin and elsewhere, Nanchang may be quite typical of modern China, which in the next two decades is projected to become the most noxious source of greenhouse gases in the world. (Even in the remote mountain country in the south part of Jiang-xi, settlements far too numerous for such poor land clutter the valleys between mutilated hills.)

True, it is winter now, and bleak. But last summer, in the green month of July, I flew southwest in clear weather from Harbin, crossing parts of five provinces en route to Beijing, and also northwest from Beijing across Inner Mongolia. The lesions of human activity visible from the air scarred every landscape south of the Gobi Desert.

One might suppose that this hammered landscape would have taken the heart out of these people who hurry so hard in all directions over their soiled city—another consequence of socialism, with its inevitable stunting of the human spirit, or so the West would like to think, ignoring the fact that unrestrained capitalism has had that same effect on its own defenseless poor. Heedless "progress," pumped to fever pitch by global markets, promises to become a great tragedy for the Chinese people, directly threatening their country's ecological well-being. From the boreal forests on the Amur to the giant panda's bamboo forests in the Sichuan foothills and the tropical rain forests of southern Yunnan; from the grasslands and glaciers of western Qinghai (where nuclear facilities and toxic waste dumps are said to be concentrated) to the fertile lowlands of the Yangtze basin, including the Poyang lakes, this land was once unequaled in biodiversity, with 1,186 species of birds (more than are found in all of North America) and such beautiful large mammals as the tiger, black bear, snow leopard, wolf, and giant panda, beautiful hoofed animals of many families, and the legendary hellbender, a hundred-pound salamander of mountain streams.

Today, reckless deforestation and erosion, pesticides and industrial pollution, assure the ongoing destruction of wild creatures. The country has suffered a dangerous loss of arable land to big dams, drainage schemes, and ill-considered development, and also the fouling of an estimated 80 percent of China's waterways (including most of the public drinking water) from chemicals and waste. (China's degraded water is considered "clean" if it is safe to drink after being boiled, a situation

certain to pervade crowded human habitats all around the world as
governments evade the looming water crisis.)

Beginning in the late 1970s, the Chinese government increased the
number of wildlife reserves from fewer than 100 to 333 in a single
decade. A number of wetland reserves—Poyang was one—were established primarily for cranes, but too often these were located in heavily
populated or industrialized regions, where for lack of public funds to
provide protection, human activities were tolerated in the reserves, not
only hunting and fishing but cutting reeds for fuel, roof thatching,
house construction, and sale to paper factories.

In Zhalong Nature Reserve in Heilongjiang—the main staging area
for Siberian cranes in spring and autumn—the red-crowned cranes depend on a patchwork of reed islets and open water for nesting and
roosting. Cutting half the reeds might actually be beneficial to the
cranes, but since the reed harvest provides 70 to 80 percent of the local
income, and because of widespread poverty and dread of famine, the
villagers feel they have no choice but to cut more.

"Cranes have great symbolic and cultural importance for the Chinese, a good deal more than any bird would have in North America,"
says Harris, whose wife, Su Liying, a Chinese biologist, worked formerly as a crane researcher at Zhalong.[8] The country people at Zhalong
have not lost their traditional reverence for cranes, she says, but subsistence and survival must come first.

In 1978, taking belated heed of the recurrent famines caused by too
many "great leaps forward," China slowed its pace and passed new laws
to limit human population, an urgent step made all the more dramatic
by India's ongoing failure to stem its human tide.[9] Unfortunately, the
shift toward free market capitalism in 1989 has been accompanied here
as elsewhere by furious industrial development and gross pollution, en-
suring a renewed assault on the environment.

By 1995, as the world's second-largest economy, China was consuming twice as much grain and red meat, 40 percent more fertilizer, and

marginally more steel than the profligate United States, all the while fueling its metastasizing growth with low-quality sulphurous coal. Aside from its effect on global warming, the resulting air pollution is lowering crop yields and crippling human health. Nine of the world's ten most polluted cities are found in China, where a third of all deaths are associated with the ruin of the air and water. (Not surprisingly, the battering of the environment has been most ruthless in recalcitrant Tibet, which is said to be a main dumping ground for chemical and nuclear wastes.) Pollution of earth, air, and water has been largely ignored in the rush toward material consumption that has seized this country in its haste to emulate our shallow and problematical Western "progress."[10]

A t a large bridge in Nanchang's outskirts, the Jiujiang road crosses the broad Gan Jiang, largest of the five main tributaries that flow into Poyang from the south. Farther north lies a paved toll road (the friendly and efficient guards laughing merrily in the tollbooth cannot be much more than twelve years old). The modern highway lasts about four miles, after which it subsides into earth road with heavy jouncing. All the way from Nanchang to our destination, an interminable rant by a shrill female voice on the car radio is ignored by Song and the driver, who try to drown her out with their own shouts. The amazing din has to compete with the driver's maniacal honking as his stiff four-wheel-drive machine barges and blares through the crowded carts and tottering bicycles and streams of pigs and geese and ducks. (Even trucks and buses make way for the ducks, whose flocks are urged into the motor traffic by crazed duckherds.) Banging and lurching north and east through the late-winter afternoon, farther and farther from the railroad that runs north from Nanchang to Jiujiang and the Yangtze, we plow ever deeper into the weary countryside.

The Poyang lakes are located at a meeting point of upper and lower reaches of a river so wide and so untamed that only two bridges span it in its last one thousand miles. In its summer seasons of monsoon and flood—July and August—the lakes may rise twenty feet or even more, engulfing a region 107 miles north to south and 43 miles west to east. This inland sea of 1,200 square miles shrinks drastically to about 200 in the dry season, when the lake empties out into the Yangtze. ("Water touching sky in summer and fall, mud with no end in winter and spring," goes a local description—or "A lake when the water is high, a river when it is low.") The inflow and outflow vary according to conditions, but by October, the shrunken lakes have parted into marshes and wet meadows, and broad mudflats without boundary, exposed by the receding water, green over quickly. By November, when the cranes arrive, sedge tubers are accessible in the shallows and watery mud, while migrant waterbirds and shorebirds make the most of the abounding fish and shrimp, mussels and snails.[11]

Poyang has a long history of commercial shooting, including the use of homemade cannons that broadcast hurricanes of shrapnel—metal junk, old nails and nuts, glass bits, and sundry pebbles. The great din further harmed the birds by making them so wary that they avoided much of the best habitat. Not until after the discovery of "the great white crane" in 1981 was the market shooting brought under control, at which time the people, obliged to give up firearms, resorted to snares and nets and even poison, which doped the birds and permitted live capture for the market. In the winter of 1983–84, the Poyang villagers killed some six hundred Siberian cranes and rare white storks and tundra swans for the manufacture of white feather fans, in addition to an estimated harvest of two hundred thousand waterfowl.[12] It was this slaughter which in 1984 prompted the Jiang-xi Forest Bureau to set aside fifty-five thousand acres as the Poyang Lake Migratory Bird Nature Reserve in the lake's northwest corner; though its nine shallow lakes merge with the main lake in the monsoon summer, they are crucial winter habitat for the four cranes.[13]

As at Zhalong in Heilongjiang, a reserve without human activity to sustain it is inconceivable in China, with its widespread poverty and straitened public funds. Though the Poyang reserve supports more cranes in winter than all other Chinese reserves combined, it also supports more human beings than cranes; perhaps seventeen thousand peasants lived inside the boundaries in 1981, before they were officially excluded.

Two of the most productive lakes for wintering cranes are Dachu Hu ("Big Divided Water") and Dahu Chi ("Big Lake Lake"), but ever since 1975, a local fishing village of a hundred people has drained much of shallow Dahu Chi through a sluice gate that feeds into the Xiu River, seining its fish—three hundred tons each year—as they pass through. For stopping or slowing the flow, the villagers demand reimbursement for lost fish, but the reserve, having little money, cannot pay. Two years ago, the resentful village drained Dahu Chi before the cranes arrived, obliging the birds to forsake the best habitat in all the lakes and forage elsewhere.

Last December, the reserve finally gained control over local water levels, recompensing the villagers for the fishing with jobs at a small local factory, but the reclamation bureau delayed the transfer of control until it had drained the lake one last time for the fish harvest. Meanwhile the reserve is threatened by ever-growing village populations as well as new immigrants to the region; the noise and activity that unsettles the shy cranes is far more difficult to control than hunting and fishing.[14]

Nearing the lake edges, the land flattens, and the dirt road narrows into tracks over long dikes that are still constructed from hand-dug earth heaved by shovel and basket from the drainage ditches between fields. Water buffalo are yoked to rough lumbering wood-wheeled carts and human beings to wooden crossbars on the shoulders, from which twin baskets of earth or heavy wooden water buckets are suspended. The burdened figures hurry along with little trotting steps. One consequence of China's modern famines has been a widespread reclamation of lake beds for agriculture, and much of the floodplain at Poyang has been harnessed by embankments, mile upon mile, with villages sprouting on the dikes and rice paddies within. Small poplars planted along the embankment tracks to stabilize the dikes are the only trees in this wet, sunken landscape except for the few old twisted hardwoods in the brick hamlets that squat on every outcrop of higher ground.

The last stretch of track follows a high red dike of washouts, ruts, and pits; in heavy rain, this dike road is not passable, since even a vehicle with four-wheel-drive toiling at four miles an hour would slide off it. The dike crosses the dry bed of a large lake for several miles before rising onto a peninsula that during the monsoon, Mr. Song says, becomes an island. Presumably this is that last leg of our journey which cheerful Pauline thought we were traveling by boat, but alas, there is scarcely any water in the lakes, only a brown haze of seasonal grasses and desiccated growth.

On a lake peninsula are some rough old farmsteads with large haystacks in small meadows, but the only wood is a small grove of planted conifers. (I am somehow relieved to see a ring-necked pheasant—the most common of the twenty-five Asian pheasants—in premature courtship of its hen.) Inevitably there is a village at the end of the peninsula, a hive of some three thousand souls—Wu Cheng, or Wu Town, after some old Family Wu, says Mr. Song. Before the Nanchang-Jiujiang railroad was completed, this river settlement at the confluence of the Gan and Xiu, which empty into the main lake not far downstream, was an important trading port on the long water route between those cities. Though its day is past, Wu Town maintains a lovely four-story pagoda at the point where the rivers meet (destroyed by the Japanese but restored four years ago) and a waterfront of archaic craft along the riverbank.

Near the old pagoda stands the walled compound of the Poyang Lake Migratory Bird Nature Reserve, where we are welcomed to the guesthouse. Night has fallen and the air is damp and cold, but on the bedspreads in our icy concrete room dance red-crowned cranes, auspicious symbols of good luck throughout the Orient. Though we go to supper in our warmest clothing, we are in high spirits, glad that the battering ride is over and pleasantly surprised by bowls of fine country cooking—white turnip soup, hot spicy buffalo, delicious gummy rice, "mock goose" (bean curd), bamboo shoots, and bitter greens.

Seated between Victor and Song Xiang Jin, I inquire of Mr. Song how the drained lakes in a time of drought might affect tomorrow's boat trip to observe the cranes. Mr. Song pauses a long moment before raising his gaze from his poised chopsticks. "No," he says finally, with that same expression of disquiet I noticed when Pauline told us that the last part of our magic journey to the Poyang reserve would be made across the water.

"No," I repeat, smiling agreeably.

"No boat," he says, not agreeably, with no trace of a smile. He returns to his mock goose.

"No boat," I say, nodding, to bring him out a little more. This time, raising his gaze from its close scrutiny of his bowl, he wears a wild and doomed expression. "No boat. No water here. Four month. No rain."

"Four months!" say I, not unduly alarmed, since fall and winter are the dry seasons. "I suppose the drought makes it more difficult to reach the cranes?"

"No *he*," says Mr. Song unhappily. "No crane." He bends once more to his mock goose, and his chopsticks fairly fly as he attacks his supper.

In China, the crane is *he*, pronounced as a guttural *heugh*. In ancient days, its clarion voice inspired music for the Chinese lute which, like a Japanese tea bowl, might be honored with its own name, such as "Crane Crying on High" (*Ling xiao he li*) or "Friend of the Crane" (*He yu*).[15] In the eighth century, Prince Yi of Wie is said to have welcomed cranes as revered guests, awarding them their own coaches, haute cuisine, and even a handsome stipend; all had the rank of civil servants, and some were promoted to generals—or so it was until the prince ordered his disgruntled soldiers to go to battle with Prince Di, at which time they advised him to send off his damned generals instead.

Victor has sensed that something is amiss, for his round-eyed head is perching like an owl on my left shoulder.

"No *heugh*," I say. "No crane."

"No crane." Unable to digest this news, my friend puts down his chopsticks.

To deal with any difficulties of translation, Victor has come armed with a yellow card prepared for him by a Chinese friend in Texas, winter home of the whooping and sandhill cranes. The card is inscribed with Chinese characters and also a transliteration, NA ER YU HE—literally, WHERE HAVE CRANE? or, more colloquially, WHERE ARE YOUR DAMNED CRANES? I thought he might produce the card in this emergency, since Mr. Song's English is somewhat blurred, especially when his mouth is full of mock goose and white turnip soup. Plainly Victor clings to the hope that I have been the victim of a laughable misunderstanding—either that or a serious international incident is in the making, since had we been told that there were no cranes at Poyang Lake, we would never have come as far as Wu Town or Nanchang or Jiangxi, or even China for that matter, but would have proceeded directly to Japan, where the beautiful *Grus japonensis* awaits us in the Hokkaido snows.

Victor's honest incredulity persuades me that I might have missed some subtle point of Mr. Song's discourse. I turn to him once more.

"No *heugh*," say I, in a calm and neutral tone designed to elicit confidence and candor.

"No crane," he agrees, going on to say that this has been the greatest drought at Poyang Lake in one hundred years.

"*No* cranes." We nod together for a little while. "Not a single one."

Oh, some few cranes, Mr. Song supposes, might perhaps be found far over in the eastern reaches, where there is still a little water. But even the main lake is now too shallow for a boat to make the five- or six-hour journey, and even if that place could be approached, a two- or three-hour trek through deep soft mud—he gestures at his waist— would be required before one could hope for a distant sighting of the cranes. "No," he says firmly, standing up. What has been prepared for us instead is a fourteen-minute film containing views of the rare species we have come so far to see.

The best meal we were served in China remains mostly uneaten as we reel outside. It is February 2, the end of the Chinese New Year—the last night of the Year of the Monkey—and the mud streets of Wu Town, in this country which loves fireworks, are racketing in staccato celebration of the incoming Year of the Rooster. Led in grim silence past small, dimly lit places of business, we are overtaken by a huge water dragon, each gauze segment of which, illuminated by two candles within and borne aloft on a pole by a shouting celebrant, is attached to the segments before and aft by the long dragon corpus; the fierce fiery head and the horn tail have their own bearers. The dragon winds away through the old streets in a great din, which in my dark mood evokes the sound of public execution.

At the Wu Town Theater, a Kung Fu movie is in progress. Song assures us that crane footage will be screened as soon as Kung Fu's adventure comes to an end.[16] Unfortunately, the theater is unheated and the film has scarcely started, and though a great deal of shouting and fighting transpires on the screen, we are in no mood to follow the plotline from one act of violence to another. Cold and depressed in the frozen theater, we hunch down and endure the ruined evening. At last, Kung Fu triumphs and the film creaks to an end, and the rest of the audience is promptly ejected, having no right to view the next attraction. Just as Mr. Song promised, and at no cost to ourselves beyond the sickening expense of the whole stopover in Hong Kong and China, we are treated to wondrous footage of the cranes, with some old swans and pelicans thrown in.

Out in the street, the dragon passes, still banishing the demons from Wu Cheng. Though we do our best to find amusement in the dragon, we are still stunned by the aptness of the last scene of the feature movie, in which the battling Kung Fu puts a stop to the evil machinations of his alter ego by reaching between the loser's legs to grasp and crush his testicles. Onscreen, this dramatic denouement was craftily signaled to the slow of wit by the breaking of a large raw egg in a bare hand, an image that elicted a scream of empathetic agony or perhaps a strange wild cheer; for ears untuned to rural Chinese modulations, it was difficult to determine which.

The dung-smeared cobbles knob up through the mud like prehistoric bones of ancient China. Stumbling and sliding, we make our way back to our cold concrete chamber and crawl fully clothed onto our pallets under those bedspreads adorned with dancing cranes.

In a grim dawn, too cold for sleep, I rise and leave the compound and walk down toward the old pagoda at the confluence of the Gan Jiang with the Xiu He. In the dense ground fog off the river, the base of the pagoda is invisible; only the two upper tiers float mysteriously in a dim misty glow caused by the small red fire of the shrouded sunrise. The ethereal effect is very beautiful and uplifting to the spirit—an auspicious portent. Soon the Gan Jiang emerges from the mist, and ghostly gulls, and the dark forms of the archaic craft left stranded by low water.

Victor is in no mood for auspicious portents. He notifies Mr. Song at breakfast that we shall not be staying for three days, as planned, but will go to Nanchang this afternoon in the hope of changing our Hong Kong flight to tomorrow morning. Meanwhile, we set off in the reserve's old boat for Meixi Hu ("Plum West Lake"), not far downriver, which is still said to contain a little water.

Like most of the rivercraft, this one is constructed of long logs laid one upon the other along each side of the hull and warped fore and aft into the conformations of a rude bow and stern; caulked and decked, the whole rude hulk is topped with a boat-length shanty sided with varnished wood.

In gray sunlight and a cool wind from the east, the heavy boat with its one-cylinder engine put-puts down the olive-yellow Xiu past the Gan confluence. Passing large torpid flocks of geese along the mudbanks, it turns east up a tributary stream that descends from Dachu Hu, now nearly dry. Shortly the boatman runs it hard aground under a steep bank and we clamber up to the edge of a flat savanna haired over thinly with the brown grass of drought. A local man is there to meet us. Dispensing with greetings, he turns his back and sets off toward the south, and we trail him two miles or more toward some white dunes. Here work gangs are shoveling sand into wicker baskets and carrying the baskets on lath shoulder poles to a tilted door-sized screen or sieve agitated manually by a man seated on the ground. The heavier sand that does not fall through the mesh is poured off into a basket between his legs, from which it is dumped by others into sacks to be transported by cart back to the river and thence to Wu Cheng. After much laborious handling of this kind (we later learn), the sand will be used in some sort of construction in Japan—surely at such infinitesimal profit that one cannot imagine what these men at the bottom are paid. The sand miners are housed in a humble tent camp where burned rice has turned cold in a black pot on a dead fire.

Beyond the ridge of dune lies Plum West Lake, where the shallow water is scarcely half a mile across at the widest point. Peasants on this shore are scything the brown grass and stacking the hay on wood-wheeled carts drawn by yoked buffalo, and across a fading lake scattered with egrets, the bank rises to a small farm community with terraced gardens climbing up to the last trees of a low ridge that in other epochs must have formed part of the basin rim of greater Poyang Lake; another hamlet atop scraggy dunes is visible not far to the east. Everywhere around the lakes of the reserve, farmers work terraced gardens—rice, green onions, cabbages, carrots, black mustard—on the high ground. "Too many people," I mutter to Victor as we scan with binoculars; too many mouths to be fed by such marginal land, and too populous for cranes.

Yet in the far west corner of the lake, a mile away, three white shapes too large for egrets are moving slowly as they forage; their posture eliminates any waterbirds but cranes.

Almost giddy with well-being and relief, I suggest to Victor that he check those white spots with his spotting scope. After forty years of intense bird study all over the earth, Victor has a quick sharp eye and extensive background knowledge far superior to my own. In rare impatience and ill humor, he ascertains with one quick sweep of his binoculars that what his hapless partner has located are not cranes at all but stooped rice gleaners in white shirts.

Recalling the ignominy of *Grus equus* in the wind-blown reeds on the Russo-Mongolian border, I check my birds carefully again before suggesting with unworthy glee that he have another look. "Siberian cranes," Victor murmurs in strange muted tones, as if these accursed *Grus leucogeranus*—a pair of adults with a brown-mottled juvenile—are the last straw in the whole miserable debacle. But when finally he straightens from the telescope, he is grinning broadly. That lone family of Siberians in the distance—the first "eastern Sibes" that either of us has ever seen—scarcely compares with the gala red-faced throngs shown at the Wu Town Theater the night before, but they are certainly an improvement on "No crane."

B y now the day has warmed considerably, with pale blue sky appearing through sunny mists. We return over the dry plain in good spirits, and are soon on our way downstream to the main river. At the confluence, the boat turns upriver on the Xiu He, which flows down from Jiang-xi's mountain border with Hunan Province. Just above Wu Cheng, along both banks, are communities of fishermen who live on their log boats in shanty cabins, often with family and dog and a few ducks, and always with fifteen to twenty cormorants,[17] which are used in fishing. Out on the river, the semidomesticated birds are swept from their perches along the gunwales with the same long stick that is later used to sweep them, clambering and flapping, from the water. The bird's throat is pierced with a length of stick or wire to prevent it from swallowing its catch, and some of the birds are entirely white, no doubt from the stress of enforced proximity to human beings.

On the north bank of the Xiu He, south of Bang Hu (Clam Lake), the boat retrieves the reserve's young research officer, Zhao Jin Sheng, who has reconnoitered Bang Hu that morning without seeing a single crane. A few miles upriver, we walk east toward Sha Hu (Sandy Lake), which proves to be as dry as all the rest. Our last hope is the view from Sha Hu hamlet, where we climb to the roof of the three-story community building which overlooks Dahu Chi across the river.

Even before climbing the stairs, we spot two Eurasian cranes, dozing on the edge of the brown lake bed. Beyond them on a low embankment more cranes can be seen in misty sunlight, and one group appears shorter and darker than the rest; I feel certain these are hooded cranes. We hasten to the roof via bamboo ladder, passing a fervent Ping-Pong match on the second floor. On the roof, Mr. Zhao looks through the scope and confirms that the darker birds are *Grus monachus*. "Another lifer," Victor whispers, stunned.

Here at Poyang, the four crane species may forage near one another,

Hooded crane (*Grus monachus*)

but they do not compete. The Siberian will rarely feed out of the water, the white-naped prefers the water edges and the mudflats, and the hooded favors higher ground in areas of emergent vegetation. The Eurasian may be seen foraging according to opportunity in all or any of these habitats; however, it is found most commonly in agricultural fields that may be some distance from the water.

Last summer in Mongolia, we saw hoodeds feeding with white-naped cranes, and these two also consort amicably on winter territories in Japan. As we hasten downstairs to cross the river and approach them, I risk the fierce retribution of the crane gods by assuring Victor that somewhere in that flock of hoodeds and Eurasians, we are bound to find his "lifer" white-naped crane.

Angling across the current, we go ashore half a mile upriver, to ensure a better sun angle for viewing. Coming up over the bank, we startle a reddish tawny animal, not much smaller than a wolf. More like a wild thing than a feral dog, it does not make a sound, just wheels and flees, peering back over its shoulder while still on the dead run, not toward the lone farmhouse downriver but straight out across the dry floor of the lake bed, disappearing on the far side. The animal passes so close to the cranes that it seems sure to flare them, yet the flock pays it no attention, a sign that this animal is a known element of their wild world.[18]

In the line of nine hooded and thirty-four Eurasian cranes, feeding along on the wild celery tubers under the dry grass, is Victor's first *Grus vipio*—a magnificent specimen, what's more, walking tall among the other cranes, with a snowy nape that extends all the way down to its silver-gray mantle, and a full mask of carmine skin that entirely surrounds its imperious golden eye.

My old friend and I shake hands, then sit down in the sun in the warm grass. Not speaking, we rest a little while, watching the cranes. "In all my years of birding," Victor murmurs happily at last, "I have never experienced such a reversal of fortune." Despite "the worst drought in a hundred years," we have seen all four of Poyang's cranes in a single day. Yet at the bottom of our contentment lies the inevitable sense of sadness and foreboding that one feels about the fate of beautiful rare creatures whose last habitats and populations are disappearing to make room for ever more members of our own species.

Soon the cranes rise in small groups and fly away toward the east part of the lake where there is water. The silver mists adrift over earth and river have dispersed higher in the sky, where the cranes are flying swathed in soft warm blue. Tomorrow, February 4, will be the first day of the Chinese spring.

At Nanchang, having weathered an interminable jouncing through the winter dark, we are rewarded by a good supper at the Sunshine Restaurant (the dishes include "carp with live head," which seems more enticing than "goose web and fish maw," the most expensive entrée at a restaurant near our Hong Kong hotel). At the Sunshine, we are regaled by a band of jolly young people eager to try out their piquant English. Like Miss Chen Shih who came to my rescue in Harbin last summer, they are cheerful, self-confident, and unaffected. The liveliness and generosity and innocent goodwill of so many people encountered in this country, the young people especially, is an antidote to the folly of our preconceptions.

Next morning at the Nanchang airport, urged by affable travelers to try some Chinese words, we receive a spirited admonishment from businessmen at the coffee counter when we confuse the guttural *he* for "crane" (*heugh*) with the softer *he* for "river" (*heuh*). To complicate matters, Taiwanese, Hong Kong, and mainland Chinese businessmen patriots are all present to defend their regional inflections. In moments, the whole waiting room resounds with boisterous renditions of *Heuh!* and *Heugh!*, the shouts and laughter sprinkled with the giggles of our pretty coffee maids, who tinkle as deliciously as those cool spring freshets that I pray still fall from the Immortal Water Crags in the Nine Rivers.

SIX

Hokkaido

Cool seascape with cranes
Wading long-legged in the tideway pools
Between Shiogoshi's dunes
                    —Master Basho, seventeenth century

O n a cold winter morning of northwest wind, the snow cone of Mount Fuji lights the sky, in an aerial view never beheld by the immortal Hokusai, who painted "Deathless"—the Eternal Mountain—over and over. On previous journeys to Japan, in spring and summer, I had stayed in a Zen monastery in Fuji's foothills and climbed to treeline, but never before had I had such a clear prospect. The old volcano ruling the south horizon seemed a most auspicious sign for our journey to the north island of Hokkaido on the final leg of a long journey to crane wintering grounds in Asia, in which Victor Emanuel and I had already observed seven species of Asian cranes. The eighth was the red-crowned crane, *Grus japonensis*, which stands five feet tall (only the sarus and wattled cranes are slightly taller) and weighs up to thirty-three pounds. *Japonensis*, known here as *tsuru* or *tancho*, is the largest and heaviest among the cranes and indeed among all flying birds on earth. To observe it dancing in Hokkaido's snows is an ultimate pilgrimage for ornithologists.

Tan is the Japanese word for "red" and *cho* is "peak," hence "red peak" or "red crown," a more suitable name than "Japanese crane" for a bird that is also found in mainland Asia. Through the centuries, this most beloved of oriental birds has been embroidered on robes and wedding kimonos and variously etched, painted, and depicted on screens, scrolls, woodcut prints, doors and walls, household ware, and sundry decorative crafts in every land. The city of Maizuru, or "Dancing Crane," was named for a feudal castle with gleaming white walls and upturned dark roofs like wings. Hokusai and Hiroshige were among the artists of renown who resorted to *tancho* over and over, and Sotatsu's famed 1611 scroll, portraying a thousand cranes in its forty-nine-foot length, is still commemorated in a beloved origami in which all these cranes are cut out and folded in a single piece of paper. "Fold a thousand paper cranes and the gods will fulfill your heart's desire." After World War II, a young girl named Sadako Sasaki folded 645 (more than a thousand, some say) before she died of cancer caused by radiation from the first atom bomb: the statue depicting her with her crane origami stands in Hiroshima's Peace Memorial Park.

The snow falls in the far field where travelers spend the night.
I ask you, Crane, to warm my child in your wings.
—Japanese, anonymous

The red-crowned crane is a messenger of death and a symbol of eternal life in the legends of the aboriginal Ainu people of Japan; a traditional ballad called "The Crane and the Tortoise" celebrates the longevity of these revered creatures. One of the oldest *tancho* poems, by Yamabe no Akahito, courtier to the eighth-century emperor Shomu, stirs the heart with wordless longing:

When the tide comes in,
Flooding sandbars all along Wakanoura's shore,
To the reedy marsh they fly—
Cranes, with their resounding cry.

"The tsuru or crane is the chief of the wild birds of the country," wrote an eighteenth-century visitor.[1] Traditionally, it was reserved for the highest nobility, who hunted it with falcons (just as, in India, trained peregrines were used to hunt the demoiselle and Eurasian cranes). Not until after the Meiji Restoration in 1867 were peasants permitted to hunt and eat—and salt and market—any cranes that foraged in their fields; as the emperor's habit of dining on tancho as a New Year's Day delicacy became widespread, the species was rapidly hunted out on the main island. As late as 1875, eighteen white cranes were killed in Honshu, though a few still migrated as far south as Tokyo.[2] Crane hunting was banned in Honshu in 1889, but naturalists concluded soon thereafter that *G. japonensis* had been extirpated from the archipelago.

Today there is only the echo of crane voices in such places as Kamakura, where in the eleventh century, at the Hachiman Shinto temple, "Yoshiie at the ocean gate set free a multitude of cranes with silver and gold prayer strips attached to their legs . . . and a wind of awe rose at the spectacle of the great white birds, trailing the streamers down the Pacific sky."[3]

*T*ancho is emblazoned on the tail of the silver airplane which banks and turns toward the northeast, entering clouds.[4] When the clouds part, the plane is over the snow country of northern Honshu, the main island of Japan. Even where Honshu is still wooded, little is left of what was formerly among the most noble and variegated of the earth's beech forests; most of it has been destroyed since World War II, when the bombing and burning of Japanese cities and a consequent need for wood and plywood for reconstruction led to ruthless clear-cutting high into the mountain, with consequent erosion and silting of the rivers— hence Japan's implacable stockpiling of hardwoods from Southeast Asia, the Russian Far East, and other regions desperate for hard currency. Meanwhile, the nation's population increased and the last Honshu wetlands were drained and developed for agriculture and industry, leaving no habitat for cranes.⁵

Clouds gather again, for the weather in the north has been unsettled, with severe earthquakes in recent days. The jade-green choppy sea of the Tsugaru Strait looms through swirling mists, and eventually the volcanoes and snowscapes of Hokkaido, or "North Sea Island," the northernmost of the larger islands of an archipelago that curves for some 1,800 miles in a great arc off the Pacific coast of Asia. When the archipelago was still connected to the Asian mainland, it was already inhabited by an early people called the Jomon, who migrated from northeast Asia and might have been stranded when sea levels rose at the end of the Ice Age, perhaps twelve thousand years ago. The Jomon were hunters who may have exterminated the small Japanese tigers, and they were also mankind's first known potters (*jomon* means "cord marks," from odd ropelike impressions on their pottery). Next to come were the light-skinned, hairy Ainu. In about 250 B.C., a people known as the Yayoi from the Korean peninsula arrived in central Japan, apparently by sea, bringing weaving, metalworking, and rice planting; though the Yayoi soon supplanted the Jomon-Ainu culture, some Ainu persisted in Hokkaido and both peoples have been identified in the gene pool of the modern Japanese.⁶

The Kuriles and Hokkaido are the traditional homeland of the Ainu, who say that the gods tossed lumps of earth across the water to create these cold islands of smoldering volcanoes and that the earliest Ainu in the region of the south coast port known as Kushiro brought tamed white cranes that escaped into the broad marshland at the foot of the Akan Mountains. Invading Ainu from the Kuriles hunted cranes with bows and arrows, and in the eighteenth century, many were killed, salted, and exported to markets in Honshu. Subsequently, the cranes dwindled even on Hokkaido, from where they vanished at the turn of the last century.

Tancho miraculously reappeared late in 1910, when a duck hunter was so startled by the sudden apparition of a huge white bird that he missed his shot. In 1924, a man named Haruji Saito located a small flock of cranes in the great marsh north of Kushiro called Kushiro Mire, where in the long cold Hokkaido winters, they had to depend on the last open riffles in the icy rivers for their food and roosting. Crane hunting was prohibited, and the bird itself was made a national monument by the Ministry of Culture to help save it from extinction; during the thirties, 6,670 acres in the center of the marsh were set aside as a special sanctuary. Somehow the birds survived the war years, but in a bad freeze in 1952, the remnant band of thirty *tancho* that hunched, half starved, around a hot spring had to be rescued by the corn and grain put out by local farmers. Soon this mission was adopted by the community and its schoolchildren, who set up a number of feeding stations in the northwest region of the marsh where most of the cranes gathered in winter.

In the next decades the birds increased, but the human population was increasing, too, with ever more roads, houses, and power lines. Power lines take a heavy toll on cranes wherever they occur, with a particularly severe mortality among concentrated winter flocks. In 1971, twenty out of twenty-three killed cranes died in this way. Around the villages of Akan and Tsurui, the wires are flagged for visibility and restrictions are imposed on photographers and well-wishers, who may startle the cranes into the hasty flight which causes most of the accidents, but the growing web of overhead lines remains the greatest cause of *tancho* mortalities, accounting for 70 percent of the deaths among the brown-necked juveniles.

Since the cranes vanished from April until September, it was assumed that these Hokkaido birds were winter migrants from mainland Asia—they were still referred to in the literature as "Manchurian cranes"—and that in breeding season most would return to the mainland, since only a few local nests had been reported and since the nearest breeding territories in Ussuria were only a few hundred miles away. But after 1972, when a young American crane biologist named George Archibald came to Hokkaido to study *G. japonensis*, its natural history was drastically revised.

Dr. Archibald's obsession with cranes began in 1967, when he abandoned his studies in medicine for ornithology. In the summers of 1966 and 1967, he worked at the Alberta Game Farm near Edmonton, where methods of raising sandhill crane chicks in captivity were being developed. Later in 1967, he visited the famous ornithology department at Cornell University, where Dr. William Dilger suggested that he do his thesis on crane phylogeny (the evolutionary history of crane genera and species). From 1968 to 1971, he studied the comparative behavior of cranes at the Cornell Laboratory of Ornithology, establishing a crane breeding station on a former mink ranch using seventeen captive birds obtained from William Conway, the curator of the New York Zoological Park; it was Conway who counseled him to avoid academe in favor of an active life in conservation.

In 1971, while finishing his doctorate, Archibald shared adjoining offices at the Cornell Laboratory of Ornithology with another young graduate student named Ronald Sauey, with whom he discussed the possibility of establishing a permanent international center dedicated to the study and preservation of the world's cranes through research, habitat conservation, and the breeding of endangered species; the idea was to establish a species bank in case a population threatened in the wild could be restored or at least maintained by introducing birds from the captive flock. In addition, their "international crane foundation" would institute programs to educate concerned people about what must be done to ensure that their local cranes survived. The main obstacles included political disputes and intermittent warfare on the Sino-Soviet border regions and elsewhere in the east Asian countries where half the earth's crane species were found: as Archibald told Sauey, "We'll have to open a whole new branch of the UN." In the winter of 1971–72, the India-Pakistan border war caused Archibald to put off a first visit to the Siberian cranes at Keoladeo in Rajasthan and come to Japan to study *japonensis* instead.

In Hokkaido, Archibald noticed that the juvenile birds that came to the winter feeding stations were far more numerous than could be accounted for by the few reported nests. Until now, he had not questioned the Japanese assumption that these cranes were migrants from the mainland, like the hooded and white-naped cranes that came to the island of Kyushu in the south. But that spring, when the juveniles departed with the adult cranes, then returned after a day or two, he began to suspect that the adults must be nesting somewhere in the region and had driven these juveniles off their territory. That cranes were silent and flew little in the summer, when their nest mounds in the labyrinthine marsh would be hidden by high reeds and sedges, would explain why most of them had gone undetected in the mostly roadless and untraveled Kushiro Mire.

That spring, with the assistance of the Hokkaido crane expert Dr. Hiroyuki Masatomi[7] and an endorsement from the New York Zoological Society[8] and a local airplane company, Archibald raised two thousand dollars for an air survey of Hokkaido's marshes. The solitary nests guarded by huge white birds were easily located—fifty-three, in fact, in about three hours—confirming his guess that the Japanese population of *japonensis* was nonmigratory. As recent studies of their distinct unison calls have shown, the Hokkaido cranes have been separated from the mainland population for thousands of years.

The postwar industrialization of Japan brought extensive wetland drainage to create ever more habitat for human beings. Because Kushiro's climate was too cool for rice paddies, its marshes were mostly left alone, until finally Kushiro Mire was the largest wetland in all the four main islands of Japan that remained relatively undamaged. Before long it came under great pressure from developers (who have learned to call their business "reclamation"), and not until 1987 was part of it finally set aside as a national park.

The *tancho* at present has a more or less stable population of about six hundred birds—roughly half the size of the mainland population—all of them resident in southeastern Hokkaido, with nearly a third nesting in Kushiro Mire. The great marsh already supports as many cranes as the limited habitat can handle—possibly more, to judge from the fact that the size of the territory normally maintained by each pair of cranes has been steadily shrinking since their numbers rose after the 1950s, until finally they were adapting to small bogs and pasturelands. In 1988, the closest nests were only about seven hundred yards apart; by 1991, that distance had contracted to about three hundred yards, and today some of the territories are even smaller. (Compare this to the mainland *japonensis* whose "immense habitat needs have led to their decline over much of their former range . . . One pair . . . requires many hundreds if not thousands of acres of shallow wetland in order to breed successfully.")[9] Not surprisingly, the smallest Kushiro Mire territories produce no chicks.

Meanwhile half of the 71,900 acres of the sanctuary have been drained and converted to industrial, agricultural, and residential use, with ongoing deforestation and drainage all around its perimeter; this not only degrades adjoining wetlands but reduces available food as the breeding pairs are forced closer together. Unless new range can be established farther west on Hokkaido and perhaps on Honshu, the future of *japonensis* as a viable population in Japan will remain uncertain even with the assistance of man.

The white-naped and hooded cranes that winter on the large southern island of Kyushu cross the Korea Strait from the peninsula. It is thought that tens of thousands of *Grus monachus* (known here as "the black crane") wintered formerly throughout the archipelago from north to south and also in the southern part of the Korean peninsula and southeastern China; but like *tancho*, the black cranes were much diminished by hunting in the post-Meiji decades and again during World War II. Since then, they have been harmed by development of the fallow grainfields and rice paddies where they foraged, until finally, as in Hokkaido, local people took up their care and feeding.[10]

In the winter of 1974, on Kyushu's Araseki plain, outside Izumi, Archibald made an estimate of twenty-two hundred *monachus* and a like number of *G. vipio*.[11] By the early 1980s, the Araseki populations of these two species had more than doubled, to about five thousand each, a number which represented most of Asia's hooded cranes and nearly half its white-napeds.

Large winter congregations at Araseki and elsewhere are evidence not of crane prosperity but, on the contrary, of disappearing habitat and confinement to limited areas. In breeding season, habitat loss may cause cranes to breed at greater densities on territories of lower quality, as in Hokkaido, while on winter grounds, as in Kyushu, the crowding increases the risk of fatal epidemic, such as an outbreak of the herpes virus or mercury pesticide poisoning. Ironically, artificial feeding could become the greatest danger to both flocks, yet if winter feeding were discontinued, the cranes, forced into farmed fields, might cause unacceptable crop damage and local resentment.

In recent years, Kyushu farmers have been experimenting with prefabricated greenhouses for growing vegetables in winter; at the same time, their abandonment of rice paddies to weeds and undergrowth have diminished the cranes' night roosts in water, which may be as critical as winter forage. (It is hoped that a few crucial fields will be secured and set aside for the beleaguered cranes.)

Beset by increasing mining, lumbering, and military activity on its Siberian breeding grounds and by industrial development in South Korea, *G. monachus* is also threatened in Japan.

K ushiro is a fisheries, coal mine, and paper mill port on Hokkaido's Pacific coast. The mills have exhausted the local forest and now import rough unmilled timber from the Pacific Northwest of the United States and Canada.[12] "Newsprint and cardboard," says Yulia Momose, who met us at the small airport. "It's the cardboard plant that smells."

When George Archibald first came to Kushiro to study red-crowned cranes, he lived with the family of Dr. Shoichiro Satsuki, and though Dr. Satsuki died in 1986, his family continues to look after George and his many friends. The two pretty Satsuki daughters have studied in the United States and speak good English, and Yulia and her ornithologist husband, Dr. Kunikazu Momose, have kindly offered to serve as our expert guides.

Yulia takes us straightaway to the haunts of *tancho*, which in winter are largely confined to the Kushiro marsh. The marsh is replenished by several small rivers that flow down from the Akan Mountains, which rise to the snow-peaked volcano known as Akan-Fuji. The 100-square-mile marsh is the heart of Kushiro's crane conservation area, supporting about 53 of the estimated 160 nesting pairs that are presently breeding on Hokkaido; the other large group breeds in the coastal region of Nemuro, which lies east of Kushiro on the farther side of Cape Shiretoko. Most of the Nemuro birds will gather in winter in the northwest region of Kushiro Mire.

Yulia's first destination is Tsurumidai (Crane Lookout), a feeding station on the Watanabe farm, where observers are engaged in the annual crane census. The countryside is frozen deep beneath the heavy snow that will cover the ground from November to April—Hokkaido receives more snow than any location at this latitude on earth—but the day is bright, without much wind, and it is pleasant out-of-doors if one stamps hard enough. Among the stampers at Crane Lookout is George Archibald's old colleague Dr. Hiroyuki Masatomi, an elderly ornithologist with the wispy beard and gentle manner of one of those sages of yore who were borne up to the heavens on the backs of obliging cranes.[13]

Whooper swans with jet-black legs and golden bills are basking in the snow light, fat with corn.[14] Assorted tits and woodpeckers flitter about a bird feeder, and a large golden thrush (White's thrush) hops about nearby. Soon the first nervous *tancho* alights and comes stalking in across the snow, but it flares and flies off again before reaching the corn. There are no cranes at the next feeding station,[15] but from a small bridge on the road we see a group of half a dozen in the black winter water of the Hororo River, a swift, narrow creek that descends the mountains into Kushiro Mire.

Near the Akan River is the main feeding area, Akan-cho Tancho, which is supervised by the former owner, Mr. Yamazaki; here we catch up with Yulia's husband, Kunikazu, of the Yamashina Institute of Ornithology, who oversees the crane census at this station. While we are there, twenty-three cranes arrive for the daily offering of *ugui*, a coarse fish of the carp family that is netted in the mountain lakes and delivered live to the crane station every week. Wary, the *tancho* stalk about and preen and even dance a little, without much fervor—it is cold and they are here to feed. As Mr. Yamazaki flings the flopping fish onto the snow, the cranes draw closer, and more fly in from the Akan River.[16] The elegant big creatures take their time, making no effort to compete with the crows, black kites, and white-tailed eagles that circle and swoop in graceful arcs, snatching the flopping red-finned *ugui* off the snow without alighting. The birds are but an *ugui* throw from the wood barricade of a small building for visitors, which has hot tea, a food counter and souvenir shop, and even an observatory on the second floor.

Beyond the field where the cranes dance and feed is a line of spruce trees along the Akan, and beyond the river rise low wooded hills. In pairs and family groups of three or (rarely) four, the great white birds swing in through the conifers. They alight so daintily on long black legs that the toes seem to strain to touch the snow and even lift a little at the final second, as if flinching away from the frozen surface. When seen against a background of bright crystals, its immaculate white, its blood-red crown and velvety black plumes, explain why most people who know one crane from another regard *japonensis* as the most magnificent of all.

When George Archibald first visited Japan in the winter of 1972, he was familiar with eight species of crane but had never laid eyes on *japonensis* in the wild. He thought it the most extraordinary of all the cranes, not only in the elegance of its plumage but in the complex patterns of its dancing, which as in most cranes reinforces the pair bond and helps to relieve aggressive tension in the individual bird as well as in the flock. Like most *Grus* species, *japonensis* rises onto its toes, elevates the mantle feathers on its back, and flares its wings in "butterfly posture" to enlarge its aspect and appear more imposing to its mate and to any rivals, but unlike the others, it continues this presentation by lifting outspread wings high above its back and turning its neck to set off its crown against the satiny black plumes of its tertials; then, pointing its long sharp bill at the heavens and cocking its small tail, it curves its neck back over its mantle to form its famous "arch."

Siberian crane (White crane)
Grus leucogeranus

Red-crowned crane
(Japanese or Manchurian crane)
Grus japonensis

White-naped crane (Daurian crane)
Grus vipio

Eurasian crane (Common crane)
Grus grus

Demoiselle crane
Anthropoides virgo

Hooded crane
Grus monachus

Brolga
Grus rubicundus

Sarus crane
Grus antigone

Wattled crane
Grus carunculatus

Black-necked crane (Tibetan crane)
Grus nigricollis

Blue crane (Stanley crane)
Anthropoides paradisea

Sandhill crane
Grus canadensis

Black crowned crane
Balearica pavonina

Whooping crane
Grus americana

Gray crowned crane
Balearica regulorum

CRANES IN THE EASTERN HEMISPHERE
(winter ranges not indicated)

● **National Park or Wildlife Refuge Site**

0 *Miles*   500   1000

0 *Kilometers*   1000

Kara Sea

R U S S

SIBERIAN

Kunevat River

Ural Mountains

Ob River

DENMARK

SWEDEN

NORFOLK
Norwich

THE NETHERLANDS

EURASIAN

ENGLAND

GERMANY

SWITZERLAND

KAZAKHSTAN

DEMOIS

FRANCE

HUNGARY

Caspian Sea

SAMARKAND

SPAIN

Lenkoran●

Fereydunkenar●

*Takla Makan
Desert*

Great Himalay

AFGHANISTAN

●Kabul

MOROCCO

IRAN

Lake Ab-e-estada

Delhi

Indus River

PAKISTAN

NEPA

RAJASTHAN

SARUS

ALGERIA

Jaipur

S a h a r a   D e s e r t

●Ahmedabad

GUJARAT

I N D I A

SENEGAL

Area of detail

BLACK CROWNED

CHAD

SUDAN

Nile River

Blue Nile

THE SUDD

ETHIOPIA

EQUATORIA

WATTLED

UGANDA

KENYA

Lake Victoria

*Serengeti
Plain*

I n d i a n

GRAY CROWNED

Ngorongoro Crater

●Kilimanjaro

O c e a n

TANZANIA

A t l a n t i c

O c e a n

ZAMBIA

*Etosha
Pan*

*Okavango
Delta*

ZIMBABWE

WATTLED

NAMIBIA

Zambezi River

BOTSWANA

GRAY CROWNED

WATTLED

TRANSVAAL

Dullstroom●

BLUE

Johannesburg●

WATTLED

NATAL

EASTERN TRANSVAAL
(MPUMALANGA)

SOUTH AFRICA

KAROO

CAPE PROVINCE

*Takla Mak
Desert*

AFGHANISTAN

HINDU KUSH

Kabul●

Great H

Indus River

PAKISTAN

Delhi

NEPA

Bharatpur●

Ganges R

●Khichan

Jaisalmer●

Jaipur●

Great Indian Desert

RAJASTHAN

KEOLADEO
NAT'L PARK

*Little Rann
of Kutch*

Ahmedabad●

GUJARAT

I N D I

Arctic Ocean

SIBERIAN

SAKHA REPUBLIC (YAKUTIA)

SANDHILL   Chukotskiy Peninsula

CHUKOTSKIY (SIBERIA)

Kolyma R.

Lena River

Yana R.

Indigirka R.

I   A

HOODED

Sea of
Okhotsk

Kamchatka

Lake Baikal

Irkutsk   Chita   Lake
Ulan   Dalainor
Ude   DAURIAN
STEPPE

WHITE-NAPED

Amur River

Sakhalin
Island

Kurile Islands

Ulaan Baatar

Selenga R.   Uldz R.

HEILONGJIANG
PROVINCE   ● Khabarovsk

PRIMORSKI
KRAI

OUTER MONGOLIA   Choybalsan

Harbin

Gobi Desert   Kerulen R.

JILIN
PROVINCE

INNER MONGOLIA AUTONOMOUS REPUBLIC

Vladivostok

RED-CROWNED

Mountains

Koko Nor
(Qinghai Lake)

Beijing   ● Gulf of
Chihli

N. KOREA

Sea of Japan

JAPAN

AN   AU

CHINA

● Seoul

S. KOREA

Yellow
Sea

Korea Strait

35°

K-NECKED   SICHUAN
PROVINCE

Yangtze River

Shanghai

mandu

Poyang Lakes   Jiujiang

BHUTAN   JIANG-XI
PROVINCE   Nanchang

Area of detail

Okinawa

● RUSSIA

Sakhalin
Island

Blagoveschensk

CHINA   San Jiang
(Three Rivers)
plain

Khabarovsk

ZHALONG
RESERVE

Pacific
Ocean

HEILONGJIANG
PROVINCE

Harbin

Amur River

Ussuri
plain

Ussuri R.

PRIMORSKI KRAI

Kunashir

Hong Kong

Lake Khanka

Sikhote-Alin Mountains

Songhua R.

HOKKAIDO

Me-Akan

JILIN PROVINCE

Spassk

Me-Akan
Kushiro

THAILAND   Mekong River   LUZON

EASTERN
SARUS

Vladivostok

Angkor Wat   VIETNAM   PHILIPPINES

Tonle Sap   South
CAMBODIA   China Sea

NORTH KOREA

Panmunjom   DMZ

Sea of Japan

JAPAN

Yellow
Sea

Seoul   HONSHU

SOUTH
KOREA

Korea Strait

Mount Fuji

PAPUA
NEW GUINEA

Araseki plain   KYUSHU

Pacific Ocean

Torres Strait

n Mountains

Darwin   Gulf of   ● Cape York Peninsula
Carpentaria

CHINA

AUSTRALIAN SARUS

Normanton   ● Cairns
Atherton

TIBETAN
PLATEAU

Morr Morr

Gilbert R.

NEW
CALEDONIA

BROLGA

Chomolungma
(Mount Everest)

QUEENSLAND

Phobjika Valley

andu   Paro   BHUTAN
i   Thimphu   AUSTRALIA

RAI   ASSAM

Sydney

BANGLADESH

MYANMAR

Ganges R.

© 2001 Jeffrey L. Ward

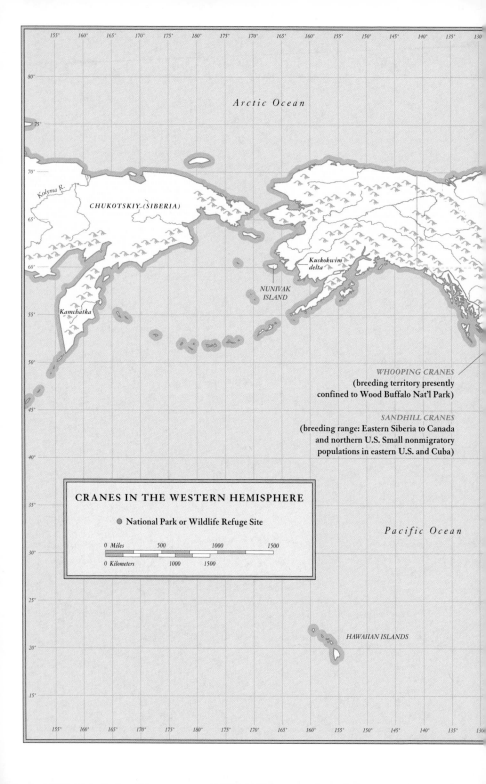

Arctic Ocean

Kolyma R.

CHUKOTSKIY (SIBERIA)

Kamchatka

Kuskokwim
delta

NUNIVAK
ISLAND

WHOOPING CRANES
(breeding territory presently
confined to Wood Buffalo Nat'l Park)

SANDHILL CRANES
(breeding range: Eastern Siberia to Canada
and northern U.S. Small nonmigratory
populations in eastern U.S. and Cuba)

Pacific Ocean

CRANES IN THE WESTERN HEMISPHERE

● National Park or Wildlife Refuge Site

| 0 Miles | 500 | 1000 | 1500 |
| 0 Kilometers | 1000 | 1500 | |

HAWAIIAN ISLANDS

GREENLAND

N U N A V U T

RTHWEST TERRITORIES

C A N A D A

ALBERTA

SASKATCHEWAN

Rocky Mountains

Great Plains

NECEDAH NAT'L REFUGE

GRAYS LAKE
NAT'L REFUGE

INTERNATIONAL
CRANE FOUNDATION

Platte River
Kearney   Baraboo

PLATTE RIVER
REFUGE

Missouri River

Sagaponack

PATUXENT
RESEARCH CENTER

U N I T E D   S T A T E S   O F   A M E R I C A

BOSQUE DEL APACHE
NAT'L REFUGE

Mississippi River

MISSISSIPPI SANDHILL
REFUGE

Okefenokee Swamp

Orlando

White Lake

Lake Marion

Kissimmee prairie

ARANSAS NAT'L REFUGE

CHASSAHOWITZKA
NAT'L REFUGE

Yeehaw Junction

Lake Okeechobee

EVERGLADES

M E X I C O

Gulf of Mexico

Atlantic Ocean

C U B A

*Isle of
Pines*

Caribbean Sea

© 2001 Jeffrey L. Ward

THE EVOLUTION AND RADIATION OF THE CRANES

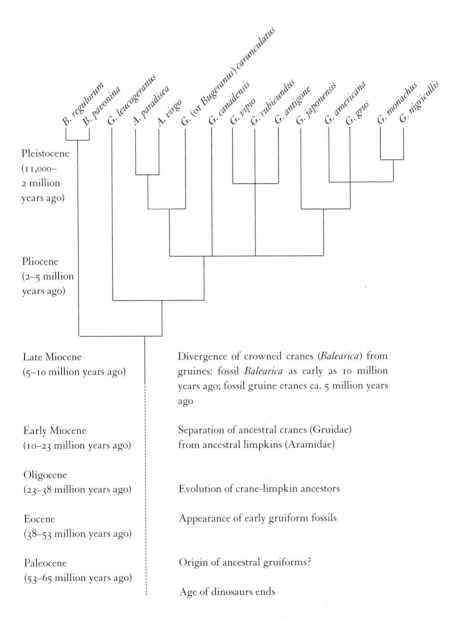

Pleistocene
(11,000–
2 million
years ago)

Pliocene
(2–5 million
years ago)

Late Miocene
(5–10 million years ago)

Divergence of crowned cranes (*Balearica*) from gruines: fossil *Balearica* as early as 10 million years ago; fossil gruine cranes ca. 5 million years ago

Early Miocene
(10–23 million years ago)

Separation of ancestral cranes (Gruidae) from ancestral limpkins (Aramidae)

Oligocene
(23–38 million years ago)

Evolution of crane-limpkin ancestors

Eocene
(38–53 million years ago)

Appearance of early gruiform fossils

Paleocene
(53–65 million years ago)

Origin of ancestral gruiforms?

Age of dinosaurs ends

Assembled with many thanks to Dr. Carey Krajewski and Dr. George Archibald.

Red-crowned crane (*Grus japonensis*)

"When I saw *japonensis* raise its wings and arch its back during its dancing, I realized that this species had gone far beyond the others in its threat-posturing and pair-bonding behavior," George had told me in Siberia. "Later I learned that the Siberian did something very similar, and that in this respect, these two are different from the others. I hesitate to say 'superior,' since one could argue that these two are inferior in their adaptations, being so specialized in their wetland habitat. All the same, of all crane species, these two excite me most." (Having handled so many in captivity, he attributes unusual intelligence to *japonensis*, which is particularly inquisitive and ingenious, with a marked ability to take things apart.)

G. japonensis has developed the most elaborate courtship dance among the cranes but also—since this big bird can be dangerous to others of its kind—the most complex threat displays and postures to vent its excitement and lessen the chance of attack and combat on the winter roosts and feeding grounds where the birds must crowd together. In his early research years ago, monitoring a night flock near the feeding stations, Archibald heard a peculiar *whooshing* accompanied by a ghostly flash out of the dark. The sound and sight turned out to be quick thrashings of the wings in which the white primaries picked up ambient light; he speculates that this wing stretch and "flap threat" (analogous to the flap threat of the white-naped crane in daylight, when its dark primaries are more visible) is a warning—an adaptation of well-armed birds that are fiercely territorial even in winter, yet must roost communally at night.

What interested George most, however, were crane unison calls, which became the basis of his doctoral thesis at Cornell University;[17] the unison call has evolutionary significance which is partially reflected in crane anatomy. In his thesis (which was based on his study of eight crane species in the wild and in captivity), George affirmed that the *Balearica* were more "primitive" than other cranes—that is, closer to the crane ancestor—not only in the relative simplicity of their calls but also in the unspecialized trachea, or windpipe, that goes directly from the neck to the lungs.[18]

The unison call of the Siberian crane—originally assigned to the genus *Grus* on the basis of morphological similarity to *G. americana*— was so divergent from the calls of other *Grus* as to call that taxonomic status into question; for this reason and many others—the two have numerous affinities—Dr. Archibald proposed that it be included in the *Bugeranus* genus with the wattled crane. In the crowned cranes, the different calls of the main geographic races supported prior arguments for *Balearica*'s separation into two species, and also the separation of the mainland and Japanese populations of *G. japonensis* into distinct races or subspecies. A few years after Archibald published his thesis, his exciting findings were substantially borne out by skeletal and external anatomy studies, as well as comprehensive studies of crane DNA.[19]

A red fox comes trotting from the spruce (its pelage is a warmer red and lacks the black points—ears, paws, and tail—of its New World kinsman), staying belly to the snow as it slips among the cranes. Biting at the flopping fish, it manages to make off with two at once, dropping them in a snow hollow at some distance from the birds, then trotting back to secure more. No doubt the bold fox is keenly observed by the beady black eyes of the vixen and their kits back in the spruce. In spring, the fox preys on the crane nests, taking eggs as well as chicks, though probably its predations are less than those of the loitering crows. Mr. Watanabe at Crane Lookout has seen a fox attack and kill an unwary adult crane that it caught foraging in a ditch, permitting the fox to leap onto its neck from the bank above.

Like Mr. and Mrs. Watanabe, who are elderly retired people, Mr. Yamazaki's father began crane feeding many years ago in the freezing year of 1950, when it was clear that without man's help, Hokkaido's dwindling cranes might not survive. Two years later, Mrs. Watanabe encouraged children from the school she ran behind her farm to feed the cranes. A crane club founded in 1957 at the Akan high school was active until recent years, but not until 1965 did Akan and the nearby village of Tsurui (Crane) help the farmers pay for the dispensed grain and hire Yamazaki and a Mr. Ito as watchmen and caretakers.

In the evening, Yulia's sister Rori, a musician, with their lively mother, Mrs. Yoshie Satsuki, treat us to a wonderful seafood supper at Kushiro's oldest restaurant, Yatsunami. Yatsunami means "eight waves"—that is, eight generations, for eight is a lucky number, Rori tells us. As for Kushiro, it derives from an Ainu word variously translated as "Place Where People Gather" and "Throat," as in river narrows. There may have been Ainu settlements on this coast even in A.D. 794, when Japan's first shogun, or "general for subduing the barbarians," was sent out to deal with rude invasions by "a wild blue-eyed people called Emishi, from the northern island of Hokkaido, who gathered together like ants but dispersed like birds."[20] To the Ainu, the white cranes were "the marsh gods." Like the Chukot of Siberia, the Australian Aborigines, the American Indians—in short, most indigenous peoples in the countries of wild cranes—the Ainu developed a crane dance, but in Ainu culture only the women danced the slow ceremonial step, while a chorus of their sisters clapped and sang in imitation of the marsh god's cries. Though a few old folks of Ainu parentage might still be found during Rori's childhood, their descendants are almost entirely assimilated; only recently has there been a movement among those claiming Ainu blood to preserve some traditional culture, as has happened in North America and Australia.

According to Rori, many farmers here resent the cranes, which consume the maize needed for their livestock and dig up the new shoots of the spring crops. Even so, nobody kills *tancho* anymore. Despite its long history in Japanese culture, the red-crowned crane has only been the "national bird" since the 1950s, when that peculiar honorific was borrowed from the Americans. (In a discussion of the late film director Akiro Kurosawa, whose greatness went unappreciated in his own land for many years, Rori remarks tartly, "We Japanese tend to appreciate certain virtues of our country only after other countries admire them first.")

At Akan-cho Tancho that first afternoon, the circling white-tailed eagles were joined briefly by a Steller's sea eagle, which was too wary to swoop down to take a fish and soon flew away. Steller's sea eagle roughly resembles a huge North American bald eagle, but its white head and yellow beak are much more massive and it has bold white patches on the black wings. A concentration of these uncommon birds occurs in winter on Hokkaido's northern coast, near the town of Rausa on the Sea of Okhotsk, where fish schools throng the Nemuro Strait between Hokkaido and Kunashir, the southernmost of the Kurile Islands that curve north toward Kamchatka. At Rausa, eagles of both species are commonly seen with captured fish out on the pack ice, with roosts of hundreds and hundreds of enormous raptors in the ravines that come down the coast.

In two days, we are to accompany the Momoses to the valleys above Kushiro, hunting and counting the wilder cranes less habituated to the feeding stations, but meanwhile, we will cross the island in search of the Rausa eagles. Early next morning we set off by bus from Kushiro northeast to the Okhotsk coast, leaving the frozen port behind as the narrow road climbs the wooded hills, crossing black streams and sunny snowfields and dairy farms with black-and-white Holstein cattle. White peaks of volcanoes appear to the north and west, and bamboo and birch give way to conifers until the whole range of snow mountains comes into view. The highest are dormant Akan-Fuji, which rises over five thousand feet, and Akan-Fuji's female consort, smoking Me-Akan.

The mountain road descends once more toward the Nemuro Strait, crossing the base of Cape Shiretoko and striking the coast at Shibetsu, where it turns northeast along the Sea of Okhotsk. The pretty fringe of black rock coast lies at the foot of steep-sided hills that are parted by narrow gorges and black streams, and brown dippers teeter here and there on the ice-shined rocks.

A few miles offshore to the north rise the pale cliffs of the Kurile Islands. By the coast road stands a large sign which portrays frowning citizens staring out to sea with raised clenched fists in symbolic protest of the loss of the southern Kuriles to the Soviet Union as World War II came to an end. Strangely, in this far corner of the nation, the Japanese characters on the sign are accompanied by an English translation which reads, "Give us back the Occupied Islands!" The largest and southernmost of the Kuriles is Kunashir, whose beautiful snow peaks and high cliffs are only fifteen miles away across the strait.[21]

Instead of the predicted pack ice, the strait on this bright February 9 is an open cold clear blue, broken here and there by the white hulls of trawlers. Along the shore road, perched on spruce and birch, are numbers of white-tailed eagles, and on the smooth surface of the sea swim goldeneye ducks, red-breasted and common mergansers, pelagic cormorants, and some small murrelets that are too far offshore to identify.

Snow, at times heavy, comes and goes. In moments the sea is shrouded over, turning gray, as a snow squall rushes in from the northwest. Kunashir fades to shadow and then vanishes. Soon the bus arrives at Rausa, a busy fishing port with a big seawall and inner harbor, and the sun, reappearing, glints on the massive saffron beak and bold white wing patch of a Steller's sea eagle, squatted on the jetty, attended by crows and a crowd of gulls—mostly slaty-backed gulls, but also ice-white glaucous gulls, a few glaucous-wings, a single mew gull, and what look like two immature specimens of the beautiful black-tailed gull that I first saw last summer across the strait on the Siberian coast.

At Rausa, where deep snowbanks choke the village streets, we are met by Yulia Momose's friend Michihiro Tazawa, a tall young ranger of the Shiretoko National Park. After a warming lunch of ramen (stretched noodles) at a village shop, Tazawa escorts us farther up the coast in a parks vehicle, hunting for eagles. The run of walleye pollock has been small this year and the pack ice late in coming (another sign of global warming to almost everyone on earth except the profiteers of the oil and automotive industries). Therefore the sea eagles are scattered and rather scarce. Most of them, coming from offshore, convene on the breakwaters and outer jetties, and also in large trees on the steep slopes that overlook the harbor and the fishing fleet. Here there are groups of a dozen or twenty—not the hundreds predicted, but an imposing array of mighty raptors all the same.

There is also an astonishing abundance of the beautiful harlequin duck, which occurs uncommonly in winter on both coasts of North America, in pairs or small scarce flocks. Close to the rocks swim nine harlequins together, six of them drakes in fresh spring plumage, and farther north along the shore, pair after pair, flock after flock, are gabbling and diving through the shining surface of the silver water. We shrug and grin and stop our foolish counting, having already seen more harlequins on a single mile of coast than we recorded between us in decades of impassioned birding.

At six next morning we set off with the Momoses from Kushiro, taking a road that follows the Shitakara River upstream toward the Akan foothills. Deciduous woods climb to the spruce ridge, and behind the ridge rises the white cone of Akan-Fuji. Our boots squeak on the snowy road that leads along the frosted trees by the small Shitakara (in the Ainu language, "Place of Elms," though the elms were destroyed long ago, and the Ainu, too). The day is clear and very cold——4 degrees Fahrenheit, according to Mr. Yamazaki, brother of the caretaker at Akan-cho Tancho, whom we found at the observation place on the Shitakara. Smiling in delight, he points at eighteen or twenty *tancho*, still roosted a little way upstream, and we stoop to peer at them between the icy branches.

Beyond the bend, the white forms hunch in icy mist. At a place where the soft and deep dry snow descends to the very edges of the ice, the still shapes create a black-and-white barrier across the stream.

The cranes are waking. One preens a little, but the rest seem to await the first cold rays of sun before starting to shift and move about in the black riffle of unfrozen current. Though not in danger from mammal predators (the wolves and tigers are extinct, and the bears hibernate), the cranes of Kushiro still roost in streams; few if any are caught by the ice, though they sometimes fly up banded with ice anklets.

Most are preening, moving a little, the black-and-white patterns shifting mysteriously in the frozen mist. Two raise long necks, point their bills skyward, and utter together the loud wild call that I first heard on the breeding grounds in Siberia. The unison call rings across the brittle cold of the dawn valley, cracking it like ice.

Though we crouch two hundred yards away, well-screened by

bushes, the alert and sharp-eyed birds are well aware of us, yet they do not fly nor appear disturbed as we straighten at last and move away; the wary *tancho* seem to know that this two-legged beast is no longer an enemy. Perhaps one day they will regain the confiding trust that is so moving in wild creatures of remote places which man reached very late, such as the Galapagos, or where for centuries man has honored a prohibition against killing, as in certain Buddhist regions of the Himalaya.

I n connection with their census for the Tancho Protection Unit, a private foundation for the study of cranes led by Drs. Momose and Masatomi, our friends lead us on a survey of the Onbetsu River drainage to the west, where last year they located those less sophisticated cranes that rarely appear at the Kushiro stations. Last month's earthquake damage—landslides and big cracks in the road—is very apparent in these hills west of Kushiro. In places the Onbetsu road has fallen away into the valleys, and a herd of sika deer in gray winter pelage waits large-eyed at the wood edge, peering out at the fractured road as if making sure it is still safe to cross.

From Onbetsu, a road heads into the mountains, and here there are work crews, for the lower Onbetsu has been blocked and diverted by the landslides. Though the upper river is still clear, we see no cranes, only a white-tailed eagle, broad-backed in a tree, and a lone dog in the river meadows, running toward dog destinations across the shining snow. Eventually a side road leads up a tributary called the Muri (an Ainu place-name, "Foggy Village," long since gone), where a few old farms lie strung along the valley. A pair of cranes appears on the bend of the mountain creek, then three more a little ways upstream, then another two that join the first pair, feeding on small insects and larvae under stones overturned in the streambed, all the while moving unhurriedly away. At a bend, these four dance lightly up onto a sun-filled snowbank, forming a bright black-white composition counterpointed by the white-black-white of snow and winter water.

I wondered why *G. japonensis*, which in these snows of the far north endures the coldest temperatures of any crane, has a longer bill and neck and legs than the black-necked crane in the mountains of Bhutan, whose shorter neck and legs and more compact and heat-efficient body are evolutionary adaptations to cold climates. Is *japonensis* intrinsically the most cold-hardy of the crane species, or has this hardihood come about through changed circumstances and conditions, such as the necessity of surviving these frozen winters in what was formerly a breeding habitat of spring and summer?

Its lordly weight and modest flying capabilities relative to other cranes, and also its elaborate bustle and white primaries, suggest to Dr. Archibald that *japonensis* may originally have been a nonmigratory form that was extirpated from a more southerly range. Mainland *japonensis* migrate south to the Koreas and the China coast: I wonder if these Hokkaido birds, joined by the Kunashir group, might have wintered formerly on the main island of Honshu, or if *japonensis* was a nonmigratory race widespread in the archipelago, with Hokkaido the northern limit of its range.

Kunikazu Momose is courteous enough to find this question intriguing, but in the absence of good evidence, he assumes that even in the old days, some of these *tancho* migrated and some did not. Those that did not are the ones that survived.

Like other northern *Grus*, *japonensis* has sparse black filoplumes on the bare black skin of the "forehead" and also on the rough warty comb of the crimson crown; in cold weather or migration, the crown may darken as blood is withdrawn until it becomes obscure under the filoplumes, or it may disappear almost entirely under the white nape, which is drawn forward like a hood. Today, despite the intense cold, the vermilion crown is bright as a fresh blood spot on new snow.

Tancho's striking appearance is enhanced by its black secondaries and white primaries, the reverse of the arrangement seen not only in *leucogeranus* and *americana* but in large white long-distance fliers of many families—geese, gannets, pelicans, albatrosses, certain storks and gulls—all of which have black primaries or at least black wing tips: the melanin in the black feathers is thought to strengthen them and reduce fraying during long hard migrations. White primaries are uncommon in large birds except in all-white birds such as egrets, and the contrasting black secondaries seen in the red-crowned crane are perhaps unique.[22] In slow-flying *japonensis*, migration is neither long nor arduous; the Amur birds fly no farther than the Korean peninsula and the coast of China, and the Hokkaido population is essentially nonmigratory. Wing efficiency is therefore less important, leaving the species free to develop more elaborate epigamic or display markings for threat and courtship. Unlike less elegant animals, cranes do not part abruptly after mating but stand side by side, crimson crowns flushed and long bills pointed toward the heavens, after which, in unison to the end, they close the mating ceremony with appropriate ruffling and bowing.

In oriental symbology, in which red-crowned cranes are prominent, the striking black-and-white pattern created when the bird spreads its wings and arches its black neck was much admired by Chinese philosophers as a manifestation of the yin-yang principle of bad and good, dark and light; that solitary note of brilliant crimson reconciles the "dark-light" dualities that return eventually to the One, the universal, the quintessential source of all existence. In this brilliant winter light, against black tree trunks and white snow, the red jewel moves and turns like the quick heart of life, as the dark evergreens, in their impenetrable stillness, breathe the imminence of the great mystery looming behind.

These hillsides, clear-cut years ago, have healed themselves in second-growth oak and birch wood with some larch and spruce. Elsewhere they have been replanted with lines of unbroken conifers, supporting little wildlife. Reforestation, Yulia says, has become "a passion" in wood-hungry Japan. The scattered farms appear well-kept if not prosperous, and many more small birds are to be seen here in the Muri than in the Kushiro valley, or even in the wooded mountains, upland pastures, and seaside bushes on the way to Rausa, where the only passerine glimpsed all day was a solitary tree sparrow on a frozen street. The fawn-and-blue Eurasian jay is common here—six together in the sunlight peck seeds from a manure heap in a cattle pen—and we also note four dusky thrushes, the great tit and the marsh tit, a spotted woodpecker, and a brown-eared bulbul in fresh country colors that looks nothing at all like the soiled street specimens one sees in Tokyo.

Farther upriver, three red-black-white heads come up over a snowbank on a bend. The heads turn in the shining light against a dark background of steep wooded hillside already overtaken by afternoon shadow. We are able to get closer, though not close. Sun-silvered creatures, moving gracefully without haste and yet swiftly in the black diamond shimmer of the Muri River—a vision, a revelation, although what might be revealed beyond this silver moment of my life I do not know.

A few years ago, the local school down near the Onbetsu confluence established a crane-feeding program administered by an old gentleman, Ichiro Sato, who feeds the cranes in a pasture outside his small farmhouse near the school. The cranes, Mr. Sato assures us, will arrive about 3:30 P.M.—late afternoon at this time of the year, not long before they go to roost—and each will peck up fifty grains of maize before resting awhile, perhaps eating a bit of snow to wash these down.

Whether or not they draw the line at fifty grains, Mr. Sato's cranes are certainly not greedy. (The seeming reticence of all crane species in the presence of food is one of their numerous attractive traits; although omnivorous, they will not gobble rotted vegetables in fields as ducks and geese will.) The white cranes come sailing down the valley at the time appointed, swinging up into the frozen wind until it fills their broad, cupped wings and they step lightly down out of the air. Even then, they gaze around before they feed. They may preen a little, dance a little, or stand upon one leg, lifting the other foot into their breast feathers to warm it after delicately shaking off any ice or snow. Though dependent upon man, these cranes are wary. In the farmyard of a house that ignores visitors, they seem somehow less acculturated, less demeaned than those in the *ugui* tourist show at Akan-cho Tancho.

Still steeped in winter, the *tancho* remain silent after the low rolling greeting call made in flight as they glide in, but sometimes newcomers are challenged by a loud unison call from a pair already there. Eventually more than twenty come, including five brown-headed juveniles from last spring's nests; the young still show brown feathers in their bustles as well as a pale brown spackle on the white mantle. This spring, although not yet mature, they will come into full adult plumage, at which time they will be driven off by the breeding parents.

When the cranes have fed (I forget to count the grains), they move away a little and, joined by the immatures, begin to leap and bow, using the cold twilight wind to pick them up, legs dangling, four or five feet into the air. As the sun sets behind the wooded ridge and faint stars appear in the fading blue above, the white birds dance forward and lift off the snow into the north wind. They bank away toward the Muri River, which they will follow down along the ridge on the north side of the valley to an open stretch of the Onbetsu. There they will form their line in the black water and feather-shift and preen and hunch and place their heads under their wings and settle for the night.

Soon all that may be seen in the near-dusk are the last pairs of white wings flicking upward, the black plumes of the trailing edge like ancient oriental symbols, even to the sharp black blade in the middle of the wing that points straight forward like a compass needle. At first that strange mark seems to spoil the black-white symmetry of the great wings, but in fact it intensifies their beauty, like that twisted pine-tree silhouette on a high ridge over the Muri valley that redeems the dull perfection of the moon.

SEVEN

The Accidental Paradise

So that the crane and cloud may share the lovely, lonely sky
Their passage heightens briefly
Upon the wind that wafts them imprecisely . . .
What though the wind into the void should lead them
While they live and let nothing yet divide them . . .
So for that while they may be from all places driven
Where storms are lashing or the hunt beginning:
So on through sun and moon's only too similar shining
And fly from
Everyone.
And bound for where?
For nowhere . . .
—From the opera *The Rise and Fall of the City of Mahagonny*
by Kurt Weill and Bertolt Brecht
(translated by W. H. Auden), 1931

I n the late autumn of 1950, the red-crowned and white-naped
cranes migrating southward down the Korean peninsula from the
watershed of the great Amur River and descending into the wetlands of the Chorwon basin and along the Imjin and the Han river es-
tuaries on the Yellow Sea were flared by an uproar of explosives and
artillery in immense and scaring bursts of noise and light. A few
months earlier, in June, the North Koreans, disputing the boundaries
imposed by the Western powers after World War II, had invaded the
South through the Panmunjom valley, and the Korean War was under

way. Though *Grus japonensis* and *Grus vipio* had overwintered in these marshes long before there was a border—and long before *Homo sapiens* first turned up on the peninsula—the disruption was intolerable for the wild cranes, which require broad reaches of silent open country and clean water.

It has been remarked that birds failed to develop the intelligence of mammals because avian problems can mostly be resolved by flying away from them. In any case, it seems conceivable that some of the white-naped cranes may have fled the region, joining those of their kind that did not overwinter in Korea but only tarried there to rest and feed in the course of a longer migration across the Korea Strait to Kyushu, in Japan. (Before World War II, as a captive state of the Japanese empire, Korea had remained largely undeveloped, and the natural histories of its wildlife, never well known, had passed mostly unrecorded, but Korean ornithologist P. O. Won would eventually discover that 287 white-naped cranes had been counted in the winter rice fields of Izumi, in Kyushu, as early as 1871.)

The red-crowned crane, on the other hand, had no history of migration from the mainland to the archipelago. The Amur and Zhalong *japonensis* migrate to coastal regions of China north of Shanghai (Jiangsu Province) while the Ussuri–Lake Khanka population winters in Korea.[1] Yet just as some *vipio* may have persisted on a southeasterly course down the peninsula and perhaps followed others across the salt water to Kyushu, a few red-crowneds may have wandered south and west to China, joining others of their kind at the delta of the Liao River,[2] north of the point where the Great Wall of China comes down to the Gulf of Chihli, or following those *japonensis* which continue south along the coast to Yancheng on the Yangtze delta where the largest-known flock of *japonensis*, five hundred birds or more, convenes in winter.

Some birds of both species doubtless struggled to survive in what remained of their winter habitats on the peninsula, which in those years endured grinding poverty and famine; since cranes are large, conspicuous, and good to eat, it seems most likely that the scattered birds were gunned down, poisoned, snared, and otherwise destroyed wherever found.

The armistice signed at Panmunjom in 1953 established a new frontier at the narrow waist of the peninsula between the Republic of Korea (ROK) and the Democratic People's Republic of Korea; this time, the border was consolidated by mines and tank traps, fortified embankments, and high steel fences topped with barbed wire. Aggressively manned by the hard-nosed soldiery on either side, the barriers forbade all access to a so-called demilitarized zone, roughly defined by the thirty-eighth parallel extending from the Yellow Sea all the way east to the blue Sea of Japan. The DMZ was buffered on the South Korean side by a "civilian control zone" (CCZ) of comparable width, where controlled farming—but no habitation—was permitted. Since a region from which *Homo sapiens* has been excluded is inevitably hospitable to other species, what had been created, in effect, was a no-man's-land several miles across and 149 miles long (about 375 square miles altogether), with streams and springs that remained open all winter—the most fiercely protected wildlife sanctuary anywhere on earth, and an accidental paradise for the great cranes.

Because the combatants would have been indifferent to an accidental refuge even had they realized it existed, the return of *vipio* and *japonensis* after *sapiens* stopped shooting passed as unremarked as their wartime disappearance. Not until November 1961 did an American army lieutenant named Ben King, stationed in South Korea, report to American crane authority Dr. Lawrence Walkinshaw that a flock of some twenty-three hundred white-naped cranes, apparently en route to Japan, had rested for a few days on the mudflats of the Han-Imjin estuary at the Yellow Sea.[3] In the years that followed, both *vipio* and *japonensis* were reported in the winter months along the Imjin and also in the nearby Panmunjom valley, but not until the early seventies was it discovered that both species had returned to the well-watered plain of the Chorwon basin, in the border country of the central mountains, which had mostly been abandoned after the cease-fire and had now become a grassland. The Han-Imjin estuary and the Chorwon basin—the two regions most bitterly contested during the war—had emerged as the best crane habitat left in Korea.

By January 1996, South Korea was in the throes of feverish development as one of the strongest economies among those tigerless states of the Pacific Rim called "the Asian tigers," in recognition of their ferocity in financial matters. Burdened by military rule, hazardous location, and uncertain future, the border region was lagging well behind the rest of the nation in its economy, but recently the boom had drawn attention to the former war zone as the last large tract of undeveloped land on the peninsula. Koreans on both sides were aware that from an economic point of view (the near-unanimous point of view in the new Asia), a valuable resource was being "wasted." And so there was talk of large-scale industrial and municipal development of the buffer zone, even though the North and South remained in a state of war.

The threat to two of the rarest and most beautiful of the earth's creatures in the name of commerce was real and imminent. Already the staging area for white-naped cranes in the Han estuary—Korea's greatest concentration of this species—was much degraded due to high salinity caused by dam and embankment construction upriver, with invasive reeds replacing the sedges that supplied the cranes with tubers. With elimination of a critical winter habitat, this much diminished species would be threatened further. Such a possibility was alarming to conservationists, particularly Dr. George Archibald. In the winter of 1996, he invited me to join him on a journey to the DMZ with concerned Korean friends, seeking ways to avert such a calamity.

All but destroyed during the war, when it was still a small provincial city, modern Seoul, viewed from the air at night, is a vast, radiant display of colored lights set about the inky reaches of the great Han River. On January 27, 1996, I am met at the Seoul airport by George Archibald, accompanied by Dr. Kim Sooil, an assistant professor of environmental biology at the Korean National University of Education and an adviser to the Ministry of Environment, and Mr. Chung Kwang-Joon, a Seoul businessman; like Dr. Kim, Mr. Chung is a charter member of the Korean Association for Bird Protection (KABP), founded in 1980 with the assistance and encouragement of George Archibald, in his capacity as roving ambassador for the world's cranes.

Korea sometimes calls itself "the Land of the Morning Calm," but at night, due to congested traffic caused by new construction on all sides, the trip into the city is a long one. The welcoming doorbell of my Seoul hotel room simulates birdsong, but nostalgic longing for its lost harmony with the natural world can only be elegaic in the new Korea.

Early next morning we set out for the DMZ in a glad flock of ten or twelve KABP members, all of them males in winter plumage—black-and-white checked caps with black earflaps, suitably emblazoned with red-crowned crane insignia. Brandishing a white banner that honors the ICF, they boisterously hail Dr. Archibald as "Archie" (even while addressing one another formally as "Mr. So-and-so"). "We are not yet a scientific society," confesses Dr. Kim, an informed and dedicated conservationist and the only professional naturalist in the group. "We are still working with the heart rather than the brain." Yet in his opinion, and George Archibald's, too, the KABP, which has recently established a winter feeding program for the Chorwon cranes, may be the beginning of a shift in national consciousness in regard to wildlife.

Before departure, Mr. Chung leans forward and pinches my thigh minutely here and there; he wishes to satisfy himself, as it turns out, that I am wearing long johns, for the Chorwon basin, scene of so many bitter winter battles, is the highest and coldest region in the country. "That's why I love Koreans, they're so uninhibited," comments Dr. Archibald, who is rather uninhibited himself. "At least when you run into a bad one, you know it right away."

I ride north in the good company of Kim Sooil, who teaches me a lot about crane history in this country during the drive. In Korea as in Japan, when one speaks of "the crane," one refers to the red-crowned crane, known as *turumi*. The white-naped in both countries is referred to as "the gray crane"—an entirely inadequate name for a splendid black, white, and silver-gray creature with a fierce golden eye and a fiery red disk on the side of the face—perhaps the *turumi*'s only rival as the most beautiful of the world's cranes.

Here in Korea as elsewhere in the Far East, the red-crowned crane is the esteemed companion of sages, scholars, and musicians, who are often portrayed standing face-to-face in reverent communion with a bird of their own height. A traditional Korean dance emulates the stately and elegant movements of *turumi*,[4] and old-time Koreans of the aristocracy would dress in the pure white raiment of the crane with a black headpiece constructed of bamboo and horsetail; a red sash might be worn, but only by the most eminent among them. However, during the infamous Japanese occupation of 1910–45, Dr. Kim recalls, his desperate countrymen commonly killed and consumed cranes, even sold their plumage to the Japanese oppressors.

"In Korea, too, *turumi* is well known to bring long life and good fortune, and crane images are seen everywhere at the New Year, when we

White-naped crane (*Grus vipio*)

make our wishes," Kim Sooil continues. "And now—because they are most numerous in the border region where so many young men died—the crane is our symbol of peace. And that is because reunification is our dream."

Kim Sooil's parents, born in the North, are still heartbroken by the "two Koreas," and later I note that my long-john consultant, Mr. Chung, refers to Mount Paektu, in North Korea, as "the highest mountain in our country." Like most older Koreans—he is sixty-two—he has never reconciled himself to the partition, which only extended the humiliation brought down upon his country by thirty-five years of Japanese occupation.[5]

Kim Sooil grew up in a dictatorship under the late President Park Chung Hee, who used the ideological dispute between Communism and the West to scare his people into submission, much as the North Korean government does today. The paranoia on both sides is chronically inflamed by the North's acts of hostile terrorism, and despite token efforts by a Board of Unification, most of these men are resigned to the idea that a real healing of the national wound is far away.

An ICF research associate named Fran Kaliher has spent the last six winters in Korea monitoring the cranes; her research is presently directed toward anticipating what political reunification might mean to the crane habitat and to forming plans to protect the most critical areas, notably the Chorwon, a main wintering site as well as staging area for birds migrating to and from Japan. "The site seems to be evolving into a typical Korean scene of vigorous economic development and consequent loss of biodiversity," Kaliher says. The extensive rice fields of the CCZ, restored to production in the 1970s, are especially critical to the cranes, which depend on the waste grain of the harvest for their primary food. Still uncluttered by plastic greenhouses, the valley has broad fields and paddies, streams, springs, and reservoirs that are open all winter for foraging and roosting.[6]

As recently as 1993, the Northerners withdrew from the Nuclear Nonproliferation Treaty and warned their people to ready themselves for renewed war. What is feared most in the South is a last desperate military adventure, perhaps a nuclear or chemical attack designed to obliterate the People's Enemy together with the People. The nervous South is ever strengthening and upgrading its defenses, even though everyone knows that North Korea is on the point of economic implosion and collapse. (As the South's president, Kim Young Sam, remarked that year, "North Korea is like an airplane in trouble that could crash at any time.")

(Two months after our departure, North Korea, blustering about renewed war, announced that it would no longer respect the DMZ because South Korea was illegally deploying weapons. In this winter of 1996, the people of the North were already suffering desperate shortages of food and fuel: the schools were closed for lack of heat and electricity, and bikes and oxcarts were replacing trucks and cars. By maintaining its forces at the DMZ, the United States was trying to stave off the effects of a sudden disastrous collapse of North Korea that might cause massive refugee problems and renewed war.)

Ten years ago, the presence of a third rare crane—the hooded crane, *Grus monachus*—was confirmed in the wetlands of the Naktong and Kumho rivers, in the South. The Naktong flock was especially precious because of the crowded conditions at Izumi and Araseki in Japan, where wintering *monachus* gleaned the harvested rice paddies with wintering *vipio*. By the time *monachus* was discovered in South Korea, it was already disappearing: in the economic boom that would make this country the wonder of the new Asia, a vital winter habitat for this shy woodland species of Siberia was being devastated by marsh reclamation and construction. Only a few years ago, the Naktong flock was estimated at 250 birds; this year, perhaps 80 pick disconsolately around the proliferating domes of the white vinyl greenhouses, while two of this small country's seven automakers build new factories on the last undeveloped tract across the river.

"*Grus monachus* has lost," Sooil pronounces gloomily as we drive north along the river. "There is no more hope for our hooded crane." Passionate about wildlife since boyhood, he makes no attempt to disguise his sorrow over the decimation of his country's birds, including

the waterfowl abundant until recently along the Han, where the last
wetlands and marshy edges were tidied up with concrete embankments
for the 1988 Summer Olympics.

The Korean peninsula emerged from the sea about four billion
years ago. Like much of the Pacific Rim, it had volcanic activity,
and outcroppings of igneous rock are visible in the border mountains.
Though the west part of the peninsula, where Seoul is located, slopes
gradually toward the Yellow Sea, with broad river basins and coastal
plains, much of the country is hilly or mountainous; a humid monsoon
climate supports a mixed temperate forest, now mostly gone, along
with the spirit of Keum-Su-Kang-San—"the embroidered rivers and
mountains"—as the peninsula's beautiful landscapes were once called.[7]

As the road goes north, the country changes, but in fact there is no
real country to be seen, only clusters of plastic greenhouses crowded between stubbled rice paddies and small pinched yards and habitations,
all the way from Seoul's interminable outskirts to the CCZ. Everywhere the sore eye turns, there is new construction. The only wild
things are the black-billed magpie and the tree sparrow, and even these
street-smart city scavengers are few.

The drive to the Chorwon basin is no more than seventy miles, but
the unbroken traffic, icy roads, and snow make the going slow as the
road climbs into the hills. With the ever-increasing army checkpoints
and military vehicles comes a grim shift in the atmosphere that intensifies all the way north.

Winters in Chorwon are cold and dry due to the prevailing northwest winds out of Siberia. Because the basin is part of a long valley
stretched between the two Korean capitals of Pyongyang and Seoul, the
flat Chorwon plain, with its rich and valuable volcanic soil, runs deep
into both Koreas, which is why this region, known in the war as "the
Iron Triangle," was so fiercely contested in the weeks preceding the
armistice accord of 1953. The basin itself is located in a mountain cirque

and its floor is broken by sudden small steep mountains—those strange rock towers seen in the mists of so many renderings of oriental landscapes—which because they were given strategic importance became the scenes of a huge and senseless loss of life.

Entering the CCZ, where human habitation is forbidden, one has a brief illusion of farm landscape, but military camps and fortifications obtrude everywhere, with sentry posts and bunkers on every rise. Near the first antitank barriers is the ruined shell of what was once the North Korean Communist headquarters. The only woods—thin fringes of second growth on rocky outcrops and along the roads—are surrounded by barbed-wire strands hung with inverted red triangles marked LAND MINES, some of which (but by no means all) are left over from the Korean War. At one checkpoint, an ominous sign reads, OBEDIENCE IS EQUIVALENT TO LIFE, which Dr. Kim, who served three years in the ROK Army (North Korean boys, he says, serve ten), renders cheerfully as "Obey or Be Killed."

The snow diminishes and the sun comes dimly through the winter fogs shrouding the paddies. Over a hill behind a hollow war-blackened building, two white-naped cranes in misty silhouette cross the winter morning. Farther on, a family of *turumi*, whiter than the new snow, share a paddy with white-fronted geese, and another white-naped family inspects a snowy corn patch on a rocky hillock, ignoring its decrepit scarecrow as it picks unhurriedly among the scattered stalks. (In this cold weather, *G. vipio* has drawn its white nape feathers over the crimson skin, all the way forward to its golden eyes.) Soon numerous cranes of both species appear, mostly in small family parties in fields and along embankments, rarely venturing closer than five hundred yards to any road.[8]

Before the war, the wintering cranes were probably quite few, since the waste grain in hand-harvested fields was consumed by the ducks and chickens turned out into the paddies by the peasants. Today the human inhabitants are gone and the fields are machine-harvested in early autumn; for the cranes, which appear in late October and November, the paddies offer plentiful grain, together with mudfish (loaches), frogs, and snails. (The water creatures are more prized by *japonensis* than by *vipio*, which everywhere throughout its range shows a preference for tubers.) In addition to food, the treeless fields provide protection for the wary birds, which like an unobstructed view in all directions. Readily disturbed by eagles, vultures, soldiers, farmers, and sightseers, the cranes may quit the CCZ to take refuge in the DMZ during daylight hours. Toward dusk, they return into the fields to feed and roost, usually in shallow water, where the approach of any predator can be detected.[9]

In terms of their phylogeny or evolutionary history, these two hardy *Grus* of the DMZ—perhaps the most beautiful in all their family—represent two different clusters of crane species that may have separated millions of years ago. Roughly speaking, the two groups are distinguished when alighted by the placement and extent of bare red skin on the head and the arrangement of secondary or tertial plumes of the folded wings in the bustle or tail.

All eleven species of the genus *Grus* (which includes, for the moment, the disputed Siberian and wattled cranes) show an area of comb or bare rough red skin somewhere on the head (the fully feathered head is one reason the two crowned cranes are assigned to *Balearica* and the demoiselle and blue cranes to *Anthropoides*); in the location and extent of this comb, no two *Grus* species are alike. For purposes of courtship display or to communicate aggression, the bare red may be engorged and enlarged by contraction of muscles in the neck that withdraw the feathered skin; in all *Grus*, the intensity of red increases in the breeding season. Conversely, as has been noted, the red may be dulled and contracted almost out of sight to indicate fear and submission, or at high altitudes, or in cold weather.[10]

The red-crowned crane, *Grus japonensis,* represents a cluster of closely related migratory birds which Dr. Archibald calls the Group of Five—the red-crowned, Eurasian, hooded, black-necked, and whooping cranes—in all of which the crimson patch, located on the crown, is set off to striking effect by the black-and-white patterns of the head feathers.[11] The white-naped crane, *G. vipio*—the sole migratory member of its group and the only one found north of the subtropics—belongs to the Australasian cluster called the Group of Three, typically represented by the sarus and the brolga, in which the bare red is located on the face; in the sarus and brolga, the red area extends down onto the neck. Together with the Siberian and wattled cranes, which are also red in the face, these three probe and dig for tubers deep in mud. All "digger" species—whose faces must be rinsed—have naked red or olive-green skin in the front of the head down to the bill (an adaptation possibly analogous to the naked head and neck which permit certain vultures and storks to worm into rotting carcasses without soiling and caking their feathers).

The prominent feathers that conceal the modest tails also vary according to the group. A raised bustle composed of highly modified tertial plumes of the inner wing, enhanced by an airy effect created by decomposed barbs, characterizes the Group of Five (and the sandhill); in the Group of Three (and the Siberian, wattled, and *Anthropoides* cranes), the modified tertials are draped over the tail in plumes of varying length. Since elaborate plumage might be an impediment on long migrations, the white-naped, Siberian, and demoiselle have more modest tail plumes than the sarus, blue, and wattled, which wander seasonally but are essentially nonmigratory; in the latter species, the graceful arc of the long-pointed "tail" may touch the ground. (In crowned cranes, which have longer tails to start with, bustles or plumes could only detract from their exquisite golden crowns.)

In their food habits, *japonensis* and *vipio* are typical of their groups; *vipio* mostly digs up tubers, while *japonensis* mostly picks and snatches live food and greens. The Five share long tracheas with an elaborate coiling in the sternum, a character also developed by the white-naped crane when it adopted the migratory habit; the anomaly, as usual, is the Siberian crane, which has only limited coiling of the trachea despite the longest migration of all cranes except those lesser sandhills that nest in the Siberian Arctic and return east to Alaska before migrating as far south as central Mexico.

According to the North Koreans, forty to seventy *turumi* presently winter on their east coast, and about fifty on the west. Neither locality lies far north of this border, and Kim Sooil, who recalls bitterly that the North Korean soldiery shot four of the *turumi* back in 1977, tends to view those birds as mere wanderers from these main flocks of the DMZ.[12]

"North Koreans say their conservation is better than ours because they have an official warden to prevent poaching," Sooil remarks wryly, imitating his impression of the shrill mechanical tone heard in the North: *Poaching not is possible! This is People's Republic! Poaching not is possible!* When Sooil asked the man if this were really true, the North Korean insisted, *Yes! Our Dear Leader say so!* (Fran Kaliher makes the point that the "better conservation record" claimed by the North is mainly attributable to a moribund state economy that has stifled development. This disaster for the North Korean people may one day be a blessing in terms of a healthier human environment and wildlife habitat, both sadly damaged in the frenzied capitalism which has seized the South.[13])

Last year at a crane meeting in Hokkaido, Dr. Archibald conferred with North Korean conservationists who supported the idea of preserving the DMZ. He was further encouraged by Japanese ornithologists lately returned from North Korea who said that this relatively undeveloped country still has forest marshes and large wetlands that might provide good habitat for migrant cranes—a valuable resource for ecotourism when the day comes that the peninsula is reunited.[14] Also, a movement is under way to establish a Korean Peace Bioreserve System with the DMZ at its heart but extending farther north and south, with parks, greenbelts, and faunal corridors like those being established for tigers across the border in the Russian Far East; it is hoped that North Korea will participate.[15]

In a bare paddy lies a dead water deer, encircled by a coven of huge cinereous vultures, carrion crows, and a white-tailed sea eagle. As if attracted to this morbid scene—though not to the grim feast—a northern harrier courses the brown paddies and a rough-legged hawk sits hunched on a dead tree, mobbed by five magpies. Both sea eagle and

roughleg are now endangered species in this country, and raptors are
generally rare throughout South Korea.

The water deer, a small, rufous, long-haired species in which the
male is fitted out with tusks rather than antlers, is an abundant creature
in the DMZ, and a few roe deer and wild goats—goral—may still be
found at higher elevations. The zone also claims the last foxes in this
battered country. Rumors of Asian leopard, not uncommon throughout
the peninsula until systematically exterminated after the war, remain
unfounded, since nobody has cared to test the myriad land mines and
the hair triggers of the soldiery by entering the DMZ in search of
tracks.[16] But greenfinches and a northern shrike, Siberian, rustic, and
yellow-breasted buntings, turtledoves and a lone buzzard (*Buteo buteo*)—all common birds no longer common in Korea—venture out of
the DMZ into the CCZ to join the magpies and the crows, which prosper everywhere in the wake of man's disruptions. (Under pressure from
the South Korean farmers, the boundary of the CCZ has withdrawn
steadily toward the north, narrowing the sanctuary of the cranes.)

I n the center of the valley, a high and heavily fortified earth wall sev-
ers and extinguishes the north-south rail line that once ran like a
spinal cord down the peninsula. At the foot of the wall, the old railroad
station is still intact, but the last train, war-blasted, lies in rusted ruin.
On the wall itself, overlooking the DMZ, stands a large tower with a
top-floor observatory fitted out with tourist telescopes and a diorama
depicting what lies in the forbidden territory to the north. Beneath the
tower are two high steel fences topped with rolled barbed wire, then an
open strip, close-cropped and mined, and finally the woods and undergrowth of the DMZ itself. Though all of it is second growth (of little interest beyond a study of a half century of natural plant succession), and
though George assures me that the situation is less desperate in the east
and south, this is the only undeveloped land I have seen in South Korea.

At the observatory snack bar, where we warm chilled bones with kimchi (pickled cabbage) and hot noodle soup, we are joined by Sun-woo Young Joon, director of the ecosystem conservation division of the Ministry of Environment, which Dr. Kim serves as an adviser. Mr. Sun-woo, a tall, open-faced young man, is sincere and hardworking, Kim Sooil assures us, and indeed he takes very careful notes as Dr. Archibald explains why this unspoiled zone is so critical to *turumi*, South Korea's "bird of peace," and also why it is far more critical to the country's future than any of the proposed alternatives, which include a brand-new "Chorwon City," featuring some sort of North-South university, a nuclear waste site for the country's ten or twelve reactors, and yet another auto factory which South Korea would be better off without, to judge from its choked highways and soiled air. (More recently, Chorwon officials proposed a parking lot that will feature a concrete crane statue covering a spring that is used frequently by the real ones.) The *turumi* that winter here, George continues, represent almost a quarter of all red-crowned cranes on the Asian mainland; as for the "gray cranes," even those that do not overwinter depend on the DMZ and CCZ for four to six weeks before traveling on to Japan. In short, no other region in Korea, North or South, is so critical for crane conservation. The wild creatures know nothing of such man-made folly as the "CCZ" and "DMZ," but they recognize a sanctuary when they see one.

Whether or not the two countries are reunified, conservationists hope to promote this border region for tourism, a more lasting and constructive source of income than the onrushing development the Koreans have in mind. What the ICF and the KABP are urging is a true crane sanctuary with a roadless area in which most of the dike tracks between paddies will be closed to visitors on foot to minimize human disturbance. Also, George says, it would be wonderful to bury the utility poles and wires, hard to see in winter mists, which cause so many crane fatalities each year. Most important of all is a continued ban on vinyl greenhouses in former paddies, which eliminate the birds' main source of food. (The ban is already under pressure from the farmers, who resent any conservation strictures that might devalue their land. "Dry-ground agriculture," with its year-round utility and its fast-moving specialty crops such as fresh green vegetables in wintertime and fresh-cut flowers—"planeloads of roses for the Moscow mafia," as George puts it—is a lot more profitable than humble rice from the ancient earth.)

Ideally, the roadless area could be enjoyed from an observatory and tourist center for those who come to see the DMZ (including the two tunnels into South Korea which the northerners have been caught digging in the past few years); the sentry posts and army lookouts could serve as blinds for the viewing of rare cranes, which for the moment are increasing: in 1993, an estimated 292 red-crowneds and 346 white-napeds overwintered here, with perhaps 2,000 migrants from Kyushu passing through in spring.

Like all enlightened conservationists, Dr. Archibald knows that parks and sanctuaries work best when local interests and opinions are considered. What he suggests to Mr. Sunwoo is ecotourism from which local people benefit right from the start—not a strict refuge but some sort of "people's park" that allows for private use of the best farmland. In a country poor in arable land, the rich Chorwon soil which is said to grow Korea's finest rice is worth billions of dollars; its local owners will never relinquish it without a fight, which might include a vengeful slaughter of the cranes.

In 1970, the red-crowned, white-naped, and hooded cranes were granted official designation as Natural Monuments Nos. 202, 203, and 228, respectively. Chorwon itself has become Natural Monument No. 245, and the Han estuary is No. 250. But as Mr. Sunwoo is doubtless aware, monument status protects neither birds nor habitat. Mr. Sunwoo assures us that the Ministry of Environment is seriously considering alternatives to industrial and municipal development. He seems sincere, perhaps because we want so badly to believe him.

Over the landscape in the winter dusk comes an insensate blare of amplifiers—propaganda hurled by each ideology at the other's head, in a Babel of hollow metallic voices lost in a tinny din of martial music. "People's Revolutionary Opera," George conjectures. On the South Korean side, an empty church serves only to support an enormous cross.

The cross is visible from near and far, as if to show to those godless Communists across the no-man's-land that the God who permitted the ungodly slaughter in this place of so many thousands of young men, white, black, and Asian, may still have relevance.

I drive back to Seoul with So Il Sung, a former journalist turned freelance photographer, who like most if not all of the KABP members in our party understands the significance of the DMZ, remarking of his own accord that no comparable "wilderness" is left in South Korea. It is evening now, long after dark, yet heavy road traffic with blaring horns and glaring lights plagues us all the way south into the city. Of necessity, Mr. So has grown used to these poisonous fumes, but he does not like them. "Too many people, too many cars," he sighs. Seoul has 10 million people, with 450 new mouths for every 110 that close for good each day; the adjoining city of Inchon, on the coast, boasts 4 million. Though the government recommends one child per family (and has instituted economic "disadvantages," according to Mr. So, for those who indulge themselves in more), the numbers of new humans—and new housing, new cars, and new highways—grow and grow. On the city outskirts north of Seoul rise garbage mountains built hundreds of feet into the sky, crests graded flat in glittering plateaus to provide more space for human habitation. These artificial eminences have replaced the real hills that were bulldozed flat in the early throes of the nation's modern progress.

The Freedom Highway north along the Han is the latest expression of the national yearning for reunification. Opened to traffic in 1992, the new highway (and a wide strip between highway and riverside) is strongly fenced and heavily patrolled by ROK soldiers against invasion or infiltration from the river and its estuary. On its inland side

lie bottomlands where Ilsan City has been created to take care of Seoul's
overflowing population. The rest of this floodplain is covered by white
vinyl greenhouses like pale fungi, thousands upon thousands, mile after
square mile, with no room for a fallen sparrow in between.

Near the confluence of the Imjin and Han rivers, the mountains of
North Korea rise from the morning mist. A flock of twelve to fifteen
vipio crosses the river bottoms of the Imjin delta below Imjinjak, where
North Korean refugees living in the South come to send prayers and
express reverence for their lost homeland, and where a few months ago,
five North Korean "spies" were shot to death crossing the river—by a
"fledgling" ROK soldier, growls Kim Sooil, who denies that those unlucky North Koreans might have been defectors rather than agents.

At Imjinjak, our party must show special passes before crossing the
Imjin into the CCZ. After so many miles of traffic and construction,
this landscape of fields mixed with scrub woods is refreshing, even
though the woods are second growth, heavily land-mined. At one place
where we stop along the way, my kind KABP friends yell in alarm
when I step off the tarred road to see a bird; from where they stand beside our van, they cannot see the farm track I am using.

A UN checkpoint manned in part by U.S. soldiers is the only place
along the border where outsiders may enter the DMZ itself. Here our
party is taken in hand by a hard-faced ROK military policeman bearing
prominent sidearms and a hand grenade. With an official blue pennant
fluttering from the car window, we proceed north to Taesongdong, a
token village on the DMZ border, where after more paperwork, we
are permitted to climb to the ROK Army observation tower. Young
soldiers in camouflage greens automatically cover their clipboards to
guard top-secret contents from our prying eyes; they warn us with
rough gestures against taking pictures. Even our viewing of the empty
valley is treated with frowns of professional suspicion, since they cannot
know—and would never understand—that these foreign devils have
not come to ferret out defenses but only to peer about, looking for
cranes. When we leave the tower a few minutes later, the soldiers jump
to their feet with shouts and wild salutes.

Taesongdong is known as "Freedom Village": the blue-and-orange-trimmed North Korean housing directly across no-man's-land is called "Peace Village." Unlike Freedom Village, Peace Village appears devoid of human life, and the mountains beyond it are stripped bald, as if to wipe out the last shadow or cranny where some counterrevolutionary or capitalist running dog might seek to hide. Peace Village claims the tallest flagpole in the world—as high as a radio tower, which it resembles—and it flies a gigantic North Korean flag of red, white, and blue. Here at Freedom Village, the pole is less huge but the flag is bigger— "the biggest in Korea," Dr. Kim assures us.

Below Taesongdong is a sort of pagoda in an artificial grove of pine and cedar, marking the place where uncounted thousands of soldiers on both sides—no doubt much like these young boys watching us now—fought and screamed in agony and terror before they died. In this genocidal epoch when the human animal is destroying its own kind almost everywhere on earth, what hope can there be for cranes and tigers? And yet . . .

Beyond the pagoda rise more walls and more fortified steel fences. Miraculously, a water deer scampers over an embankment and vanishes into the scrawny growth around a bunker. The fortifications descend to the valley floor, the only place where patrolled farming is permitted; the bullock cart that creaks along, running the gauntlet of weapons, seems lonely indeed. Here the fallow wetlands of the DMZ are being obliterated by drainage and cultivation, and inevitably, the cranes are missing. George Archibald shakes his head, ready to leave. He is disheartened by their absence from this valley where twenty years ago he recorded ten *japonensis* families—forty-two birds altogether—and several hundred *vipio*.

Our permit allows a visit to Panmunjom, where the official border neatly bisects a wooden table on which the armistice was signed. Here one may visit a North Korean museum that reveals American atrocities, but we decline this educational opportunity, electing to go bird-watching instead. With two armed ROK marching behind, we walk the DMZ's south border on dirt roads that might resemble country lanes were it not for that amplified blare echoing across the landscape. Before long, we are halted by a roving patrol led by a large leashed dog. One of our guards has retraced his steps a ways to direct a vehicle, violating the rules by leaving our official escort one man short. In this urgent military crisis, twenty men unlimber automatic rifles and crouch on the road shoulder in full combat alert until our guard returns and we are permitted to proceed.

Oblivious of all this martial nonsense, a water deer fawn scrambles over a grassy bank, and flocks of pretty parrotbills forage busily in the sedges. We record a spotted woodpecker and some raptors, doves, and pheasants, then a Daurian redstart and a flock of Naumann's thrushes, blowing in fits and twitters through the winter trees.

On a frozen pond the ice creaks eerily with lugubrious deep gurgles that echo up and down the edges, as if a dragon had been awakened from cold-blooded torpor in the mud below. Dr. Archibald describes how from this place in 1974, he saw a small flock of white birds he could not identify flying across the bare mountainsides across the valley. Eventually the birds turned and came straight for him across the DMZ, but not until they alighted right in front of him did he realize that they were crested ibises, a species thought to have been extinct in Korea for several decades.

Two winters later, he tried in vain to capture a lone survivor. The ibis flew into his mist net, but because the frozen net was brittle, the bird broke through. It did not appear the following winter, when he supposed that the species had probably disappeared from the peninsula.[17]

Rumors persist of a single crested ibis that abides near an old shaman's hut by the Imjin River. Though no one has much confidence in such a tale, we visit this place because it overlooks a long stretch of good crane habitat across the Imjin. Entering the winter paddies, we follow an embankment path toward the river. In a corner of the snowy fields, the brave men of the KABP, bright checked caps flashing, discover mist nets set for songbirds left by the local people. One net is twisted by the struggles of two buntings and a parrotbill whose bodies the trappers have not bothered to retrieve; our men break the bamboo net poles with excited shouts. Next, they find a poisoned goose that apparently reached the ditch before it died, and Dr. Kim recalls that five poisoned *vipio* were found on these flats last year. No shooting is permitted in the CCZ, but man is never at a loss when it comes to killing. "What a species we are!" George Archibald exclaims, after this long morning, astonished anew by the destructive and murderous proclivities of man.

Across the Imjin, which is clogged with chunks of dirty ice, the terrain is torn up and raw, and scarred by the dead chemical colors of earth-moving machines and plastic sheeting, flapping like blue shrouds in the winter wind. In this place, a mile upriver from the Freedom Bridge, the South Koreans are building a new span for another new highway to the border, against the great day of reunion with the North. The ice upriver from the bridge is a roosting place for thousands of white-fronted and bean geese, and stalking the paddies on river bench above, on the littered edges of the bridge construction, is a flock of twenty-six white-naped cranes, which in this setting look unnatural, somehow degraded.

O f the two thousand *vipio* that fly south through the Koreas, about half are going by way of Chorwon, and perhaps 85 percent of the whole migration will fly on to south Japan. A few may join the hooded cranes at Naktong River—unlike *japonensis*, which rarely ventures farther south than this border region. The *vipio* and *monachus* that winter in Japan return north to breeding territories in China and Russia by way of the Koreas, resting not only at the Han-Imjin and the Chorwon but the Kumya estuary wetlands on North Korea's eastern coast and also the Tumen River delta just across the Chinese border in Jilin Province.[18]

The wintering cranes of the Han-Imjin region are thought to come south from breeding territories in the Three Rivers plain in northeast Heilongjiang, while those at Chorwon may have followed a more easterly flyway from the Amur drainage and around Lake Khanka, on the Russo-Chinese border. Since the red-crowned crane is no longer found in South Korea below the CCZ, and since its total numbers in the wild—including the nonmigratory population in Hokkaido—are less than half those of the white-naped cranes, the loss of Korean wintering grounds would seem to be more serious for this species.

China today has six to eight hundred wintering red-crowned cranes; Japan has about six hundred. Either population could decline in the coming years due to loss of habitat. However, as George Archibald points out, the winter sanctuaries of *japonensis* along the China coast appear more stable than any important winter territory of the white-naped crane, which is threatened not only by the proposed development of the DMZ and CCZ but by encroaching development and crowding at Izumi and by the disruption of the Poyang lakes ecosystem threatened by the completion of the Three Gorges dam. Therefore the potential loss of the Han estuary might be most harmful to this more abundant species. With reunification, the Han-Imjin estuary may become an industrial port. Already, degradation of the river below Seoul has spoiled the delta, making it increasingly unlikely that the white-naped cranes once abundant here will return to overwinter.

In the CCZ, a *japonensis* family is feeding in the vicinity of some new bunker construction where little chimneys like weird metal mushrooms stick up out of the ground, permitting the humans crouched below to breathe. At Imjinjak, a large flock of wild ducks rests in dry rice fields just below the bridge, and farther down the estuary thousands of waterfowl of many species are scattered out across the pewter water. However, since these wetlands are fenced off, the only people close enough to appreciate the birds are the armed patrols in green camouflage garb, faces daubed with simulated mud and modern helmets concealed under humble straw, guarding their republic from assaults upon the coast that seem less and less likely to take place.

Weather is sudden in Korea, and a blizzard sweeps in from the Yellow Sea (known to Koreans as the Western Sea) over vast mudflats laid bare by an outgoing tide even greater in its rise and fall than the tide in the Bay of Fundy. *Japonensis* in particular likes to probe these saline mudflats for crustaceans, but any chance of locating the white cranes swirls away in flurries of thick snow. We have seen few cranes in the Han-Imjin, and there seems small doubt that their numbers are diminishing.

With the Naktong habitat of the hooded crane all but destroyed, and the Han-Imjin under so much stress, it appears that the last refuge of the rare cranes will be the Chorwon basin, where for the moment their numbers appear stable. In ancient times, before settlement by early agriculturalists, the rich Chorwon soil supported a noble forest in which tiger, leopard, and black bear were quite common. In the centuries that followed, the forest was cleared away, and the wild creatures had to adapt to mankind as best they could. Then came the din of modern war, and afterward a great silence. As some wild things recovered and the land cleansed itself, the migrant birds returned. The cranes increased until their rolling call was heard up and down the valley. But now, as another century draws to a close, it appears that the cranes may fall silent again.

To see such creatures in these sullen borderlands, skirting barbed-wire fences and embankments, highway construction and utility poles, in a ruptured landscape torn by loud and unnatural noises, is deeply saddening. One can only marvel at the endurance of wild animals and their strong instinct toward survival, which offer such hope as we have that these magnificent creations of our land and life can persist long enough for mankind to come to its senses and leave a place for them. Unless we act swiftly to protect the few redoubts these wild cranes have left, then they must fail.

However our own species decides its fate, the last great cranes will fly north and south as they have done throughout the long millenniums, all unaware that this strange upright beast whose violent activities have doomed their kind is the only one with the capacity to save them.

Toward dusk on that first afternoon at Chorwon, large crane flocks appeared at a point just north of Hagel-ri, or Sapsulbong, an abrupt small mountain 920 feet high that stands by itself in the middle of the basin. During the Korean War, Sapsulbong acquired its nickname—Ice Cream Mountain—perhaps because of the cone shape it acquired from relentless battering by artillery on both sides. This nondescript small hill changed hands fourteen or fifteen times in the fierce fighting that took place in the last weeks of the war, before its costly inclusion in South Korea could be settled at Panmunjom. After the war, peasants excavating the rubble around its base to make new rice fields unearthed a pit of human skulls and bones several yards deep. Off to the west, in the mists of the mountain cirque, rises Pork Chop Hill, another hellish slaughter ground of that aimless war that broke the Korean homeland in half and remains in bitter stalemate fifty years later.

Watching these great and ancient birds flying through the mists in a damp cold where so many young soldiers quaked in fear and wretchedness, watching them stalk these silent winter fields veined with so much human blood, one is beset by somber, confused feelings. "I feel all the more blessed that I can observe such beautiful creatures, knowing the horrors other men had to endure here years ago," George Archibald murmurs quietly, sharing my own dark mood. In the dimming sun, we watch the birds drift down over the silent land. To protect these cranes as harbingers of peace and morning calm—how respectful that would be, however late, to the young soldiers on both sides who lost their lives so horribly to no sane purpose.

EIGHT

Outback

Now they are standing close together
Others are flying
Closely approaching
Others are following from Karangarri

They are remembering
Now they are telling
Others are flying from Karangarri . . .
—*Didjeridu* song, traditional Aborigine

Until recent decades, the only member of the crane family known in Australia was the brolga, a beautiful pearl-gray bird with an eight-foot wingspan, which is still widespread throughout the northern and eastern regions of the country but much diminished everywhere else; its greatest remaining concentrations occur along Queensland's east coast in the large freshwater swamplands of *bulkuru* sedge in which it spends most of the year, and from Arnhem Land east around the belly of the Gulf of Carpentaria to the Cape York Peninsula—hot, saturated, and inhospitable regions of trackless swamp and soggy flatwoods, crocodile rivers and savannas. It is also found in limited numbers in southern New Guinea, "from Frederick Henry Island to the Fly Basin."[1]

Then, in March 1961, the brolga's sovereignty was challenged by exciting reports from Queensland, where a flock of sixty to eighty odd-looking "brolgas" had turned up in the croplands of a farm community on the Atherton Plateau where no cranes had ever been reported. The birds departed in November with the onset of rains, but in March of the following year they returned on the winds of the dry season, bringing others with them. In 1967, three juveniles turned up in a flock of twenty-four adults, with three more the following year. Though their breeding grounds were still unknown, a few of these strange cranes were being reported from the eastern side of the great Gulf of Carpentaria, near the small Outback settlements at Normanton, Burketown, and the Archer River.[2]

One reason, perhaps, why the Atherton birds had passed unnoticed was that, like the brolga, the strangers were uniform gray in color with red on the upper neck and head; at any distance, the two species are quite similar. But in 1961 observers noted that these Atherton cranes appeared slightly larger and darker than the brolga. Their legs were pinkish-red instead of grayish-black and the bare red skin of the head extended three inches farther down the neck—differences that might well have escaped the untrained eye when the two were not standing close together. Also, the Atherton bird lacked the discreet black wattle seen under the brolga's chin. With confirmation of these field marks, the birds were identified as sarus cranes of the Southeast Asian race, *Grus antigone sharpii*, which presumably had strayed from New Guinea across the one-hundred-mile Torres Strait to the Cape York Peninsula of Queensland. The Atherton discovery was all the more exciting because this eastern sarus, formerly common in seasonal wetlands, lowland plains, and river deltas, had all but disappeared in the long years of chronic warfare in Southeast Asia and was now an endangered bird. (Other than a native bustard, the brolga's closest known kin in Australia before the advent of the sarus was the plains wanderer, a small quail-like bird of the dry Outback which ventures everywhere on tiptoe, as if unnerved by its awesome responsibility as the sole representative of its family; like so many of its relatives, it is presently endangered.)

Though fascinated by reports of *G. a. sharpii* at Atherton, George Archibald's main purpose on his first trip to Australia in 1974 was to study the endemic brolga, *G. rubicundus*, which was readily observed during the dry season at the agricultural farms in the dry Outback of northwestern Australia, where sorghum and cotton crops were irrigated by reservoirs that filled during the monsoon rains. There the big birds not only picked at the new sorghum plants but dug deep and yanked them, roots and all. The farmers refrained from shooting or poisoning "the red-necked cranes," which had become increasingly unpopular.

In his field notes, Dr. Archibald described how the brolgas took wing in the full heat of midmorning. "Normally a few cranes launch themselves into the air, more follow at intervals, and soon the whole sky is filled with brolgas . . . a true aerial ballet, with birds climbing skyward on thermals and becoming finally pillars of brolgas floating up and down on layers of hot air. Softer and softer their voices become as they gain altitude and finally vanish into the blue sky. I have often wondered just what the brolgas do way up in the heavens; I imagine they soar around in the cool air looking over the vast brown landscape below . . . Throughout this part of the day, the world loses the brolga—not even their calls can be heard."[3] That year he captured three pairs of "desert cranes" for transferral to the ICF in Baraboo, Wisconsin, where they duly became the first of their species ever to reproduce outside Australia.

Because the eastern sarus reported from Atherton had escaped notice until 1961, it was still assumed that these birds had arrived in recent times; it also appeared that they were multiplying rapidly. In 1984, when the flock's numbers were estimated at about eight hundred, or ten times more than the first flock reported at Atherton, its nests were finally located in a remote and desolate equatorial region of swamp forest and savanna some twenty miles inland from the Gulf of Carpentaria in far west Queensland. Since this was also a known breeding ground of *rubicundus*, the potential competition between sibling species using the same habitat raised intriguing questions.

Accompanied by an Australian colleague, Andrew Haffenden, Dr. Archibald traveled that year to the Morr Morr cattle station in that region. The two confirmed that the sarus was not only established but that its nests outnumbered brolga nests in a ratio of approximately three to two, which suggested that the sarus might drive out the brolga in competing for food and nesting territory or overwhelm the endemic bird through interbreeding.[4]

At this time, it was still assumed that these "new" cranes were eastern sarus, *G. a. sharpii*. In 1991, DNA tests would determine that the Australian population was genetically distinct. Reclassified as a geographic race or subspecies, the bird was awarded its own trinomial, *Grus antigone gilli*, in honor of a Mrs. Gill who first reported it at Atherton.

Just as the eastern sarus is smaller and darker than the Indian, *gilli* is smaller and darker than *sharpii*, with darker ear patches and a more fully feathered throat. Its DNA (as well as its ethology and morphology) established that while it had spread from the East Indies to the island continent rather recently in the long span of geologic time, it had not arrived in the 1960s nor even in this century but twenty-five thousand years ago, at the very least. (The ancestral brolga had appeared long, long before, perhaps during the Pleistocene when the seas withdrew into the Ice Age glaciers, leaving vast marshes on the Sula shelf and the Gulf of Carpentaria. Even today, when deep straits part the high mountainous islands, there are no real obstacles to the wanderings of cranes.)

More than a decade would pass before Dr. Archibald returned to the Morr Morr station to monitor the progress of the new cranes, tending to crane business in Korea on the way. "I'd love to repeat the survey to determine who is winning," he wrote me in November 1994. "Let's go together. It would be a super chance for you to experience the Aborigines"—the station was owned and run by native people—"and we could gain fresh insight into the interactions of *antigone* and *rubi-*

cundus." Our expedition would take place during the three months of the rainy season—"the Wet"—when both species established territories and nested, with a visit to Korea on the way.

In early February 1996, we flew south from Seoul to Cairns, on the northeast Queensland coast, where we were joined by Andrew Haffenden and his wife, Suzanne. Next morning we headed west by chartered plane, climbing the steep jungle wall of the coast escarpment. The light aircraft flared numbers of big sulphur-crested cockatoos from the rain forest beneath, but at the top of the escarpment, the white cockatoos, rain forest, city, and sea dropped away abruptly behind the green horizon. The plane leveled off and headed west across the base of Cape York Peninsula, a forbidding landscape of dry rock plateaus and hard ravines gouged deep by narrow torrents; the few dim foot tracks wandered off into sparse scrub without the smallest trace of destination. To the north rose a high inland escarpment—the peninsular divide, where caves with Aboriginal rock paintings had been located, Andrew told us. A lone glinting in the distance to the south was the agricultural settlement on the Atherton Plateau where the sarus cranes were first reported.

In the last two hundred miles of the flight to Morr Morr, not a sign of man was seen, nor a distant smoke. Not one dim path crossed the scrub and rusty iron soil of the dry plateaus, the jagged steep ravines. In such emptiness, the light aircraft felt inconsequential, like a blown feather. Eventually, the terrain relented, descending slowly as broad swamps appeared and small creeks gathered into rivers, flowing north and west to the vast and empty gulf, but the brown land greened only a little as it subsided into equatorial heat. Beyond Gilbert River, muddy truck tracks could be seen, and scattered cattle, then the glint of tin roofs and the straight scar of a grass airstrip; strange lumps humped toward the brush edges as the plane came in. The grassy savanna on both shoulders of the airstrip turned out to be fine stomping ground for *Macropus agilis*, the agile wallaby, which cavorted in dozens like huge dark brown rabbits.

The Morr Morr Pastoral Company, forty-seven miles by rough muddy track from the nearest settlement at Normanton, runs twenty-seven thousand head of cattle on a ranch extending forty miles north to south by sixty miles east to west. In the dry season, its scattered thousands of beef cattle are rounded up by cowboys, assisted these days by a helicopter, and the cowboys are mostly Aborigines.

According to an old native man named Finley Gilbert, interviewed in 1984 by Archibald and Haffenden, the first white men from the gulf coast had come to the Gilbert River region in horse-drawn wagons early in the century, establishing homesteads before sending for their wives and children. This had happened during his parents' lifetime, Finley said. His people were terrified that the white men would "shoot them out" as they had done to other native bands up and down the coast; instead, the whites gave them bags of flour laced with strychnine, and many died. (According to Andrew, the story of the poisoned flour is widespread and near-mythic among the Aborigines; while genocidal use of strychnine certainly occurred, its use in this region has never been confirmed.)

Brought up in the bush along the Gilbert River, some eight miles from Morr Morr (formerly Delta Downs, established in 1912), Finley Gilbert was known on the station by the name of his home territory. His people preferred meat to plants, taking wallabies, turtles, monitor lizards, and freshwater crocodiles in all seasons, also emus, cockatoos, and bower birds, snakes, fish killed by spears or by poison from a tree pulp tossed into the water, and the eggs of ducks, geese, and cranes. While the men hunted, the women gathered honey, figs, lily tubers, nuts, and berries, in addition to wild yams, turnips, and bananas. The band was locally migratory, which permitted the wild foods to recover quickly from seasonal harvest.

In the rainy season, Finley's people would set up a little circle of palm-leaf shacks with a fire in the middle. Each man would build his own shack. If a man was a good hunter, he was given a wife; if he was very good, he might have three or four. Men fought to the death over their women, with the winner taking the wives; for women, the penalty for adultery was execution. When food was abundant, the tribe held a

festival called a corroboree, building a bonfire and eating before dancing and singing began; many of the songs and dances honored cranes.

At Morr Morr, Finley Gilbert said, there had been a village of about
one hundred people. When the whites came, his people were divided
up between the cattle stations, penned like beasts, and worked as slaves.
When they ran away, trackers were paid to hunt them down and bring
them back for punishment. Meanwhile, they were decimated by the
whites' diseases.

The workers had no days off and no pay—and no concept of pay,
says Andrew. Most of them didn't really run away but went on walkabouts for spiritual or personal reasons. They had no concept of nine-
to-five jobs that awaited them day after day, much less forty-hour
weeks. A man did what was necessary to take care of his present needs;
if other matters came up, he attended to them. When he ran out of
what was needed, he would work again. The white people did not understand this. They imagined the "Abos" were running off and were
therefore lazy, feckless, unreliable—in short, what the white man has
habitually thought about forest people in Africa and the Indian people
in the Americas and traditional people everywhere who are not yet
bound by rigid linear concepts such as time-as-money that constrict the
human spirit in the West. Even so, the station housed, clothed, doc-
tored, fed, furnished tobacco, and otherwise took care of the band's subsistence, though as few as four out of twenty people (children included)
might be working.

Toward the end of the 1960s, the Aborigines were granted equal pay
and the right to vote; they were no longer maintained by the stations.
Unaccustomed to cash or the concept of saving, the ranch hand would
spend his salary at once, often on alcohol, and was therefore unable to
take care of the others, which, as Andrew says, led to a "breakdown in
the traditional sharing pattern in the group, which led to the loss of
other important aspects of the culture."

Some years ago, the government bought the million-acre Delta
Downs station for $2.5 million, renamed it Morr Morr, and gave it to
the native people, who duly hired a white man to manage it. Finley
died in 1990 at age eighty-seven, and his remnant band lives mostly at

Normanton in a sad state of alcoholic decrepitude and poverty, like so many displaced native peoples the world over.[5] Such tragedies are perhaps inevitable—Andrew thinks so. Overcoming the problems by ensuring only opportunity for those able to benefit is the stark solution, in his view, and one that has worked positively in certain areas of the Outback, "but at great cost to most of a generation, and with the inevitable loss of much of the knowledge carried by the native people."

In 1984, the station employed nineteen stockmen, or cowhands, as well as cooks, handymen, vegetable farmers, and fence builders. By the time of our visit in early 1996, the crew had drifted away to Normanton for the rainy season. I wanted to inquire about traditions of crane myth, songs, and dances in this region, but the one Aborigine who came through the station during the six days of our stay spoke little English, seeming quite content in his own silence.

The Australian sarus, though undiscovered by the whites until 1961, has long been distinguished by the Aborigines as "the brolga that dipped its head in blood" or "the red-legged brolga"; the true brolga has blackish legs. (George Archibald's Aboriginal guide called it "Big Red.") In any case, the native hunters preferred the red-legged bird because it was larger and fatter than the brolga. It was also warier and more difficult to hunt; the sarus takes wing quickly when disturbed, while the brolga usually stalks away before deciding to take flight. Sometimes the brolga is referred to by white ranchers as "the native companion," since captive chicks raised by Aborigines may follow their owners on foot travels and even on the job on sheep or cattle stations.

Perhaps because of its narrow range and roughly similar appearance, the sarus had never become a totemic creature like the brolga, which in the myths makes its first appearance "long ago back in the Dreamtime." In a typical account, the best dancer in the land was a beautiful young girl named Brolga, who imitated the dances of the birds and made up wonderful new ones of her own, so that people of other tribes often came to see her. One day, Brolga went off by herself to a big coolibah tree on the dry red plain near her camp.

Brolga began to dance in its shade, moving with the shadow of the old tree's branches. As the wind swayed the tree, Brolga swayed, dancing out into the sunlight. The early morning sun fell on her face, and with her arms floating out, she spun for the sheer joy of it. As little puffs of dust rose from her feet, an evil spirit, Waiwera, saw Brolga and decided he must have her. Quickly he spun himself into a whirlwind, a willy-willy, and flew down onto the plain and swept her up in a great roaring of wind. When her tribe came hunting for her at the old coolibah tree, her tracks had been covered by the wind, but they followed the track of the willy-willy and at last caught up with Brolga; bravely, they rushed at Waiwera, hurling spears and boomerangs. Waiwera spun Brolga upwards, spiraling her away into the sky, and poor Brolga vanished forever. But at that moment a child cried out, Look! A strange bird we have never seen before! And from behind a coolibah stepped a beautiful tall gray bird that slowly stretched its wings and began to dance before it flew away—a bird which the Aboriginals, ever since that day, have named for Brolga, because Waiwera had been unable to take with him Brolga's elegance and love of dancing.[6]

As a totemic animal, which may be invoked in time of mourning and even circumcision, the brolga is the subject of numberless tales, dances, songs, and ceremonies. According to Andrew, brolga stories are the responsibility of those who hold the brolga totem, which is often no more than a small stick buried near the ceremonial ground.[7] Before it rotted, its custodian would dig it up and wander about until he found another stick that contained the brolga spirit. Usually the totem would be passed down to his son, and nobody performed a brolga dance or song without the custodian's approval.[8]

Songs and dances at corroborees in the heart of crane range in northern Australia are performed by men only—a solo or paired dance, or a group of dancers in a circle or in a line, "advancing with bird-like hops, arms outstretched like wings. The chirping sounds made by the dancers intermingle . . . with the bird-call refrains of the singers."[9] Generally they are accompanied by the dry rhythms of beating-sticks and the long hollow wood horn called the *didjeridu.*[10]

> Now they are standing close together
> Others are flying from Mamururi
> Up there circling Ngiwalkirri
>   *Kurruwurwur!*

Kurruwurwur is a name for the brolga; another is *wuraywuraywuray.* Unlike the white man's rendition, "curaduck," both native words wonderfully evoke its low, rolling, plaintive voice.[11]

> Now they are standing close together
> Others are flying
> Closely approaching
> Others are following from Karangarri
>
> They are remembering
> Now they are telling
> Others are flying from Karangarri . . .

Although Morr Morr continues to be owned by the tribal people, it is presently managed by a young white man, Darren Gakowski, who lives in a small house in a compound off the end of the airstrip with his wife, Christine, and their small children; his mechanic and handyman at the station is a Polish immigrant and lifelong loner known as Wally. Husky and affable, Gakowski is a sometime bronc and bull rider, and he is curious about North American rodeos, espe-

Brolga (*Grus rubicundus*)

cially the Calgary Stampede, which he is happy to hear I once attended.

Near the buildings, one is greeted by the loud harangue of the big blue-winged kingfisher called the kookaburra, a ubiquitous bird wherever it occurs; it shouts after us on this first afternoon in the thick heat as we head off on a track into the swamp forest, on the first hunt for cranes and nests. The forest here is limited almost entirely to gum trees (eucalypts) in a broad range of species, including—to name only a few—the pale ghost gum and the lemon-scented gum, the beefwood and bloodwood, silver box, gutta-percha, and the Darwin woolly butt, lightly interspersed with cabbage palms, pandanus, melaleuca,[12] and an acacia species known as lancewood.

Down the cattle trail in the wet open woods fly small swift flocks of beautiful red-winged parrots. We enjoy four species of large cockatoos, including the uncommon red-tailed black and the common pink galah. An immense goatsucker called the tawny frogmouth mimics a large gray wood knot on a limb; in a swamp pool are primitive pied geese, whose partially webbed feet permit roosting in trees. A pied butcher-bird (named for its shrike-like habit of spiking lizards and other prey on twigs like cuts of meat) delights us with its mellifluous bold song. Otherwise few perching birds are seen or heard, for a severe hurricane in early January has devastated their habitat in the weak trees of the gum forest. The only cranes seen all afternoon are a small group of sarus, crossing low over the stunted and storm-broken wood.

A t Morr Morr, heavy rains arrive in the late afternoon and continue in rushing bursts throughout the night, with perhaps as much as four inches by dawn; then the air clears, and the soft mornings are beautiful. Darren Gakowski, on his way to Normanton for camp supplies, drops us off on the track about five miles from the station, in the savanna woodland where the farthest nest sites were located on the 1984 expedition. At once we find brolgas establishing a site, to judge from the fact that the pair does not fly but stalks swiftly away through the high grass only to circle back between the trees; when they take wing, it is only to cross in front of us and alight again not far away, bare faces gleaming in the morning light. The brolga's whole face is rough red comb with sparse black bristles; under its chin is a discreet black wattle, and like the sarus (and the wattled crane), it has a bare crown of olive-green-gray skin. Otherwise, this five-foot bird is an elegant pearl gray, shading to a darker gray in the primary and secondary feathers of the wing. (Both species may be tinged reddish-brown from the ferric oxides in the water.)[13]

As a rule, the brolga nests on higher ground than the sarus, safe from potential flooding, an adaptation that may reflect its longer experience in this terrain.[14] These brolgas seem to be nesting late, possibly because of the great storm here in December. Not wishing to distract them from their courtship, we move on quickly, hunting northeast through the woods in the general direction of the cattle station.

On a reed platform at the edge of a clear savanna pool set about with white ghost gum and shaded by an overhanging tree is a sarus nest containing two large ivory eggs glowing like treasures.[15] Nests of the Australian sarus are often unsuccessful; on the other hand, their long nesting season permits them ample time for a second attempt. During this period, *G. a. gilli* undergoes a complete molt of its flight feathers, which renders it flightless for six weeks. By contrast, the brolga never molts so completely that it becomes flightless, nor does it roost in water at night but perches instead on a small elevation, perhaps in deference to its only predator, the crocodile.

Toward midmorning, the brolgas spiral upward on the thermals, seeking relief from the steaming heat; we only wish we could soar with them, to escape the waterlogged windless air and the wet heat in the lungs and the pernicious leeches and mosquitoes.[16] Here and there, a thin shade provides protection from an equatorial sun that burns hot while remaining mostly hidden behind the heavy gray shrouds that gather for the rains of afternoon.

Although oppressed by the fierce and humid climate, I love this morose landscape for its emptiness and silence, unbroken by man-made sounds of any kind, and also for a paradisal freedom from pollution in the air and water, a lost blessing almost everywhere on earth. In this rare place, one can drink without harm from rain puddles in the track and even from the forest pools used for cooling by the cattle; the mild tang of manure is tolerable, I find, when pouring with sweat in a green oven of 100 degrees Fahrenheit with 100 percent humidity, especially when the alternative is dehydration. At midday we gasp and suffocate

on the long treks back to Morr Morr—the "death marches," we call
them. Yet even in extremis, staggering along, we cannot stop our discussions of the ways of cranes.

Since his student days, George Archibald has been fascinated by
crane phylogeny, and because I, too, am stirred by the evolutionary
history of living creatures and the adaptations made across great spans
of time, I pick his mind hard in these sweltering days. Like all great
teachers, George is generous with his information and eager to hear
ideas and speculations, even those offered by unqualified others such as
myself.

Ever since the late nineteenth century, the very similar *antigone* and
rubicundus had been considered sister species. But recent studies have
indicated that the outwardly dissimilar brolga and white-naped cranes
were the true siblings and that *antigone* had diverged from its common
ancestor with *rubicundus/vipio* about 230,000 years ago—astonishing,
since in every aspect of morphology and behavior, the sarus and brolga
appeared far closer to each other than to the white-naped crane. In another surprise, the studies have made clear that the eastern sarus is
closer to the Indian sarus than it is to the Australian, a finding which
dispels any idea that *G. a. gilli* was a recent immigrant from Southeast
Asia: indeed, evidence points to an ancient migration of approximately
one million years ago.[17]

Small genetic differences between close relatives can be caused by
rapid speciation: the sarus and brolga were separated so recently in geologic time that they still hybridize. Nevertheless, new mitochondrial
DNA evidence has caused Archibald to speculate that an Ice Age ancestor might have diverged into western and eastern populations, one of
which gave rise to *antigone* and the other to *vipio* and *rubicundus*; this
ancestor, immigrating to the great southern island and adapting to austral habitats and climate, theoretically evolved into the ancestral brolga.
A subsequent wave of eastern sarus, he continues, interbred successfully

with that early brolga to produce the "Australian sarus," smaller and less red in the face than the eastern sarus though somewhat larger and darker than the brolga.

In the end, however, none of the studies, anatomical, behavioral, or molecular, has clarified the relationships between the five species groups indicated by the several studies, probably because crane radiation and the diversification of these groups has been too rapid to leave firm evidence of the shared ancestral and derived characteristics that define lineages.

At present, George is less interested in crane DNA than in the ethology of each species, believing that behavioral evidence can be as strong as DNA as an indicator of evolutionary history. (Penned together in mixed flocks, for example, *antigone* consorts more readily with *rubicundus* and *vipio* than with the northern cranes.) In attempting to understand the sympatry of the two Morr Morr cranes, what interests him most are their vocalizations (the unison call and about fourteen others) as well as their dances, threat displays, and feeding habits.[18] For example, he wonders why the sarus (*G. antigone*), in all its races, has the loudest call of any of the cranes, despite the fact that compared to its northern congeners (which need to be heard over long distances during migration), it has a trachea only moderately coiled; the brolga (*G. rubicundus*) has a similar trachea but a lower voice, made more resonant by a gular throat sac that the sarus lacks.

In all our walkabouts over the days, we find no better place to observe cranes than the riverine swamp near the far end of the airstrip, where pairs of both species unison-call at potential invaders of their territories. Besides the many mated pairs, small restless flocks of unpaired young fly overhead, sometimes eight to ten birds at a time. George is astonished by the numbers, calling this the greatest density of breeding cranes he has ever encountered anywhere on earth.

Of all the world's cranes, the brolga and sarus of the Gulf of

Carpentaria are perhaps the least afflicted by the dire consequences of man's rise to civilization. To a degree unequaled anywhere except Antarctica, the ecosystems are pristine and uncontaminated, though the world draws near. At night, because the sky is clear, stars fill the canopy, burning bright right down to the horizons. Fortunately for the cranes, this equatorial savanna is a wet green hell that few would consider a fit habitat for human beings. It is also marginal pastureland for domestic cattle (though—because it is fragile—cattle may yet spoil it).

Of the two species, the brolga forms larger flocks, and in "the Dry," which lasts about nine months, hundreds will congregate at agricultural farms in northern Australia, while others fly east to coastal regions of Queensland. But most will fly north to the gulf, scarcely twenty miles from Morr Morr, where they feed on *Eleocharis* tubers in the salt marshlands.[19] The brolga, which uses salt marsh and other saline wetlands more extensively than other species, has developed specialized salt glands near the eyes through which it is able to secrete concentrated salts—an illustration of how rapidly adaptations may appear even in species such as *rubicundus*, which has only recently (in geological terms) split from its ancestor.

The eastern sarus *G. a. sharpii* that winter in the Mekong Delta also subsist on *Eleocharis* tubers, but here in Queensland, when it leaves the breeding grounds, the Australian sarus *G. a. gilli* resorts to dry grassland and savanna areas, scattering in pairs and little flocks to hunt seeds, insects, and small vertebrates. George posits two opposing theories to account for this. The first sarus, arriving from the East Indies, would have encountered thousands of brolgas in the coastal marshes; quite possibly this tuber competition from a closely related species drove them to adapt to grassland niches of the Cape York Peninsula, and later to man's croplands, such as the cornfields of the Atherton Plateau. Conversely, he speculates that the Mekong Delta muds its ancestors were used to were softer than the hard salt flats of this shallow coast, and that, lacking the brolga's heavy digging bill, the sarus adapted to hunt-and-pick feeding during the Dry. Thus most if not all of the Morr Morr sarus will fly south to Atherton, where seven to eight hundred may inhabit a wetland known as Bromfield's Swamp.

Each day, we observe hundreds of cranes and other waterbirds—green pygmy geese, little cormorants, darters, whistling ducks, egrets; also, the white-and-chestnut Brahminy kite, a beautiful raptor I recall from an expedition to New Guinea many years ago. One morning we admire the creation of the great bower bird, that inspired relative of crows and birds of paradise which in its courtship throes constructs an elaborate bower for its intended—in this case, vertical stick walls about one and a half feet high and two feet long, enclosing a neat avenue paved minutely with white bone shards and bits of scavenged glass, sorted carefully according to color (blue, green, and white) and pointed up by a plastic scrap as unreally red as a maraschino cherry.

Another day, we come across fresh claw prints and the tail track of a fair-sized crocodile on the bank of a small creek where we have stopped to rest. Saltwater crocodiles, or "salties," which are said to grow up to twenty feet in length and are generally considered the most aggressive of all crocodilians, come far up into these rivers in the rainy season; not long ago, Darren Gakowski tells us, a saltie cruising the bank under the water's surface stalked, seized, and killed a woman along the Gilbert River, many miles inland from the gulf.

Aside from large crocodiles, the only dangerous creatures here are snakes; Australia claims the eleven most poisonous species on earth, including the king brown found at Morr Morr. One afternoon as we head for the airstrip, Andrew encounters a king brown just outside the compound. As a lifelong friend of snakes, I holler at him not to let it go before I look at it. Pinning its neck with a forked stick, he picks it up and turns it over for inspection. Having handled poisonous snakes since boyhood, neither of us feels we are being reckless, but his poor Suzanne, quite understandably, is extremely scared, upset, then very angry with us. Chastised, we release the graceful creature and watch it whisper its way into the grass.

Though the brolga still numbers in the tens of thousands, its last great redoubt is this wilderness of roadless swamplands and wet woods around the belly of the gulf and northward on both coasts of the Queensland peninsula. Much of this empty region is already cattle range, burned over regularly to create grassland. In southeast Australia, the brolga population has been much diminished by agricultural drainage of its favored wetlands of *bulkuru* sedge (*Eleocharis dulcis*). Intrusive development, which alters wetland hydrology and the succession of plant species, can only increase in a global economy, with unknown consequences for the cranes.

"The ephemeral nature of critical crane breeding habitat, combined with the long-lived nature of the birds, has combined to give a false sense of security as to the health of crane populations based on numbers only," Andrew Haffenden has written. "Politically, much of the suitable habitat is under Aboriginal control, and the political will is toward economic improvement of these areas. While some conservationists rhapsodize about the special caring relationship of native people with their environment, experience has shown that over time, Western goodies hold greater sway than traditional values. And for our part, there is little ethic in believing that one group of a nation's people should live with less than the rest of us enjoy so that the country as a whole can have a conservation commitment . . . This may mean that the very short term presents one of the last chances to securely establish the current populations of cranes in Australia."[20]

The sarus appears to have increased since the first reports in 1961; at Morr Morr, they outnumber the brolgas about two to one. In the twelve years since my friends counted them, the three-to-two ratio of sarus nests to brolga nests has remained stable, yet in this region the brolga is holding its own; the sarus domination that was predicted has not occurred, probably because brolga reproduction is more efficient, with a higher survival rate. For example, by nesting some distance from the water on dry ground, the brolga ensures that the rising water never floods the nest when the rains come, but surrounds it instead with teeming shallows where new chicks are taught to feed.

While the two cranes share the same general habitat at Morr Morr, there exists a distinct ecological separation. The sarus prefers small, wooded swamps while the brolga favors more extensive long-lived marshes where the deep wet mud is easier to dig. With swamp drainage and the coming of cattle, which churn up the mud and expose it to the air, the marshes dry out earlier each year, sealing the tubers in hard earth; also, the cattle destroy much new growth in the savanna woods, converting it to a grassland habitat better suited to the feeding of the sarus. In the rare instances when the two species roost or feed in the same place, they maintain separate flocks.

Perhaps because they are genetically so close and compete for nesting territories, the brolga and sarus here at Morr Morr may respond to the calls of the other species, but already the sarus has developed some unusual vocalizations which may inhibit interbreeding with the brolga.[21] Unison calls may form an adaptive barrier against interspecific pairing, yet they are not infallible, since on several occasions George picked out hybrids in the pairs and flocks circling low over our heads. Because the two cranes are mutually fertile, they could conceivably create a "hybrid swarm" that might overwhelm the biological barriers between them, in which case the hybrid might eventually obliterate both parent forms and emerge as the sole species on the continent. On the other hand, if the hybrid shows decreased fertility or is otherwise unfit, or is selected against as a prospective mate because of its odd appearance, a reproductive barrier may develop, in which case—although hybrids will occur—the two cranes will remain largely distinct.

To judge from this second trip to Morr Morr, in 1996, the sarus population in northern Australia has remained stable for more than a decade; it does not seem to exceed one thousand birds. Nor, as yet, does interbreeding threaten to eliminate the brolga in favor of a hybrid, as was feared. Hybrids are few, and there is no evidence as yet that they are fertile. Asked if hybrids might lack critical adaptive traits, George nods. "Attractiveness to the parent species," he laughs. "The hybrid may have every necessary trait except the ability to turn somebody on."

One day, reeling into the mess-hut shade after a death march, Dr. Archibald strips to his shorts and prostrates himself belly-down on the cool concrete floor, in dire need of "thermoregulation" of his roasted body. When Darren Gakowski brings a telex, George raises his head just far enough to squint, then shrieks, leaps to his feet, and dances a crane dance, red eyes closed in fervent gratitude, a seraphic smile bathing his face. The "Sibes," he whispers, have returned to Bharatpur, India, for the first time since 1993.

From Australia, the Craniac would proceed straight to Bharatpur. I traveled to Bali and central India on tiger research, then north to Delhi, where I encountered a beaming Dr. Archibald and his Russian colleagues Sasha Sorokin and Yuri Markov; they had just arrived from Bharatpur, where they had communed with those last three Siberian cranes. They were off in the next hour for the Buddha's birthplace at Lumbini, in lowland Nepal, to see the densest breeding population of sarus cranes found anywhere on the Indian subcontinent. As for me, I was en route to South Africa, in quest of *Anthropoides paradisea*, the blue crane.

NINE

Equatoria, Ngorongoro, Okavango, and Transvaal

During the night the hippos bellowed from the Nile, a distant sound, the first murmurings out of the heart of Africa. The first light shone on a new land of long grass and small acacia, with occasional great solitary baobab. The grassland danced with antelope and birds—tropical hawks, doves, pigeons, guinea fowl and francolins, bee-eaters, rollers, hornbills, the myriad weavers . . . At the edge of a slough stood two hundred crested cranes.
—Peter Matthiessen, *The Tree Where Man Was Born*, 1972

On cloudless days in 1961, I rode atop the cargo of a truck bound south across the desert from Khartoum to the villages of the Blue Nile, in the region of great swamps known as the Sudd. On the grassy north-south track, as the truck rumbled past a drying slough in the broad thornbush savanna, a wild two-note honking rose above the clatter of the engine. On the bank, a legion of mighty birds—at least two hundred—stood in sun-blazed ranks, bold white and gold and chestnut wings set off by the dark slaty-gray body and long neck topped by a red-black-and-white head crowned by a spray of elongated feathers on the nape, like spun gold in the bright sun of Equatoria—so vivid in their patterns, so astonishing, that even today, the image of those birds opens like a bright flower in my memory. (How wonderful it seems that even the boldest colors of creation are never garish or mismatched, as they are so often in the work of man.)

In those days—the winter of 1961—the black crowned crane, *Balearica pavonina*, was widespread throughout a range which extended from Senegal and Mauritania east to Sudan and Ethiopia.[1] Its habitat was well-watered *sahel*, that long swath of savanna country which in West and Central Africa separates the Sahara from the equatorial forests to the south. More recently, a southward expansion of the desert sands and a northward overflow of human beings have narrowed and destroyed much of its habitat. Meanwhile, the diminished birds have been hunted for food or captured alive for sale as guardians or pets which keep yards clean of insects, spiders, and small reptiles. In Nigeria, a trade in live cranes is the main reason that the national bird, once common in the north *sahel*, is nearing extinction in that country—one of the few crane populations anywhere whose habitat degradation is not the foremost cause of its decline. ("One is continually being reminded by Nigerians that theirs is the most densely populated nation in Africa," one observer noted as early as 1962, "and that perhaps, therefore, there is no place for wildlife.") Resignation to the disappearance of wild creatures vital to tribal myth and culture seems to pervade most of West Africa, where *Homo sapiens* is rarely absent from the landscape. Birds and mammals, in particular the primates and forest antelopes—and even totem creatures such as the ground hornbill—have been reduced to "bush meat," to be snared and shot at once, before others find it. In recent years, a severe drought that has persisted since 1973 has helped reduce *B. pavonina* to perhaps thirteen thousand birds in all West Africa; it is already close to extirpation in several lands besides Nigeria, and is still declining. In 1978, in Senegal, Gambia, and the *sahel* of the northern Ivory Coast, I came across one solitary pair, alert and wary at the far end of a drying pan in Senegal's Niokolo-Koba National Park. Like many West African states, Senegal is draining and filling its last wetlands for new agriculture in the struggle to stave off widespread famine in its growing population, and in Chad and Cameroon, the situation is no better. In Sudan chronic civil war between Muslims in the north and Christians in the south, with its accompanying hunger and disruption (already in progress forty years ago when I passed through), has caused crowned cranes to be taken for food, but at least it has stalled the draining of the Sudd, which is now the great stronghold of the species.[2]

"Once upon a time," George Archibald relates, "an African king was lost and dying from thirst in the desert. A herd of antelope came by, but they refused to lead the king to water. Later some elephants appeared, but they, too, refused to help the king. Then a flock of cranes spotted the king. They brought him some water, then carried him to an oasis. To thank them, the king gave each a golden crown, but the other animals were so jealous that they stole the crowns. When the cranes complained, the king gave them gold-colored feathers to wear instead—true crowns that could not be stolen. These were the first crowned cranes."[3]

The poet Homer in the eighth century B.C. described "cranes which flee from the coming of winter"; Aristotle remarked that "these birds migrate from the steppes of Scythia to the marshlands south of Egypt where the Nile has its source." Aristotle's cranes were Eurasians or demoiselles, which both migrate as far as southern Sudan. Eurasian cranes also winter in small numbers in North Africa, from Morocco and Algeria to Egypt, and many come south to the agricultural Nile valley; the demoiselle bred formerly in mountain valleys and plateaus in northwest Africa,[4] but most occurred here in migration from the Caucasus region of the Black Sea and the Caspian, crossing the Red Sea to winter as far south as the junction of the White Nile and the Blue in Equatoria.

In Uganda, I made my first acquaintance with *Balearica pavonina*'s sibling species, the gray crowned crane (*B. regulorum*), a widespread and prominent bird of well-watered open country which replaces *pavonina* from Uganda and Kenya south to the Cape of Good Hope (excepting the broad band of dry mopane forest that separates Tanzania from southern Africa.)[5] *Pavonina*'s dark slate grays are replaced in *regulorum* by dove-gray plumage, and *regulorum* is noticeably larger, with prominent carmine wattles under the chin. Both birds share the bold ivory-and-chestnut wings set off by black primaries, or "flight feathers," and also the gold-crowned harlequin head with its bare pink skin and bold black-and-white pattern, although the placement of the pinks and whites is different.

Forty years ago, the gray crowned crane was ubiquitous almost everywhere one traveled outside the forest. "Below the camp, the water trails of courting coot melt the surface of Momela, and beyond the lakes, in a realm of shadow, Kilimanjaro's base forms a pedestal for the high cumulus. Birds fly from this dark world into the sunlight of Momela—a quartet of crowned cranes, wild horn note calling from across the water, and ducks that hurry down the clouds . . ." This remembrance (like the chapter epigraph) comes from my first African journals,[6] and *B. regulorum* has delighted me many times in the four decades since, most recently as a bird-safari guide in the cool mountain air of Tanzania's Ngorongoro Crater. Hearing that ancient two-note call, quite unlike the rolling woodblock rattle and horn of the *Grus* species and yet immemorially the voice of cranes, I turned to see a family of four crossing the crater from the high west wall over the black lumps of grazing rhino, buffalo, far elephants, and on across the canopy of tall yellow-barked acacias in the open marshy wood on the crater floor, the morning sun flashing in the vivid semaphore of broad black-and-white wings against the high dark forest rim, the nape on fire, streaming back behind. And in the great stillness of time and the earth's morning that this huge crater evokes, I could hear an echo of that ancestral Balearian back in the Eocene.

The brief, gooselike vocalizations produced by *Balearica*'s uncoiled trachea do not resemble the unison call so prominent in the *Grus* cranes,[7] nor do these birds flap their wings during the process.[8] Unlike the gruines, the crowned cranes sometimes nest semicolonially and roost in trees. The arboreal habit may account for the larger tails of

Balearica, which must brake when it alights upon a limb, and also for its long prehensile hallux, or hind toe, useful in perching. The short bill— shorter than the head—is stout and blunt rather than spear-shaped, and comes equipped with ovoid nostrils; and a pad of soft black feathers on the forehead leads back to the crown, that spray of golden strawlike feathers on the nape which is peculiar to this genus and makes it the most exotic of the cranes.

Crowned cranes are close kin to the trumpeters, a gruid family limited to South America, which suggests to Dr. Archibald that the trumpeters derived from early Balearicine ancestors which spread to the southern continent. It could even be argued that in their different adaptations and behavior, bold and bizarre plumage, and more compact body shape and general aspect, the crowned cranes seem closer to the trumpeters than to other gruids, and are therefore unlikely *Grus* progenitors; it may be that the modern *Grus* evolved quite separately from a common ancestor of *Grus* and *Balearica* which has long since vanished from the earth.

The first crane-like birds, which appeared in the age of dinosaurs, were somewhat similar in body dimensions to a modern crowned crane or its smaller and more aquatic relative, the limpkin. The ancestral cranes and limpkins appear to have separated from their common ancestor in the late Paleocene or early Eocene epoch, about fifty-four million years ago, when the continents were largely composed of humid tropics.[9] The "Balearian," or "crested," cranes, as they were called in early texts, are the last survivors of ancient genera of the early Eocene.

The broad distribution of balearicine fossils in both time and space suggests that these strong cranes might have explored the trans-Atlantic or trans-Bering land connections between North America and Europe that were open at various times during the early Tertiary period. The last fossil balearicines have been located in deposits from the early Pliocene (five million years ago) of Europe; the modern genus *Balearica* had already appeared in late Miocene deposits in Wyoming (ten million years ago). It is assumed that *Balearica* was already in Africa in the same period.

In features of their skeletal anatomy, the *Balearica* closely resemble the many pre-Pliocene fossils from North America and central Asia. Anatomically and behaviorally, this genus is "primitive"—that is, lacking certain specialized characters found in modern or typical cranes. Nonetheless, *Balearica* is assumed to be a forebear of the very different cranes whose ancestors evolved in the early Miocene, some twenty-two million years ago.

This epoch of worldwide cooling and drying brought a great expansion of open-country grassland with standing water, an ecosystem very hospitable to cranes; this climate change is a probable cause of the rapid speciation in the Gruidae which took place about five million years ago and again three million years later.[10] Because of its high number of endemic species, Eurasia has traditionally been considered the source of the crane radiation, but one could argue for any of three continents as likely sites, and in fact, the original geographic source is not yet known.[11]

The new cranes first appear in the late Miocene on the fossil record of Europe and shortly thereafter in western North America. A leg bone (tibia) of today's sandhill crane (*Grus canadensis*) dating from the Pliocene, nine million years ago, has been found in Wyoming, and by the mid-to-late Pleistocene (two million to ten thousand years ago), many if not most of the modern cranes were occupying their present ranges, having completed the diversification of the gruines into what are recognized today as five main lineages.

The new cranes were better adapted to the cold, not only in more dense and compact plumage but in the habit of spring and fall migration, which permitted use of northern food resources in summer while sparing them the rigors of the northern winter. The evolution of cold-resistant cranes was hastened by the waxing and waning of the glaciers, which cut off one population from another, causing the ancestral gruids to radiate into geographic races which, with continuing isolation, evolved into groups of closely related sibling species. Divergent evolution may be rapid, causing marked differences in size and appearance.

In time, a closely related cluster of five northern *Grus* adapted to the Asian wetlands (*G. japonensis*), tamarack bogs (*G. monachus*), and alpine grasslands (*G. nigricollis*). Perhaps the most recent of the five was the whooping crane of North America (*G. americana*), which developed farthest from the source. (A second cluster of three "southern" cranes—the sarus, brolga, and white-naped—is discussed in chapter 7.)

Most of these *Grus* show intriguing affinities with one another, to the point of occasional interbreeding. Whether or not eastern Asia was the radiation point of the *Grus* genus, it was certainly the heart of *Grus* distribution. (China alone can claim eight cranes, whereas the New World claims but two.) Not one of the endemic *Grus* of eastern Asia—the sarus, red-crowned, Siberian, white-naped, hooded, and black-necked cranes—has ever been recorded on another continent.

Like most gruids, the two crowned cranes nest in the vicinity of water, and like the rest, they are believed to nest each year and mate for life in the event that their nestings are successful. Among all cranes, the *Balearica* produce the largest clutch, sometimes as many as four eggs, though rarely do more than two of the chicks survive. During the shared four-week incubation, the idle partner perches on a branch nearby; before incubation is completed, each egg, originally pale blue, turns an off-white shade, marked with green and brown by way of camouflage. As in most cranes, the chicks are a warm fluffy brown streaked with dark brown and white (though some are more golden or gray). After hatching, the nest is usually abandoned quickly, even in the cold highlands of western Kenya, and the hardy chicks are never brooded. After hiding them in the reeds (it is not known how; perhaps they are concealed beneath marsh vegetation), the parents fly to a nearby tree, descending next morning to call them out of hiding. At three months, the chicks are fledged, and a year later they come into full plumage; though still sub-adult, they resemble their parents, crown and all.

In Tanzania, *regulorum* may breed from January until the rainy season in May, tossing together a rough nest of dried grasses and sedges in the shelter of deep reeds. It frequents marshy sloughs and pools bordered by farm fields, and will often roost in the tall village trees. Until recent years, its adaptability to man's habitations and activities, its unspecialized feeding habits—it mainly preys on insects, especially locusts, which are snatched deftly when startled up out of the grass by its stamping feet—and a semi-sacred status in much of its range spared it the sharp decline of *pavonina*, but now this species, too, is being extinguished by the inexorable spread of human beings and their herds, by overgrazing of savanna pasture, and by the cumulative loss of wetland habitat. In recent years, in western Kenya, conservation groups have persuaded local people that plentiful clean water for fish ponds and tree nurseries makes far better economic sense than draining the wetlands for more subsistence farming, and perhaps this idea will take hold in time to help crowned cranes.

At the end of the millennium, the gray crowned crane, widespread but scattered, has an estimated population of eighty-five to ninety thousand birds, more than all other cranes of Africa put together, but it is steadily declining in Uganda, Kenya, and Malawi, and also in southern Africa, where fewer than ten thousand now remain.

S outhern Africa, where *B. regulorum*'s range is shared with the wattled crane, *Grus* (or *Bugeranus*[12]) *carunculatus*, and the blue crane, *Anthropoides paradisea*, is the only place on earth where all three of the presently recognized genera of cranes occur together.[13] One theory holds that in warmer epochs, the crowned cranes evolved in northern continents, then moved south throughout Africa, followed by ancestors of the wattled and blue cranes; *carunculatus* may have emerged in the vast wetlands of the Zambezi drainage in the Central African plains, whereas *paradisea* appears to have evolved in the southern veld where it was joined by the wattled crane's expanding population. (It is presently supposed that early demoiselles, wandering south, found good habitat

Wattled crane (*Grus carunculatus*)

in southern Africa, where a nonmigratory population became established. Isolated from northern demoiselles by mopane forest and equatorial tropics, this geographic race evolved into a distinct species, named originally in honor of the explorer H. M. Stanley but known more commonly today as the blue crane.)

Though all cranes are drawn to wetlands, the more recent species seem to have been shunted toward the margins of shared range by those which arrived ahead of it. Thus the blue crane—once a southern race of the demoiselle and, therefore, perhaps the most recent crane species to emerge on the African continent—has adapted to dry uplands almost entirely. Like the demoiselle, the blue is a short-billed grassland species (though not so short-billed as the crowned cranes) with short toes suitable for running; like all cranes, it is an omnivorous feeder, taking insects, small reptiles, and even rodents with its seeds and grains. George Archibald suggests that the crane ancestors were upland birds, which later resorted to wetland habitats to escape predators and there developed specialized traits, like the three white species, which depend almost exclusively on marshes.[14]

Largely because the cranes of the *Grus* genus show an area of carmine skin somewhere on the head, the demoiselle and the blue crane are usually assigned to their own genus. (*Anthropoides*'s fully feathered head may be a direct inheritance from the *Grus* ancestor, to judge from the fact that all *Grus* cranes start off in life in this condition.) Yet the demoiselle has many affinities with the Siberian, while the blue crane is genetically quite close to the wattled crane—so close that these two occasionally interbreed, despite a daunting discrepancy in size. (The dark offspring, reportedly even larger than the wattled, shows the puffy head feathers of the blue.) For these reasons and others, some authorities lump the two *Anthropoides* into the genus *Grus*, while others include the wattled crane in *Anthropoides*.

Like the blue, the wattled crane may have originated as a nonmigratory southern population of a northern bird, possibly a proto-Siberian; though wattled and Siberian are still classified as *Grus* by most taxonomists, George Archibald proposed years ago that the Siberian be grouped with the wattled in *Bugeranus*. These big wetland cranes share significant behavioral traits such as high-pitched calls, idiosyncratic bill movements, and (in the males) a rapid uncoiling of the neck at the outset of the unison call that is seen in no other species; there are also unusual anatomical and skeletal features, such as a strip of bare comb that extends along a groove on the upper mandible and an atypical single-looped trachea that intrudes only slightly into the sternum. In addition, both have narrow leg bones, long furculae, or wishbones, relative to the sternum, and the longest bills among the cranes (for feeding in deeper shallows).

As in the case of the sarus and the brolga, convergent evolution (similar habitat adaptations) probably explains the superficial similarity in sternum, trachea, and other characters independently derived from separate ancestors. Alternately, resemblances may arise from primitive features found in the gruine ancestor and retained independently in their own lineages. Drs. George Archibald and Carey Krajewski favor this explanation, and they presently agree that *carunculatus* might best be grouped with the *Anthropoides* cranes, since, like the demoiselle and blue, the wattled crane has a fully feathered crown and elongated tertiary feathers of the inner wing that form plumes draping down over the tail and it, too, has unison calls of a fixed length that are initiated by the female. (Like *Anthropoides*, the male Siberian emits one call for each female call, but in this queer bird, either sex may initiate the calling and the sexes call alternately, with the female voice identifiable by its higher pitch.)

Carey Krajewski's work on crane DNA and phylogeny has strongly influenced George Archibald's conclusions. "The refining of my thinking has been based on his superb research," George has told me. In recent years, based on DNA analysis, Dr. Krajewski has recommended the inclusion of blue and demoiselle, wattled and Siberian in the genus *Grus*. Dr. Archibald, too, would be content to see all cranes other than *Balearica* assigned to a single genus. However, he says, if *leucogeranus* were to be excluded as some sort of taxonomic misfit, it should not be relegated to *Anthropoides* or *Bugeranus* but be placed in its very own new genus; although never isolated geographically, this elusive species is only distantly related to modern *Grus*, including the wattled crane.

*A*nthropoides paradisea* has the most limited distribution of any of the fifteen cranes, yet until quite recently this beautiful blue bird was so abundant throughout much of its range that the fledgling newsletter of the ICF, in its winter issue of 1975, could say of this species, "It is a pleasant change to report on a crane that is holding its own against man's 'progress.'" As late as 1980, the blue crane population, still benefiting from widespread grain farming and the extirpation of predators from farm regions, was called "healthy throughout South and Southwest Africa" and "nowhere endangered."[15] If this was accurate, then a dangerous decline of the species started soon thereafter.

As with the black crowned crane in Nigeria, its status as South

Africa's national bird has not spared the blue crane from persecution and destruction, mostly from widespread poisoning in the croplands, intentional as well as indirect, through pesticide spraying and related causes. Farmers resented its depredations on their crops where it wintered in the fallow wheat fields of southwest Cape Province, and the national bird was also destroyed in the Transvaal, Natal, Free State, and the Karoo, where the crowned and wattled cranes often perished with it. Illegal poisoning is still widely practiced; in recent years, 675 blue cranes were killed in a single field by grain soaked in commercial insecticides.

Not surprisingly, *paradisea* declined from about twenty-one thousand in 1980 to fourteen thousand ten years later. In the general transfer of land after the 1994 elections, many of the larger farms were split up among African farmers, and fast-spreading settlement and new agriculture drove out the cranes. None, in fact, are found around native farms, which Dr. Archibald sees as "the death knell for the blues." Already the species is largely gone from Transkei, Lesotho, and Swaziland, with serious declines in the Transvaal, Free State, eastern Cape Province, and Natal. Today fewer than one thousand persist outside the commercial farm fields of the southwestern Cape and the dry plains of the Karoo, where they still hold their own in modest numbers.

Oddly, no blue cranes are found in the great grasslands of Central and East Africa. Sixty to eighty *paradisea* frequent Namibia's Etosha Pan, and a few stray into southern Botswana; otherwise, the species is restricted to South Africa. (The reasons for this may be related to the utter absence of cranes from South America, or to the mysterious absence of crowned cranes in Botswana's huge Okavango Delta.)

In 1992, Victor Emanuel and I led a bird safari to Namibia, where I hoped to see the small nonmigratory flock of blue cranes at Etosha Pan. We found gray crowned cranes at Etosha and the wattled crane a few days later in the Okavango, but the blue remained hidden from our sight. When I stopped over in South Africa in late February 1996, on my way home from Australia and India, *paradisea* was the only crane I had never beheld in the wild.

E ast from Johannesburg to the Transvaal, the road crosses grass-lands and broad farmlands, broken here and there in the clear distances by tree plantations, coal mines, and coal-fired electricity installations. In 1975, twenty-nine pairs of blue cranes were found nesting at higher, colder altitudes in the Steenkampsberg, at the eastern edge of the Transvaal's highveld, where they had been extirpated as a breeding bird since the turn of the century. Seven years later, in 1982, thirty-one nest sites were located there in the Belfast-Dullstroom region. Although by 1995 the local population had declined to fifteen birds, with just five nests, it seemed the best place to start looking.

At Belfast, I turn north under swift rain clouds. Climbing the Steenkampsberg, the road arrives in the picturesque village of Dull-stroom, named for one Wolterus Dull, a nineteenth-century pioneer, and noted for pretty gardens and bountiful wildflowers. In a subalpine climate with an annual rainfall of thirty-two inches, the Dullstroom region is cold in winter, fitfully warm in summer, and damp all year round. It is too mountainous for commercial agriculture, and the highland shepherding of its early days has given way to forestry and trout farming. Today it is a last sanctuary for all three of South Africa's cranes.

The crowned crane nests on high ground in the marshes, choosing the warm spring in December and January when there is more water; the blues nest in the same season in dry grasslands. For reasons not well understood, the wattled cranes nest mostly in the austral winter, at the peak of the dry cold season in July.[16] Thus the three species coexist without competing in this region, using their habitats in different ways.

George Archibald had given me a letter of introduction to fellow craniacs in Dullstroom, but alas, they are away; on the telephone at the Dullstroom Inn, I try in vain—it is a Sunday—to reach crane researcher Kerryn Morrison or Frans Krige, director of the Verloren Valei (Lost Valley) Nature Reserve, a haunt of cranes. That afternoon I explore instead a red dirt road northwest of the village which climbs up to Transvaal's highest mountain, called De Berg. In a hillside field near the De Berg road runs a little band of springbok, a small gazelle that in the wintertime may consort with *paradisea*, perhaps because the wary blues cry out in warning at the smallest sign of danger; not far away, a herd of twenty large roan-colored blesbok pause in their ruminations in order to observe me observing them. Though I see no cranes, I renew acquaintance with a number of African familiars, such as the hadada ibis and the jackal buzzard.

Kerryn Morrison, who awaits me at the inn's pub, is a friendly young woman who is doing her master's thesis on the habitat needs of South Africa's three cranes. Over a beer, she delivers the glum news that the blue cranes on the Steenkampsberg have finished nesting and are now well scattered; with autumn nearing in the southern hemisphere, the pairs will have led the juveniles to lower altitudes, to forage in the crops of corn and wheat. She knows of one late pair with chick, but even if that chick has not yet fledged, the family may be difficult to find; also, away from the main road, many of the mud tracks are impassable because of heavy rains.

However, we shall try. Early next morning, we travel south about fifteen miles toward Belfast before turning east on the dirt road to Elandskloof, then south again down a long hill into a narrow valley with rocky tableland rising on each side. Finding no cranes, we return to the hilltop, where Kerryn points out the *paradisea* nest site in a rock outcropping on a grassland ridge. The blue crane establishes its territories in these dry uplands (and also in the near-deserts of the Karoo and Namibia, so long as water is not too far away), but even here the birds are threatened by grassland conversion to monotype forests of pulp-paper species such as pines and eucalyptus planted in hard rows that support no life. Unlike the crowned cranes, which build loose nests, *paradisea* deposits two brown-blotched eggs in a mere scrape among the stones. The chicks, gray-downed with tawny heads, may follow the parents off into the grass within the hour, for like the demoiselle, the blue is quick to abandon the eggshell bits and other signs of its chick's humble abode.

Suspended in the highland air, a long-tailed widow bird with bright red scapulars performs its ecstatic courtship flight, writhing and undulating like a black jellyfish in the sea; a flock of small dark falcons crisscrosses and darts over the grass tops like enormous swallows.[17] Gazing about her, Kerryn murmurs that the juvenile must have fledged, in which case the family would have left to join a nomad flock; once again, it appears, *A. paradisea* has eluded me. But even as she speaks, two ghostly white crowns appear in the blowing grass tips on a rise a short distance to the west, and in a moment, two tall silver-blue birds emerge from the golden grasses in the clear mountain light of the late austral summer.

A. paradisea has long loose trailing plumes that arch gracefully as they curve down to touch the ground—actually, modified feathers of the inner wing that like the long tail of the widow bird may be shaken and "shimmered" like black snakes during display. When the cranes turn to inspect us, their heads look oddly round or swollen due to the loose tufted feathers on the head and upper neck. Then their large chick crops up beside them, as if sprouted from the earth. Had we come along even a minute later, we might have missed them. I take a deep breath, content at last, yet knowing already a vague regret that my search for the wild cranes of the world is at an end. Swiftly and yet without haste—that is the elegance of cranes—the three *paradisea* move away, and soon the pale heads vanish in the grasses.

Near the main road on the return, a cape vulture flops up out of the veld, and farther on, a flock of bald-headed ibis eyes us askance from the wet meadows; both species are presently endangered. In a ranch pasture a black wildebeest is grazing, and also a small herd of Burchell's zebra; like the springbok, both introduced species on the Steen-

kampsberg. The native steenbok is here, too, and Kerryn tells me that
duikers—the red and the blue—inhabit the riverine woods that trace
the streams across the high plateau.

From Dullstroom, having said goodbye to Kerryn, I drive out the
De Berg road to the Verloren Valei Nature Reserve, a beautiful tract of
about twelve thousand acres acquired from farmers in 1985 to protect
its twelve pairs of wattled cranes as well as its unspoiled ecosystem of
mountain grassland and the alpine marsh ponds known as vleis. There
I find its director fashioning an artificial leg for one of the pen-raised
paradisea that are fed daily near the reserve office. Frans Krige tells me
that blue cranes in small nomad flocks are sometimes attracted to the
tamed ones, and that four birds which arrived earlier this morning are
foraging higher on the stony ridge behind the headquarters cottage. As
I climb nearer, the wild blues take off and glide down across the entrance road, alighting prettily in dancing steps beside a small rock outcrop scarcely fifty yards away.

Frans Krige says that two pairs of wattled cranes—one with a
fledged juvenile about five months old—are still resident on the reserve, and we drive up onto the higher plateaus to look for them; on a
rocky ridge, my guide takes time to point out the lovely yellow-breasted
pipit and the orange-breasted longclaw, and also a superb pink gladio-
lus. The first glimpse of *Grus carunculatus* is a flash of white in a deep
green meadow of an alpine marsh between two ridges.

Though its main populations are now located in the vast lowlands
of south-central Africa and the Zambezi delta, *carunculatus* was formerly scattered in small numbers in high-altitude wetlands north to
Ethiopia, where a little-known group still persists on alpine moorlands
at thirteen thousand feet in the Bale Mountains, cut off from the pressures of the world below by tracts of montane forest.[18] It also inhabits—
or formerly inhabited—local regions in Malawi, Angola, Zimbabwe,
western Tanzania, Mozambique, Namibia, Zaire, Zambia, and Botswana (the Okavango Delta[19] and the Makgadikgadi pan), but only in
Zambia's floodplains does the species occur in any numbers. There the
vast Kafue flats north of the Zambezi River, a seasonally flooded, ripar-

ian wetland roughly 160 miles long and 35 miles wide, holds the largest concentration of *carunculatus* left on the continent—perhaps three thousand of the estimated twelve thousand that remain. But as in the Amur and the Yangtze, the Kafue cranes are seriously threatened by massive hydroelectric dams and ever-increasing wetland exploitation.

In 1990, some twenty-five hundred wattled cranes were reported in the Zambezi delta but failed to breed because of unstable water levels; the enormous Cabora Bassa (558 feet high) and Kariba dams upstream, which diminish or eliminate the annual floods that overflow the delta, enriching its good soil, are doing great harm to the huge wetlands and their complex ecological systems. (The delta's fertile western edge, fed by undammed streams, may still support twenty to thirty pairs of wattled cranes.) Here as elsewhere, the fishermen and farmers, their traditional livelihood destroyed by vast international projects and economic forces beyond their control, have turned to bush-meat hunting, and so the delta wildlife dies away.

In South Africa, *carunculatus* has been extirpated from Cape Province and Swaziland, in part because the wetlands are burned over in the austral winter when the cranes are nesting, and streams are dammed to supply irrigation for commercial fish ponds; it is also reduced by poisoning and power-line collisions. Today the species is mostly found here in Eastern Transvaal (now known as Mpumalanga)[20] and in the uplands of KwaZulu-Natal.

Like the three cranes of Asia and North America, the wattled crane, white of head and upper body, declares its territory by building its nest platform in the middle of a marsh or pond where the open water all around makes its presence conspicuous to others of its species. The most aquatic of African cranes, it may even create a pool around the nest by digging up plants with its powerful bill and piling and packing them into a platform. Yet for all its preparations and precautions, *carun-*

culatus has the lowest reproduction rate of any crane.[21] In South Africa, it rarely troubles to lay more than one egg, and when it does, the second is abandoned promptly when the first chick hatched is led off into hiding.[22] Furthermore, it has the longest incubation period (33 to 36 days) and fledging period (90 to 130 days) of any crane, which increases the exposure of its eggs and young to danger and calamity. It rarely strays far from its territory, being quite content with sedge tubers, rhizomes, and water lilies; its principal food is the fleshy tuber of a spike rush (*Eleocharis*), which provides carbohydrate reserves for the hard seasons.[23] Apparently less attracted to small vertebrates than other cranes, *carunculatus* picks out grass seed, grains, and insects on the infrequent occasions when it forages in fields.[24]

Round eyes of antelope—rufous oribi, gray reed buck—observe us solemnly as we strip off our boots and socks and set out across the marshes. Frans Krige knows the myriad vlei flowers—two elegant orchids (green-and-purple, salmon pink), a big pink *Nerine*, and a lovely *Lobelia* of pale blue. Eventually we draw close to the great cranes, whose long necks rise like white columns as they gauge man's approach.

Carunculatus, over five feet tall, with a seven-foot wingspread—tallest of all cranes except the Indian sarus—is a huge creature that from any distance appears white when alighted, though its folded wings are actually a pale gray-blue; a dark chocolate band separating the white upper body from the gray-blue mantle encircles the belly like an honorary sash, conferring an ambassadorial style and manner. As in most cranes, the sexes are indistinguishable, though the male tends to be taller and more dominant. Like the sarus and the brolga, *carunculatus* (named for the red caruncles on its face) has a bare greenish brow; its long large bill is yellowish and straight, and the red skin on the side of the white head extends from the bill back to the orange-yellow eyes and down to the pendular white wattles.

"Their name is the only inelegant thing about them," I wrote admiringly of the first wattled cranes I ever saw, twenty years before in the Chobe region of the Okavango. "As they stride along the marsh edge, the wattle is scarcely apparent; what one remembers is the long sweep of the neck . . . Days later, I see the five again, stately and beautiful, consorting with impala in the sun and shadow of a glade under an open canopy of thorn trees . . ."[25]

Wary but not frightened, the birds stalk imperiously across our path before deigning to alter course a little, tending away; they do not protest with strident calls as most cranes do. Being nonmigratory and mostly sedentary, with little use for loud heraldic calls, *carunculatus* is rather silent, as if aware that its voice is the least melodious among the cranes; even its unison call, that strong clue to *Grus* phylogeny, is meager and screechy, without resonance, as if rusty from disuse.[26]

The second pair with its large juvenile is found in another marsh over the ridge, and we watch this group a long while from the crest. There are fifteen wattled cranes on the Steenkampsberg plateau, less than a quarter of the number found as late as 1982; last year (1995) there were five nests, from which only two chicks survived. Threats to local cranes include impoundments for irrigation, which drown good habitat and create dead lakes that fill up behind the concrete; overgrazing and wetland burning in the winter (which often destroys *carunculatus* chicks, since this species may breed almost year-round); aerial spraying and agricultural poisons; commercial tree farming, or "afforestation," of the grasslands, which quickens runoff and erosion and carves the gouged dongas, or barren small ravines, that scar worn landscapes everywhere in Africa. None of these ills directly afflict the cranes in Verloren Valei, yet here, too, all three species are declining. Even the well-intentioned removal of the sheep and cattle thought to be overgrazing the crane habitat and trampling the nests worked against the cranes; the herds had done more good than harm, providing nutrients the cranes needed by turning over and fertilizing the soil.[27]

Two months before my visit, more than sixty gray crowned cranes were counted in the Steenkampsberg, but at this season, the "crownies" are scattered, hard to find. Frans Krige gives me directions to a likely haunt about twenty miles from Dullstroom, behind the higher ridges to the west, but by the time I leave Verloren Valei in the late afternoon, the black clouds to westward have collapsed in broad walls of heavy rain, which continues well into the evening.

TEN

Down the Edges of the Distant Sky

Down the edges of the distant sky
The hail storm sweeps . . .
While far above the solitary crane
Swings lonly to unfrozen dykes again
Cranking a jarring mellancholy cry
Thro the wild journey of the cheerless sky.
—John Clare,
"The Shepherd's Calendar," 1827

I n 1979, more than three centuries after it was last reported (in 1653), the Eurasian crane, *Grus grus*, returned to England as a breeding species. More astonishing still, the cranes reappeared in the same reach of East Anglian marsh—not out of mysterious ancestral memory, as one might like to imagine, but because those remnant marshes in the Norfolk Broads, still preserved by landed families, were probably the best habitat they came across in their westward wanderings on the winds from Europe.

Twenty years earlier, between 1958 and 1963, numbers of *grus* were turning up in England, as many as six together, though few of these strayed birds appeared in Norfolk; like most vagrants and accidentals, they failed to establish themselves in Britain, where large open marshes are all but gone. In October 1963, an unusually heavy *grus* migration

Eurasian crane (*Grus grus*)

from the Baltic States and eastern Europe passed through West Germany and Holland, with some forty birds counted in the Channel Islands, and doubtless most of that year's visitors to England came from these flights—not a long detour in light of the German finding that under favorable conditions, "gray cranes" are capable of a nonstop flight of twelve hundred miles.

In September 1979, two *grus* appeared at Hickling Broad, from where they soon moved to the marshes near Horsey Mere on the Norfolk coast. Joined by a third bird on October 10, they were duly photographed by documentary filmmaker John Buxton, a landowner at Horsey. In early October, an exhausted adult with an otherwise unidentified "rubber object" wrapped around its bill had been captured near Ipstead, in Norfolk, and this bird was released among the others in March 1980. The four cranes came and went throughout the year and two overwintered in Norfolk; all the next year, these two behaved like a mated pair, although no nest was found. The following spring, the cranes brought off a nesting, for a brown juvenile was seen flying behind the adults later that summer—the first wild crane bred in Great Britain since about 1600, when extensive drainage of the Norfolk Broads began. By 1989, four young had been raised and *grus* was precariously reestablished—no longer a "vagrant" but a full-fledged resident of Britain.

Saint Columba, while living at Iona off the coast of Scotland in the sixth century, bade a monk to tend a weary crane from Ireland. Geoffrey Chaucer had the crane on his short list of common English birds in *The Parliament of Fowles*, circa 1382: "The crane, the giant, with his trumpet sound." The "common crane" was still a breeding bird of England when the clergyman Edward Topsell, in 1614, published *The Fowles of Heaven, or History of Birdes conteyning their true and lively figures with the whole description of theire natures*: "They are most delighted to live in fenny places, lakes, and standinge pooles or ryvers . . . they love the warmest places best, and therefore when they remove from Countrey to Countrey it is observed by the people from whom they flie, that . . . winter is cominge."

Topsell describes the appearance, biology, mythology, and many other aspects of this "noble and princely creature" (and also provides true and lively figures and whole descriptions of the natures of the "Balearian Crane" mentioned by "Plyny and the Auncients" and the "Crane of Japan . . . sent to the Pope by the Princes of Japan"), including the unique *asperam arteriam,* or "throat bole"—the trachea—which permits it to cry out "with a shriller and more continuall voice, being ne'er weary, though he flie out of sight. And this is the true cause why their voices be hearde before their bodies be seene." He cites quotations from Virgil and Dante, to whose ear crane voices were "clangorous" or "clamorous"; Topsell also observes that "As swine are said to gruntle so Cranes are said to jangle."

"The Latynes call the Grues of their gruntinge voice . . . the Italyans Grua and Gru, the Spanyards Grulla and Gruz . . . The word 'congruity' derives from cranes because they live, agree, and fly together," Topsell claims, citing the Latin *congruere,* "to consent." (*Congruere* contains the word *grue,* which is the French name for the crane and also the French nickname for a streetwalker, evoked, no doubt, by her long-legged stalking gait or possibly her jangling calls, or both, or neither.)

Among the crane's many medicinal attributes, "Their flesh is profitable against cancers, ulcers, palsies, and wind in the guts . . . The brains has been used against sores in the seat . . . and the fat of cranes (said Pliny) mollifies hard swellings and tuberous bunches." This bird-struck clergyman avers that "the Eagle is the enemy to cranes, as is the devil to every good Christian man or woman," and that "the Gentlemen of England make use of cranes in their escutcheons."

But "the crane is now only an occasional visitant," Edward Blyth observes in his classic *Monograph on the Cranes,* which appeared in London in 1881. He notes a record of "four specimens shot and several other seen" by a Mr. H. Stevenson in 1869, who "remarked that the occurrence of so many of these rare visitants in the one season was the more remarkable, as he was not aware of more than four examples having been killed in Norfolk during the last half century."

As the so-called common crane of Europe, *Grus grus* had been described at length in the taxonomy assembled by Linnaeus in his *Systema Naturae* of 1735. However, he placed the seven species that were then known to him in his "Order *Grallae,*" along with the trumpeters, the ostrich, and most large wading birds. Linnaean taxonomy persisted until Blyth belatedly recognized the cranes as a distinct family, composed of the genera *Balearica* and *Grus*; he recognized also that, relative to *Balearica*, *Grus* cranes had long and convoluted trachea, long bills, and elongated nostrils (which in crowned cranes are ovoid). Blyth's mighty work was the foundation for all subsequent crane systematics, which after two centuries is still disputing the number of crane genera and species.

Under regional names, *G. grus* appears much earlier in Western art, at least as far back as the six-thousand-year-old paintings at Tajo Segura cave in southern Spain. In historic times, this species has adorned innumerable books and paintings, tapestries and ceramics in Europe and farther afield. It is sometimes depicted standing on one leg, clutching a stone in the raised claw—the sentinel bird which, nodding off, will reawaken when the stone drops into the water.

The breeding range of *grus* extends all the way across northern Europe and Siberia to the Russian Far East and Japan; therefore "Eurasian crane" might be a better name, since it is "common" only by comparison to its uncommon relatives.[1] Like most cranes, *grus* is declining in many parts of its range, but it seems to be recovering somewhat in Europe, where it is no longer hunted. Before its return as a breeding bird of England, its westernmost range was Sweden, which has a large estimated population of some twenty thousand pairs. In recent years Germany has succeeded in restoring the "gray crane" as a nesting species, and (perhaps a consequence of global warming) an increasing number are overwintering in France, including a flock of several hundred in the Lac de la Forêt d'Orient, east of Paris. The large Scandinavian and Russian populations migrate southeast in autumn, many gathering in Hungary[2] before crossing the Mediterranean to Algeria; farther east, they go to Asia Minor and continue south through Israel to Africa, ascending the Nile valley as far as Sudan and Ethiopia.[3] Still farther east, the Asian *grus* winter in the Caucasus, in Pakistan and India, and in southern China and Southeast Asia, with a few turning up in Kyushu, in southern Japan. *Grus grus* is the one foreign crane that occasionally wanders to North America; since it also flies to northern Africa, it is therefore the only species occurring on all four continents where cranes are found. In 1999, lone birds turned up in Quebec and Indiana and also on the Platte River of Nebraska, among the great companies of sandhill cranes, another adaptive and prosperous species which has been called its ecological counterpart in the New World.

In late May of 1995, wishing to see the European bird in its westernmost breeding territory in East Anglia, I took the train from London to Norwich, where I was met by Durwyn Liley, a young English ornithologist who was completing his graduate thesis on the ringed plover and was also very keen to see those cranes. Accompanied by his sister Chez, we set off at once, heading northeast toward the Norfolk Broads and Hickling Marsh—the largest reed beds left in England—and pausing only to admire the village of Potter Heigham with its beautiful twelfth-century thatched-roof church and a tower which in earlier days, before the seas withdrew, had been a lighthouse.

From high dunes on the shingle coast northwest of Horsey, listening hard over the sea wind for crane clangor and jangle, we scan the inland pastures and wet meadows to no avail. In the late afternoon, a farm track leads us inland to the embankments that confine the mere, where an ancient mill with skewed and broken arms shelters a barn owl. We note lapwings, redshanks, little gulls, and greylag geese, reed and sedge warblers, and also the common cuckoos which usurp their nests. A marsh harrier appears, and soon there comes the bottle-blow of a hidden bittern—both of them uncommon birds in Britain and both of them predators on the nests of *grus* (which would make haste to do as much for them). Not until evening does a solitary crane appear out of the west, approaching swiftly with powerful deep strokes, gliding in and alighting not a hundred yards away from where we crouch behind clumps of the white-blossomed hawthorn known in spring as "maythorn."

Toward dusk, an elderly man in green fatigues equipped with recording equipment and a rifle appears in the canal in a small punt propelled by an assistant. This is John Buxton, whose name has been provided me by George Archibald and who has given me directions to the marsh over the telephone; Mr. Buxton informs us that the crane we saw was the male of a nesting pair, alighting near its nest. A second pair has lost two egg clutches to predators, he says, but seems to be making a third try a bit farther to the east, near Horsey Mere. We are kindly invited to come around to Horsey Hall for coffee the next morning.

Horsey Hall is hidden from the coast road by an old small wood between dune and marsh which shelters a lovely Saxon church of the ninth century. Its south side opens on a prospect of wet meadow; beyond shines the blue water of the mere and the white church steeples of villages far away on its inland shore.

John Downs, a tanned, husky man in neckerchief and shorts who lives across the lane from the church in the wood, is the manager of Horsey Farm; his wife, Jeddie, a spritely person in the black rubber "wellies" worn by most country people in rainy England, was formerly nanny to John Buxton's children. It was Sir John's father, Sir Anthony Buxton, who gave part of this marshland to the National Trust in 1948; subsequently, a canal embankment path was built from the Horsey windmill near the coast road to the old Brograve Mill which housed the barn owl. Sir Anthony, who died in 1970 and is resident in the church-yard, was the person who taught Jeddie Downs about wild birds, and a good thing, too, because on that epochal day of September 1979, it was she who first spotted, recognized, and reported the Eurasian crane. "Flew straight down into the marsh," she marveled, "right in front of the car!"

Ordinarily, *grus* seeks out and defends a large territory in remote swamp forest or sub-Arctic tundra; the nests of two adjacent pairs can be ten miles apart, since the sight and sound of other *grus* seems to inhibit the breeding and nesting of this shy species. Here in Norfolk, *grus* has adapted to nesting in the open marshland, with the two pairs less than a mile apart. Thus it appears that *grus* can contract its territories according to the circumstances, like the close-nesting *vipio* in the valleys of eastern Mongolia and *japonensis* in the crowded marshes of Hok-kaido.

O ut-of-doors on a spring morning of warm sunlight, not common on the Norfolk coast, we enjoy good coffee and good talk with John and Bridget Buxton; we are shortly joined by a small dark chat (the black redstart, uncommon in Britain but widespread in Asia) which hops across the lawn. Mr. Buxton, who has produced a number of notable documentaries for Survival Anglia, hopes to work more closely with George Archibald in the future, since only four of the fifty eggs laid by the cranes have produced chicks that were successfully raised to adulthood. After fifteen years, Buxton sighs, there are only six or seven cranes—a meager reproductive rate that he ascribes to flooded nests, foxes, and avian predators but also to human disturbance, mostly from boaters and damned waterborne "twitchers" (bird-watchers such as the Lileys and myself, ticking off species on their dratted lists), not to speak of trippers, picnickers, and sundry louts who tramp uncon-scionably across these meres and marshes. But of course we know that with England's waterlands all but gone, this "noble and princely bird" can never prosper here again.

Hard wind and fleeting sun and rain: we search for cranes all day in the coastal meadows. In a sunny oak and hawthorn wood, out of the wind, restored by good bread and cheese and a cool beer, we listen to spring flutings of the song thrush. On the coast at Cley, pink sea laven-der blooms in the small marshes behind the dunes, and the handsome falcon called the hobby, last seen in Mongolia, hurtles down the shore. Though sharp-eyed Durwyn turns up both of the two vagrant Euro-pean thrushes (a bluethroat and a rock thrush) he has located with the help of his rare-bird radio alert, we find no cranes.

Dusk finds us at our lookout on the dike embankment. All is quiet.

Persuaded that *grus* is roosted for the night, we are on the point of leaving when a single crane appears low out of the west, crossing the marshland and alighting to fierce calling—four series of shrill synchronized trumpetings—at the same location as the previous evening. Almost at once another comes across the wind from somewhere farther inland, setting its wings and gliding down to the unseen nest farther east toward Horsey Mere, where its mate greets it with all due clangor and jangle. Having located the nearer site in the maythorn just over the canal, we hide and wait, and soon the heads rise from the wind-tossed reeds to peer at the queer forms on the embankment. Content, we withdraw from the marsh and head south across the twilight toward Norwich, where I ring up John Buxton with that day's report, neglecting, however, to inquire whether or not, as a Gentleman of England, he made use of cranes in his escutcheon.

ELEVEN

The Sadness of Marshes

> They were looking down from a great elevation and all they saw
> was at the point of coming together, the bare trees marching in
> from the horizon, the rivers moving into one, and as he touched
> her arm she looked up with him and saw the long, ragged,
> pencil-faint line of birds within the crystal of the zenith, flying in
> a V of their own, following the same course down. All they could
> see was sky, water, birds, light, and confluence. It was the whole
> morning world.
>
> —Eudora Welty, *The Optimist's Daughter*, 1972

In Wisconsin in 1994, on a visit to the Lac du Flambeau Anishinabe, I inquired about crane traditions in this widespread people of the north-central states and southern Canada. Like most American Indian tribes—most traditional peoples, for that matter—the Anishinabe (or Chippewa or Ojibwa) revere the crane, which is so admired for its oratorical abilities that it is called "Echo Maker" or "Speaker for the Clans." Among the five original clans or totems, the *Ah-jii-jak*, or Crane (the whooping crane is *Wabishki Ah-jii-jak*, or White Crane), shares the chieftainship with Loon, but it is Crane who sits in the place of honor, nearest the water drum and the east door of the Midewiwin Lodge. (In this wooded country west of the Great Lakes, *Ah-jii-jak* would be the greater sandhill; in the legends of the Alaskan Tlingit, Crane would be the lesser sandhill or little brown crane.) In a Cree tale, Crane carries Rabbit to the moon, a task that even Eagle has refused, and is rewarded with a beautiful red crown. It is said that "Crow and Cheyenne warriors carved flutes from the crane's hollow leg bones and played them as they rode into battle, brandishing their sage-smoked shields and wearing lances fringed with eagle feathers."[1] In the Southwest, where Crane is ubiquitous in fables, legends, pictographs, and petroglyphs, there is a Sandhill Crane Clan at Zuñi pueblo, and the Tewa people of San Juan pueblo have a tradition that the dances of kachinas and sacred clowns are directed by Crane Old Man. (Crane Old Man may also represent the whooper, since that bird is prominent on a wall of murals at Pottery Mound, New Mexico; the white crane formerly occurred as far south as the highlands of central Mexico and may have been the totem that inspired the Aztecs to call themselves the Crane People.) The great war leader Tecumseh depended on "crane power" in his heroic attempt in the early nineteenth century to unify the Indian tribes against the invading white men; the unity symbol used by the peace movement in the sixties was originally a Hopi Indian sign derived from the footprint of the crane.[2]

A t the turn of the century, the whooping cranes that nested formerly in southern and western Wisconsin and along the Mississippi headwaters were failing to appear, and within thirty years, Wisconsin's sandhill cranes were also disappearing, due to hunting and habitat destruction. In 1929, when a young Forest Service biologist named Aldo Leopold could find but five pairs of sandhills in the state, he chastised the museums for continuing to collect specimens. Not until crane hunting was outlawed did Wisconsin's scattered population begin a slow recovery, adapting gradually to smaller wetlands closer to human habitation.[3]

In late September 1994, during a visit to the International Crane Foundation in Baraboo, Wisconsin, George Archibald took me to the

Narrows, an elevation which overlooks the forested Baraboo hills—the largest deciduous woodland in the state—and also a broad area of ancient marshy bottoms that he hopes to see converted to crane wetlands. In an autumn cornfield, near a picturesque red barn and a hillside turning swiftly to fall colors, a dozen greater sandhills picked and fed. To the north lay the counties of Leopold's classic *Sand County Almanac*; we visited his old writing shack on a sand hill which he had replanted with red pines and other native trees. "The Shack" is maintained by Nina Leopold Bradley, who lives in a pretty woodland house not far away; the sandhill crane, his daughter says, made Dr. Leopold an impassioned advocate of conservation. ("Wherever the truth may lie," he wrote in the preface to his book, "this much is crystal clear: our bigger-and-better society is now like a hypochondriac, so obsessed with its own economic health as to have lost the capacity to remain healthy . . . Nothing could be more salutary at this stage than a little healthy contempt for [our] plethora of material blessings.")

When the ICF was founded in 1973, its primary mission was the raising and maintenance of the rare cranes for long-term protection and potential restoration to the wild. That ambition expanded as the world's cranes declined and more and more species became endangered, until finally, with its first black-necked and wattled cranes (in 1993), it had successfully bred all fifteen species.

In recent years, the foundation's emphases have shifted from rare crane reproduction to public education, the study and perpetuation of fragile ecosystems, and international cooperation with regional organizations to preserve crane habitat within the context of general biodiversity, which the ICF is already establishing in China, Korea, Africa, and Southeast Asia.

Crane City at the ICF is a twelve-acre complex of sturdy sheds and ample pens roofed and separated from one another by mesh wire, with the view of the next pen blocked by green plastic "walls" to deter these

Sandhill crane (*Grus canadensis*)

often fractious birds from agitating or attacking one another. The cranes are timid before forming pairs, after which they become increasingly territorial and aggressive, obliging their handlers to wear heavy gloves and eye shields. Entering the pens, we are accosted several times; the white-napeds and the Siberians, George says, are the most feisty. Some dance with him when he leaps up and down, waving his arms— a sort of *Grus* impersonation that has led to significant insights about the imprinting of cranes on surrogate parents, which in turn has led to experiments with crane-costumed feeding and the rearing of young birds in preparation for release into the wild and a life unmanipulated by human beings. (The method was first tried successfully in 1982 by George's wife, Kyoko, using local sandhills.)

Prowling the Crane City pens, my inspired guide pointed out such fine anomalies as the flesh-colored bill in the blue crane and the flesh-colored soles on the feet of *Grus nigricollis*. We paused to enjoy a small flock of wild sandhills that flew over low, calling out to the captive birds, creating uproar. Back in Archibald's office, as goldfinches, bluebirds, and magnolia warblers came and went outside his window, I wondered aloud if the two crowned cranes, with their arboreal perching habit, had retained any webbing between the toes. Excited as a child, the Craniac sprang from behind his desk as if set free. "Let's go find out!" he cried, with the spontaneous enthusiasm and curiosity that has made him so very effective as a crane champion. We hustled over to the public pens, where we soon determined that *Balearica* indeed possessed the bare vestige of webbing between central and outer toes that is found in *Grus*.

In late winter and early spring, all over the Gulf Coast, the Southwest, and northern Mexico, the sandhill cranes grow restless. Calling and circling, they gather up their flocks, until at last the cycle of the turning earth propels them on their annual migration. Heading northward from the Gulf Coast, from the Muleshoe Wildlife Refuge of west Texas, New Mexico's Bosque del Apache National Wildlife Refuge, and the fifty square miles of bitter lake called Wilcox Playa in southeast Arizona, the skeins of birds funnel like sand grains into the narrow waist of the great hourglass of the continent's central flyway and descend to the great staging area along the Platte River in Nebraska, where most will arrive by early March. Here the flocks feed and feed again, accumulating the spring instincts and life energies that will urge them aloft to call and circle, summoning their cohorts in pursuit of winter as it withdraws into the north.

Seen from the airplane as it descends toward the Platte, the crane flocks circle the cold sky over the winter farmland and the sandhill country of small marshes and rolling hills on the north side of the broad valley for which this bird was named. Below the plane's wing, the Platte, flowing east out of the Wyoming Rockies, is the largest of the prairie rivers that water the Great Plains. Here in south-central Nebraska, it crosses the mighty flyway where oxbows, shallow lakes and marshes, river edges, and harvested brown fields sustain the greatest assembly of cranes and migrant waterfowl left in America.

The Platte, "too thick to drink, too thin to plow," was the great river road toward the far west, serving the Mormon and Oregon trails, the Pony Express, and the first transcontinental telegraph line, railroad, and highway. Much of what is now valuable cropland in this broad landscape was originally sedge meadow that furnished abundant tubers for the cranes. Even so, the cranes (and waterfowl) were less numerous before the advent of row-crop agriculture and its harvest waste made a vast food supply available to tide the birds over these cold days of late winter and early spring.

Unfortunately, in this semiarid region, farming requires massive irrigation. Diversion of the Platte began around 1880, and over the next century, the demand for reservoir storage and hydroelectric power for growing populations in towns and cities as far away as Denver has drastically depleted its flow, diverting perhaps 70 percent of the normal volume before it reaches this stretch of the river. With water low, aggressive vegetation has encroached upon the banks, making brushy islands of the larger bars while narrowing the open channels that cranes require for roosting. As the wetlands become woodlands, crane habitat has shrunk from two hundred miles of river to this sixty-mile stretch between Grand Island and Kearney where the crane companies crowd dangerously in the few reaches of open water that remain.

Seen from the air, the reduced Platte is little more than a wide shallow creek through cottonwood and wet meadow, set about with the fresh reds of spring willow. The shifting sandbars, parting the braids of the wandering channels, may be mere shallows surrounded by deeper water; for roosting cranes, the bars afford a clear view of the willow banks and river woods from which a hunting coyote would have to wade and swim. Spreading away on both sides of the river are broad brown stubbled fields scattered with corn left over from the harvest, inviting the prodigious daytime gleaning that strengthens the migrants for the ordeal of their journey to the half-frozen nesting grounds farther north.

I am met at the airport by Ken Strom, director of the Lillian Rowe Sanctuary, established on the Platte in 1974 and administered by the National Audubon Society; he takes me at once to the river. Here silver-brown bird legions forage in the stubble and green winter wheat behind the banks—no fewer than ten thousand cranes in sight at once, the crane clamor resounding through the closed windows of the car. Absorbing the silence of their mighty sound, we watch them for a long time without speaking, as one might watch storm surf from the dunes, or a prairie fire. At sunset, the restless waves of feathered life overflow into the shallows and out along the bars, brown in one light, silver-gray a moment later. In hiding in a mesh-and-deadwood blind as we let the multitudes alight around us, drifting and falling from on high in sky-darkening numbers and unearthly clamor, we lose ourselves, escape into the roar that is bearing us away.

The sandhill crane, *Grus canadensis*, has a widespread, broken distribution, occurring formerly over most of North America. *Canadensis* includes from two to six geographic races, depending on the philosophy of the authority. Among the putative races, three—the lesser sandhill or "little brown crane," *Grus canadensis canadensis*; the intermediate or Canada crane, *G. c. rowani*; and the greater, *G. c. tabida*—are migratory and relatively numerous, while three others (in Mississippi, Florida, and Cuba) are nonmigratory and relatively few.[4] (A fourth nonmigratory group was extirpated early in the twentieth century from the coastal marshes of Louisiana; it was last seen in 1907.) Including all races and populations, the species is presently estimated at 650,000 birds, more than three times as many as the Eurasian crane and almost as numerous as the other fourteen species put together.[5]

The crane thousands observed on this cold clear afternoon of early spring include all three migratory races of *G. canadensis*; the great majority are lessers, but there are also about thirty thousand greaters and a somewhat larger number of so-called Canadas. (The typical greater—which has probably been divided into eastern and western populations since the Pleistocene—appears twice the size of the lesser, and even the intermediate, when seen with the two others, is readily distinguishable by size.[6])

G. c. canadensis, with numbers estimated at 450,000, is by far the most far-flung race, with a vast Arctic and sub-Arctic breeding range in the Northwest Territories and Alaska[7] that extends westward to the islands of the Bering Strait; from there, an estimated 65,000 will fly onward to the Chukotskiy and Kamchatka peninsulas and 1,500 miles along Siberia's Arctic coast to the Indigirka and Kolyma rivers in Yakutia, where their range joins that of the Siberian crane. In autumn, the Crane from the East, as the Yakuts know it, returns to Alaska before heading south to widespread wintering grounds in the southwestern United States and as far as Chihuahua, in central Mexico; its journey of some five thousand miles in each direction is the longest made by any crane.[8]

Ken Strom is a veteran of the 1992 expedition to Black Dragon River. Other Amur friends, including George Archibald and Sergei Smirenski, greet us that evening in Kearney, where they compare the Platte River with the Amur and also the Indus in Pakistan, all of them large shallow braided rivers with shifting sandbars that attract migrating cranes. The Amur is afflicted by border tensions between nations and the Indus by the swarms of human beings on its banks, but neither, as yet, has suffered man's attempts to harness it with dams. In Wyoming and Colorado as well as Nebraska, the Platte is bound tight by more than forty dams, with forty more still pending: if these are constructed, more than 80 percent of this already diminished river will be lost, and with it, the most critical crane migration sanctuary in North America. Indeed, sandhill legions on this river, dancing and bugling in spring and fall, are by far the greatest crane assemblies on earth.

From another blind early next morning, George Archibald and I watch a ghostly shape emerge from the gray daybreak light and form itself as Coyote; it picks its way through deadwood and willow, working upriver. Across the shallows, forty yards away, the bar is hidden by companies of waking sandhills, but one woebegone bird is well off by itself, hunched down on a bare point. Soon the coyote emerges from the brush and slips into the shallows, swimming without haste toward the bar. Challenging the raider with shrill guard calls, the bird flocks shift to clear a path but do not fly, knowing what this animal is after. Subtly it alters course, tending gradually toward its quarry, and in that moment the lone bird snaps its head from beneath its wing. At once the coyote resumes its path, trotting and swimming across bar, braid, and shallow, and emerging on the farther bank of the main channel; it pauses to shake water off its coat before slipping into the willow brush without a backward look.

Sunrise. Most of the cranes are a pale rust color except on the head and upper neck. *Canadensis* in spring daubs its dun feathers with clay, continuing to paint itself all the way north, using wet and decaying marsh vegetation and sometimes the mud itself; the earth tones will serve to camouflage the bird in the northern terrains where it will nest.[9]

The Eurasian crane confines its efforts to its mantle or back feathers, while the Siberian—whose snowy plumage does not lend itself to camouflage—is content with a few swipes across its nape or a rough circlet at the base of its neck. The Siberian's token self-adornment may be no more than desultory ritual performed prior to courtship, a vestigial trait of some ancestral crane that was cryptic in coloration, reduced over the ages to the "old behavior" of an overspecialized and quirky bird. Real camouflage in that species would be nonadaptive, since like all white cranes, the Siberian depends on its high visibility to flare rivals of its own species off its territories.

Soon after the sun fires the horizon, the crane armies rise in stupendous celebration, crossing the black winter trees along the river. "Then, with this great hurrah, they went up and were gone. It felt like they'd ripped my heart out and taken it with them."[10] The sound brought back a moonlit night of many years ago when, stalking a huge roosted flock of geese, I crawled painfully on hands and knees across a frozen potato field, inching into the very edges of the flock before heads shot up and the outriders sounded the alarm. Five thousand Canadas took off in a mighty yelping roar around my ears, the hard heavy wings beating the air and the climbing silhouettes blotting the moon and turning the night dark—an exaltation of life never matched until this dawn when the sandhills rose in thunder, swirling and climbing and parting into wisps and strands in the fiery suffusions of the sunrise.

George Archibald finds the sandhill's voice the loveliest among the cranes, despite its "broken" rattle, since it lacks the plaintive stridency of those *Grus* species possessed of longer tracheas. Whispering as we watch and listen, we continue our discussions of crane evolution begun in other years on the Amur River.

Though research on fossil birds has been quite limited except in North America, it has been generally assumed that the crane subfamily originated in the Old World, since eight of its fifteen modern species breed in eastern Asia. But as George observes, their present distribution does not ensure that Asia was their place of origin: the ancestral forms might have originated in North America. After all, the earliest fossil species of *Balearica* were found in North America, and the first fossils of cold-hardy ancestral *Grus*. George imagines an unspecialized bird of cryptic appearance, a sort of proto-sandhill, but the Eurasian crane is also an unspecialized and successful species of modest size and cryptic plumage, and either of these grayish birds, in his opinion, might have resembled the *Grus* ancestor that spread from North America to Asia before the great radiation of modern crane species occurred.[11]

Some proto-*Grus* would have remained in North America, where they evolved into the sandhills. Others followed *Balearica* to Asia, where certain populations became isolated in separate habitats by glacier movements and the changing climate of the oncoming Ice Age. If the *Grus* ancestor was most similar to *G. grus*, then *G. japonensis* (which in its head pattern is very similar to *grus*) was perhaps the first of the modern cranes to radiate from this *grus*-like ancestor, since it differs more from its sibling species than any other crane in the Group of Five and is also the most evolved in its courtship behavior. Next, perhaps, came the hooded crane (*monachus*) of the northeast Asian woodlands, which at higher altitudes would evolve into *G. nigricollis*, the black-necked crane. (A few years later, George said blithely, "I have changed my mind," having concluded that *japonensis* developed separately from that ancestor which gave rise to the *grus* and *monachus* lines, which led respectively to *americana* and *nigricollis*.[12])

In a general hypothesis based on his unison call research, and not seriously contradicted by DNA evidence, the *Grus* ancestor had spread farther west on the Asian continent, evolving in the uplands as an early demoiselle and in the wetlands as an ancestral Siberian; subsequently, these cranes spread into Africa, where an early Siberian was a forebear of the wattled crane and an early demoiselle ancestral to the blue. In southern Asia, the radiating *Grus* evolved into the sarus (*G. antigone*), which in the increasingly cold climate of the Pleistocene would divide into nonmigratory and migratory populations; the northern migrant became the ancestral white-naped crane (*G. vipio*), which would later develop a *vipio-antigone* descendant, the brolga (*G. rubicundus*); the sarus, white-naped, and brolga formed the group of closely related "diggers" which George refers to as the Group of Three. (Most modern *Grus* are untroubled by cold and snow so long as there is food, but the behavior of captive birds makes clear that the loose-feathered tropical species—the crowned cranes, sarus, and brolga—cannot tolerate winter cold in outdoor pens.)

As I have mentioned, curiously—despite the presence of nonmigratory *G. canadensis* as far south as Cuba—there is no evidence, past or present, of cranes in South America, even though promising habitat exists in the Amazon Basin, the llanos of Venezuela, the high-altitude puna of Peru, the great Pantanal marshes of the south-central continent, and the plains of Patagonia.[13] Perhaps it was disease, George says, or possibly usurpation of the cranes' ecological niche by an ancestor such as the huge and fearsome *Diatryma*.

Unless *leucogeranus* can be called a *Grus*, *canadensis* appears to be the earliest modern species to evolve from the *Grus* ancestor. The un-

Robert Bateman 2001 ©

Brolga (*Grus rubicundus*)

Black crowned crane (*Balearica pavonina*)

Wattled crane (*Grus carunculatus*)

Blue crane (*Anthropoides paradisea*)

Whooping crane (*Grus americana*)

Sandhill and whooping cranes (*Grus canadensis* and *Grus americana*)

Juvenile whooping
crane (*Grus americana*)

Juvenile sandhill
(*Grus canadensis*)

specialized sandhill never developed "newer" characters such as the striking face patterns that distinguish other *Grus*. In the throes of courtship, the sandhill may engage in violent head bowing and leap twelve feet into the air with wings partly opened, but it lacks the lateral wing displays, including the "butterfly" charge posture, that are common to all of its *Grus* kin.

Yet as a bird of generalized habits and appearance, *canadensis* shares characters and habits with every other species. As in the demoiselle and blue, the bill of the sandhill is short enough to take seeds in the uplands, yet long enough to permit the wetland foraging of other *Grus*. It is notably unfussy in its domestic arrangements, nesting according to local conditions on dry dunes or in bogs, on arid plains (in Cuba), marsh hummocks, and the rough edges of golf courses (where, unlike most cranes, the nesting hen often permits a close approach, perhaps to divert itself with a better look at *Homo sapiens*).

Excepting the Siberian and wattled cranes, whose placement in this genus is still debated, the sandhill is the only *Grus* excluded from the two main groups of Palearctic and Australasian cranes, even though it has clear affinities with both—for example, it shows red on the crown like the Group of Five but also on the side of the head (down to the eyes) like the Group of Three. In addition, it shares traits with the Siberian, which DNA analyses have established as the most "primitive" and atypical of the eleven species presently assigned to *Grus*. Even more so than the Siberian (and the Eurasian), it indulges regularly in feather painting. Like the Siberian, it performs a rapid seesaw head-snapping during the unison call. It is even "primitive" like *Balearica* in its lack of the open-wing display, and also in its shorter trachea.

That the sandhill shares distinctive traits with every other crane strengthens its status as an "ancient one," as does the fact that it is the earliest of all modern species on the fossil record, turning up in its present form among Wyoming fossils nine million years old. It moves me (for strange reasons I cannot fathom) that the elegant creature rising in companies from the bars of the Platte on this March morning is the most ancient of all birds, the oldest living bird species on earth.

Drifting down the horizons, the crane armadas call and call. Gazing after the last faint strings, Dr. Archibald sighs in a wonder and contentment that always seems to refresh itself among the cranes. "I think we could build the whole Gruidae group out of these sandhills," the Craniac says gleefully, rubbing his hands to warm them.

At midday, awaiting the evening flight of cranes, we travel south and east across the Little Blue River country, traversing an immense flat plain with grain elevators, corn bins, and nitrate factories arranged variously on the horizons; our destination is a "rainwater basin," a shallow pothole the size of a large lake, where we join a bald eagle in intent observation of great crowds of snow geese, white-fronted and Canada geese, canvasback and redhead, mallard and pintail, scaup, widgeon, and teal. In the evening, returned to the river, I enter a good blind with a wire-mesh roof strewn lightly with sticks, where I listen for a while to the spring redwings and a solitary cardinal, setting up his territory from a perch in an old cottonwood by the water. Soon a horn note comes downwind from a sky losing its light, and within minutes, the first thousand cranes are circling the river woods and gliding down into cropland and meadow, from where they will make the short flight to the channels. Soon the legions come straight in, many thousands at a time, filling the river dusk with yelps and beating wings; the birds are still falling as the darkness comes, falling among black limbs of old broken cottonwoods, falling until bar and shallow are shrouded in shifting shapes, the nearest scarcely fifty feet away. Already some are quiet. They drink from the silver glitter of the braid as evening deer step out from the night willow and move in peaceful silhouette among them.

As in all migratory cranes, the spring journey to the breeding grounds is far more urgent than the return in autumn. In a week or two, even as the last sandhill squadrons lift from the river bottoms, calling to their kind to follow as they circle higher into hard March skies, a few families of whooping cranes come from the south. Arriving later in the season, not lingering long, the unsociable whoopers ignore the last sandhill clusters or chase them from their feeding grounds and roosts.

Sandhills, like whoopers, are principally diurnal migrants, taking advantage of the warm thermals and using "spiral-gliding" flight where possible to conserve energy.[14] Both species are thought to drive off their last year's young during spring migration, and since juveniles lack the reproductive urge that might propel them farther north, they often wander.

Forming orderly companies over the river valley, the circling sandhills take their bearings on distant breeding grounds in the sub-Arctic, fanning out like flights of mighty arrows. Many of the lesser sandhills will point toward the Yukon delta in the far northwest and the shine of the north Pacific; and some will cross the ice-strewn water of the Bering Strait, gliding and soaring on cold Arctic winds toward the white horizons of Siberia.

TWELVE

Grus americana

In 1831, according to contemporary report, the whooping crane was common in the fur countries of Canada, and was even then so tenacious of life that there were known instances "of the wounded bird putting the fowler to flight, and fairly driving him off the field." This information will be of small surprise to people familiar with this spirited species . . . The most statuesque of North American birds, standing over five feet tall, the whooping crane moves nearly a yard with each long graceful stride; its fierce, fiery eye and javelin beak, backed by a mask of angry carmine skin, might well give pause to any creature wishing harm to it . . .

The whooper was one of the first birds remarked upon by the explorers of this continent, and the wild horn note of its voice . . . contributed to its early legend. Its dislike of civilization was evidenced by its swift disappearance from the east coast . . . During the nineteenth century it retreated west of the Mississippi, and by 1880 was a rare bird everywhere. It was last seen in Illinois in 1891, and a nesting in Hancock County, Iowa, four years later, was the last recorded in the United States.

—Peter Matthiessen, *Wildlife in America*, 1959

At the time of the first Europeans, the whooping crane, never abundant, had an estimated population of fifteen thousand birds. Four decades ago, when the above elegy was written, only twenty-six remained on earth, a number which had varied little since the 1920s; a whooper nest found in 1922 by a game warden near Kerrobert, Saskatchewan, was the last one discovered anywhere in

North America. A magnificent bird was vanishing from the earth, and any hope that the last flock might prevail seemed small indeed.

Historically, the breeding range of *Grus americana* extended from Illinois north and west through the central prairie states and provinces into central Alberta; it wintered discontinuously from the highlands of central Mexico and the Gulf Coast of Texas and Louisiana to the southeast Atlantic seaboard and the Delaware and Chesapeake bays. By the time of the widespread prairie settlement after the Civil War, however, it was already uncommon, with no more than fourteen hundred scattered birds.

By the turn of the century, whooping cranes no longer bred in the United States; by the 1930s, they were gone from prairies of Canada. Twenty to thirty still arrived each fall in the coastal marshes of Texas, but those that wintered on the King Ranch and the Blackjack Peninsula did not reappear after 1937.[1] In August 1940, a small nonmigratory group of thirteen whoopers, only recently discovered at White Lake in the Louisiana swamps, was scattered by hurricane and flood; a juvenile observed before that storm was presumed to be the last wild whooper born in the United States.

In the winter of 1941–42, after a century of shooting, egg collecting, and habitat destruction, including the draining of large areas of Gulf Coast marsh to create rice fields, only fifteen *Grus americana* returned to the salt marshes at Aransas—far too few, it was thought, to overcome inbreeding in addition to the many hazards of a long, arduous migration. Nor was there a way to protect the flock once the birds left Texas, since the home of the crane, far north beyond Saskatchewan in the continent's vast sub-Arctic territories, remained a mystery. The situation was so dire that the National Audubon Society and the Fish and Wildlife Service joined forces with the Canadian Wildlife Service to sponsor joint field investigations of *americana*'s natural history in order to learn what might reasonably be done to help the surviving birds.

Then, years later, the cranes brought six young south, and by 1950, their precarious numbers had climbed to thirty-three; in the next three years, however, twenty-four were destroyed during migration, mostly by hunters in Saskatchewan. There a body of farmers, complaining that the

Canadian Wildlife Service and other groups associated with the Crane Project were wasting money on a doomed bird potentially destructive to their crops, vowed publicly to shoot the pesky things on sight. With the count falling dangerously again, the Audubon Society solicited public interest and support, broadcasting the crane's dramatic story all along the known migration route—Texas, Oklahoma, Kansas, Nebraska, the Dakotas, Montana, and Saskatchewan—and especially in the environs of known resting places such as the South Saskatchewan, Platte, Niobrara, Cimarron, and Red rivers. The campaign was successful, the shooting stopped; the nesting territories remained unknown.

On June 30, 1954, after an intensive nine-year search, *americana*'s breeding ground was discovered accidentally when a fire patrol flying over the Salt River–Fort Resolution region of the Northwest Territories, east of the Rockies and west of the rocky barren country of the Precambrian shield, spotted a pair of great white birds with a brown juvenile in a wilderness of pond, muskeg, and wet meadow; the first nests were found in the following year by a team led by Robert P. Allen of the Audubon Society. The cranes had taken refuge, as Allen would report, in "a sheltered and remote spot, far from the normal paths of mankind, with natural features that provide food and water, protection from lightning-set fires . . . and without other animal inhabitants that might provide a serious threat as predators."[2] Better still, all the nests were located within Wood Buffalo National Park, a huge fastness of black spruce, birch, and willow on the border of Alberta and the Northwest Territories, not far south of Great Slave Lake. The migration route of the last flock, from the Northwest Territories to the Texas coast, was 2,600 miles long, a flight exceeded in North America only by those lesser sandhills that journeyed between the Siberian sub-Arctic and central Mexico.

In that year of discovery, 1954, not a single juvenile arrived in Aransas, but subsequently the *americana* population, protected at both ends of its migration route as well as at Cheyenne Bottoms in Kansas and other resting places on the way, began a slow recovery, although its situation remains precarious. A half century later, it is still by far the rarest of the cranes.[3]

In 1957, on a field research trip for a book on America's vanishing wildlife,[4] I paid a visit to the two survivors of the storm-lost Louisiana flock in their sad, cramped pen behind the New Orleans zoo. From there I went on to Aransas, where the twenty-six birds of that winter's company, scattered across the salt meadows and boggy pools and creeks of the barrier island marshes, were readily observed from the Audubon boat, which slowed here and there in the canals to view a wary crane. Dwarfing the herons and egrets, they stalked like avengers over dark green spartina. (They will also forage in the upland, where they hunt for small live food; the refuge lands are burned over in rotation, about five thousand acres a year, to make small prey more accessible to the cranes and other creatures.)

In the black primaries of the white wing and the black alula feathers at the wing crook, concealed when the wing is folded, the whooping crane much resembles the Siberian, which also appears pure white at any distance; in its bare black forehead and crimson crown, it resembles *japonensis*, to which it is more closely related; and like *japonensis*, it has a long black beak used to probe for animals in mud. However, its bustle is white, not black, and its red crown, black lores, and red line straight back from the bill form a distinctive mask.

Grus americana has a coiled trachea over five feet long, the longest in its family, but in its vocalizations and visual displays (as well as the striking arrangement of its black-and-carmine mask), the whooper is virtually identical to the Eurasian crane *G. grus*, which supports George Archibald's theory that in long-lost eons, an ancestral *grus* spread eastward across Beringia to North America, where it survived competition with the native sandhills by adapting to aquatic habitats and evolving into a larger and more specialized white bird of open wetlands—in short, the whooping crane.[5] It is no coincidence that, among the fifteen crane species that fly the earth, the rarest and most imperiled are the three white species. Like emblems of the purity of water, earth, and air that is being lost, the white cranes are dependent on pristine wetlands, and in this they are the most specialized in their subfamily. Unlike the three which are most numerous and successful—the sandhill, Eurasian, and demoiselle, all creatures of modest size and subdued appearance—

the white cranes, in varying degrees, have failed to adapt to the spring shoots and harvest gleanings of man's agriculture.

Though most have left Wood Buffalo by the end of September, the last migrants may not turn up at Aransas until December; pairs accompanied by new-fledged juveniles are often the last to arrive. Whoopers migrate in scattered family groups but all follow the same general route; on their winter marshes, despite some territorial feeding, they are essentially a single flock, vulnerable to swift destruction by hard storm, like the Louisiana flock in 1940. Mostly they forage on the inshore side of the Intracoastal Waterway, which in the year (1941) that the cranes reached their low ebb of thirteen birds was dredged right through the six thousand acres of marsh habitat by the Corps of Engineers, at a loss of about fifteen hundred acres to the refuge. Every day, the main channel is plowed by cargo ships of the chemical and petroleum industries which surround their narrow habitat, and the risk of a serious oil spill is increased by the oil drilling and extraction industries nearby. In the years since World War II, much more habitat has been lost as the marsh banks erode in the heavy wash of propellers; as their walls collapsed, the brackish feeding pools behind the banks, with their crane fare of blue crabs, fiddlers, and clams, poured away into the channel, until an estimated 20 percent of the refuge had disappeared. Not until the turn of the millennium did the corps see fit to protect the banks with a heavy matting of interlocked tiles, off-loading the spoil from channel dredging inside this barrier and seeding it with marsh plants instead of dumping it at sea. The cranes have not resorted to this man-made habitat as yet, but it is hoped they will.

Beginning in 1967, a team of Canadian and American researchers removed one egg from the clutch of two in each of the wild nests in Wood Buffalo in order to create a captive flock at the Fish and Wildlife

Whooping crane (*Grus americana*)

Service's Patuxent Wildlife Research Center in Laurel, Maryland. In 1975, forty-nine whoopers turned up at Aransas, and that spring, in a bold attempt to establish a second migratory population, fourteen fresh eggs from Wood Buffalo were placed in the nests of sandhill cranes at Grays Lake, Idaho, to be hatched, reared, and led by their foster parents on an eight-hundred-mile migration from Grays Lake to the Bosque del Apache National Wildlife Refuge in New Mexico. This was a much shorter and less dangerous flight than the journey from Wood Buffalo to Aransas, and for a time, it seemed that this cross-fostered flock, reared from 380 surplus whooper eggs transplanted between 1975 and 1988, and increasing to thirty-three fledged birds by 1984, might actually perpetuate itself and prosper.

Sadly, the migrating whoopers collided repeatedly with power lines that were avoided by the smaller and more agile sandhills, especially in Colorado's San Luis Valley, an important staging area in spring and fall migration. Others would perish of cholera and tuberculosis, apparently contracted from the snow geese with which they shared the winter grounds at Bosque del Apache. Others still were struck down by golden eagles and shot by local hunters, who resented being fined or imprisoned for shooting big white birds which they professed they had confused with snow geese.

Much more serious, however, was the growing realization that no pair bonds were forming or were likely to form in the brave new flock, presumably because the whoopers—which could be taught new migration routes by men and sandhills but not the instinct for the appropriate behavior needed to awaken a breeding response in their own kind—had imprinted on sandhill signals, to which their prospective mates were unreceptive; the sole chick produced was a sandhill-whooper hybrid. The experiment was given up in 1988, though the doomed flock continued to travel north and south for the next decade, slowly dwindling in number. By the winter of 1990–91, when eleven were reported killed at Bosque del Apache, only thirteen remained of the eighty-five fledged at Grays Lake over the years. On a visit to Bosque in 1998, I saw but two whoopers among the sandhills; the lone bird that survived the millennium died in 2001.

As early as 1979, crane specialists, including George Archibald, were discussing the establishment of a nonmigratory flock in central Florida. A century ago, those whoopers which bred in the north-central states—Wisconsin, Minnesota, Iowa, the Dakotas—had been regular winter visitors, to judge from the fact that in the half century between 1870 and 1920, 250 were reported shot—surely a fraction of the actual kill in what was then a rough frontier state. A whooper collected by a taxidermist near St. Augustine in the late 1920s was the last recorded casualty, and another seen in the Kissimmee prairie of Osceola County in 1936 was the last known sighting.

(These records do not reflect the imaginative accounts of whoopers dancing in the Florida backcountry classic *The Yearling*,[6] nor some problematical observations made by my late acquaintance, the painter John Little, in his Florida boyhood: "Whoo-pahs? C'antless duhz-ens of 'em back in the swamp behind the house," Little once assured me. When I raised an eyebrow, he became indignant; did I doubt the testimony of a Floridian born and bred? Had he not seen those whoopers with his own eyes? "C'antless *duhz-ens* of 'em! And ever' las' one jus' a bee-*you*-tifull pow-dah blue!")

That the lost Louisiana flock had survived in similar habitat was a compelling argument for the Kissimmee, a vast marsh-and-savanna country of shallow lakes, palmetto scrub, fenced cattle range, and game management areas with a dearth of human beings and a plenitude of surrogate parents in the form of nonmigratory "Florida sandhills" (four to six thousand, including those across the Georgia border in the Okefenokee Swamp) and also an increasing winter population of the very similar "greater sandhills" which came south each fall from the north-central states. These visitors were identified in the 1970s by Florida Game and Wildlife Commission biologist Lovell Williams, who was first to notice that a large fraction of the local flocks disappeared each spring.

With a young field researcher named Steve Nesbitt, his colleague on the commission, Dr. Williams investigated methods of establishing young captive whooping cranes in Florida. Although more aquatic and carnivorous than the sandhills, whoopers resort to the same general habitat, and the hope was that the resident sandhills might lead released whoopers to good forage locations and safe roosts in shallow water. In 1979, a release program was proposed to the whooping crane recovery teams in the United States and Canada.

In experiments during the 1980s, in preparation for the proposed release, eggs of the nonmigratory Florida sandhills were replaced in twenty-three wild nests by eggs of the migratory greater sandhills to establish whether crane migration is innate (as in certain shorebirds and other birds) or whether the instinct is awakened by the leadership of the parents returning north. In the absence of parents, the introduced juveniles, though they might wander, were more likely to return to the release area than set out for the north—so it was hoped, and so it would turn out. Some juveniles of the introduced greater sandhills tended to drift south in autumn, in response to some ancestral instinct or the passage of other migrants overhead, but they did not migrate northward in the spring.

Local backlash against the Grays Lake whoopers in New Mexico had prejudiced federal bureaucrats against introducing them elsewhere; also, the mortalities inevitable in induced migration seemed too great in such a precious bird. But during the 1980s, federal resistance was overcome as the improved chances of nonmigratory birds released in sparsely inhabited ranchland became clear. By now, the ICF had become very successful in raising captive cranes, and in 1989 it was entrusted with some of the surplus eggs from the Fish and Wildlife Service's Patuxent flock so that it could help produce young birds for the release program.

Meanwhile, in the Texas flock, the winter count had risen to forty-five by 1964, eighty-five by 1976. A decline in the early 1980s returned the flock to seventy-odd birds, but that troubling drop was followed by six good breeding years—so good that in the winter of 1989–90, 146 whooping cranes arrived at Aransas. With the wild flock doing so well, and both the ICF and Patuxent producing numbers of young birds reared in isolation by crane-costumed keepers, the time had come for the Florida release.

The first "cohort" of new whoopers, eight from the ICF and two from Patuxent, arrived in Florida in the second week of January in 1993, two years ahead of schedule. The release site was the Three Lakes Wildlife Management Area in the broad, well-watered country between Kissimmee and Yeehaw Junction.[7] One of the least-damaged regions left in Florida—it had fifty pairs of resident bald eagles[8]—its largest settlement was tiny Kenansville, at the south end of Lake Kissimmee; lakes Marion and Jackson, entirely enclosed in the wildlife management area, were uninhabited. With abundant foraging and nesting sites, and with cattle ranchers sympathetic to the project, the Three Lakes seemed ideal.

To minimize injuries in transport and in the pens, all of the newcomers were fledged juveniles, approximately six to eight months old, or about the age when they would normally be banished by their parents; this is also an age when young whoopers show little aggression toward one another once the hierarchy within their flock, or "cohort," has been established. To keep them from wandering too far and getting lost, the birds were fitted with restraint harnesses called brails, which keep one wing at a time from full extension; off balance, they cannot fly from the conditioning pen. (After two weeks, the birds are recaptured in the pen and the brails are switched to the other wing, to prevent any atrophy of muscles.) This temporary restraint, together with the food made available at the pens, would establish "place loyalty" and keep the cohort from scattering too widely to maintain an effective breeding group upon maturity.

The hope that local sandhills would lead these pen-raised birds to safe roosts and good feeding areas was quickly abandoned. *Americana* and *canadensis*, while not competitive except on breeding territories, turned out to be mutually indifferent—all but one quirky whooper female which regularly chose the company of sandhills over that of her own species, inviting the suspicion that she had somehow become imprinted on surrogate sandhill parents at the ICF or Patuxent before coming to Florida. While most would eventually learn to follow the lead of the local sandhills, the whoopers were initially attracted to other white species, mainly the great egret, and would actually call out to large white birds with black wing tips similar to their own, such as white pelicans, wood storks, and white ibis.

On March 9, 1993, at the release pen on the east shore of Lake Marion, about forty miles south of St. Cloud, I introduce myself to project director Steve Nesbitt, who introduces me to his colleagues, biologist Marty Folk and veterinarian Dr. Marilyn Spalding. Folk lives in St. Cloud, and his team is monitoring the cranes on a daily basis.[9] The unroofed pen, 100 by 400 feet, is surrounded by high steel-mesh fence to discourage predators; formerly at the lake edge, it is now high and dry due to sinking water levels caused by unusual drought.

The two months since the first release have been discouraging. Almost half of the first batch of precious whoopers failed to roost at night in open water and have been lost to bobcats, which usually leap onto the bird's back and bite through its spinal cord at the nape. Optimal roosts for both *americana* and *canadensis* are hard-bottomed shallows up to sixteen inches deep, such as a submerged sandbar surrounded by deeper water, with no shore vegetation to impede a 360-degree view. Such roosts, which permit the birds to jump straight up to escape a threat (normally, cranes prefer to run before taking flight), may be used year after year, as in Nebraska's river Platte. Water roosting, like migration, is instinctive, but as with migration, the instinct may perish if not fired by parental example.

Unfortunately, the new birds do not follow when the sandhills fly over in late afternoon but dally until the crepuscular hour preferred by hunting cats. Accustomed to vegetation in their pen rather than water roosts, some hide in reeds and bushes where wild parents would never lead them; others move around at night on the dry land. One has been killed right outside the pen and the other four in a nearby marsh too dry and shallow for safe roosting. In recent weeks, in belated predator control, eleven bobcats have been trapped and "removed" from a one-mile radius around the release site to give the new birds a chance (this has also been done with bobcats and coyotes at Aransas.)[10]

We watch from hiding as the new birds walk up and down inside the wire cage. These pen-raised cranes have never beheld a human face, having been fed and tended since emerging from the egg by peculiar hooded figures garbed in white in simulation of crane parents, a tactic pioneered at the ICF. All have lost weight while acclimating to central Florida, and two are sickly, but the other five leave the pen regularly and are flying strongly. About 3:20 on this hot muggy afternoon, after brief dancing activity, the five fly from the pen, land nearby, and walk down to the lake edge. At 4 P.M., Folk enters the pen in a white sheet to feed the laggards some fresh crawfish he has netted earlier in the day, after which two more fly out and sail down to the lake.

The veterinarian wishes to check the remaining birds, but when approached, the less peaked of the two flies out to join the others; the last bird is herded against the fence and captured. Dr. Spalding takes a bacterial swipe from the hard ivory-colored eye and also a scrape from the inside of the bill. Like the sandhill and most other cranes—and like many other ground-feeding species, such as the woodcock—the whooper may probe in underwater mud with a soft, flexible bill tip that detects small prey; I hold the malleable bill while Spalding takes the bird's temperature and a feces sample from the cloaca. There is little sign of food in the cloaca and the bird is generally emaciated; Spalding thinks its illness may be peritonitis, since these creatures of omnivorous diet will pick at and sometimes swallow bits of glinting metal. (One bird required an operation to remove a treble fishhook from its inner throat.[11]) So chronic is this habit that the galvanized steel mesh of the release pen must be checked with a metal detector for loose bits and shavings.

The five strong birds are already wandering some distance from the pen, chasing armadillos and white ibis; recently they roosted for the night two and a half miles away. After a year or so, if all goes well, this first cohort will form loose pairs, even though they will not reach sexual maturity until they are three or four years old. Judging from sandhill behavior, the researchers assume that the females will disperse more widely, extending the family gene pool by finding a mate elsewhere; the young male eventually returns to winter near the natal area, where he may be tolerated by the male parent during his attempts to establish a neighboring territory of his own. The dominant males will control the territories nearest the release site; the territories radiate outward as more pairs are formed.

Americana may be less immune to subtropical disease than the native *canadensis*; its past failure to breed in Florida might have been caused by a virus known as EEE.[12] All juveniles introduced to Florida in the winter of 1993 were inoculated against EEE, but in the future this practice will be discontinued. As Dr. Archibald says, "Their wild offspring can't be inoculated and protected, so we may as well learn whether a virus will defeat us before we spend millions of dollars on something that can't work."

O f the fourteen cranes released in the winter of 1993, only five survived the first year—a sickening 60 percent rate of mortality—and the following year was even worse, with a 73 percent mortality among nineteen new birds, almost all of it attributable to bobcats; the Florida researchers were now engaged in systematic bobcat trapping and removal. The release methods had been much improved, with a change from fixed steel pens to mobile plastic ones; the new pens have one end submerged to encourage water roosting and can be moved farther into the water or withdrawn, according to flood or drought conditions. Both Patuxent and the ICF were now introducing water into their rearing pens, with the chicks being trained (by following crane-costumed keepers) to enter the water and roost before dusk, when bobcats became most active. (The coyote, which is spreading south from north-central Florida, has so far been a minor threat, and the alligator, too.) Even so, the researchers have concluded that twenty new birds every year will be needed to carry out the full experiment.

By October 1995, a few pairs had begun to form, and that year the mortality rate of the new birds fell to 50 percent, which meant in effect that seventeen of the fifty-two released in the first three winters were established and free-flying. The next year, forty-eight were released, with 40 percent mortality—in effect, a 60 percent survival rate, very close to the optimum that had been hoped for.

By early 1997, the 1993 survivors were mature, and one of the new pairs had been observed in advanced breeding behavior, building a series of nest platforms on the edge of Lake Hart, in the Moss Park area southeast of Orlando. George phoned me to say that the young ICF male was "beautifully paired" with a female from Patuxent, and the first Florida eggs were expected any day. Last year, he said, this pair drove the sandhills out of a large wetland and built several nests; this year they would surely produce the first wild whoopers born in the United States since that lone juvenile reported in the 1940s after the hurricane that destroyed the wild nonmigratory flock in Louisiana.

In late February 1997, with directions from Steve Nesbitt, I drive north from Lake Okeechobee to Lake Marion, in the region north of Yeehaw Junction. Though the Three Lakes is still the home area for the released cranes, the young adults are wandering as far north and west as Suwannee County, and south into Palm Beach and Charlotte counties, almost as far as the Caloosahatchee River.

Approaching Lake Marion on Joe Overstreet Road, I am pleased to see the uncommon caracara; over the lake flies a troupe of black skimmers and three glossy ibis. As Nesbitt has predicted, a pair of whoopers with the bright red crowns of breeding season stalks the public landing, and a single bird stands like a white sentinel in the near distance— possibly the unsociable lone male that shuns the company of cranes of any kind.

Two sandhill cranes pass overhead, and the young whoopers stretch their necks skyward in a unison call, in warning that this boat landing area is their territory. Observed by an impassive eagle on a high dead limb, they dance a bit, but otherwise, throughout several hours, they show less evidence of reproductive intent than of unseemly domestication, thanks largely to the ministrations of a lakeside camper who plies them daily with bologna. (Eventually, the crane team asked the man to stop, and finally to leave the camp, since he could not seem to break his bologna habit. Subsequently, the acculturated pair had to be driven from the landing area, in an effort to break their unhealthy affinity for human company.)

Next morning, I drive northeast to Narcoossee and an area between two small lakes known as Moss Park. Two years ago, and again last year, a pair of whoopers reconnoitered the locality; this year they have constructed several nests. The function of these "starter nests" is not entirely understood, except that they serve to work off excess energy while courtship instincts and breeding relationships come into focus and the main nest site is established. Multiple copulations then occur, and the one or two eggs are laid, two days apart. The false nests may later serve as resting platforms for the chicks, while the parents stand guard beside them, in the shallow water.[13]

At Moss Park, where I am met by Marty Folk, we launch one-man canoes at the canal leading to Lake Hart. Marty is encouraged by the much-improved survival rate of recent years and positively exhilarated by the possibility of whooper eggs and chicks. He is a small tidy sunburned man with glasses, straight black hair, and a sudden grin which bursts onto his face at the very thought. Even now, more new cranes are being released six miles north of Lake Marion on the Overstreet Ranch, where the grazed land provides much less cover for bobcats. With the new mobile pens and improved release methods, the project should continue to reduce mortalities, he says, and the whoopers already established are bound to lead the new cohorts to safe roosts in water.

These days the ICF birds are being released in late October or early November, to avoid the onset of winter in Wisconsin; the Patuxent birds join them after New Year's, from January to early March, but no later than April 1, when bobcats with new kittens are especially active, and when territoriality among established whooper males might cause the newcomers harassment and stress. With no experience of adults, the young birds inevitably invite attack, not having learned to lower their heads and necks to signal submission.

Male cranes, being generally more aggressive than the females, zealously guard and defend their nesting territory. Threat behavior usually suffices to drive off intruders, but cranes can be formidable fighters. Dancing forward, wings half spread, they launch their attack with the long claws of the feet, bowling over the opponent which, once down, may be killed by the javelin beak. (On one occasion, in Putnam County in northern Florida, a sandhill pursued by a whooper was seen by Dr. Spalding to plummet from its flock like a shot bird; she performed a necropsy which located and identified a lethal stab wound in the back of the head.)

P retty Lake Hart has marshy long-grass edges set about with woods of slash pine, swamp maple, and live oak. Nearing the canal mouth, we coast in the woodland silence. The crane pair seems to be calling from just around the point, behind the trees. A moment later the great birds cross directly overhead, huge in the blue sky over the shining pines; they circle twice at treetop level before turning away. This pair has built eight "starter" nests around Lake Hart, causing high expectations, but they have yet to produce eggs, nor will they do so.

In June, the male will disappear and the female, maintaining ritual behavior on their territory, will call alone each morning. Because older females sometimes solicit the attentions of unpaired young males (which discourages interbreeding between siblings), a substitute male is captured at Three Lakes and sent off as soon as possible, wearing a hood to keep him from orienting himself and flying straight back home. At Lake Hart he is grounded for three days by heavy rain and wind, after which, in no way disoriented, he takes flight and returns at once to the Three Lakes. In December, the unlucky female finally joins a group of sandhills; she is found shot in a flooded pasture soon thereafter.

Three more cranes are killed by flying into power lines, yet despite the mortalities, the crane flock is growing. By May 1998, some sixty whoopers are exploring the middle peninsula, among which fourteen have formed pairs. This is a year of serious drought, with both spring and summer dead dry, and there is little courtship activity and no nests or eggs. But in 1999, two of the several pairs that completed nests produce the first egg clutches in the project. Though one clutch is lost to a mammal predator (probably a raccoon or feral hog, both common ani-

mals along the marsh edge) and the other to flooding after heavy local
rain, the release methods seem almost vindicated—almost, but not
quite. In the seven years since my visit to the first group, nearly two
hundred whooping cranes have been released without a single chick to
show for it.

In the first winter of the new millennium, fifteen pairs of whooping
cranes have established territories by early February, and by March,
three nests hold eggs. More exciting still, a chick hatches on March 16,
2000—the first wild whooping crane born in the United States in sixty
years. A second egg hatches on March 18, but ten days later, the
younger chick is seized by a predator—in all likelihood a great horned
owl, since in mammal predation, both chicks (and sometimes a frantic
adult) are usually taken.

On April 11, I meet Steve Nesbitt at the game commission office in
Gainesville; we drive south to St. Cloud, where Marty Folk awaits
us in a mall parking lot. I congratulate him for the well-deserved success represented by the first crane chick. "I think it's still there," Marty
says, "and I hope you see it." Steve Nesbitt grunts, noncommittal; they
talk logistics for a few minutes. Marty will continue north to a ranch
near Okahumpka where a flock of twenty-four young whoopers has
convened; Steve and I will go to Okahumpka the next day.

We set off south again toward the nest location, kept strictly secret
for fear of possible disruption caused by unwise bird-watchers and the
media; Nesbitt smiles at my suggestion that he blindfold me and spin
me around ten times before we go there. At supper with friends the
previous evening, this weathered ornithologist and expert crane man
was shy and quiet, but this morning we have a lot to talk and laugh
about. A native of Washington, D.C., and a graduate of Oklahoma
State University who has worked in Florida since 1971, Steve is a
grandson of the late Dr. Ira Gabrielson, the esteemed director (1940–46)
of the U.S. Biological Survey (which became the Fish and Wildlife Service), who was Steve's beloved mentor throughout his boyhood and

early youth.[14] A friend and strong supporter of Rachel Carson in her battle against the use of DDT and other chemical pesticides, Dr. Gabrielson had kindly assisted my research for *Wildlife in America*, which appeared in the same period as *Silent Spring*.

Spreading away on both sides of the county road that leads south from St. Cloud is what was formerly the alluvial plain of the Kissimmee River, the main headwater of Lake Okeechobee. From the road, it looks like savanna grassland broken by saw palmetto and wax myrtle, pine groves and oak hammocks, but in fact it is pocked by potholes and small marshes that retain water and food for cranes even in this time of drought. The greater sandhills have already headed north, but Florida sandhills are common in this flat country, and a pair that is herding its gray chick off the road shoulder scarcely lifts its wings as our truck passes, and a caracara crosses the savanna toward a stand of long-leaf pine.

Assured that the whooper project has been classified as "experimental nonessential" and that therefore their lands will not fall under the jurisdiction of the Endangered Species Act and be subject to seizure, local ranchers have given permission for crane releases on four or five sites outside the state management area. They are generally tickled to have cranes, Steve says; all they ask for is protection from careless birdwatchers and others who leave cattle gates open and create disturbance.

We turn off through a locked gate into open ranchland, where a dirt track leads us several miles to a slash pine hammock overlooking a broad marsh. Across the savanna and beyond the treeline of pond cypress, laurel oak, and bay trees that marks a water course, a pine ridge rises on the east horizon. Nowhere in this broad landscape is there sign of man, no grind of bulldozers nor whine of chainsaw nor distant howl of tires, nor even the dull drone of an aircraft.

The nest site lies south of the pines, perhaps a hundred yards away. Before the eggs hatched, this site was fiercely defended; other whoopers were the first to be driven off, then sandhills and, as hatching neared, the herons and ducks which compete for the precious food resources needed to sustain the chicks in their first days.

On March 28, that horned owl (or eagle, hawk, or crow; for small chicks, the most dangerous predators are avian) took the second chick, an event less unfortunate than it might seem, since the survivor's chance of reaching adulthood is much improved by the undivided attention, protection, and feeding it inherits with its sibling's death.[15]

In its first ten days of life, the whooper chick remains close to the nest. (The *japonensis* chick may scramble out if its parent moves any distance to confront a predator, hiding itself in the dead reeds in the vicinity of the nest, as if counting on its own gold browns for camouflage; probably this is also true of *americana*.) The chick's first growth occurs in its long legs, and as soon as it is strong enough to keep up, it is led away from the exposed nest into the shelter of the marsh; crane chicks can run, swim, and keep up with the adults within twenty-four hours of hatching. (It was noticed at Grays Lake that young whoopers would respond instinctively to alarm calls from their sandhill foster parents by fleeing toward open water in the way of whoopers instead of taking cover in the vegetation as sandhills do—apparently an early manifestation of the more aquatic, and open country, orientation of the whooper.)

Stalking through low bushy growth, the male is foraging off to the east, near a bayhead of palmetto, bay, and myrtle. To judge from his unrelenting vigilance—the fierce-eyed red-black-white mask rises every few moments to scan the marsh—the chick is with him, although invisible, since the maiden cane, sedge, and dry low brush reach its parent's belly. (Now that its own nest site has been abandoned, the whooper pays no attention to a sandhill on a nest close to the bayhead.) With that bare crown of bright red caruncles set off by the flesh-colored lore of breeding season at the base of the black bill, and the satin-white head fixed by the spear of bare red skin that runs back from the bill below the eye, the warrior male looks furious and formidable.

The marsh pool dances with the shining leaves of the blue-flowered pickerel weed and the fresh green bed of maiden cane at the water's edge behind it.[16] The white crane moves slowly with head lowered to

its downy chick; it seems less bothered by the faraway rumble of a passing truck on the county road than by the close passing of a northern
harrier, then a great blue heron. Separated from the observers by a shallow pool perhaps forty yards across, the male walks and picks with its
invisible companion; when he raises his head, the crown is livid in the
sunlight.

Crane chicks swim well soon after hatching, in order to keep up
with their parents in a flooded marsh, and adult cranes retain vestigial
webbing, though they seem to swim only in emergencies. (George
Archibald once witnessed distraction behavior in which a blue crane
swam and fluttered across open water to lead dogs away from her
chicks.) Presumably whoopers can swim, too, and this might tempt
them to flutter across canals and sloughs during their six-week molt in
spring, thereby risking attack by an alligator, which has no place in
their race memory of prairie potholes.

Soon the female returns from across the marsh, cupping broad white
wings and spreading black fingers as she sails in and alights delicately
beside her family. (As in the Siberian crane, the black primary feathers
disappear the instant the wing is folded.) Her white neck arches in a
long graceful curve as she points her black bill at her toes—the chick has
run to her, though I can't hear its wild peeping. Some twenty-seven different calls between whooper chick and parent have been described so
far, Steve Nesbitt whispers. At the smallest danger to its chick, the adult
utters a purring rattle, distinctly menacing, and this warning becomes
more high-pitched and prolonged when a real enemy appears, whether
bobcat or bald eagle—an occasional crane predator, like the golden eagle
in the West. When the threat seems imminent, the parent utters its sharp
guard call, which may be directly followed by attack.

For an hour we watch the white cranes closely and still the chick remains half hidden, a fleeting shift of light brown haze in the dry brush.
At one point, the pair gives its unison call and jumps into the air, dancing forward with uplifted wings toward the bayhead as if to drive off
some phantom threat; a moment later, darting its long neck, the male
snatches up a two-foot mud snake with a dull reddish belly. He shakes
it hard, flings it down, then picks it up and carries it to the chick before

pecking and tugging it to pieces.[17] The pair catches two or three more snakes and a few crayfish, which are all thrashed, chopped, and presented to the chick; its fare may include insect larvae, water beetles, shellfish, young muskrats or baby alligators, turtles, mice, ducklings and other fledglings, and also the berries, grains, and acorns found on higher ground. Each little while the parents stretch long necks and peer about them, shining black bills dripping water in the sunlight, and still they do not lead their young into the open.

From the thicket behind comes the melodious trill of Bachman's sparrow, not a common bird; Steve lifts a finger to his ear and smiles. We are enjoying the warm sun and dry scrub smells, the sad whistle of titmouse and fine lisp of a pine warbler, the ringing notes of Carolina wren and urgent chirrup of a bobwhite quail, which presently shows off its spring colors in the sunlight at the base of a near palmetto.

Perhaps a half hour after midday, the white cranes turn toward us. In three long strides they step into the clear on the green carpet of maiden cane around the pool edge. A moment later I am staring at the chick—the first wild whooping crane born in the United States in sixty years, the first born east of the Mississippi in well over a century, and so far as is known, the first of its species ever born on the Florida peninsula. When it stretches its neck and peers around in imitation of the wary adults, it is tall enough to reach the belly of the parent, which stands as tall as a small human being. This historic chick, warm golden brown, with a short bill not yet black but pinkish orange, resembles a large downy pullet with no tail.

The cranes forage near the pond edge for an hour or more. The chick tries to preen its downy body but shortly gives this up, the better to blink and settle down in the fresh green and rest its long legs until it is time to hurry and tumble toward a parent bringing food. When we leave quietly in the early afternoon, the crane family, undisturbed, is moving gradually in the general direction of the nest site, and the chick has disappeared again into the grass.

"I hope it makes it," I say fervently, thanking Steve Nesbitt for a fine day in the field, "and I also hope you and Marty know that your project is successful, whether or not this chick survives." He nods. "We've shown it can be done," he says, "so I guess we can say that the theory has been validated." Steve is a modest and unassuming man, and his satisfaction is tempered by the knowledge that this fragile creature is the solitary heritor of those 211 *americana* raised, transported, and released since 1993, and many thousands of dollars, and decades of frustration and patience and hard work. If man wants the last wild land and life to illuminate his world, he will have to pay dearly to undo his damage, and he must. The time is past when large rare creatures can recover their numbers without man's strenuous intervention.

Steve Nesbitt is confident that a Florida whooper population can be established—indeed, *would* have been established had it not been for this drought. After all, eighty-eight to ninety birds have survived to roam over large areas of central Florida, among which thirty are trying to form breeding pairs. The reproduction of young birds will rise dramatically when the drought breaks and water levels rise and food for cranes—and their competitors and predators—is plentiful once again over wide areas.

Next day on the cattle range at Okahumpka, north and west, we observe groups of this year's cohort of new cranes from the shade of a tall hammock on a ridge; a few still have smatterings of juvenile brown feathers on the head. Of the twenty-four that have gathered here, eighteen draw near in separate groups, walking and feeding, flying overhead, "whooping" their powerful bugle call—*ker-loo, ker-lee-oo,* as some describe it—across the wind. Gusts of spring passerines blow through the oak wood—bluebird and blue grosbeak, orchard oriole, palm warbler—as before us the cranes drift back and forth between wind-glittered blue ponds inset in the hollows of brown hills.

In 1998, 182 wild whooping cranes, including 30 juveniles—a record—flew south to Aransas for the winter. By October 2000 an estimated 267 were flying wild, including the 88 to 90 now in Florida, with another 104 birds in captive breeding flocks in addition to 38 more presently scheduled for release. This year the total *americana* population is still below the minimum number thought to be needed for full recovery, and meanwhile there is a growing need to increase genetic diversity in wild populations, perhaps by such means as transposing captive-laid eggs into wild nests.

In 1999, the project celebrated a 70 percent survival rate among the first-year cranes, higher than had ever been expected, and the first year of the new millennium may be even better. Of the thirty new birds released in 1999–2000, twenty-five are still alive and flying around Florida—in effect, about as many *Grus americana* as existed on earth four decades ago, when I first wrote about them. In the brief annals of crane conservation, this is an exciting success, yet *americana* at the turn of the new century remains much the rarest of the cranes, effectively limited to that single flock that leads its young on a perilous migration some twenty-six hundred miles from the border of the Northwest Territories to a small eroding corner of the Gulf Coast very vulnerable to oil spills and winter storms. The fierce nature of the species offers hope that it may yet prevail, but it cannot survive without strong assistance and commitment from the creature that drove it to the abyss of extinction in the first place.[18]

That young whooper on the Kissimmee prairie struck me as so singular and so pristine that the idea of banding this historic bird seemed inappropriate, apart from the stress that is inevitable in wild animal capture and handling; after all, I suggested to Steve Nesbitt in a phone call two weeks later, this bird would always be easily identifiable as the one white crane flying free of bulky leg bands, and its chances of survival could only be improved.

Steve knew what I was feeling and in fact agreed. Nonetheless, it was decided that it must be banded, the better to monitor its movements and whereabouts. The banding was scheduled for late May, and by the first of June, Steve said, it should be flying. He spoke cautiously. At five weeks, it was doing very well, but he knew that among sandhills in Florida and whoopers in the Northwest Territories, about 50 percent of all chicks hatched would perish before they flew, the great majority by predation, and that they are most vulnerable in the two weeks after hatching and again in the few days before fledging.

(For cranes of all ages, risk of death increases markedly in time of drought, when the birds are obliged to abandon the home territory for an unfamiliar area, and water and food—and cranes, competitors, and predators—are dangerously concentrated in the disappearing marshes.)

On May 22, when the chick was sixty-six days old, within a few days of fledging, the crane men gathered at the nesting marsh. Wading birds of many species were gathered at the shrunken pools to make the most of the exposed life, but the cranes were gone. The birds were located in a marsh off to the eastward, and the frantic chick was run down, captured, blood-sampled, banded, and released in a quick sixteen minutes, as the parents trumpeted wildly from the marsh edge. Before long the family, reunited and apparently untroubled, resumed its wary hunt for food.

In the next days, the cranes attempted to return to the home territory, but the pools were dry and they retreated to the capture marsh. There the torn and eviscerated chick was found in shallow water on the morning of May 25. From sign at the scene, and the manner of eating—the head gone, the bite marks, the unscattered remains—the predator was identified as a bobcat.

When I spoke with Steve Nesbitt over the telephone a few days later, he was still downcast, but he also knew that with the hatching and raising of a whooper chick to within days of its first flight, a major aim of the Crane Project had been realized. The researchers had shown that whooping cranes would form pair bonds, mate, lay fertile eggs, tend and hatch the clutch, and raise a chick in central Florida even in a year of severe drought, and that this mostly undamaged habitat had the resources to sustain a crane family long enough for a chick to grow strong and take wing. "It is no less proof," Nesbitt wrote me on June 2, "that these birds, raised in captivity and with little or no natural experience, can get it right. Everything we saw from this pair suggests that they were doing everything they were supposed to do. They were as good as the best sandhill parents I have ever seen." In one season, fifteen pair bonds had formed, three pairs nesting and laying eggs; and this pair had hatched two chicks—very unusual in a pair nesting for the first time. Barring unforeseen circumstances, therefore, the researchers could feel confident that a nonmigratory population of whooping cranes could be established in Florida. Thirty-eight more juveniles were to be released that winter (2000–2001) in the hope that the drought would break and that at least one of the fifteen pairs already formed would produce a crop of young.

In May 2000, one of those Florida pairs, as if frustrated by the drought, struck out on its own and flew to Illinois; a week later, the birds turned up near Sandusky, in northeastern Michigan—their first appearance in that state since 1882. After foraging in soybean and wheat fields (to which they would later return), they moved a mile north, in early June, to wetlands created when peat mines were exhausted and abandoned. Too late in the season, they built two nests; though no eggs were produced, it was hoped they might fly north again the following year. But after the whoopers left Michigan in November, his radio indicated that the male had been lost over the Great Lakes, perhaps in a storm. The female made it back to Florida, perhaps with sandhills, perhaps on her own.

As a rule, the birds do not wander more than two hundred miles from the release site, especially since they are pen-raised birds with no experience of migration. (Typically, the female *americana* would follow her mate wherever he led.) This male was notorious as the crane that swallowed a fishing lure with two sets of treble hooks shortly after its release in January 1996. Understandably, this caused him to act strangely. Recaptured and relieved of the lure, he had been fitted with the PTT (a platform terminal, or "satellite" transmitter) before being returned to the wild. Subsequently, he miraculously survived a collision with a power line, leaving his entangled transmitter behind. It seems appropriate that this death-defying bird should be the first to venture out of Florida, and very exciting that, without guidance by surrogate parents or ultralight aircraft, he chose a route that led him back toward the remnant prairie potholes and marshes of his ancestral breeding grounds, in the same latitude as his first home at the ICF in Wisconsin. Who can say what primordial instinct turned his beak north like a compass needle and led this pioneer and his steadfast mate on their long journey home across the heavens? And who is not uplifted by the mystery of life implicit in a question that we cannot answer?

In a remarkable experiment in 1997, four young whoopers were led south from Idaho to Bosque del Apache by an ultralight airplane piloted by an Idaho crane man named Kent Clegg; two of these birds were lost to a coyote and a bobcat soon after their arrival, and a third perished in 2000, leaving one survivor to finish out his days in the company of the aging veteran from the original Grays Lake program. However, the successful experiment inspired plans to establish a second migratory flock to be established farther east, and preparations were soon under way in the one hundred thousand acres of the Necedah National Wildlife Refuge, in northern Wisconsin. Sandhill juveniles from eggs removed from Wisconsin nests of greater sandhills which wintered in north-central Florida, raised at Patuxent in "isolation" from human beings, were trained to imprint on an artificial parent in the form of an ultralight aircraft which, putting down at small airstrips en route, would lead them south in careful stages to Chassahowitzka National Wildlife Refuge on the Gulf Coast of northwest Florida. During the winter, their adaptation to a habitat free of wild cranes (though not predators) would be closely studied. In theory, the survivors, having experience of the migration route, would return to Wisconsin on their own. Not until captive release and induced migration methods had been well studied and refined would the project turn to whooping cranes, which, as in the nonmigratory flock in the Kissimmee region farther south, would be supplemented every year until a flock of twenty-five migrating pairs had been established.

With protection, says Dr. Archibald, the whooper can make "a tremendous comeback" in its original prairie range. George is an eternal optimist but also a pragmatist; he regrets all those whoopers lost in central Florida. "We can't keep raising whooping cranes to feed the bobcats," he joked ruefully when I saw him next in Baraboo.

On September 17, 2001, at 7:15 in the morning, eight young whoopers, trained and conditioned by brief preliminary flights behind their ultralight, departed Necedah and headed south.[19] Shortly after takeoff, bird number 4, which had been slightly injured en route from Patuxent, wandered from the group; recaptured by the ground crew tracking the flight, he was set free among his mates that same evening. Given a second chance after a few days, number 4 defected again; thereafter, he traveled southward in his crate.

On October 25, during a night storm that destroyed the pen, crane number 3 was killed when she flew up and struck a power line. In November, numbers 7, 6, and 5 would delay the migration by wandering and lagging, but on November 14, all but number 4 made the day's flight. A stretch of bad weather followed. By November 23, it was realized that on eighteen days out of thirty-eight, no progress had been made due to rain, snow, hail, high winds, and fog. (The longest flight was two hours and nine minutes, the shortest just thirty-eight minutes.) But the next day, after a journey across seven states, the cranes made their first landing in Florida, and on December 3, after more weather delays, the seven arrived at Chassahowitzka, near Crystal River, completing a journey of 1,217.8 miles in forty-eight days.

At Chassahowitzka, the salt-marsh shelter pen where the birds returned for food was 350 by 150 feet, and its wire fence was buried two feet in the ground to discourage bobcats, alligators, and feral hogs. Nonetheless, two birds were lost to predators over the winter, leaving just five to prove the worth of the experiment by returning north in spring without adult or ultralight to guide them. To the great joy and excitement of observers across the country, all five birds departed Chassahowitzka on April 9 (in the same week that the wild Texas flock headed north from Aransas), flying 217 miles, far into Georgia, that first day. Grounded by bad weather, they flew on as soon as possible, and on April 14 all five crossed over into Tennessee—though number 7, a female low in the group's peck order, proceeded separately and chose her own route thereafter. On the sixteenth, the four reached the south shore of Lake Michigan and turned west over Gary, Indiana, to Chicago, where they descended and spent the night in a forest park in the city outskirts. Delayed by weather on the seventeenth, they flew north next day, arriving at Necedah on April 19—all but number 7, who tarried south of Madison, Wisconsin, before completing her journey to Necedah. (However, she never rejoined the others, moving east to Horicon National Wildlife Refuge for the summer.)

In eight flying days, the five cranes had returned to their home marsh over roughly the same route and the same distance that had required forty-eight days in the previous autumn. In November 2002, four of the five flew south in just six days to Chassahowitzka, establishing beyond question that pen-raised cranes could be taught to migrate; the fifth joined the large sandhill flock that has wintered in recent years at Hiwassee, in Tennessee. Two of them would overtake (and briefly accompany) the second cohort of seventeen juveniles, brought to Necedah for training in June 2002 and led southward behind their ultralight in early October: these seventeen would arrive safely at Chassahowitzka in early December.

In north-central Florida, still afflicted by drought, the nonmigratory flock produced seven nests in the spring of 2002. The one that seemed least promising was assembled a half mile from Main Street in Leesburg, Florida, some thirty miles northwest of Orlando, on the edge of a small drought-shrunk lake with a threat of predation by dogs from surrounding houses. After one chick was lost to a bald eagle, the second was fiercely defended by the new parents, which attacked and stomped one eagle so energetically that it had to be rescued and removed to a rehabilitation center. As it turned out, this pair was to raise the first wild whooper chick fledged in the U.S. (June 6, 2002) since that lone juvenile seen in the doomed Louisiana flock that was destroyed by storm back in the 1930s.

Nicknamed "Lucky," the historic bird and its vigilant parents remained in their home area throughout the summer. In late September, I called Steve Nesbitt to find out how Lucky was doing. "He's still lucky," Steve said happily. By the end of the year, he was larger than his pen-raised parents and had already lost most of his brown feathers; although the three cranes still frequented their home lake, the adults were showing early signs of expelling Lucky from their breeding area. Steve thought he would probably join the new cohort of pen-raised birds that were being released only ten miles away.

In 2002, the rains had come at last, and though the deeper lakes were not yet filled, the conditions for breeding success in 2003 looked better than at any time in years. "We have nearly fifteen pairs," Steve said, "which could produce as many as ten or twelve successful nests." Though a happy end to the history of North America's great crane was not assured, the year 2002 was a true reward for the enterprise, faith, and plain hard work of craniacs across the country. The whooper population had risen to well over 400, including nearly 100 in Florida, nearly 200 in the Aransas flock, and another 130 in captivity. With the simultaneous success of the Necedah experiment, the fledging of Lucky, and the restoration of good Florida habitat, a new migratory flock and also a nonmigratory flock may become well established in the next decades, ensuring a future for *Grus americana*.

Notes

Introduction

1. A fit companion, since the closest relatives of the Gruiformes are the Charadriiformes, an order which includes the gulls and terns.
2. A book on tigers, *Tigers in the Snow* (New York: North Point Press), appeared in 2000.
3. The friend was Louis Crisler, author of *Arctic Wild* (New York: Harper and Row, 1958).

1. Black Dragon River

On May 23, 2000, under pressure from Russian oil interests (which emulate oil interests everywhere in their resentment of any "ecological hindrances" put in the way of untrammeled exploration and extraction), President Vladimir Putin of Russia ordered the elimination of the Committee on Environmental Protection (*Goskomekologii*), the only governmental body that oversees environmental regulation and protection in Russia; its responsibilities, which include the wildlife reserves—the *zapovedniki*—were transferred to the new Ministry of Natural Resources, whose primary duty is resource exploitation and extraction.

1. Paul A. Johnsgaard, *Crane Music: A Natural History of American Cranes* (Lincoln: University of Nebraska Press, 1998), p. 58, states that sandhill cranes pass Mount McKinley in Alaska at an altitude of 20,000 feet or more. Barheaded geese have been recorded at 29,500 feet over the Himalaya; see *The Atlas of Bird Migration*, ed. Jonathan Elphick (New York: Random House, 1995).
2. I thank Mark Cocker of London's *Literary Review* (January 4, 2002) for the following: "One of the first references to an identifiable bird species in Western literature is Homer's comparison in the *Iliad* of the sounds made by the advancing Trojan army to the bugling calls of cranes. In the thirteenth century, the Hohenstaufen monarch, Frederick II, wrote extensively on these

birds and their migrations through southern Italy in a book (*The Art of Fal-
conry*) that has strong claims to being the earliest work of scientific ornithology."

3. See Schiller's ballad "The Cranes of Ibycus," after a story in Plutarch about
   crane revenge on the murderers of the Greek poet Ibycus (c. 550 B.C.) near
   Corinth.

4. A letter from Lama Surya Das refers to "the greatly revered black-necked
   cranes, the legendary mount of the Dalai Lamas on which they traveled
   from monastery to monastery."

5. "On King George Island, off the Antarctic Peninsula, are fossil footprints of
   an enormous bird, 46 million years old. These are probably the tracks of the
   so-called terror bird, a flightless, fast-running relative of the cranes and rails
   that stood three and a half meters tall. Its clawed feet enabled it to disem-
   bowel mammals, including the two-meter-long glyptodonts, which were ar-
   mored like armadillos. Terror birds probably originated in South America,
   where they may have hastened the extinction of large marsupial carnivores.
   At the time of the closure of the Darien Gap, 2.5 million years ago, they were
   the largest carnivores in South America." David Campbell, *The Crystal
   Desert* (New York: Houghton Mifflin, 1992), pp. 50–51.

6. The word *crane* comes from the old German *Cranuh*, which like *Grus* is a
   rendition of the bird's cry.

7. The structures of cranes' wings and feathers have long been studied because
   of their adaptability to changing flight conditions.

8. The product was *qiviut*, a wool spun from the guard hairs of the shaggy coat,
   which are finer and warmer than cashmere.

9. The Siberian forest, with its vast capacity for absorbing carbon dioxide, is replacing the slaughtered rain forests of the tropics as the planet's first defense
   against global warming.

10. Officially, the International Workshop on Cranes and Storks of the Amur
    Basin, June 26–July 12, 1992. Supporting organizations included the Na-
    tional Audubon Society, Baikal Watch (a project of the Earth Island Insti-
    tute), the Wilderness Society, the Siberian Forest Protection Project, and the
    Wild Bird Society of Japan; these organizations, already at work in the Lake
    Baikal region, had now joined with Russian counterparts for the protection
    of the Amur-Ussuri.

11. Many of this country's sixty-eight reserves, set aside gradually since the days
    of Lenin, have been closely protected from the public, even as the rest of
    Russia has been despoiled.

12. Quoted in S. Brownmiller, "Flying to Vietnam," *Audubon*, November–
    December 1993, p. 78–82.

13. In 1983, through the good offices of the ICF, Chinese and Russian crane au-
    thorities had been brought together at a conference at Bharatpur, India, and
    Archibald hoped that this Amur journey on their common border would lay

the foundation for international wildlife reserves in the Lake Khanka and Mongolian border regions of their countries.

14. Although it had recognized Japanese dominion in the Kuriles since 1855, Russia confiscated the islands at the end of World War II after Japan surrendered to the United States, as recompense (say the Russians) for concessions made almost a century ago after the Russo-Japanese War. In the summer of 1992, the Russian government seemed prepared to return the southern Kuriles to Japan, in expectation of sorely needed economic aid, but political conservatives, invoking Mother Russia, were already thundering against it, and there seemed to be no imminent solution. Although few cared about these cold and foggy islands, the Yeltsin government was afraid of giving ammunition to Russia's virulent nationalist faction by conceding them.

15. This province, with adjoining Jilin and Liaoning provinces, embraces the former Manzhou, or Manchuria ("Place of Mandarin or Man People"; called by the Japanese Manzhouquo or Manchukuo), known these days as Dong Bei, "the Northeast."

16. Once the Tibetans are outnumbered, a plebiscite will doubtless return Tibet to China by "popular" demand.

17. Since our voyage on the Amur, the Sakha Republic has pledged to protect 270,000 square miles as boreal forest and tundra reserve, to offset some of the environmental damage done by the mining and timber industries and to spare its remaining wildlife, with special attention to its sacred bird, the Siberian crane.

18. Interestingly, the Yakuts have no legends about the sandhill, although it migrates almost as far west as the great Lena River and overlaps the range of *kitalik* in a coastal stretch of about two hundred miles in the Indigirka region; this might suggest that this western extension of its range has been fairly recent.

19. The Zhalong marshes were this crane's most productive breeding territory until the Cultural Revolution, when fishermen and reed cutters were permitted access to the lake; since then, Zhalong's *japonensis* population has fallen from a claimed 500 to about 180. Inevitably, the population on the Three Rivers plain has fallen, too. Dr. Ma Yiqing says that Zhalong (made a reserve in 1979) has recovered somewhat, with about 230 *japonensis* and 40 *vipio*, due to protection of reed nesting areas and other measures. The Zhalong region can claim annual visits from six species of crane: the red-crowned, white-naped, Eurasian, and demoiselle are breeding birds, and the hooded and "white crane"—the Siberian—rest there every year during migration. In addition, it has a captive flock of 90 *japonensis* reared artificially and maintained throughout the year. As a rule, the red-crowned cranes from northern China migrate to southeastern China, in particular the Yancheng Nature Reserve on the coast north of the mouth of the Yangtze River in Jiangsu Province, where an estimated 600 to 800 spend the winter. (The pop-

ulation in the delta of the Liao River, where the Great Wall terminates on the Gulf of Chihli, may be a nonmigratory subspecies.)

20. Amurzet is a contraction of Amur Zemblya (Amur Land) Ebreska (He-brew) Tovarische (Community).

21. According to American journalist Harrison Salisbury, the fire destroyed eighteen million acres of virgin taiga, ten times more land than the Yellow-stone fire of the following year. China's minister of forestry was summarily removed for failure to cut fire corridors through the parched tracts or to have equipment ready. Though a few bulldozers were finally brought in, the fire was mainly fought with wet burlap bags wielded by thousands of Chi-nese soldiers and conscripted men. More than two hundred people died, with hundreds injured.

22. As early as the late 1970s, anticipating disastrous long-term effects, Smiren-ski wrote articles against proposed dams on two main Amur tributaries, the Buryea and Zeya rivers. The dam on the Zeya, subsequently built, has borne out his most pessimistic predictions; at the time of our voyage, Russian engi-neers were searching for earthquake cracks in the dam that would necessi-tate a drastic lowering of the water level in what is now the second-largest reservoir in all of Russia.

The Khingan dam was first conceived back in the 1950s, in the days of Chino-Soviet solidarity against the West. The idea perished with the chilling of relations a few years later, but recently China has sought to resurrect it, in the light of the vast energy required for the rapid development of Hei-longjiang and the settlement of one hundred million people in this sparsely inhabited region south of the Amur. The Russians, being desperate for hard currency, are eager to sell to the Chinese their share of the huge amount of hydroelectric power that might be generated. The Chinese engineers antici-pate low costs and large profits. They maintain that the increase in water level will be small and that few fields will be flooded upriver from the dam, since there are no settlements to speak of—in short, that the region will be little affected, even the fisheries; salmon ladders and restocking will ensure, they say, that the harvest will decline no more than 5 percent.

Unfortunately, these ameliorating measures are generally inefficient and expensive. The anadromous salmon need a current to follow upstream; in the large dead lake behind the dam, they would only wander. Even if a few survived to breed, the young not destroyed in the dam turbines would re-quire a strong unbroken current to carry them downstream, since their physiology demands that they reach the sea within a certain period or perish. The less agile sturgeon requires eighteen years to mature and spawns almost entirely in the dam site region. Sturgeon are very particular about water temperature, rate of flow, and a clear river bottom, all of which would be drastically transformed in the artificial lake behind the dam, with its accu-mulating sediment. For the sturgeon, the estimated loss would be 80 percent, Smirenski says.

Ken Strom of the National Audubon Society agrees that a reservoir behind a dam is an alien habitat, since the warmer water may encourage fish diseases and permit the establishment of unwelcome species that could not thrive in open current. Also, water near the surface may be too warm for the fish seeking to ascend the stream, or—if it is drawn from the bottom—too cold and poor in oxygen.

23. Ma Yiqing et al., "Research on Red-Crowned Crane and other Waterfawls [sic] of Heilongjiang Province," and other publications, 1984–95; see bibliography of *The Cranes*, ed. Curt D. Meine and George W. Archibald (Gland, Switzerland: IUCN, 1996).

24. In the 1950s, the Chinese made an annual harvest of "several million" salmon, whereas by the 1960s, only about sixty thousand were being taken, and today but "a few thousand."

25. Mr. Noritaka Ichida is president of Japan's Wild Bird Society, and Dr. Hiroyuki Masatomi shared in Archibald's discovery, back in 1972, that the Hokkaido population of the red-crowned crane did not migrate to the Asian mainland, as had been assumed.

26. In 1996, Khingan fires wiped out all of the *japonensis* nests.

27. According to our Amur colleague Li Wen Fa, who studied this species at Xingkai Hu (Lake Khanka), the female and male brood in turns, changing places four times every day until the eggs are hatched. The chicks observed in Li's study were born from eggs laid in the second week of April and hatched in the middle part of May. Within a few days, they left the nest, and for their first twenty-five to thirty days were fed and led by the female and male in turns, after which both tended the chicks together. See Li Wen Fa, "A Preliminary Study on Crowned Cranes in the Xingkai Natural Protected Area," *Journal of Heilongjiang Land Reclamation*, 1991, pp. 67–76.

28. Khingan researchers were soon notified of a few sightings of banded *vipio* on winter territories in south Japan, and a pair banded as molting adults in 1985 returned to Khingan every year after, including 1992, when it raised two chicks. Based on its territorial behavior, Andronov believes that this is the same pair first recorded here in 1972 by Smirenski's mentor Dr. Vladimir Flint, who would later become Archibald's foremost partner in efforts to conserve the Siberian crane. Since cranes don't breed before the age of three or four, this pair would be a quarter century old. Subsequently, in a late-winter migration, four *vipio* banded by Japanese researchers would travel north across the Sea of Japan and the Korean peninsula, stopping to rest in the DMZ and on the east coast of North Korea, then the Russian shore of Lake Khanka, before heading west to breeding grounds in the San Jiang plain.

29. The long-term lease would be underwritten by the Wild Bird Society of Japan; the ICF would provide logistical support for staff operations and local education.

30. The entire expense of the large Chinese delegation to the Amur conference was underwritten by the ICF with the understanding that the Chinese

would provide hospitality to the Russian biologists who hoped to visit the Xingkai Hu Reserve the following year.

31. A few months later, I would hear from Archibald and Harris that the Chinese and Russians were already working on a cooperative crane program at Lake Khanka, to commence in the spring of 1993. Harris also reported that the white-naped crane banded that morning at Khingan turned up at Khanka in the early autumn, flew on to another staging area in Korea's DMZ, and arrived safely on its winter grounds on Kyushu, in southern Japan, transmitting useful information all the way.

32. The Chinese officials were Chen Jing Lu, chairman of the Mishan County Forest Bureau in Heilongjiang, and his deputy, Yu Chang Shen, the director of Xingkai Hu Reserve.

33. The first scientist to explore Lake Khanka, from 1868 to 1870, was Lt. Col. Nikolai Przhevalsky, whose name is commemorated in the Mongolian wild horse, *Equus caballus przhevalsky*. In the 1930s, the lake region was studied further by geographer Vladimir Arseniev, a student of the Amur tiger and the author of that masterpiece of Ussuria exploration, *Dersu the Trapper*, from which the great Kurosawa film *Dersu Uzala* was made.

34. This whole flat plain of the Ussuri was formerly lake bottom, and when that ancient lake began to dry, the northern taiga penetrated this far south; all but the coast range was cleared by Russian settlers in the nineteenth century.

35. Later that morning, farther south, near the Ilistaya River, we spotted four white-naped cranes over the marshes.

2. On the Daurian Steppe

1. The official source for birds on the International Union for the Conservation of Nature and Natural Resources "Red List" is A. J. Stattersfield, D. R. Capper, and E.C.L. Dutson, *Threatened Birds of the World* (Barcelona: Lynx Edicions, 2000).

2. Under the Soviets, coal mining commenced in the 1980s. With only 10 percent of its territory surveyed, Mongolia can claim abundant copper, fluorspar, and coal, as well as tin, tungsten, uranium, and gold. The country is rich in other minerals, but at present there is no capital to exploit them. Oil exploration is under way, and there is discussion of a modern railroad. Yet because its land is vast and its population small, Mongolia has a precious chance to institute environmental protections, as Bhutan has done, and manage its grasslands for the benefit of wildlife as well as of its people.

3. I thought this was superstition until I found it confirmed by an authoritative account in Tim Severin's *In Search of Genghis Khan* (New York: Atheneum, 1992).

4. The great nineteenth-century ornithologist Edward Blyth disapproved of the "unsuitable" attempt by "some ornithologists" to suggest that *Grus virgo*

and *Grus paradisea* constituted a new genus, *Anthropoides*. *Anthropoides* and yet another genus, *Bugeranus*, were adopted a few years later by taxonomist R. B. Sharpe. See Edward Blyth, *The Natural History of the Cranes* (London, 1881).

5. Bold and Tseveen's excellent paper "The Cranes of Mongolia" has been translated into English by Elena Smirenski and is included in *Cranes and Storks of the Amur River*, eds. Curtis H. Halvorson, James T. Harris, and Sergei M. Smirenski (Moscow: Arts Literature Publishers, 1995).

6. *G. vipio*'s egg—greenish olive with reddish-brown blotches—is almost indistinguishable from that of *G. grus* and *G. leucogeranus*, and rather typical in its murky colors of most eggs of *Grus*.

7. In dry years, the last wild flock of whooping cranes, which breeds in remote Wood Buffalo National Park, on the border of the Canadian Northwest Territories, may lose chicks to wolves, and very likely the same would be true here.

8. See James T. Harris, "Managing Nature Reserves for Cranes in China," *Proceedings of the Sixth North American Crane Workshop* (Regina, Saskatchewan, and Grand Island, Nebraska: North American Crane Working Group, 1992), pp. 1–11.

9. See Peter Matthiessen, *The Shorebirds of North America* (New York: Viking, 1967).

10. The nest was discovered by Dr. Juri Pukinski of St. Petersburg's Institute of Zoology.

11. It was thought that these two were especially close until DNA tests established that *grus* was actually closer to *nigricollis*, the black-necked crane. (See chapter 4.)

12. In their monograph on the Daurian crane, Drs. Tseveen and Bold conclude that its main range in Mongolia extends "from the eastern spur of the main Hentei ridge along the middle channel of the Hurkh River, north to the Russian border and down the Kerulen River to the south and east, including the entire Onon River basin, the entire flood-land of the Uldz River and its tributaries, and all the numerous valley lakes between the Onon-Uldz and Uldz-Kerulen Rivers." A secondary range is the lower Kerulen, connecting to the China range at Dalainor, and possibly there is another in the delta of the Har Buhyngol River in the Orhon-Selenga drainage, 118 miles to the west. The invariable nesting habitat is swampy herb-sedge margins of small grassland ponds, lakes, and rivers; the birds avoid those salt or brackish waters that we passed in that far northeastern corner of the country where three nations meet.

13. Formerly some wintered in the Ganges basin in Bengal, but these birds have been hunted to the point of extirpation.

14. *G. vipio* has been observed infrequently west of Ulaan Baatar but to date no breeding pairs have been reported.

15. Two months later, a white-naped crane banded in the Daurski Nature Reserve was tracked by telemetry to a resting area in the Yellow River delta and from there on southward to the Poyang lakes.

16. In captivity, territorial birds and plain old cranks—the Siberians and red-crowneds are considered the feistiest—attack their keepers regularly with claws and bill, and they can be dangerous.

3. Gujarat and Rajasthan

In the fortnight after our departure, the remnant Kunevat flock at Keoladeo was augmented by a pair of two-year-old subadults raised from wild eggs by foster parents. They were kept in a thirty-square-foot enclosure while habituating to the presence of the five wild birds nearby, which might lead them on their northward journey. The situation of this *leucogeranus* population was now so desperate that almost any scheme was worth a try, but one had to wonder if two young cranes that had never migrated would get their signals straight, and even if they did, if they would be strong enough to survive the risks and hardships of the journey to the sub-Arctic tundra. As it turned out, the two captive birds learned to feed themselves quickly when released, but they failed to associate with—or were not accepted by—the others in time to accompany them when they left on migration at the end of March. The two ended up in the Jaipur Zoo.

In 1996, a report came from Burma of forty-five eastern sarus (*G. a. sharpii*) at Kyadet, and also fair numbers in the Irawaddy delta; the sarus had also reoccupied two large marshes south of Mandalay. However, these birds are still subject to the geopolitical chaos and dislocation caused by a brutal military dictatorship that is now internationally condemned for the oppression, relocation, and murder of its Karen tribespeople; in its struggle to remain in power at all costs, this regime is inflicting poverty and starvation on Burma, with an inevitable assault on the region's wildlife, including its remnant cranes.

1. This is the region of Gujarat that suffered the catastrophic earthquake of January 2001, in which more than twenty thousand people lost their lives. It is also, with Kutch and Saurashtra, the region that in theory will benefit from irrigation by way of the "Wonder Canal" and the disastrous grid of dams that has all but destroyed the great Narmada River valley and its people. (See Arundhati Roy, *The Greater Common Good*, Bombay: India Books, 1999.)

2. *G. a. sharpii* was first described by the taxonomist R. B. Sharpe in 1895 in the *Bulletin of the British Ornithologists' Club*, vol. 5. Sharpe was the noted ornithologist who established *Anthropoides* and *Bugeranus* as new crane genera, along with five others that failed the test of time.

3. The Burma sarus is thought to be clinal—that is, intermediate between the Indian and Southeast Asian races.

4. Since then, the ICF has helped raise funds to complete the dikes and sluice

gates. Knowing that otherwise, in a poor country, the reserve will not succeed, the ICF has advocated controlled fishing and grazing and monitoring of water levels to promote growth of sedges for the cranes and melaleuca trees for commercial harvest.

5. The breeding grounds were located by Jeb Barzen of the ICF.

6. The birders were led by Bob Fleming, an expert on Himalayan wildlife whom I knew many years ago in Kathmandu; it was Fleming who told Victor Emanuel about Khichan.

7. The late Ronald Sauey, who co-founded the International Crane Foundation with George Archibald, went to Keoladeo to pursue his doctoral thesis on the Siberian crane, based on six winter visits and twelve months in the field between 1974 and 1983. See Ronald Sauey, "The Range, Status, and Winter Ecology of the Siberian Crane (*Grus leucogeranus*)," Ph.D. dissertation, Cornell University, Ithaca, New York, 1985.

8. Mr. José Luis Copete of Barcelona has drawn my attention to a 1998 article in *Ibis* by P. Provencal and U. G. Sorenson (*Ibis* 140: 333–35) citing a medieval Egyptian text by An-Nuwayri which seems to describe *G. leucogeranus* in the winter of 1315–16 in the Nile delta, far west of its present westernmost winter range near the Caspian Sea; also, a relief of six cranes, apparently *leucogeranus*, from 2510–2460 B.C.; and a painting from 1991–1785 B.C. portraying the netting of this species. All three references are from Egypt, from which, suggest the authors, the species may have been extirpated long ago by hunting.

9. The possibility of a remnant population in "extreme northwest Russia" is mentioned in *Handbook of the Birds of the World* (Barcelona: Lynx Edicions, 1992); but where do these birds, if they exist, pass the winter undetected?

10. The cranes' feeding difficulties were reported by filmmakers Stan Breeden and Belinda Wright, known for their fine documentary on the Indian tiger.

11. Jim Harris once observed eastern Siberians at Poyang Lake in China which had led two chicks southward on migration, a very uncommon accomplishment in this species.

12. Captive flocks are now established at the ICF (thirty birds), Vogelpark Walsrode in Germany (fifteen), and Oka State Nature Reserve southeast of Moscow (twenty-five).

13. In 1993, a large tiger-poaching operation at Ranthambore was uncovered. Returning to India with another wildlife group in March 2001, Victor and I saw a number of tigers, not only at Ranthambore but in three other tiger parks as well.

14. *The Atlas of Bird Migration*, ed. Jonathan Elphick (New York: Random House, 1995), p. 25. A friend has told me: "On a migration route, observers used a telephoto lens set up to track a full moon and snap a picture whenever something entered the film-plane; from the size and shape of the birds, it was concluded that they were geese at 29,000 feet." Jack Turner, personal communication with the author, November 11, 2000.

15. All birds are marvelously efficient mechanisms in their use of oxygen. Air at

Everest's peak, nearly six miles high, provides only a third of the oxygen at ground level, yet a Ruppell's griffon was flying more than a mile higher than Everest when it was sucked into a jet engine at 37,900 feet. The high-fliers have developed special respiratory adaptations such as sacs that hold the inhaled air after it passes through the lungs, then return it through the system before exhalation, providing the bird with two hits of oxygen on every breath; they also have an adaptive hemoglobin that absorbs oxygen very quickly at high altitudes, meaning that more can be extracted. Once the blood is suffused with oxygen, capillaries hurry it deep into the muscles, instilling vital energy.

16. This unison call, "swinging their heads up and down in an arc while performing a musical bell-like duet," is unique among the cranes. Used most commonly in threat display, it is always initiated by the male, which may dispense with the duet entirely and call alone. (In some *Grus*, the male usually initiates the unison call and may call alone should his mate fail to join him; in others, the female is the instigator and initiator.)

17. This name is mentioned by Salim Ali and Dillon Ripley in their *Handbook of Indian Birds* (Bombay, 1969).

18. The Siberian's unison calls, courtship displays, and idiosyncratic behavior have persuaded Archibald that it has no business in the *Grus* genus. DNA researcher Dr. Carey Krajewski agrees with Archibald that *G. leucogeranus* is the most primitive of the Gruidae and should probably be assigned to its own genus. Since they share an identical trachea, a rapid seesaw head snapping, and an odd "shoulder tuck" in preparation for the unison call, it might be assigned to the *Bugeranus* genus in which some authorities have already placed the wattled crane. This bird shares characters with *Grus*, *Bugeranus*, and *Anthropoides*, but its phylogeny and taxonomic status remain unclear.

19. George Archibald, conversation with the author, September 2000.

4. At the End of Tibet

In a referendum of 1999, Bhutan's people—scared off, perhaps, by the economic disaster inflicted on the Russians by special interests inside and outside the country, who pushed for capitalism and "democracy" too greedily and too soon— voted to resist so-called progress and democracy by retaining their royal family. That same year, on the other hand, television was permitted into the country, so the long-term consequences may be the same.

1. *G. nigricollis* was also the last crane to come to the ICF, in 1980.

2. Four nests and seventeen birds were counted in 1982.

3. In recent years, a few pairs have returned to Arunachal Pradesh.

4. Bhutan has been criticized internationally for human rights violations against the ethnic Nepali of the southern lowlands, some of them resident for generations, who are systematically being driven from the country.

5. As of September 2000, there were 250 at Phobjika, 150 at Bongdeling, 1 to 20

at Bumthang, and 8 to 10 at Kotaka, or 409 to 430 wintering *cha thung thung* altogether.

6. Archibald has noted the same phenomenon among the hooded cranes wintering in Kyushu, in Japan, which pay no attention to local farmers but take flight the moment any stranger shows himself.

7. According to their DNA, the two closest relatives among *Grus* cranes are *nigricollis* and the hooded crane, *monachus*—also a stocky bird, from which it is thought the black-necked crane may have derived. Instead of a black neck and whitish body, the hooded has a white neck and blackish body. Archibald theorizes that on the nest in the dark woods of its swamp breeding grounds, the hooded crane's white neck blends in with the birch trees so prevalent in Siberian forests. Conversely, the black neck of *nigricollis*, which breeds in a treeless habitat at high altitudes, has a thermoregulating function, absorbing the thin heat of the cold sun.

5. In the Nine Rivers

1. The other rare white cranes of the northern hemisphere, *G. americana* and *G. japonensis*, make do with territories of 1.1 and 1.5 square miles, respectively (and in Hokkaido considerably less).

2. See Peter Hessler, *River Town* (New York: HarperCollins, 2001).

3. See Arundhati Roy, *The Greater Common Good* (Bombay: India Books, 1999).

4. In fiscal 1992, China was granted more loans from the World Bank (over $2.5 billion) than any other country, much of it in the form of funding for the Three Gorges. In 1997 and 1999, Morgan Stanley Dean Witter, Salomon Smith Barney, Credit Suisse, and Merrill Lynch were among the many Western corporations eager to underwrite the China Development Bank bonds, joining the World Bank as sponsors shortly before the Bank itself withdrew its funding for the Three Gorges dam in a hail of international condemnation.

The Chinese government makes much of an early report by Canadian experts that the Three Gorges dam would have projected benefits to seven provinces in developing electricity and industry, while its vast reservoir, in a dry region, would protect and benefit the People's agriculture. Yet in order to swallow the vast floods, the reservoir would have to be emptied before the monsoon, while to provide the hydroelectric power, it would have to be kept full. And nobody has dealt satisfactorily with the risk of earthquake, which might drown thousands, or the dam's frightening vulnerability as a military target, or the immense tonnage of silt (and raw sewage: 265 billion gallons of human waste each year) that will accumulate behind the dam, or the effects of silt deprivation on annually flooded farmlands below the dam which feed a third of China, or the further damage to the land from saltwater incursions caused by the reduced head of water at the river mouth.

Nor have the technocrats concerned themselves with the cultural dese-
cration of China's revered "River to Heaven," which descends nearly two
thousand miles to the sea from four miles above sea level in the glaciers of
Qinghai and Tibet, not to speak of the heartbreaking loss of the 126 miles of
Qutang, Wu, and Xiling river gorges, the most beautiful on our earth. The
mist over Wu Gorge has been celebrated by poets and painters for two thousand years, and the precious archeological sites, some of them ten thousand
years old, date back to early peoples of the late Ice Age.

There is little mention in the Bank's report of the massive, cruel displacement of a million people from ancestral towns and villages, gardens,
and temples engulfed by the rising water, who are being forced to abandon
the revered graves and habitations of their ancestors and cultural traditions
that go back many centuries. ("For such people, dispossession has genocidal
consequences," writes Howard Berman, in *Tibet Environmental and Development News* 7, p. 4.) Already the besieged Tibetans fear that the hordes of displaced Yangtze poor will be resettled in Kham (eastern Tibet), which can
neither afford nor feed them. (Crane people are additionally concerned that
the refugees may be resettled in northern Sichuan and/or on Chongming Island in the lower Yangtze, a critical breeding range and a winter sanctuary,
respectively, for the black-necked and hooded cranes.)

The Canadians claimed that such an enormous transfer of human beings
would be feasible, but I have been told by writer Catherine Caufield, a par-
ticipant in the Amur conference who has since published *Masters of Illusion*
(New York: Henry Holt, 1996), a disturbing account of World Bank ambi-
tions, that the Canadian report has been sharply criticized by more objective
hydrologists for telling the Chinese government only what its dam proponents wished to hear. A few years later—very late for the millions of poor
souls whose lives are being destroyed—the Canadian group, like the World
Bank before it, changed its mind: a transfer of refugees on such a scale, it
now decided, was not really practicable after all.

A brave group of fifty-three Chinese engineers and academics have been
appealing to their government to reconsider the consequences of the dam,
and apparently the government, already uneasy about the huge corruption
scandals that have accompanied the dam's construction, is encouraging opinions from independent environmental groups to balance those of the strong
pro-dam clique within the government; at the same time, the government is
leery of a political green party which might ignite popular outrage over the
innumerable environmental botches that now plague the country. The
anti–Three Gorges fight is being led by a well-connected and therefore well-
defended and influential heroine named Dai Qing. "From the beginning,"
Dai Qing said in 1993, "the Three Gorges dam has been a political project
promoted only by those who would have personal and financial and political
gain." (Why, after all, should the Chinese leadership be any wiser than the

Big Dam proponents in the Indian government, or, for that matter, the United States, which is already talking about dismantling some of its dams?)

In any case, manipulation of the water flow by the Three Gorges dam will permanently alter the hydrology of the Poyang lakes—a system already severely damaged by watershed and wetland degradation. Saving the Poyang habitat might possibly depend on diking the northwest lakes and marshes and pumping water in during the spring and summer to simulate the waxing and waning of the Yangtze; otherwise the dam may fatally degrade the winter habitat of 99 percent of the earth's last Siberian cranes.

For the Yangtze itself—though the full consequences of the dam are as yet unclear—the great dam will slow the formation of new delta land through sedimentation, resulting in the loss of winter habitat in the coastal marshes north of the Yangtze in Jiangsu Province, where the delta extends eighty miles from north to south and normally gains new deposits a half a mile in width each year; this is the region of the Yancheng Nature Reserve, which in winter provides good habitat for five to seven hundred red-crowned cranes, the largest population of *Grus japonensis* anywhere on earth. It will also affect aquatic plant communities and wildlife habitats throughout the lower basin, and probably extinguish the rare Yangtze dolphin and the Chinese alligator (animals which, in the year 2000, numbered roughly two hundred and five hundred, respectively).

5. This exciting news was revealed at an international crane conference sponsored by the ICF at Keoladeo/Bharatpur in early March 1983.

6. A team led by Japanese ornithologists Drs. Kiyoaki Ozaki and Hiroyuki Masatomi, who would attend the Amur conference a few years later, made an estimate of 2,626 Siberians at Poyang Lake. They also found large congregations of white-naped, hooded, and Eurasian cranes and surprising numbers of the rare Oriental white stork, which we had observed in 1992 on their nests near the Amur. (Vagrant red-crowned and sandhill cranes turn up rarely at Poyang; George Archibald saw a sandhill there in 1985. That so few red-crowneds have strayed upriver to Poyang is surprising when one considers the numbers of this species at Yancheng Nature Reserve on the Yangtze's northern delta.) The 1,165 white-naped cranes were many more than could be accounted for by their known nesting territories in the Amur drainage, and also an astonishingly high count for yet another crane that was thought to be endangered; the discovery would lead to our Mongolian expedition and its search for *G. vipio*'s main nesting grounds a few years later. Like the black-necked crane and the Siberian, the white-naped had been miraculously resurrected, if not yet on the breeding grounds at least on paper.

7. As many as 800 Siberians have been reported at Zhalong in April and early May. Zhalong can also claim the largest number of nesting red-crowned cranes (about 180 in the year 2000) in the Amur drainage.

8. See Su Liying, "Human Impacts on Cranes in China," in *Proceedings of the International Crane Symposium: People, Water, and Wildlife*, ed. H. Whitaker (Washington, D.C.: National Audubon Society, 1992).

9. Among developing countries, eastern Asia leads the way in effective family planning, which began in China. Taiwan, Hong Kong, South Korea, and Singapore have lowered reproduction below the replacement level of 2.1 children per mother.

10. See Lester Brown, *Who Will Feed China?* (New York: Norton, 1995); also Orville Schell, "China's Faustian Bargain," *Travel and Holiday*, November 1992.

11. An aquatic fauna and flora that includes 270 species of aquatic plants, 92 aquatic invertebrates, 65 mollusks, and 120 fish is a cornucopia for the 130 bird species in the reserve area, which include, besides the four species of cranes, the rare black and white storks.

12. See George B. Schaller, "Saving China's Wildlife," *International Wildlife*, January–February 1990, pp. 30–41.

13. See Jim Harris, "Managing Nature Reserves for Cranes in China," in *Proceedings of the Sixth North American Crane Workshop*, ed. D. W. Stahlecker (Grand Island, Nebr.: North American Crane Working Group, 1992).

14. In 1998, many villagers had to flee when their rickety settlements were washed away by heavy floods at Poyang Lake.

15. See Dorothea Scott, *A Flight of Cranes* (Baraboo, Wisc.: International Crane Foundation, 1982).

16. Kung Fu films, manufactured in Hong Kong, are never shown there, we were told, being designed for simple folk out in the provinces.

17. *Phalacrocorax carbo*, known in the West as the great cormorant.

18. On our return through Hong Kong, we described the strange canid on the riverbank to Simba Chan of the World Wildlife Fund, who had served as a translator at the Amur River conference. He was now directing the Mai Po Bird Sanctuary outside the city. Simba showed us our "lifer" black-faced spoonbill, a species down to about three hundred birds, with its last breeding marshes in North Korea badly threatened. He said that Jiang-xi Province and the Poyang Lake region in particular was one of the last places in China where one might hope for a glimpse of the Asian wild dog, known as the dhole, a creature that fit our description of the animal we'd seen. (Jiang-xi was also a last redoubt of the South China tiger.) A few years later, I would see many dholes in central India, and though the Indian animals appeared less reddish and more tawny, I believe it was a dhole we saw at the Nine Rivers.

6. Hokkaido

In Kyushu in recent years, the numbers of *G. monachus* and also *G. vipio* have actually shown a slight increase: on January 7, 1999, 2,535 white-napeds and 7,904 hoodeds were counted at Izumi; on January 10, 2000, there were 3,093 white-napeds, 8,811 hoodeds. Over the long term, however, both species remain threatened. In any case, it is still true that many more *monachus* appear each winter than known nesting territories on the Asian mainland can account for.

1. Engelbert Kaempfer, *The History of Japan, 1690–92* (Glasgow: I. Maclehose and Sons, 1906).
2. "This beautiful bird used to be rather common, but now that it is permitted to become a prey of anyone has been almost exterminated." Thomas W. Blakiston, "Catalog of the Birds of Japan," *Transactions of the Asiatic Society of Japan*, vol. 8 (Yokohama, 1880).
3. Quoted in Peter Matthiessen, *Nine-Headed Dragon River* (Boston: Shambhala, 1986).
4. Both Japan Air and Lufthansa use the red-crowned crane as the tail logo on their aircraft.
5. *Tancho* was still a widespread resident of Honshu when the birth of the scholar Oe no Masafusa (1041–1111) was commemorated by Akazome Emon, his great-grandmother:

> I wish I could live
> Long enough to see him soar
> High above the clouds
> When his cloak of crane feathers
> Has grown out with the years.

From the translation by Donald Keene, *Seeds in the Heart* (New York: Henry Holt, 1993).
6. Interestingly the Ainu, whose few descendants still persist in the far north and south of the archipelago, have a Y-chromosome genetic connection with the Tibetans, who may have moved south out of northeast Asia only a few thousand years ago.
7. Also his assistant Tamaka Kitagawa.
8. Now the Wildlife Conservation Society.
9. On the San Jiang plain of Heilongjiang, both *G. japonensis* and *G. vipio*, the white-naped crane, nest only in extensive wetlands, but as we discovered last summer in Mongolia, *vipio* becomes tolerant of the proximity of its own kind where food is plentiful and man leaves it alone.
10. Crane feeding also took place on Honshu, Kagashima, and Yamaguchi.
11. George Archibald, *Animal Kingdom*, April 1974.
12. North American mill crews are losing their jobs in consequence of unrestrained free trade.
13. Dr. Masatomi, a Hokkaido native who had accompanied Dr. Kunikazu Momose to the Amur crane conference, was formerly director of Kushiro's Municipal Museum; he and Momose have become Japan's foremost authorities

on *G. japonensis*. See H. Masatomi and K. Momose, "The Status of the Tancho or Red-Crowned Crane in Hokkaido, Japan," in *Cranes and Storks of the Amur River*, eds. Curtis H. Halvorson, James T. Harris, and Sergei M. Smirenski (Moscow: Arts Literature Publishers, 1995).

14. Corn is rich in fats and carbohydrates, which release large quantities of heat energy for resisting cold, and in the winter, even captive cranes prefer it to food pellets.

15. A former farm sold by Mr. Tsudui Ito to the Wild Bird Society of Japan.

16. In winter flight, a *tancho* occasionally tucks its legs beneath it rather than expose them out behind.

17. "All fifteen crane species have a unison call—the loud duet given by mated pairs and characterized by various posturings of the neck and wings . . . The unison call is a duet consisting of a series of calls given within the same time period by a male and female crane . . . Because the structure of the unison call is genetically determined and has many vocal and visual characteristics, it was selected as a character to reveal crane taxonomy." See George W. Archibald, "Crane Taxonomy As Revealed by the Unison Call," in *Proceedings of the International Crane Workshop*, ed. James C. Lewis (Stillwater, Okla.: Oklahoma State University, 1976), pp. 225–51.

18. By this criterion, the Siberian and wattled cranes are slightly more advanced, with a trachea that makes a slight downward impression in the sternum or breastbone; that impression is deeper still in *Anthropoides*. In the sandhill and in the Australasian cranes (*antigone*, *rubicundus*, and *vipio*), the trachea actually penetrates the sternum for half its length and coils back on itself before exiting. In the Palearctic cranes (excluding *vipio*), it penetrates the whole length of the sternum and loops back on itself twice before continuing. The long trachea may be partly an adaptation to high-altitude migration, warming the near-frozen air before it sears the lungs. The Eurasian crane, with its extensive tracheal coiling, migrates high over the Himalaya, while the demoiselle, with moderate coiling, navigates the Himalaya by way of its passes and deep valleys; the Siberian, ever the exception to the rule, flies directly over the Hindu Kush with almost no coiling at all.

19. See D. Scott Wood, "Phenetic Relationships Within the Family Gruidae," *The Wilson Bulletin* 91, pp. 384–99. "Archibald performed the first comprehensive analysis of cranes based on a coherent set of characters," wrote George's close colleague Dr. Carey Krajewski (then of the University of Wisconsin), a leading authority on the subject. "His study of crane unison calls led him to identify clusters of similar species. Archibald's work verified the distinctness of crowned cranes (*Balearica*) and suggested an unexpected relationship between *Bugeranus carunculatus* [the wattled crane, known by other authorities as *Grus carunculatus*] and *Grus leucogeranus*." Intrigued by the continuing dilemma posed by *leucogeranus*, Krajewski had embarked on a comprehensive molecular study of the cranes, using a DNA hybridization technique. His work confirmed Archibald's finding of a deep separation be-

tween the *Balearica* and *Grus* cranes, and also his identification of five distinct superspecies, or species groups, among the gruids; in fact, four species groups in the DNA study precisely matched the unison call groupings. As for the fifth, Archibald had proposed grouping *leucogeranus* in the genus *Bugeranus* with *carunculatus*, but Krajewski questioned this solution; his own study suggested that the elusive Siberian, despite its many affinities with the wattled crane, was too distantly related to be placed in the same genus. See C. Krajewski, "Phylogenetic Relationships Among Cranes (Gruiformes: Gruidae) Based on DNA Hybridization," *The Auk* 106, pp. 603–18. "One of the most interesting taxonomic questions within the Gruidae is the systematic relationship of *Grus leucogeranus*. Its skeletal morphology and unison call are very similar to *Bugeranus carunculatus*. However, its external characters relate it to *Grus americana*. The electrophoretic data demonstrate that *G. leucogeranus* is biochemically identical to *A. virgo* and very similar to *G. americana*. Although it appears in a major cluster with *Bugeranus*, it is still very separate from that species." See James L. Ingold, Sheldon I. Guttman, and David R. Osborne, "Biochemical Systematics and Evolution of the Cranes (Aves: Gruidae)," in *Proceedings of the 1983 International Crane Workshop, Bharatpur, India*, ed. George W. Archibald and R. F. Pasquier (Baraboo, Wisc.: International Crane Foundation, 1987), pp. 577–84.

George Archibald, however, continues to believe these two birds have too many affinities, behavioral and anatomical, not to have shared a common ancestor. He reports that in the spring of 2001 a flock of twelve brown juvenile Siberians turned up at Dalainor in Inner Mongolia, and another six brown juveniles at the Muraviovka refuge on the Amur. A flock of juveniles unaccompanied by adults is an extraordinary anomaly among the cranes; the only other instance that he knows about is a flock of juvenile wattled cranes reported the same season from the Zambezi delta in Mozambique. "This is only more evidence, it seems to me," George says, "of the phylogenetic relationship between these two."

20. Quoted in Matthiessen, *Nine-Headed Dragon River.*
21. According to Mikhail Dykhan, the young director of the Kunashir Wildlife Refuge who attended last year's conference on the Amur River, only one pair of red-crowned cranes had attempted a nest the year before, although three or four pairs cross the Nemuro Strait each spring.
22. Interestingly, juvenile *G. japonensis* in first-year plumage, still brown on head and neck, have vestigial black tips on their white primaries, revealing ancient kinship with the other two white cranes.

7. The Accidental Paradise

The tide of materialism in South Korea may be retreating at long last. On March 29, 1996, two months after our departure, the environmental news bulletin *Greenwire* would report that in a recent poll of 1,500 South Koreans by the government-funded Korea Environmental Technology Research Institute, an astonishing 85 percent of the respondents worried that pollution was getting worse each year, and cited "habitat loss" as the greatest environmental problem after the pollution of the air and water. They also stated that the environment was more important to the country than economic development.

In 1998, a new group of seventy to eighty hooded cranes was found wintering in estuary wetlands of South Korea's Suncheon River. In the years since, a development of that area planned by Suncheon City has been turned aside by the efforts of our friend Kim Sooil, who had thought this species was finished in South Korea; Dr. Kim presently represents the Northeast Asian Crane Site Network in Japan, whose director is none other than our friend from the Amur River and Hong Kong, Mr. Simba Chan.

Since our visit, North Korea has set aside its nuclear weapons program, and South Korea and the United States have canceled their annual military maneuvers near the DMZ. In June 2000, the two presidents of the Koreas, expressing amity and hope, met at Panmunjom for preliminary discussions of reunification. A group called the DMZ Forum, backed by environmental organizations, wished to see commercial development replaced with a cross-border "Peace Park." Unfortunately, the U.S. military, on the specious grounds of protecting American security, refuses to help ease the border tensions by removing its myriad land mines, despite the international treaty, already signed by more than eighty nations, prohibiting use of these devices, which have uselessly killed, crippled, and maimed the bodies and the lives of thousands of defenseless human beings. And as of this writing, there was no telephone or mail service between the two Koreas.

1. The *japonensis* that migrate to the Kongwha Islands on the west coast of South Korea might come from some region in between.

2. At the Liao delta, there may be a nonmigratory group; if so, this is the southernmost breeding population of *japonensis*.

3. Dr. Walkinshaw, who died in 1993, was the author of many publications, including *Cranes of the World* (New York: Winchester Press, 1973).

4. Similarly, in the Young San Ceremony, an elaborate tribute to the Buddha, the monks are clad in long-sleeved gowns. "Their dances featured stately walks and bows at an unhurried pace," said Jack Anderson in *The New York Times*, October 24, 2000, reviewing a performance in New York.

5. One thinks of India and Pakistan and the two Germanys and the fragmentation of the former Yugoslavia and other places where simplistic "solutions" such as partition, arrived at by powerful and impatient foreigners with scant acquaintance of the country, too often condemn millions of defenseless people to decades of misery and strife. Yet as hard pragmatists, these KABP businessmen have taken careful note of the financial burdens that devolved upon West Germany when it reunited with its impoverished Communist sibling.

6. Other crane species occur in the CCZ as accidentals. Last year, a Siberian crane and a lesser sandhill crane turned up in the same season, the first bird far northeast of its usual wintering grounds at Poyang Lake and the second a laggard juvenile that may have failed to accompany its parents on the return migration from Siberia across the Bering Strait to North America.

7. Archeologists have found evidence of early Asian agriculture all over the peninsula. Linguistically, the Koreans are related to the Tungus of the Amur watershed and the Mongolians of central Asia and, more distantly, the Inuit peoples, the Hungarians, and the Finns; also, there is thought to be an ancient link between these northeastern Asians and the indigenous Jomon of Japan.

8. It has been noted by Korean ornithologist P. O. Won that "the response to vehicles was mostly flight and the response to noises was mainly alertness. The frequency of disturbances caused by human beings was comparatively low, but when disturbed by humans, the cranes would fly away the farthest." See S.-H. Pae and P. O. Won, "Wintering of Red-Crowned and White-Naped Cranes, *Grus japonensis* and *Grus vipio*, in the Cholwon Basin, Korea," in *The Future of Cranes and Wetlands: Proceedings of the International Symposium, June 1993*, eds. H. Higuchi and J. Minton (Tokyo and Sapporo, Japan: Wild Bird Society of Japan, 1994).

9. *Japonensis* roost in family units, standing on one leg or sitting on the ground, while *vipio* convene in large loose flocks and rarely or never sit down. Both peck and eat the snow and ice when the water is frozen, at which time they roost on the open ice out on the reservoir. Fran Kaliher has noted that the roosting cranes prefer icy surfaces even when ice covers only 5 percent of the area. See W.-S. Lee and Fran Kaliher, "Population and Distribution of Wintering Cranes, South Korea," unpublished report to the ICF, 1995. See also Curtis H. Halvorson and Fran Kaliher, "A Current Assessment of Cranes Wintering in South Korea, January–March 1992," in *Cranes and Storks of the Amur River*, eds. Curtis H. Halvorson, James T. Harris, and Sergei M. Smirenski (Moscow: Arts Literature Publishers, 1995). Archibald comments that cranes generally prefer to sit down on the ice, feet tucked under the breast feathers, head tucked under the wing, which is better insulation for more area than exposing one leg to the air by standing in the water.

10. In all adults, the bare skin is thinly haired with bristles.

11. In the black-necked crane, *G. nigricollis*, the white is reduced to a bold spot just behind the eye.

12. George Archibald and Jim Harris agree that, based on present knowledge, both Imjin and Chorwon are more important than any known winter habitat in North Korea. More recent reports tend to indicate that *japonensis* is more common in North Korea (an estimated 300 to 350 birds) than in the South (200 to 300), though the DMZ birds may skew both of these rough estimates. See *The Cranes*, eds. Curt D. Meine and George W. Archibald (Gland, Switzerland: IUCN, 1996).

13. "Granted, it gets harder and harder each year to ferret out those qualities and scenes which drew me to [this country] after an initial aversion in my first encounters during the mid-1980s," Fran Kaliher observes in a letter to the author on March 15, 1996. "But by a twist of circumstances I was detained there long enough, in an 'immersion' situation, to be exposed to its subtler, more sensitive and spiritual facets, and it has won my heart. Despite the present slide toward mimicking Western excess, indulgence, and materialism, there are yet outposts of moderation and simplicity, and a counterculture cognizant of deeper tradition and meaning."

14. Both Koreas signed the Biodiversity Treaty at the Earth Summit at Rio de Janeiro in June 1992.

15. See Ke Chung Kim, "Preserving Biodiversity in Korea's Demilitarized Zone," *Science* 278, October 10, 1997.

16. There may still be a few tigers in far northeastern North Korea. On February 26, 1998, tiger biologists Dale Miquelle and Dima Pikunov of the Siberian Tiger Project would find traces of what might have been tiger or leopard near Hwachon, in the vicinity of the DMZ.

17. In 1979, George Archibald urged ornithologists in China to look hard for remnant ibis, and in 1981 an estimated seven individuals were spotted in the Tsinling Mountains of Shaanxi Province, a mountain range that also supports giant panda. Nests were located and protected, and a few prefledged birds were collected to start captive populations. Today there are more than one hundred in captivity, and a similar number in the wild. The Chinese are now considering the possibility of releasing captive birds back into the wild within the original range of the species in China.

    In 1981, the last five wild ibis in Japan were taken into captivity. Perhaps because of their advanced age, they did not breed. In recent years, captive birds have been brought from China to Japan and these "mainland" ibis are breeding in captivity in Japan. Only one or two old captive birds of the original Japanese populations survive.

18. The lower Tumen forms the border of China, North Korea, and Russia where these countries converge, and the international Tumen River Area Development Project will involve South Korea (and perhaps even Mongolia) in an intensive industrial development complex—textiles, chemicals, pharmaceuticals, mining, timber, shipping—in what is proposed by the global marketeers as northeast Asia's first international free-trade zone. China has plans for a massive irrigation and hydropower system to supply the Tumen, and inevitably, environmental problems are appearing in the headlong and to date unregulated development of the 150-square-mile wetland delta. China and North Korea are building the usual "friendship bridges," and new rail links are already under way.

8. Outback

In November 2000, the ICF would receive a letter from Australian crane researcher Tim Bevard in regard to an October survey of crane populations on the
Atherton Plateau. For three decades, the group roosting in Bromfield's Swamp
had remained stable, with about eight hundred birds, but many more cranes
than previously thought were passing the Dry in other wetlands on the Atherton
Plateau, which presently supported a flock of about five thousand cranes. "The
great majority" were sarus; furthermore, Bevard reported, there were "lots" of
hybrids and mixed pairs. Thus, the outcome of this evolutionary struggle between brolga and Australian sarus is still in doubt.

1. H. J. Lavery and J. G. Blackman, "The Cranes of Australia," *Queensland
   Agricultural Journal*, March 1969.
2. Lavery and Blackman, "The Cranes of Australia."
3. George W. Archibald, "The Australian Brolga: Crane of the Desert," *The
   Brolga Bugle* 1, 1979, p. 3.
4. Archibald and Haffenden also removed the second eggs from sarus nests,
   to be taken to the United States and reared at the ICF for eventual rein-
   troduction into Thailand, where the native crane had not been reported
   for almost twenty years. Eventually eighteen birds were raised from the
   twenty-four eggs gathered at Morr Morr, and six of these were presented
   to the Crown Princess of Thailand later that year. None of the Australian
   sarus sent to Thailand have been released into the wild, to avoid interbreeding in case the native race should reappear; they have mainly been
   used as surrogate parents, incubating eggs and rearing chicks for *G. a.
   sharpii*. (See Prakash Gole, "The Status and Ecological Requirements of the
   Sarus Crane, *Grus antigone*," Ministry of Environment and Forests, India,
   1989.)
5. Finley Gilbert is not his Aboriginal name; according to Haffenden, once a
   person dies, his name is not spoken again.
6. Adapted from *Gulpilil's Stories of the Dreamtime*, compiled by Hugh Rule
   and Stuart Goodman (Sydney: Wm. Collins, 1979).
7. Haffenden has been educated in these matters by elders of the Aurukun
   community, about 250 miles north of Morr Morr on the west coast of the
   Cape York Peninsula.
8. Sometimes, however, a brolga story may be owned by a separate person.
9. See Alice M. Moyle, *Songs from the Northern Territory* (Canberra: Australian
   Institute of Aboriginal Studies, 1974). In recent years, the Aborigines have
   been contacted by American Indian emissaries, who are also contacting
   Ainu traditionals in Japan; the Native Americans are encouraging them to
   preserve their languages and tribal ways, including the crane traditions so
   widespread and similar among Indian peoples. One messenger from North
   America was astonished and physically shaken by a crane song accompanied

by *didjeridu*. Asked the purpose of the song, the singer "hesitated a few moments, then looked directly at me and said, 'It is used to call the young people together so they can seriously consider their responsibilities as human
beings to continue the Human Life Stream.' After some more long moments, still looking directly at me, he continued, 'And to call all the faithful
[People] together from the Four Directions.' " (Letter from Craig Carpenter,
April 22, 1993.)

10. The *didjeridu* is not used in the Morr Morr region.

11. Oddly, the Papua New Guinean word for the endemic brolga is *groos*, pronounced as in *Grus*; apparently the people hear the crane's loud, grating calls
with the same ear as Europeans. Similarly, some linguists hear "brolga" as
"burulga," which imitates the low growling "talking" of the birds.

12. The melaleuca was not nearly so dominant on its home range as it has become in swamplands all over the Everglades and southern Florida.

13. Lavery and Blackman, "The Cranes of Australia."

14. Here at Morr Morr in 1984, George Archibald found a floating sarus nest so
massive that one could stand on it, a phenomenon never reported in *sharpii*,
quite possibly because so few *sharpii* nests have been described.

15. The eggs are elongated ovoids in shape, as in most cranes.

16. The Indian sarus also soars, but we did not observe this habit in *G. a. gilli*
(which may dissipate overheating through the large area of bare skin on the
head).

17. George Archibald also learned that in his Group of Five, *japonensis* (not *grus*,
as he had thought) was the earliest species to split off from the ancestor, and
that this species was also the most different from the others and the most
evolved.

18. In the Group of Three, "the male raises his forearm and spreads his primary
wing feathers" during the unison call, whereas in the Group of Five, the females utter "a piercing, scream-like call to initiate the display" while the
males "show varying amounts of wing feather erection." See George W.
Archibald, "Crane Taxonomy As Revealed by the Unison Call," in *Proceedings of the International Crane Workshop*, ed. James C. Lewis (Stillwater,
Okla.: Oklahoma State University, 1976), pp. 225–51.

19. In winter, in its Southeast Asian marshes, the eastern sarus, like many
aquatic cranes, feeds almostly exclusively on tubers of an *Eleocharis* sedge,
whereas on its breeding grounds, scattered out in pairs, it takes insects and
small vertebrates to better feed its young.

20. Andrew Haffenden, letter to the ICF, September 3, 1995.

21. Archibald sees this as further evidence of the sarus's long millenniums of
evolution in Australia. New vocalizations tend to be more pronounced
where the breeding territories overlap, as they do here; the traits of each
species diverge more than they do where the ranges are separate (a principle
of evolutionary biology), since the birds' very proximity drives them deeper

into their respective quirks and niches to avoid interbreeding. During the loud and elaborate "duet" known as the unison call, for example, the sarus female initiates the calling with her customary double note, which is answered a moment later by the male; however, once the duet has started, she breaks the normal pattern of short swift calls exchanged in duets by both species, switching instead to three or four long calls (the "guard call") to each male response.

9. Equatoria, Ngorongoro, Okavango, and Transvaal

At latest estimate, perhaps forty thousand black crowned cranes (*Balearica pavonina*) survive in West and Central Africa and in Sudan.

1. At that time (1961), *Balearica pavonina* was the single species of "crested crane," with four geographic races known as the Sudan, West African, East African, and South African crowned cranes.

2. "Stretching from the Atlantic coast to the valleys of the River Nile, the savannas and floodplains of the Sahel are among the most beautiful and threatened lands of Africa. This region was once an oasis for nomadic herders and wildlife, but in recent decades it has been ravaged by the southward march of the Saharan desert and ever-increasing competition for its limited resources . . . Requiring a mosaic of wet and dry habitats in seasonally flooded lowlands, [the cranes] are denizens of the great floodplain systems of the Sahel, including the Senegal valley, the inland delta of the Niger River in Mali, the Waza River of Lake Chad in Cameroon, and the extensive Sudd wetlands in southern Sudan . . . In the past thirty years, they have been decreasing and are near extinction in many parts of West Africa, including Nigeria (circa 30,000 in the early 1970s), where they are the national birds." Rich Beilfuss, ICF *Bugle*, November 2000.

3. George Archibald, ICF *Bugle*, February 1993.

4. The last confirmed sighting of a small relict flock of twenty to thirty breeding demoiselles, threatened by hunting and egg collecting in high grasslands of the Atlas Mountains of Morocco, was made in the 1980s; nobody has investigated since, so they may still be there.

5. The two races or subspecies of the gray crowned crane, *B. regulorum*, are *B. r. gibbericeps* and *B. r. regulorum*—respectively, the East African and South African crowned cranes.

6. Peter Matthiessen, *The Tree Where Man Was Born* (New York: E. P. Dutton, 1972).

7. The unison call is also found in a gruid relative, the pearl-gray kagu of New Caledonia.

8. Only in *Balearica* are the unison calls similar in both sexes and also random; they are mainly a clamor of the "guard call" used in alarm or threat. And

only *Balearica* makes "boom calls," lower in pitch, usually when the guard calls have finished.

9. In their wake, the huge-beaked and carnivorous *Diatryma*, a giant relative of the rails, preyed on the small early mammals of that period.

10. C. Krajewski, letter to the author, August 15, 2001.

11. " 'Adaptive radiation' describes the pattern of diversity within single branches of the tree of life. The fifteen species of living cranes (which along with several fossil taxa, comprise the avian family Gruidae) constitute an unusual adaptive radiation among vertebrates in that they are, for the most part, rather recently evolved yet have a nearly cosmopolitan distribution. Most of the spectacular radiations among animals, including Darwin's finches and the marsupials of Australia, are geographically constrained. Indeed, geographic isolation of a few individuals in an area with open ecological niches is the most general model of adaptive radiation, but one that clearly does not apply to cranes . . .

"We believe that these gruine lineages arose rapidly, probably as a result of intercontinental dispersal and isolation during the Miocene. The ancestral gruine may have inhabited North America or Eurasia, but the species groups must have diverged in distinct areas: *canadensis* in North America, *anthropoides* south of the present Mediterranean, *antigone* in Australasia south of the Himalayas, and *americana* in eastern Asia. (The whooping crane is an Ice Age colonist of North America.)" Carey Krajewski and George W. Archibald, "The Evolution of Cranes," 1994 (unpublished).

12. It interests me that the two *Balearica* are closer in their anatomy to the other endemic African cranes—*A. paradisea* and *G. carunculatus*—than they are to the other *Grus*.

13. "The most species-rich areas are not necessarily the most taxonomically diverse. For example, . . . even though Asia has twice the number of [crane] species as Africa, the phylogenetic endowment of the continents is quite similar." J. C. Haney and M. E. Eiswerth, "The Plight of Cranes: A Case Study for Conserving Biodiversity," in *Proceedings of the Sixth North American Crane Workshop*, ed. D. W. Stahlecker (Grand Island, Nebr.: North American Crane Working Group, 1992).

14. George Archibald, personal communication with the author, February 5, 1997.

15. C. A. Van Ee, "Notes on the Breeding Behavior of the Blue Crane," 1981, quoted in *The Cranes*, eds. Curt D. Meine and George W. Archibald (Gland, Switzerland: IUCN, 1996).

16. In the Okavango, the wattled crane nests in August, right after the high water of the rainy season starts to recede, taking with it any further threat of flood.

17. The western red-footed kestrel.

18. Personal correspondence with James Malcolm, Ethiopian Wildlife Conservation Organization, Addis Ababa, March 1994.

19. Aerial spraying for tsetse fly in the Okavango Delta has harmed the cranes.
20. The count for this region in the year 2000 estimated about 230 individuals.
21. The wattled crane was also the last species to be bred in captivity.
22. South Africa is marginal habitat for *G. carunculatus*, and two chicks are reported more frequently in its main range in the vast swamps of south-central Africa.
23. Two hundred or more species of spike rush are distributed worldwide, and a number are utilized by cranes; in addition to Africa, one species sustains the brolga in northern Australia and another the sarus in the Mekong Delta, and another the sandhill in Wisconsin.
24. In the Dullstroom region, they turn up regularly in the fields with the other cranes, says Kerryn Morrison, especially when tending young.
25. Peter Matthiessen, *Shadows of Africa* (New York: Abrams, 1992), p. 70.
26. George Archibald speculates that this crane is mostly silent because its territoriality is so well established by its very large size and striking patterns.
27. It is thought that a recent crane decline at the Umgemi Wattled Crane Reserve in KwaZulu-Natal had the same cause.

10. Down the Edges of the Distant Sky

In recent years, the Buxtons have engaged a full-time warden to discourage intrusions in the nesting area as well as predators, and the small flock of *G. grus* has increased to about fifteen, including, most recently, young from at least two and possibly three nests.

1. *G. grus* is "not numerous, but more common than other cranes," according to *A Field Guide to the Birds of the U.S.S.R.* by V. E. Flint et al. (Princeton, N.J.: Princeton University Press, 1989).
2. A staging area in Hungary's Carpathian Basin attracts about seventy-two thousand birds, far more than can be accounted for by the estimated populations on the breeding territories or winter grounds.
3. The *G. grus* of Siberia migrate mostly to Iran (the south Caspian), India, and southern China.

11. The Sadness of Marshes

In the millennial year 2000, George Archibald retired as director of the ICF in order to write a book; he was replaced by the exceptionally competent and dedicated Jim Harris. On a trip to Cuba to study the local sandhill race, he discovered that these birds lived in dry country with no close dependence on water; he speculates that this race may be evolving into a flightless bird.

George's small office in the barn of his pretty farm near Baraboo overlooks wet meadow pasture, and in the late winter of 2001, when I happened to ring up,

I found him ecstatic: a pair of greater sandhills was nesting in full view of his window. With the fresh delight of one seeing it for the first time, he described the beauty of the snow falling and the stillness of the great bird on its nest, marveling at the feather insulation that kept the white flakes from melting. Spring passed and the grass grew tall; he never knew if the nest had succeeded until the early June morning when I called again to pester him about something else, and the crane family stepped out of the tall grass onto the new-mown pasture. "Two chicks!" George cried. "There they are!"

1. Jack Turner, *Teewinot: A Year in the Teton Range* (New York: St. Martin's, 2000).
2. Recently, an Indian friend in spiritual training who went to Australia to help enlist Aborigine support for a solidarity movement for traditional peoples sent a letter relating his encounter with an Aborigine singer and their discussion of cranes as birds of wisdom and harmony. He described to this man how, years ago, he and I had watched a pair of sandhill cranes in their spring courtship dances in the snow edges near a remote lake in eastern Oregon, "then turn to us and dance for us as they touched us with their wonderful Unity Powers." Craig Carpenter, personal communication with author, April 1993.
3. Today an estimated thirteen thousand inhabit Wisconsin.
4. In 1960, the estimated forty Mississippi sandhills were probably saved when a proposed highway through their only known range along the Pascagoula River in southern Jackson County was turned aside. These birds—a little darker than their migratory kin, with a dark disk on the side of the head—went unrecognized as a separate race until 1972; since then, this small group has been augmented by a captive propagation program initiated at Patuxent Wildlife Research Center (now the Patuxent Environment Science Center). The first releases were in 1981, with a total of 245 as of 1999. These birds and their wild-born descendants constitute about four fifths of the present flock in what has become the Mississippi Sandhill Crane Wildlife Refuge on the Pascagoula.
5. The sandhill, Eurasian, and demoiselle comprise nearly three quarters of the IUCN estimate of 1.22 million cranes on earth.
6. The lesser stands three and a half feet tall, with a six-foot wingspan; it weighs seven or eight pounds. DNA studies have established that the greater, intermediate, and lesser sandhills are probably clinal, with gradual changes in morphological characters and no positive means of distinguishing between them other than the pronounced size discrepancy in *G. c. canadensis* (the lesser) and *G. c. tabida* (the greater); see *The Cranes*, eds. Curt D. Meine and George W. Archibald (Gland, Switzerland: IUCN, 1996), p. 1,085. For example, the greater sandhill and the nonmigratory "Florida sandhill" are virtually identical. Many authorities now conclude that the distinctions be-

tween all these geographic populations are too small to justify taxonomic separation—that the validity of these so-called races, in short, exists mostly on paper, and that essentially there are but two "good" sandhill races, the lesser and the greater.

7. The group that nests on sand dunes on Banks Island in the Canadian high Arctic, surrounded by a sea of ice, is probably the most northerly breeding crane; it is said to be smaller than the lesser sandhills of the mainland, with smaller eggs and a briefer nesting season.

8. In cranes, as in sandpipers and plovers, there is "staggered migration," in which those that migrate farthest north also migrate farthest south. Paradoxically, the larger sandhills, with a better ratio of heat engine to body surface loss and therefore more resistance to the cold, do not migrate so far north, but neither do they need to migrate so far south.

9. Archibald wonders why this species bothers to revert to its gray plumage, since even as a chick it is more reddish than most cranes and repaints itself this color every year. (I had noticed that chicks of the Florida sandhill and also the demoiselle were gray, and apparently this is also true of the blue, black-necked, and Eurasian cranes.) A hooded crane at the ICF once painted itself all over, like a sandhill—another symptom, George suspects, of the *Grus* ancestor erupting in the modern species.

10. Sil Pemberton of Kearney, quoted in Anne Raver, "Beside a River's Troubled Waters, These Harbingers of Spring Dance On," *The New York Times*, March 21, 1993.

11. Traces of what may be ancestral gray crop up in the triangle of gray feathers behind the red crown in both *grus* and *americana* and also in *americana*'s tertials, in the dark grayish neck plumage in *japonensis*, and in the ear coverts in *vipio*, the white-naped crane.

12. George Archibald, conversation with the author at Baraboo, Wisconsin, September 2000.

13. A DNA study is now in progress to determine which sandhill population is most closely related to such South American gruid relatives as the trumpeter and the sun bittern.

14. Ronald Sauey, "The Range, Status, and Winter Ecology of the Siberian Crane (*Grus leucogeranus*)," Ph.D. dissertation, Cornell University, Ithaca, New York, 1985, p. 136.

12. *Grus americana*

In the fall of 2000, a fresh shipment of young whoopers was released at a new location south of Lake Wales, in central Florida—a private tract with a private lake unused for water-skiing, fishing, or other recreation that might disturb the cranes—and as a result, nineteen of the twenty-one were still alive and flying when I spoke with Steve Nesbitt on June 9, over six months later. Unfortunately, the great drought had continued through the winter and during the nest season, and although fourteen to sixteen pairs had formed, as they had in 2000, only two nests actually produced eggs. In the first of these, the eggs simply disappeared, possibly due to abandonment but more likely through predation. The second nest was located in a small cypress swamp in the middle of a large development not far from Tampa, and the few residents who knew about it cooperated with the Florida Game and Wildlife Commission in keeping the secret. There was no pressure on the birds and no disruptions; furthermore, when after thirty-five days the researchers went in to check the eggs, the whoopers challenged and attacked them, fighting off intrusion. As they had suspected, the eggs were infertile. Furthermore, the swamp had completely dried, which might well have been fatal to any chicks.

Steve Nesbitt was full of admiration for the spirit and tenacity of the cranes—not only their spirit in defending that nest but the fact that they had persisted in nesting in the face of the terrible drought: 2000 had been the worst nesting year on record for the native sandhill crane, and 2001 was expected to be worse. However, he said, there had been signs that a normal summer monsoon had begun, and there had been some rain; he was very hopeful that the drought was ending, which in his opinion would ensure the successful outcome of the whooping crane project. "In the first breeding year after the drought," he promised, "we'll have whooper nests coming out of our ears." To increase genetic diversity in these birds, some captive-laid eggs may be transposed into wild nests.

Meanwhile, the surviving female of the wandering pair of whoopers which had built nests in northern Michigan has not seemed interested in a new mate, and in early June 2001 she disappeared. Perhaps she has perished, but possibly she has retraced her route north. (This spring, another pioneering crane from the Florida flock had turned up in southwestern Virginia.)

Steve Nesbitt doubts that last year's flight to Michigan involved any innate knowledge of old whooping crane migration routes. Since the Florida whoopers will call out to any large bird with a white body and black wing tips, he suspects that those two cranes had followed white pelicans northward. "Probably looked up and saw those pelicans spiraling high in the sky, the way they do, and flew up to spiral with them, got caught up in it, and kept on going."

1. In the same year, Blackjack was acquired by the Fish and Wildlife Service for inclusion in the Aransas National Wildlife Refuge (formerly the National Migratory Waterfowl Refuge).
2. Robert P. Allen, *A Report on the Whooping Crane's Northern Breeding Grounds*, supplement to Research Report No. 3 (New York: National Audubon Society, 1956).
3. Much credit is due to years of commitment and hard work by Canadian and American field ornithologists, in particular Robert Allen.
4. Peter Matthiessen, *Wildlife in America* (New York: Viking, 1959).
5. That the sandhill showed no sign of occupying the whooper's niche when

the near-extinct whooper vanished from most of its range suggests that the sandhill was never an aquatic species.

6. "The dance . . . resumed. The birds were reflected in the clear marsh water. Sixteen white shadows reflected the motions. The evening breeze moved across the saw-grass. It bowed and fluttered. The water rippled. The setting sun lay rosy on the white bodies. Magic birds were dancing in a mystic marsh. The grass swayed with them, and the shallow waters, and the earth fluttered under them. The earth was dancing with the cranes, and the low sun, and the wind and sky." Marjorie Kinnan Rawlings, *The Yearling* (New York: Atheneum, 1985), p. 88.

7. Yeehaw Junction is thought to get its name from the "yee" and "haw" of the oxcarts on the old woods roads, or possibly from the Muskogee word for wolf, from the days when the small red wolf still ranged through northern Florida; in this region the war chief Wildcat hid out from the U.S. Army in the Seminole Wars of the first half of the nineteenth century. It was also the home country of the celebrated outlaws and bank robbers known as the Ashley Boys.

8. This was the largest assembly outside Alaska, and the seed population for the recovery of the eagle after the ban on DDT in 1967.

9. Folk's team included Marilyn Spalding, Jim Schmidt, and Kathy Sullivan.

10. Wolves and other creatures prey on the crane chicks in Alberta, especially in years of drought when the bogs dry up, but the Canadian Wildlife Service has avoided intervention, in line with the strict policy of its national parks.

11. Dr. Spalding would later weigh this bird and X-ray it; like the other ailing bird, it tested positive for swallowed metal. Operated on later in March, it soon recovered.

12. EEE stands for eastern equine encephalomyelitis, a virus transmitted by mosquitoes; it has plagued some of the captive flock at Patuxent.

13. Like the unison call, "a starter nest may serve to synchronize the physiology of the pair, bringing them further along the hormonal sequence that culminates in egg laying. They may also be the consequence of minor adjustment in nest site placement in response to changes in water levels." Nesbitt, letter to the author, June 2, 2000.

14. Gabrielson's own mentor had been Dr. R. M. Anderson, the last man to see the last whooper nest in the United States, in Iowa in 1894.

15. It used to be thought that the two chicks would inevitably fight over the food presented—in effect, fight for their lives and to the death, as they do, occasionally, in captivity. But it has been noted that crane chicks in the wild fight relatively little, and if they do, the parent intervenes. Sergei Smirenski, conversation with the author; see also Liao Yanfa, "The Black-necked Cranes of Longbaotar," *The Brolga Bugle*, February 1987.

16. The maiden cane–pickerel weed ecotone was also a crane habitat in Louisiana.

17. In Siberians the male provides the begging juvenile with two and a half times as much food as does the female; the whooper juvenile is fed primarily by the female.

18. The Siberian and the whooper are the most endangered of the cranes, and are given similar chances of survival, but the biodiversity benefit in saving *leucogeranus* is twice that of *americana*, since *leucogeranus* has no close genetic relatives.

19. Actually, three ultralights, working in shifts. The fastest one was used for tracking strayed birds. A fixed-wing aircraft was used for scouting the route ahead. Including the ground staff following in two vehicles, the birds were attended by fourteen people.

Acknowledgments

I am grateful indeed to my friend Bob Bateman for the beautiful paintings and drawings that contribute so much to this book, and also for his generous interest and support, together with that of his kind Birgit.

I am also grateful to Dr. George Archibald of the International Crane Foundation and to Jim Harris, who has recently succeeded him as president of the ICF; both have been generous mentors, friends, and companions in the field (Siberia, Mongolia, Korea, Australia, and the United States) since the outset of research for this book. Another great friend and field companion has been the ornithologist Victor Emanuel (India, Bhutan, China, and Japan). My warm thanks also to Dr. Sergei Smirenski and Viktor Bakhtin (Siberia), Dr. Ma Yiqing (China), Sharaid Sugarragchaa Chuluunbaatar and Drs. Ayurzaryun Bold and Natsagdorjin Tseveenmyadag (Mongolia), Raj Singh (India), Simba Chan (Hong Kong), Yulia and Kuni Momose and Rori Satsuki (Hokkaido), Dr. Kim Sooil and Fran Kaliher (South Korea), Andrew Haffenden, Mark Tredinnick, and John Stokes (Queensland), Kerryn Morrison and Frans Krige (Transvaal), and Steve Nesbitt and Marty Folk (Florida).

Mrs. Mary Griggs Burke of New York City and the Livingston Griggs and Mary G. Burke Foundation generously supported Dr. Archibald and myself in crane research in the Australian Outback, and Mrs. Gertrude Ferrar in Seoul was very hospitable. Curt D. Meine of the ICF and Betsy Didrickson, the ICF librarian, and Elena Smirenski, Susan Finn, Su Liying, Kyoko Archibald, and other friends at the foundation have been unfailingly hospitable and helpful.

The passages on crane evolution and phylogeny are largely based on the conclusions of Dr. Archibald and his eminent colleague Dr. Carey Krajewski. Throughout the nine-year process of writing this book, George Archibald and Jim Harris have kindly answered innumerable queries by mail, telephone, and in ongoing discussions at Baraboo; they have also checked the entire manuscript for accuracy and omissions. Sergei Smirenski, Kim Sooil, Andrew Haffenden, Mark Tredinnick, Kerryn Morrison, Rick Beilfuss, Jeb Barzen, and Curt D. Meine have cheerfully contributed comments and corrections on chapters concerning their regions of expertise.

My excellent and indefatigable editor and friend Becky Saletan and her kind assistant Katrin Wilde have been cheerful and diligent throughout a long and complex editing. All of the friends mentioned here have my warmest thanks, and none are responsible for errors of fact or emphasis that may remain.

Index